WITHDRAWN

Also by Gina Arnold

Route 666: On the Road to Nirvana

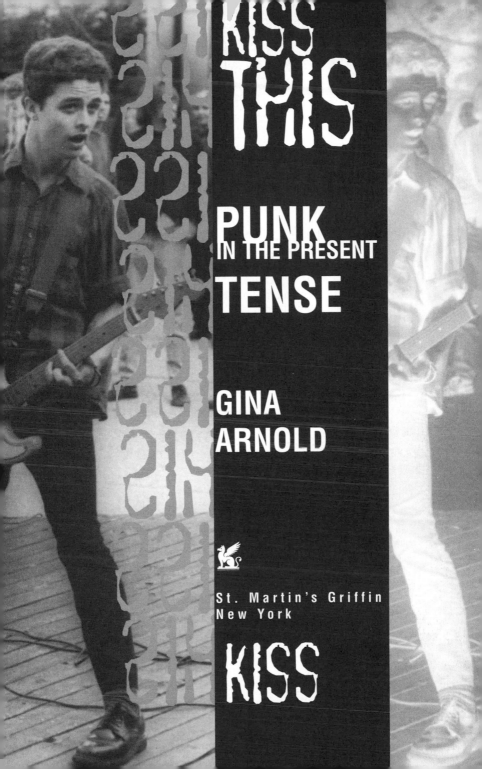

KISS THIS

PUNK
IN THE PRESENT
TENSE

GINA
ARNOLD

St. Martin's Griffin
New York

KISS

KISS THIS: PUNK IN THE PRESENT TENSE. Copyright © 1997 by Gina Arnold. All rights reserved. Printed in the United States of America. No part of this book may be used or reproduced in any manner whatsoever without written permission except in the case of brief quotations embodied in critical articles or reviews. For information, address St. Martin's Press, 175 Fifth Avenue, New York, N.Y. 10010.

Design by Maureen Troy

Library of Congress Cataloging-in-Publication Data

Arnold, Gina.
    Kiss this: punk in the present tense / Gina Arnold. —1st ed.
        p.   cm.
    ISBN 0–312–15521–2
    1. Punk rock music—History and criticism.   I. Title.
    ML3534.A76   1997
    781.66—dc21   97–19811
                                                                         CIP
                                                                         MN

First St. Martin's Griffin Edition: October 1997

10   9   8   7   6   5   4   3   2   1

Contents

Part 3:
Still Rockin' in the Free World/133

Acknowledgments

I suppose that all books are collaborative efforts, but mine are probably more so than others. This book began as an idea given to me by my editor and friend Robert Wilonsky; it was then supported through its darker days by (among other people) Greil Marcus, Tim Armstrong, and Jim Fitzgerald. Without the gracious help of those four people, it would never have been written; nor would it have worked at all without the invaluable help of the following network of people, to whom I send my love:

In (or regarding) FINLAND: Susan Marcus, Sepultura, Claire Pillsbury, Mirka Rautakorpi, Jari Mylly, and Semira Ben-Amor. In LONDON: Abner Stein, Catherine Hurley, Bill Scott-Kerr, Lindsay Hutton, Michael Arnold, Jeff Kaye and Alex Frean, Alice Arnold and Sandy Toksvig. In the CZECH RE-PUBLIC: Patrick O'Donnell, Mirek Wanek, Dita Hanzelova, Dave Rosecrans. In BUDAPEST and ISTANBUL: Kelly Curtis Management, Colleen Combs, Nicole Vandenkamp, the Pearl Jam crew, the Fastbacks (Kim Warnick, Lulu Gargiulo, Mike Musburger, Kurt Bloch), Eddie Vedder, Ira, Gracie, and Ayya. In PORTLAND, SEATTLE, MINNEAPOLIS, and AUSTIN: Louis Black, SXSW staff, NXNW staff, Jody Bleyle, Kathy McCarty, Tom Hazelmyer, Charles Peterson. In SAN DIEGO: Robert Mizrachi, Mark Woodlief, Sandra Dijkstra. In LOS ANGELES: Clark Staub, Sue Cummings, Stuart Ross, Cherly Ceretti, Brett Gurewitz, Jeff Abarta, Melissa Boag, Lisa Fancher, Robert Wilonsky, Ice T, Jorge Hinojosa, Geoff Weiss, Rob Cavallo, Isabelle and Ray Farrell, Scott Becker, Jenny Boddie, and everyone at M.S.O. In BERKELEY: Trouz Cuevas, Michelle Germain, Kava Massih, Terezia Neiman, Elizabeth Newman, Lawrence Livermore, Molly Neuman, Elliott Cahn, Christopher Arnold, Corry Arnold, Jesse Townley, Murray Bowles, Jon Ginoli, Green Day (Billie Joe Armstrong, Tre Cool, Mike Dirnt) and Rancid (Tim Armstrong, Lars Frederikson, Brett Reed, Matt Freeman). And in

SAN FRANCISCO: Vivien Arnold, Kevin Berger, and all my other dear friends.

All of these people were an incredible help, and I cannot thank them enough for, among other things, reminding me that writing about music can still be fun and edifying and worth doing; and for making me like my job again. But this book would still never have gotten written without the constant care and encouragement of my mother, Jodie Arnold, to whom it is dedicated. Thanks, Mom!

(Portions of this book have appeared in the pages of the *New Times Los Angeles*, the *East Bay Express*, the *San Diego Reader*, and *Option* magazine.)

Written by the Winners

The past is over and done with: nothing more can happen in it. It speeds away in a beam of light, immutable, impenetrable, along the endless curve of time. I've often wished I could travel out to it, not in order to change anything in it like in some stupid science fiction book, but just to watch events unfold. Everyone knows that history is written by the winners; but I'd rather like to see the losers' perspective, and then judge things for myself.

For instance, what about punk rock? I see myself in some sort of glass vehicle, jogging alongside a rock concert as it whizzes into the past. Suddenly, the curtain goes up, and boom! I'm in the audience all over again, only this time I have all my wits about me. It's the Sex Pistols at Winterland, 1978. *"I am the Anti-chr-r-r-rist! I am an an-archist-t-t-t.*

From my glass box, I can see it all. On stage, there's the Pistols, still young and vibrant, skinny and shrieking. And below them in the audience is me with my two wussy girlfriends, looking determinedly out of it in our fresh-from-Macy's back-to-school outfits, three dorky girls with horrified looks on our faces, the indecently raw shadows of our current selves.

The sight of that me will no doubt make me shudder, but the main thing I wonder about that night is what could possibly have moved me so? I was scared of the audience, and too young to rock; nor had I been damaged, like my elders, by years of boring seventies boogie and so on. I thought the people in punk bands were ugly and unsexy, and yet I loved it anyway. It was a passion that was to last about seventeen years.

I still don't quite understand what happened at Winterland that night, but rock concerts have more to do with momentum and audience excitement than with music, anyway—and something about that one opened up my universe. It was like the moment when you learn to read—or when Dorothy steps out of her house in Oz. It turned a black-and-white world to red, and for that reason alone I am curious. What was it really like? Modern technology—video- and audiotape—doesn't tell enough; it's as if there's some mysterious element missing, a sixth or seventh or eleventh sense, that gives the whole thing meaning. A million essays analyzing the thing can't capture its essential flag. That's why I want to go back there.

ii.

I was eleven when I realized the wider implications of the maxim "Beauty is in the eye of the beholder," and for some reason I can remember the occasion distinctly. I was on my way to a swim meet in Fresno, in a car that was speeding through the dull gray area called the Altamont Pass, near Livermore. My pals and I were pinching one another and singing stupid songs in the backseat as usual when my friend's mother, who was driving, said, "I love the way the telephone poles look out here, the way they line up down the highway; they remind me of giant wire dancers."

Even now, I remember looking up and seeing those chrome gray poles stretched across the golden hills of California, and the way that they were suddenly transformed by her words into an actual artlike landscape. At the time, I thought that Mrs. Nasr was a conceptual genius, but in fact her words were just a faint suburban echo of postmodern thought: of the time, in 1922, when Marcel Duchamp bought a ready-made urinal at a hardware store and designated it a work of art.

Duchamp's sculpture—entitled *Fountain*—created a whole school of philosophy, and a simply interpreted one at that, since the idea that anything is art if you look at it right seems to be one of the prime directives of the human brain when left to its own devices. Children are often attracted to the oddest of icons—gaudy advertisements and shapeless stones, and those grubby pieces of chewed-up cloth that were once a well-kept teddy: Duchamp just put a name to this type of thought process, and art and literary criticism have flown down his route ever since.

Of course, it's debatable whether Duchamp helped or hindered fine art, spawning everything from film noir to pop art, Jeff Koons, Damien Hirst, Survival Research Laboratories, punk rock, and the Cocktail Nation— but one thing is for certain: in music, his has been the most dangerous doctrine ever uttered. From the Del Rubio triplets to the Shaggs, from the Boredoms to Kiss to the Leningrad Cowboys, Duchamp's worldview has excused much that doesn't necessarily deserve to be excused, and given contextuality and meaning to other things that do. Why, punk rock itself is a curious medium: is it noise or music, or genuine art? Is it all a trick, or an excuse of some kind—a fifteen-year-long play on the children's tale called "The Emperor's New Clothes"? "Without pop culture, there'd be no culture," read a flyer in Portland, Oregon, that I recently saw, but sometimes I wonder. The phrase "pop culture" covers up a multitude of sins.

I think what people in rock, and particularly punk, really mean is that "Without self-expression, there'd be no sense of self," and this is where punk rock comes in. In the beginning, it was pure danger: telling a worn-out population of bored white kids that meaning supersedes skill and passion is more important than talent was Duchamp's *Fountain* all over again, only with electric guitars. What the Pistols got at wasn't musical or even political, but it was something ... a cry of frustration or expression of some type, a massive getting of the people's goat.

And yet, punk is no mere urinal being called by another name. It is a purer statement than that. Those early recordings had little technical skill and were backed by the most bare-bones production, but their raw power is undeniable. There is a scene in the Clash's otherwise execrable movie *Rude Boy* in which Joe Strummer is seen playing a punked-up version of the old song "Let the Good Times Roll" on a rickety old piano. It's done almost without talent—and yet it is both riveting and true, the essence of passionate intensity: it is what punk rock music—or perhaps just rock 'n' roll music—is all about.

What the Pistols and other punks wanted badly to achieve was an honest voice: a musical lack of pretense, and a sound that cried havoc with their friends and foes alike. What they got was something else entirely, a fifteen-year-long process of invading and changing the face of pop culture into something a lot more, for lack of a better word, *ironic*. Punk plays with ideas of outlawry and rebellion; it plays, also, with the notion of success and selling out. It pretends it's not sincere, but it is, at bottom, as committed to its cause as anything that came before it, positing an ideology that's as devoted to freedom and kindness as any other world religion.

The thing about punk is, it would be ashamed to admit it. It's shy or something.

iii.

The Minutemen's D Boon once said he thought that every block in America should have its own punk rock band. I think what he meant was that kids would be better off in their garages making music and yelling about their rage rather than playing baseball or watching TV: that the lessons and feelings that punk rock invokes in its makers are so spiritually uplifting that if every kid was in a band, we'd have a better society, and that's a nice idea. But alas, Boon—who died tragically in 1985—hadn't considered some of the more impractical aspects of his remark. For one thing, punk rock must feel righteous, not popular; alone, not nurtured: it has to be embattled in order to exist at all. If every kid on the block had a Mohawk, wouldn't that negate their meaning?

Also, can you imagine a world where very block had its own punk rock band? Everywhere you went, cacophonous noise ringing out of the basement; the dogs and cats all in constant hiding; and every kid, for cred's sake, claiming desperately that he was hated by his peers.

Seriously, a world full of punk bands would be an abomination, but that's almost the kind of world we live in now: one populated with punk bands who are accepted as part of the fabric of society. That's why, in March of 1996, I suddenly became aware that punk rock—heretofore the ruling concept of my whole persona—was now a meaningless philosophy. It had lost its grip on its own internal tenets; as a descriptive, it meant nothing. Like all the great art movements that came before it, it sowed its seed and the seed came up and then it was harvested and the land around it became fallow. Instead of consumers we became the consumed, doomed to be burned by the powers that be, lost through auspices of our very own making.

The realization had been coming along gradually, of course, spurred on by such things as the formation of punk rock supergroups and the entire career of Courtney Love. But the catalyst for the final revelation was the Sex Pistols' announcement that they were about to reunite for a summer tour. According to MTV, the legendary punk outfit—now augmented by the man whom Sid Vicious had replaced, Glen Matlock, who had helped form the band originally and played on *Bollocks*—were going to kick off a nineteen-city European tour in June, after which they would come to the United States.

Of course, as numerous pundits pompously pointed out, the Sex Pistols were doing it for the money. But then, Greil Marcus's assertions about art and situationalism notwithstanding, that's why they did it in the first place. As weird and groundbreaking as they may have looked, the Pistols were always just another classic case of guys whose lives were saved by rock 'n' roll. Like Elvis and the Beatles and Bruce before them, they used the genre to better their socioeconomic position: to escape from the grim and pointless confines of a London council flat, bad beer, dingy stairwells, and the dole.

Perhaps that's why the idea of them re-forming wasn't immediately distressing to me. For one thing, the Sex Pistols have always claimed for themselves the right to be despicable. And for another, it was all but inevitable. After all, "cashing in" is just another way of saying "selling out," and that phrase has dogged rock music since the beginning of history. Everyone in rock music sells out eventually; it's his fate and life cycle, as well as his God-given right. It's as sure as summer follows spring. Selling out is part of the paradigm.

Elvis sold out when he returned from the army and started making cheesy movies. The Stones sold out when they fired Brian Jones. The Who sold out with *The Who Sell Out*, self-consciously, ironically, and stylishly, but wholeheartedly nonetheless. The Beatles sold out a few months ago, with *The Beatles Anthology* and fake reunion. The Pistols held out for longer than most, but now it's time for them, too, to lie down in that shallow grave.

But that's okay. After all, everyone, even non–rock stars, sells out in the end—giving up his or her hopes and dreams and ideals and youth for the safer and more practical virtues like family, and security, and health. This is all simply part of the life process, and rock 'n' roll is, of course, all about life. That's why rock fans kick and scream about their favorite bands "selling out," because it is an intimation of their own mortality, the very first sign that all things must pass.

What fans don't ever take into account is that bands who don't sell out (so to speak) tend to look stupider than those who do. Who wants to see a Sonic Youth in their forties? Why aren't the Beach Boys now called the Beach Men? And what about that balding Danzig?

The Sex Pistols claim they can't sell out since they've predicated themselves on being the ultimate rock 'n' roll swindle, and they sort of have a point. After all, their impact, such as it was, can never be erased, whether they sell out or not. And say what you will about the canniness of Malcolm McLaren, the drug-addledness of Sid Vicious, the calculated venom of Johnny Rotten, the negativity of the statement as a whole, the Sex Pistols' music—at least *Never Mind the Bollocks*—is incredibly powerful. "Anarchy in the UK," "God Save the Queen," "Bodies," "Pretty Vacant": someone wrote that music, and it is great art, defining and describing the world we live in, and changing it in the process. It's simply not the bollocks the band claimed it to be, a play on punk or a fashion statement: it is the major soci-opolitical, cultural, and yes, artistic statement of the past era, influencing drama, literature, film, life.

At this point in time, nothing can be subtracted from the Pistols' fabulous legacy, but it did seem odd that punk rock was going to end at a specific time and place, and that the time would be a midsummer's night, and that the place would be in Finland. And as the date approached, I suddenly felt it would be nice to be there. After all, I had been at the Pistols' last concert; why not go to their next one? Perhaps, I thought hopefully, an epiphany would occur there, too. I'm fond of epiphanies. And the first one had shaped my life.

Well, once I'd thought about it, it became an obsession. Not just going to Finland to see the Pistols, but the whole idea of the end of punk. Immediately, everything began to spiral toward a kind of inevitable conclusion, from sales of Green Day's *Insomnia* to Mountain Dew commercials featuring Johnny Rotten.

Finally, the people in charge of Lollapalooza announced the lineup for 1997, and when I saw that it included Rancid, Devo, and the Ramones, I made my decision and purchased a ticket to Helsinki, stat ($278, RT from London). As a rock critic, one searches endlessly for themes and contexts in which to jams one's values. This is the only way one can make sense of the chaotic and confusing things that jut out of the genre, and besides, it imposes some kind of myth and mystery on top of one's ordinary existence, it makes a story out of what are, in fact, mere random facts. It livens up your life.

The proposed Pistols reunion had suddenly given shape to an idea—a sort of overview of the situation to date. Picture punk as a big huge snow-ball, rolling down the mountainside of life. It's taken it eighteen years to pick up enough speed in the cultural cosmos to cause its current economic strength—the very strength that makes this reunion viable. Punk was the catalyst that caused the continuum on which sit R.E.M., the Replacements, Nirvana, and now Green Day, Offspring, Rancid, and others. But the Sex Pistols reuniting is going to stop everything dead in its tracks, and kill the ball's momentum.

On the other hand, maybe that will be a good thing. Eighteen years ago I saw the Sex Pistols, and it changed my life completely. Now I feel like I was sitting right on top of that snowball as it rolled the whole way down. From that vantage point it was easy to see that culture accrues at an uneven pace, then sheds itself accordingly. But now it is everywhere—fragmented and strewn across an increasingly distant landscape, a brightly colored mass of punk clothes on sale racks and stupid bands covering Germs songs. Its shards are pretty, but they have no edges. You couldn't cut a piece of bread with 'em, and so it is of no use to anyone.

And what then?

I don't really know. I thought that if I could pick up the pieces, turn them over in my hands and inspect them up close and personal, then I would maybe find something out about it all, just like scientists do with old bones and molecules and gross blood samples and things like that. If I can't go meet the past in a tiny spaceship, then perhaps I can reconstruct it—and call it Punkosaurus rex.

And so it was that on the morning of June 20, 1996, I boarded a plane at Gatwick airport bound for Helsinki. In the departure lounge, I saw a skinny boy wearing a leather jacket, ripped T-shirt, butt duster, and Doc Martens. He was sporting a red Mohawk, and sure enough, he reappeared at the FinnAir terminal amid a host of demure Nordic matrons who were to be our fellow travelers. His name was Gary and he was from Glasgow; and—shades of Irvine Welsh!—he was twenty-four years old and on the dole. The tape in his Walkman had X-ray Spex on one side and Green Day on the other (39/Smooth, mind you, not anything as crass as Dookie), and he was going to Finland to see the Sex Pistols in part because he loved them, and in part because it was his birthday.

Gary had a friend in Tampere—he'd seen Rancid there the month before—and I was off to Lahti, so we arranged instead to meet the next day in the pit. "Meet you in the pit!" we said to one another, with self-conscious irony. And, "I'll be easy to spot," said Gary, as we parted in a terminal on the other side of the Baltic; "I'll be the only one with a red Mohawk and wearing a kilt."

As a matter of fact, he wasn't, and I never saw him again. This is the story of Gary and everything he stands for; of the punk predicament, as it were—and the glorious folly of life in the fast lane, and of the end of rock 'n' roll. Love, after all, looks not with the eyes but with the mind. Therefore winged Cupid is base, vile, and blind. . . .

PART 1

DEAD PUNK IN THE MIDDLE OF THE ROAD

Chapter 1
Hope You Die Before We Grow Up

Over hill and over dale, over park and over pale... it is a Midsummer Night's Eve in a wooded glen somewhere in the wilds of Finland. The chill blue sky is full of cumulus clouds, the air is ringing with the music of Bad Religion, and I am standing on a lovely hillside, 250 miles south of the Arctic Circle, surrounded by thousands of comatose Finnish kids, all in an alcoholic stupor. Bodies, to be exact.

Another way of putting it is, I am on top of the world looking down on creation, and the only explanation is insane. Today, eighteen years, six months, and seven days after they broke up one rainy night in San Francisco, the Sex Pistols are about to take the stage in the first stop of what's being billed as "the Filthy Lucre Tour."

Since snowboarding is one of the things that has helped sell hardcore and nuevo-punk rock to American youngsters, it is only right and fitting that the Pistols' first concert in eighteen years is to take place here at the Messila Funpark, a densely wooded lakeside snowboarding park some one hundred kilometers north of Helsinki. This weekend it is the sight of a three-day festival involving a diverse set of bands including Moby, the Shamen, the Prodigy, Sepultura, and the Sex Pistols, as well as twenty thousand young people drawn from Finland, Norway, and nearby Russia.

"It is a terrible day," a nice woman named Raija tells me on the train heading north from Helsinki. "It is as if they compete to see who can be the most sickening." She could easily be talking about the fact that the Pistols—along with so many other seventies acts like Kiss, Kansas, Deep Purple, and the Who—are about to reunite, but in fact, what she is referring to is the traditional drinking binge that marks Midsummer's Eve in this and many other Nordic countries.

In Finland, Midsummer is a vacation day akin to our New Year's Eve. Although Americans aren't too shabby with a bottle, the Finns are Olympic champions at it. Johannussattu (as it's called) is Finland's national drinking holiday, and its effects are already apparent in the glazed eyes and fucked-up faces that surround us in the train. At the station in the town of Lahti, where special coaches have been arranged to take people to the Messila Festival, I board a bus with six or seven teenagers, each of whom carries an extra-large green Glad bag full of his or her belongings: extra socks, a bed-roll, and a giant cache of beer bottles. Every time the bus comes to a halt on the twisty road up to the park, there's this enormous clatter—clank!—of glass on bloody glass.

The boy next to me, a nice, bespectacled youth of twenty-one or so, silently drinks two twenty-four-ounce cans of beers in the ten minutes it takes to get to the festival site. It is three in the afternoon.

ii.

Messila is a recreation area that also contains campsites, sailing facilities, and a gorgeous view of a lake; nearby, in Lahti, three enormous ski jumps loom prepossessingly over the dreary town.

As one approaches the park, however, one is forcibly struck by the ex-treme emptiness of the surroundings. Unlike in America, where entire cities become warzones for the duration of any rock event, you would never guess that a giant rock concert was taking place anywhere in the vicinity. The place looks deserted. In reality, the festival is occurring all around us, as we clank and clatter on up the hill.

This is partly a tribute to Finland's emptiness, and partly to the Euro-pean tradition that sees kids camping and gathering peacefully all over the Continent at a series of summer rock festivals like this one, often for days on end. While in America, any concert that draws over 50,000 people—Woodstock '94, for example—is considered a huge event, in Europe, such festivals are incredibly common.

In the United Kingdom alone, there's Glastonbury, Reading, Phoenix, the Fleadh, and T in the Park (Edinburgh)—all of them drawing in the 100,000-person range. The Continent has even more: Pink Pop in Belgium and Roskilde in Denmark, for example, both draw up to 150,000 people, five times what Messila will get today.

Typically, each of these festivals has two or three stages and tons of bands; the music usually goes from midafternoon to three or four in the morning, and tickets cost a hundred dollars. Audiences will travel from a vast surrounding area to get there before it starts, and then they camp out for days, thus alleviating some of the problems of traffic and parking that would plague any American equivalent.

For some reason, Finland is a mecca for such rock festivals. Several are held every summer, including the notorious Ruisrock Festival, headlined by Nirvana in '92, which this year features the Red Hot Chili Peppers, Bunny Wailer, and Neil Young; and, frighteningly, a heavy-metal festival this same weekend being held somewhere up near Lapland, which will feature Iron Maiden and a re-formed version of Deep Purple. (Sepultura are heading up there to play as soon as their set at Messila finishes.)

The Messila Festival, however, is particularly notorious, because it takes place on Johannussatto, the country's equivalent of New Year's Eve. Partly because it draws some of its audience from northern Russia and Estonia—countries that rival Finland for the scope of their insobriety—and partly because of the holiday it occurs over, Messila is downright bizarre. As I hike up the snowboard hill to the gates, I am struck by the difference between this and, say, Lollapalooza. There is no traffic here, no pushing, no searches, no filing through gates like cattle . . . just a long hike up a dirt path past one thousand plastic tents, along a road littered with used condoms, pools of vomit, and comatose kids who are resting by the side of the road.

At the top of the rise, however, one is met by a familiar sight: a crane has been erected, from which one can buy the right to bungee-jump, if one is so inclined. Presently one comes upon a little Lollapalooza-like concourse, complete with hippie booths selling incense, Finnish burritos, and the inevitable "Anarchy" T-shirts.

The Messila Festival is sponsored by Koff beer, one of Finland's most popular manufacturers and a name uncomfortably close to Duff beer, of *Simpsons* fame. (Duff beer sponsored "Homerpalooza.") Temporary beer halls abound on this hillside, makeshift shacks meant to look like the Old West, and each one is titled, for some reason, with the name of a U.S. town: "Memphis," "El Paso," "Nashville," and—I kid you not—"Livermore." Thanks to Koff, the whole place is reeling and hilarious, and night will never, ever fall: at ten o'clock it looks like four in the afternoon, and it's not gonna get a lot darker. I cross some more woods and stumble down the hill, and about fifty meters from the stage I am attacked by a large Finnish lad who grabs my face with the palm of his hand while snapping pics with my camera. At that moment, I thank the Lord for Sepultura, a kindly Brazilian death-metal group, whose Finnish record company has left a backstage pass at my hotel in Helsinki.

Sepultura—the name means "burial" in Portuguese—just recorded an album entitled *Roots* that utilizes the services of a Brazilian Indian tribe called the Xavantes. There is something peculiarly moving in the conjunction of this tribe's indigenous music and the band's raging death metal, particularly when it's being played up here at the top of the world, about as far from the rain forest as one could possibly be. When the Finnish air—cold and clean—fills up with a taped recording of this tribe's rhythmic chant, and thousands of Finnish kids start pumping their fists in unison, it's easy to feel like global unity has been achieved at last.

Some Americans might think that a concert featuring a death-metal band like Sepultura and a punk rock act like the Pistols is a bizarre coupling of musical styles, but Sep's Max Cavalera is, in fact, a big Sex Pistols fan. *Roots* even contains a song called "Cut Throat," which is modeled after the Pistols' song "E.M.I." and contains a chorus that goes, "Enslavement—Pathetic—Ignorant—Corporations." (EPIC, spelling the name of their famous label.)

Cavalera is excited to be opening for the Pistols today. "I got the Sex Pistols record when I was thirteen or fourteen. It was one of the only punk albums you could get in Brazil because it was released on a major label. The funny thing about us was we were little metal kids, we listened to Motorhead, GBH, Discharge. My friends were all, 'Oh, that's stupid punk stuff with stupid hair,' but I hadn't seen pictures of them—there isn't one on the album—and I thought it was fucking great. I didn't understand English then, but I loved the music, the attitude. While people in Europe and America thought of the Pistols as this punk thing, to me, they were like the logical next step after Iron Maiden, who were all played out."

Cavalera says he saw Johnny Rotten at the Helsinki airport and they nodded pleasantly to one another, but he isn't going to get a chance to talk to him here, since they have to take off for Lapland before Bad Religion's set even finishes.

It turns out that Max wouldn't have had a chance to talk to Rotten anyway, since the Pistols' arrival precipitates a sudden security lockdown. When their bus rolls up—a mere half hour before their scheduled performance—a raft of security guards starts pushing everyone away from the driveway. No one is allowed to see the Pistols up close and personal, as they are whisked from bus to trailer and onstage in private. I even see one guard manhandling Bad Religion's Greg Graffin.

When the Pistols get onstage—at 10 P.M.—the field in front of them is literally littered with comatose bodies and vomit. Thousands of young and bleary-eyed Finns are all fabulously, mythically, tremendously drunk. They are rocking and swaying to the recorded music and bellowing out insults in Unpronounceablese between taking swigs from huge plastic jugs of booze. Apparently, the hip thing to do here is to fill a large plastic bottle originally meant for automobile fluids with your drink of choice, so that it looks like the kids are swigging antifreeze and motor oil. (Either that, or they really *are* swigging antifreeze and motor oil.)

This was the Sex Pistols' first time in Finland. The band was supposed to play there in 1977, but the show, a benefit for a children's organization, was canceled when the Pistols' material was deemed inappropriate by the promoter. Tonight, the many conceptual problems presented by their re-uniting at all are compounded by audience indifference. Although hundreds of the kids in the crowd sport "Anarchy" T-shirts and multicolored hairdos, the crowd as a whole seems oblivious of the Pistols' music—since the first six songs are relatively obscure numbers like "Did You No Wrong" and "Satellite."

True, the band opened with "Bodies," but they then proceeded to play their five least-known songs, thus inducing sudden boredom in the crowd of kids who'd recently gone apeshit over Sepultura and Bad Religion. To them—and to me also—the Pistols' music sounded clean and shiny; while Rotten himself looked bored and said the equivalent of things like, "I lello, Finland! Do you want some rock 'n' roll?"

No wonder the kids started pelting them with things! Besides, that's what crowds do these days, and the Pistols must be awfully naive not to have known that. But then, perhaps the Pistols are naive. Perhaps all they ever wanted was, like Sally Field before them, to be loved. Whatever: twenty minutes into the set, Rotten threatens to stop playing, apparently angry because audience members were hurling plastic bottles at him.

"I am not your target," he yelps. "There are worse things than me in this world.... You should be fucking grateful I'm here."

Rotten made good his threat after the next song, saying, "That's it, fuck you, fuck off." Off he stomps; the rest of the band leaves with him. "Get some Finnish cunt up here to take your abuse," he adds nastily.

The poor sod with that unenviable position was one Billy Carson, an African American actor who is popular in Finland, who came onstage and berated the crowd for a second time. "Idiots! Morons!" he shouted in broken Finnish. "This band has come here after twenty years. You should treat them with respect!"

Soon, the band returned to the stage to play five more songs, including better-known numbers like "Holidays in the Sun," "Pretty Vacant," and "E.M.I."

There was little applause upon completion of the set. Only when the band returned to encore with "Anarchy in the UK" did the crowd—most of whom weren't born when the song came out—explode, dancing and cheering and singing along in English.

The Pistols wound up the set with the old Stooges song "No Fun." "This is what you've been, and what we're having," said the ever-pleasant Rotten, by way of introduction.

But despite his taunts many young fans said afterward that they were pleased with the performance.

"I liked it very much, them and Sepultura," says Marija Lammi, nineteen, of Tampere.

"Maybe they are only doing it for the money," added Annika Muhonen, fifteen, "but it's still good music. They still have something to say."

But did they? I wondered. One thing that struck me about the Pistols' show in Finland was their seeming naïveté. The tantrum could have been a reaction to the crowd's indifference, but it seemed more likely that Rotten was genuinely upset by the rowdy and inebriated audience. Perhaps the Pistols, whose largest gig prior to this one was in front of 3,500 at Winterland in San Francisco, were unprepared for the modern-day spectacle of 20,000 drunk and belligerent teenagers. Unlike younger bands, they may have been truly taken aback at the sight of such large-scale mayhem that rock 'n' roll shows now effect, and indeed, it is a distressing sight.

Since most of the band's dates in Europe this summer are at even larger rock festivals, including Phoenix, Roskilde, and ones in Prague and Slovenia, they better get used to it, PDQ. Hell, the rest of us have, however unwillingly.

Anyway, as their bus speeds off into the evening light on its way to the next gig in Munich, Messila returns to normal. Presently, headliners the Leningrad Cowboys, a Finnish band that parodies metal and C&W, play a version of "God Save the Queen," which slips imperceptibly into Elvis Presley's "Burning Love" before winding up with the all-too-appropriate lyric, "No future—less vodka for you." Truer words have seldom been spoken.

A Tale of Two Cities

Two days later, on the flight home from Finland, the airplane dips over Hyde Park, where one can see a bunch of workmen erecting the stage for the Who concert, which will occur there next week. A mile to the north, in Finsbury Park, the stage has already been erected for the Sex Pistols' London gala. By midday the Tube is full of bright-haired punks heading up the Victoria line to see the all-day concert. It is Sunday, the twenty-third of June, the day of the Sex Pistols' triumphant return to their birthplace, London.

This is the show that the Pistols want the press to be at—to help propagate and fuel the hype that's going to drive them across the Atlantic later on this summer. And when it comes to hype, the English press is happy to oblige, just as they did the first time. But unlike in Finland, where skepticism about the Sex Pistols' reunion just edged out a sense of healthy indifference, England is full to the brim with stories about punk's twentieth anniversary. Besides this much-talked-about show, there is a festival coming up in Blackpool in August that will feature reunions of X-Ray Spex and the Damned, among others.

Given the number of young Mohawked punks—the 1996 equivalent of hippies on Haight Street—you see on the King's Road now, driven by songs by Green Day and NOFX, it seems like the time for this ridiculous reunion is ripe here in the UK. And yet, according to *Timeout* and Capitol Radio, sales have been slow for this concert, despite all the hype. The Finsbury Park show costs twenty-two pounds (thirty-five dollars) and the show has sold twenty thousand tickets, most during the last two weeks, but it's totally unclear if the intended audience for these shows is sixteen-year-old nuevo-punk Rancid fans paying homage to their elders, or older fans who never got to see them in the first place.

One glance into the confines of Finsbury Park late in the afternoon of June 23, and one would immediately say the latter. This afternoon Finsbury Park is hardly an advertisement for British beauty. On the contrary, all the old punks, basking in the unaccustomed sunlight, shirts off, bellies protruding, messy hair receding, and skin like so many fish, look like nothing so much as the cast of the *Road Warrior* gone slightly to seed.

As was the case in Finland, this show also has its share of hippie booths selling sunglasses and Guatemalan wear, and looming in one corner is the inevitable crane with bungee jump. The only way you can tell you're in Britain and not America (or Finland, for that matter) is the perpetual inclusion of tea on every menu, however inappropriate the fare. Burritos, beer, and tea, for example. Bangers and mash and tea. Ninety-nine flake (a white, cold, petroleum-based product the British like to pass off as ice cream) and tea...the list goes on.

The audience's unbeatitude notwithstanding, the Finsbury Park show is hitchless—the polar opposite of Messila, except Messila was polar, and this is pleasant. The Pistols are preceded by six hours of punk, including sets by Iggy Pop, the Wild Hearts, the Buzzcocks, Stiff Little Fingers, and Fluffy; and the warm, clear weather and England's unexpected victory against Spain the European Cup soccer quarterfinals the day before have combined to cast a euphoric spell over the whole arena. People are friendly and smiling, blissed out, beaming: nothing could blow their high today, and the Sex Pistols don't even try to. Prior to taking the stage—a half hour late, incidentally—the Pistols play a tape of all the worst songs, circa 1976: Leo Sayer's "You Make Me Feel Like Dancing," for example, and "The Night Chicago Died," plus winners of the Eurovision Song Contest too terrible ever to have been heard in the United States. This was the music the Pistols meant to destroy, and the crowd immediately gets the joke, singing along with every insipid word.

It's clear that this audience is primed and ready, and indeed, when Rotten and Co. take the stage—"Are you r-r-r-ready?"—and rip into "Bodies," a giant roar of appreciation goes up as an audience twenty-five thousand people strong sings every word along. Everyone is arm in arm, laughing, dancing, singing along, as if to a Christmas carol: "She was a girl from Birmingham! She just had an abortion!"

Wheee! What does it all mean? I'm flummoxed: this whole co-option of punk—from the snowboarders who rage down the mountain to Bad Religion, to the kids who claim the Pistols as their idols—has completely bewildered me. But there's no denying that the rest of the Pistols' set is one long white riot, with the audience, warm and fuzzy and full of good cheer, chanting "No future! no future! for you" like so many idiot savants.

The next day's papers report that the concert was attended by Johnny Depp and Kate Moss, and the inevitable Gallagher brothers, Liam and Noel, who are utterly ubiquitous in London and go to everything, no matter what: a few days later one of 'em startles poor Burt Bacharach by leaping onstage at the Royal Festival Hall and telling the audience how great he thinks Burt is.

It's all very unsettling, this mixing up of cultural icons. Where is the tribal unity that made punk rock so appealing? This evening, the Pistols were introduced by two English football stars, Gareth Southgate and Stuart Pearce, the latter of whom says that *Never Mind the Bollocks* is his favorite album ever. Later, I wondered aloud if this was meant as irony; as if the Pistols were saying truculently, "Look—the same people who loathed us now love us twenty years on."

"No way," sneers my friend Lindsay Hutton, editor of the fanzine *Next Big Thing*. "It's meant exactly as it is, as the worst kind of night out with the lads drinking, part of this whole ridiculous English nationalistic football fervor."

"But Rotten's *Irish*," I say, puzzled. Ironically, later on that week, Southgate betrays England's hopes in the European Cup final by kicking the penalty which gets caught out by Germany's goalie. And Pearce, it turns out, played the same bitter role in a World Cup game in 1990.

In other words, rather than representing England's shiniest, jockiest status quo, Southgate and Pearce are currently England's biggest goats. Besides, since the British press has declared that a European Cup victory will mean a sudden general election and a certain victory for the otherwise fading Tory Party, Southgate's big boo-boo may have had lasting political consequences for the good. Nine months later, Labour gets in instead, putting an end to the eighteen-year Conservative reign that governed the era of punk.

And yet, despite that positive development, if popular music reflects popular culture, then the world's in a sorry state right now, and particularly in Britain. This week's *Melody Maker*, for example, is full of praise for the 60 Foot Dolls, a revolting Welsh band who brag in interviews that they like to (literally) take shits on their groupies after having sex with them, presumably to show them who's boss.

Melody Maker's praise notwithstanding, the Dolls' surely won't help propagate Britpop—or rock 'n' roll itself—up and over this year of dread reunions. In fact, with them and those like them in the offing, all that's left to right-thinking common people is nostalgia, and perhaps a sense of humor about events like all of these. Our stars are dying, our heroes are humiliating themselves, the latest bands are loathsome creeps—kind of how it was in '76, if I'm to believe what I read.

Most tellingly of all, backstage, an area as large as many a concert venue, is a madhouse; like something out of Robert Frank's Stones movie, *Cocksucker Blues*. It's full of minor pop stars, old punks, and American record-label employees who yak incessantly through every band. Every time a band comes onstage, the guests stream through the guest entrance onto the field to watch the show "for real," but it's all very perfunctory: during the Pistols' ecstatic rendition of "Anarchy in the UK"—which, along with the seventy-thousand-person-strong sing-along of the Lighting Seeds' "3 Lions" at Wembley the night before, may be one of the rock 'n' roll highlights of the summer—I heard a label dude yell into somebody's ear, "So . . . how's Sleeper doing in the U.S.?"

During the encore of "No Fun," I rush into the enclosure to file a story on my mobile phone. A hundred or so oblivious guests sit there drinking and laughing. One of them, an American, hurls a chair at me, apparently angry because I'm reviewing the show without watching it to the end. He doesn't explain why he isn't watching it at all, and I don't even ask.

iv.
The Punks Meet the Godfathers

Six days later, the mood of England has distinctly altered for the worse. Or to put it another way—a heartbreaking loss to Germany in the European Cup semifinals and a sudden steady rain have returned the country to its normal gloom.

It's Saturday, June 29—the day of the concert for the Prince's Trust, aka "MasterCard Presents the Masters of Rock Concert"—billed, in the oft erroneous British press, as "the largest rock concert ever held in London," "the largest rock concert held in Hyde Park since 1976," and "the largest gathering in London since the Royal Wedding in 1981" . . . as if large gatherings are something to be desired, rather than the messy and uncomfortable situations they are in reality.

The newspapers here also keep on asserting that this is the first time *Quadrophenia* has ever been performed, but this isn't true: in fact, *Quadrophenia* was performed in America in 1974. My cousin, who accompanies me today, may be the only person in the audience of 150,000 who will have seen both. The night he went in America, at the Cow Palace in San Francisco, Keith Moon passed out halfway through the show and was replaced on drums by a random member of the audience. Today Moon is being replaced on drums by Rabbitt Bundrick and Zak "Son of Ringo" Starkey.

But to continue. The MasterCard Presents the Masters of Rock™ Concert features five acts: Jools Holland, Alanis Morissette, Bob Dylan, Eric Clapton, and Pete Townshend and friends, his friends being Roger Daltrey,

John Entwistle, plus fourteen other musicians, numerous singers, and six actors who are performing *Quadrophenia* in its entirety today. The project is a benefit for the Prince's Trust charity, but it is also a huge media hype, designed to occur in conjunction with the release of *Quadrophenia* on CD. One can't help but suspect that it's also a prerehearsal for the Broadway-ization of *Quadrophenia* à la 1992's smash *Tommy*.

It's such a hype, in fact, that some clever press officer manages to get a rumor started that "special guests" will include an impromptu reunion of the remaining three Beatles—a rumor that, despite its unbelievability, keeps sadly gullible journalists in their seats to the end.

This is particularly galling, since "special guest" turns out to mean nothing more than Ron Wood, who plays along with Bob Dylan.

The MasterCard Presents the Masters of Rock™ Concert is in an enclosure running along Park Lane, stretching from Marble Arch back to about Serpentine Road, about a quarter of a mile. Although it is vast, it is also patently the smallest amount of space you could reasonably fit 150,000 people in. When we arrive, around 4 P.M. in time for Dylan, the enclosure is full—wall to wall, fence to fence, shoulder to shoulder, cheek to cheek. The whole situation makes the Finsbury Park gig—nay, it makes the Messila Festival look like the pleasantest and most unpretentious gathering ever staged.

Eventually, after much palaver, we are sent to sit in a bleacher section, along with some 5,000 other "VIPS," some of whom paid 200 pounds (360 dollars) for the privilege. (In contrast, the field costs a reasonable 8 pounds, or 13 dollars.) We are nearer the stage than most and quite near to the sections containing the royal box—Prince Charles, Pélé, Mick Jagger, boxer Frank Bruno—but we are still nowhere near a good view of the stage. It doesn't take long to realize that the best seats here are the ones outside the whole enclosure, where a couple of hundred people are lounging comfortably on the grass watching the concert on one of the perfectly visible Jumbotron screens and hearing about exactly the same audio as we are . . . for free.

Inside, however, it is not so pleasant. For one thing, it is a freezing cold day; huge gray rain clouds loom threateningly overhead. For another, we're not allowed out on the field (which looks an awful place, but still!). And lastly, we are being inundated by MasterCard cant, from the ads on the twelve Jumbotron screens that dot the enclosure, to the giant blimp that hovers overhead.

At 5:45, Prince Charles enters the arena, and *Quadrophenia* begins.

And alas, it is a mess. The staging, such as it is, is impossible to watch, the voice-over makes little connective sense, and worst of all, the size of the venue means that the sound and the visuals are out of synch, so every character—Phil Daniels as the narrator, Trevor McDonald as the newscaster, Gary Glitter as the Punk, Adrian Edmonson (ironically, the man who played the faux punk Vivian on *The Young Ones*) in Sting's role as the Bellboy—looks like he has been badly redubbed in a Japanese cartoon: their lips move, and the sound comes out seconds later. Theaterwise, it's a rout.

Oddly, the music itself actually holds up better than expected. Songs like "The Real Me," "Had Enough," "Cut My Hair," "The Punk Meets the Godfather," and "5:15" have been relatively underplayed on FM radio compared to so many other Who songs, and sound great here. Daltrey—who looks about twenty years younger than his mates—is in particularly fine form, and Townshend is quite moving on the solo acoustic number "Drowned."

The show winds up, as the record does, with an overly bombastic "Love Reign O'er Me," and an encore of "5:15." But it all comes to nothing: the audience's response is distracted and unenthusiastic. Clapton's much simpler set fares much better later in the evening, but then, here in Britain, Clapton is still God.

Somehow, I had pictured this concert as being more like the films I'd seen of the Rolling Stones' famous free concert in Hyde Park in 1969, which drew an alleged 250,000 people: all verdant grass and picnics and Butterflies Are Free. But the MasterCard Presents the Masters of Rock™ Concert is the antithesis of that: it speaks instead of money and advertising and cross-promotion and megahype. What is fun about standing in a freezing cold field for nine hours, watching a bunch of dinosaurs lumber across some far-off TV screens?

When I voice this opinion, various English people say disapprovingly, "But it's for *charity*...and a *royal* charity, at that." My cousin adds, "It's the event itself. People want to be able to say they were here. What's wrong with that?"

I say, "A lot." *Duh.* After all, people only want to say they were here because the media have impressed upon them the patent falsehood that this is an important moment. And it's only "important" because it's (*a*) large and (*b*) a "first." In this case the media—and the audience—are tools of MasterCard, and the Who, who simply want to gather together the largest amount of people they can shill to as possible.

Clearly they don't care about the artistic quality of the event, or they'd *never* hold it in a venue this size. And as for charity, why charge eight pounds and put on such an expensive thing if you're truly into raising money?

Ever feel like you've been cheated? I have, again and again—but more so in the last ten days in Europe than ever before. As I looked out at the enclosure at Hyde Park, two football-fields long, I was summarily reminded of all the things that the Pistols were fighting against in 1976 ... bloated rock concerts featuring bands like Queen, who (articles keep reminding us) headlined the last such event in Hyde Park in 1976; Led Zeppelin, whose lead members Page and Plant are seated a few rows down from me; and the Who themselves, who are about to take the stage.

In those days, bands like the Pistols and the Buzzcocks were against the glitz and pretentiousness of what now seem like minor infractions: Page's double guitar; eight-minute-long songs; rock operas; silken trousers and fringed scarfs; the occasional use of the London Philharmonic Orchestra to flesh out rock operas; backstage parties populated by Sloane Rangers and the 1976 model-equivalent of Kate Moss.

At the time those things seemed worth destroying; many of those things are here today. After all, compared to a concert held in a quarter-mile-long cattle pen, the Pistols reunion was downright honest. At least, for all its nostalgic aspects, it was fun. In comparison to this, the Finsbury Park gig, with its moderate crowd of twenty-five thousand, was like fucking CBGB's.

Despite its amusement value—and I can't deny it was amusing—the whole experience has made it clear that rock 'n' roll is very near death. It received a mortal blow in Finland, and now the bell is tolling, as loudly as can be. Yes, London is freezing with boredom now; soon it will be stone cold, immobile; and everyone in this entire city will be turned into pillars of salt. You can already see the statuary in these giant gardens—Finsbury Park, Hyde Park, Green Park, Kew.... There's Johnny Rotten, his hair in cementy spikes, and Roger Daltrey, his chin jutting out; Clapton and Dylan, like Methuselah and his dad, and of course Peter T, his arm stopped straight out midwindup. One of these people once said, "Don't look back"; but it's way too late because everybody did.

■ The Ramones, 1996
Photo by AP/Wide World Photos

Chapter 2
Rock in a Hard Place

Once upon a time, in a galaxy far, far away, there was a beautiful band called the Ramones, and the world for once agreed. The Ramones were perfect; the only perfect entity in existence.

First of all, there were four Ramones, which was the perfect number for a rock 'n' roll band. Then, they were named Johnny, Joey, Tommy, and Dee Dee, which were the perfect names for a rock 'n' roll band. (These weren't their real names, but that was okay, because in rock 'n' roll, you're allowed to be called anything you want.)

Another perfect thing about the Ramones was the way they looked: identical. They were skinny and greasy and longhaired and pale skinned, and they wore tight black jeans and black leather jackets, and they looked like they didn't give a fuck. All those perfect people who make the rest of us feel inferior had no power over the Ramones: the Ramones were perfect as they were.

But the most perfect thing about the Ramones was their music, which distilled to its very essence the good things about rock 'n' roll. Each song had only three chords, but they were, as Joey once put it, the *right* three chords. Each song had an immensely fast tempo, which made them sound even more exciting. The band played loudly, and exactly in unison—thus coining the term "loud fast rules"—and they sang lyrics that were a poignant cross between goofy and terrible and perfectly apt. They never forgot to put in a tune and a catchy chorus, and every song began with the same four words, "One two three four," and that was perfect, too.

When they first began, the Ramones played a lot of shows in their hometown of New York City, and everybody who saw them loved them immediately. People from America agreed that they were wonderful and joyous and gave new meaning to the term "genius"; people from England saw them and went home and formed rock bands that sounded just like them. The Ramones were inspirational, because they proved that you didn't have to be pretty and pretentious and sensitive and overbearing—or even particularly musical—to be a member of a fucking great rock band.

It was obvious. And because the Ramones were so good, they were allowed to make a record almost right away. After all, given the history of rock—of bands like the Beatles and the Stones and the Monkees and Led Zeppelin—it seemed a foregone conclusion that a band as simple and as affecting as the Ramones would take over the world.

But it didn't happen that way. For years the Ramones put out records with wonderful songs on them, and they toured the United States and Europe over and over again. But they never made it past what is known as cult status—they never made a record that had a gen-u-ine hit.

They should have, though. Because if "Sheena Is a Punk Rocker" had been a hit in 1977, everything would have been different. For one thing, there would have been no reign of Ronald Reagan, because America wouldn't have been fixated on *Happy Days* and nostalgic music, because the present would have been so good. Instead of dwelling on a past that never really existed, they'd have been out forming punk rock bands and dancing merrily to something new.

Yes, picture a world where "Sheena" was a hit—followed, of course, by "Rockaway Beach," "End of the Century," "Bonzo Goes to Bitburg," "Pet Sematary," and so on. Instead of wearing polyster and spandex, everyone in America would have worn cotton-blended black and white. Instead of fluffing their hair like Farrah Fawcett, they would have left it long and straight. They would have had taste, damn it. They would have had better pictures of themselves in their photo albums. They would have had some self-respect.

Alas, this never happened. The Ramones had a different history—the wrong history as it were—foisted off upon them. Valiantly, they plugged away at things, but enough is enough, and in 1995, they decided to break up.

And then a funny thing happened. When the Ramones announced their imminent breakup, certain people wouldn't let them. They literally refused to let it happen. (Can you say "Perfect"?) One by one all the bands that loved and revered and worshiped the Ramones came out in public and said, "We won't let this happen." First Pearl Jam, then White Zombie, then Soundgarden. They insisted that the Ramones please tour with them; that they extend the date of their demise till all of America had seen them and formed their final opinion.

And so, in the summer of 1996, the Ramones finally got to face Middle America: steaming hot fields full of shirtless white boys, the audience that ought to have embraced them all along, if it hadn't had magenta-colored spandex pop metal haircut bands pushed off on it instead. And a person had to wonder: Was it too late for American youth to learn to love the Ramones? The country had been given one last chance.

ii.

Forks in the River Speedway, in Newport, Tennessee, is an hour and a half from Knoxville—although it is only a few miles away from Pigeon Forge, the childhood home of Dolly Parton in the heart of the Great Smoky Mountains. Tourists pack Dollywood on weekends to attend the legendary "dinner stampedes," but the speedway scene is another trip entirely. A couple of weeks ago, Charlie Daniels and 38 Special rocked the Smokies at the Speedway—fifty thousand rednecks on reds peeing on the side of the road—and today, it's Lollapalooza's turn to turn Appalachia into Lollapalachia.

Folks around Forks think that Lollapalooza's going to draw a scary, black-shirted metalloid crowd—after all, Metallica's fan club is based in nearby Knoxville—but folks are wrong. To those on the East and West Coasts of America, this year's Lollapalooza lineup—featuring Psychotica, the Screaming Trees, Rancid, the Ramones, Rage Against the Machine, Soundgarden, and Metallica—is considered the most mainstream bill ever, a travesty of commercial, testosterone-driven acts. But as anyone who's ever spent a Saturday night in Knoxville knows, Lollapalooza is the biggest thing to hit what passes for alternative culture in the Great Smoky Mountains ever.

Of course, in 1996 "pop culture" has become a pretty loose term—thanks mostly to the influence of Lollapalooza itself. Too much has been written about the festival at this point for one to bother to recap its history or its influence; suffice it to say that, along with MTV, it has had a profound effect on pop culture. Now in its sixth year of existence, the festival has been one of the main subversions of metal-pop-country hegemony in America, and this year is the most subverted—some might even say perverted—version yet.

Lollapalooza has always provided onlookers with a glimpse of clashing genres. But few stories illustrate the moral dichotomy inherent in 1996's punk-meets-metalloid lineup better then the afternoon in West Palm

Beach when a girl came up to Rancid's Tim Armstrong and begged him to get her backstage.

The girl, a typical Floridian babe in scanty clothing, pled her case as eloquently as she could. "Please, Tim, I've got to go there. The drummer from Metallica said he'd do a line on my tits!"

Tim, who shaved his Mohawk a few weeks ago but still bears the stigma of ten years spent in hardcore heaven: "Do a line? You mean...he's going to draw a picture on your tits with a Sharpie?"

iii.

Armstrong's words sound impossibly naive—unless you consider just how low-key bands have become in the last five years. The tit-waving antics of GNR (Guns 'N' Roses) are over and done with; now it's Metallica who seem old and fogyish for behaving like the stereotypical "rock stars" of old.

This, then, is the moral and artistic dichotomy of Lollapalooza 1996—the same dichotomy that has seemingly kept audiences across the country at bay. On your left, you have Rancid, straight-edge, DIY, indie-label—short for "independent", meaning unaffiliated with a major—punk rock heroes, backed up by their homies the Ramones and, at some dates, by Devo.

On your right, the defending champions of humorless heavy metal, Metallica, who come complete with thudding bass line, high-neck guitar solos, cigars, chopper rides, Learjets, backstage babes, and onstage pyrotechnics. They are supported, to a certain extent, by the less flamboyant but equally heavy music of Soundgarden and, at some dates, Rage Against the Machine.

In theory, a tour that melds together these utterly populist elements would create a mighty strong metal indeed. But in practice, the two things have turned out to be more antithetical than gangsta rap and industrial rock, than jazz and Eurodisco, than mind-wandering indie-crap and shiny girl grunge, than Sinead O'Connor and Courtney Love.

Punk and metal, antithetical? Get outta here! On the surface, the two things seem like the least-daring mixture ever. The Melvins, for example, who are playing the second stage, have been melding Dead Kennedys with Black Sabbath since Kurt Cobain was knee high to a grasshopper.

But to audiences in places like Des Moines, Iowa, Rockingham, North

Carolina, and Ferris, Texas, the combo has proved to be scarier than a bill with the Butthole Surfers and Ice T. The initial perception was that a Lollapalooza bill featuring Metallica and Soundgarden, both of whom have number-one albums, would be far too popular to put into amphitheaters. But ticket sales for this year's Lollapalooza have been similar to other years', and about half what the tour producers expected.

How come? "I don't have any idea," tour manager Stuart Ross says, shrugging. "There's one theory that says that Metallica audiences are waiting for Metallica to come do their big two-and-a-half-hour production in an arena, and don't want to come and wade through eight hours of alternative music that they may not appreciate and crowds they may not want to hang out in. That's theory one.

"Theory two is that the alternative audience has been turned off by the fact that Metallica's on the bill. I don't agree with that, but some people hold that theory. Third is the fact that we raised the ticket price, and this is the point of price resistance.

"Then there's the issue that because we're in fields, and some of our audiences are too young to drive and some of their parents may have been hesistant to take them to a venue they're not familiar with and which they don't already know as a nice, safe environment.

"Lastly, for some reason, it's a big movie summer and it's a slim music summer. I hear that no show except for Kiss is doing well this summer."

Still, despite the warning signals, the slow sales have taken Lollapalooza by surprise. An early gig in Rockford, Illinois, drew 35,000 people, but elsewhere sales haven't been so hot. Newport, Tennessee, had an attendance of 19,000. The week before the show, New Orleans had only sold 10,000 tickets, although that had risen to 18,500 by showtime. And at Ferris, Texas—fifty miles north of Dallas, normally a huge Metallica market—sales were 17,500.

According to Ross, Lollapalooza is losing about five hundred thousand dollars in potential revenue per gig. The losses are incurred by the expense of running each gig in half-capacity fields: this year Lollapalooza, for example, is traveling with forty trucks, thirty buses, and a crew of three hundred workers at each venue. The idea was that by shoehorning itself into fields instead of playing at already existing fifteen-thousand-seated amphitheaters, the tour would be able to accommodate the many Metallica fans who would flock to see it.

In order to make money on that kind of outlay, however, Lollapalooza would have to sell over twenty-five thousand tickets per venue. But sales have been off projections—way off. The irony is, in terms of sheer entertainment value, this bill is the shit. Critics have charged that by excluding more "alternative" acts (including previous festivals' seemingly token female and rap acts) Lollapalooza has given in to the mainstream by retreating into the safety of an old-fashioned all-male, all-metal extravaganza. In fact, what they've given in to is the concept of sheer entertainment. The T-shirts say "Summer of Noise," but within that term, you couldn't get a more disparate group—or one more continually appealing to Lollapalooza crowds. There's no ultrahip act on the Matador label this year, no Pavement, no GBV. But there is nonstop great rock.

"What I like about these acts," says Mark Weinberg, twenty, guitarist for third-stage band Crumb, "is that they aren't trendy flash-in-the-pan acts like Bush, they're not one-hit wonders. They all have really deep roots. And I don't know, my favorite bands are Sebadoh and Pavement, but for Tennessee, Rage and Metallica and Rancid are so much more appropriate a definition of alternative."

Joey Ramone, of all people, agrees: "Everyone I've met here so far is pretty cool and kinda like grass-rooted, you know what I mean? Soundgarden, Rancid...It's a rock 'n' roll show. Alternative...I don't know, half those bands, like the Presidents of the United States, I don't know what the fuck to make of them, you know?

"But this is a cool bill; it's kind of a real sobering bill—it's like bands that are unique and rooted and grounded...They're real, they're not bullshit, not living in the hype world...not trendy. I'm happy about being on this bill."

iv.

"This bill" begins with Psychotica, a glammy, Bowie-influenced act led by a former drag queen in a silver body suit, silver Mohawk, and orange eye makeup—a hell of a getup to be wearing in ninety-five-degree heat. He is carried on stage on a giant silver cross. "Hello Hillbillies! We're Psychotica and our whole mission in life is to piss the Bible Belt off!"

The crowd roars with pleasure, lifting its fists in the devil salute. It's impossible to read whether this is ironic or not; but it's easy to imagine that it is done in the same playful spirit that is clearly attending every Kiss concert this summer. Psychotica's whole trip is to make fun of metal, and it's clear from the start that people get the joke.

The Screaming Trees make a wonderful counterpoint to Psychotica's outrageous, New Yorky act. Few bands look more like their audience than the large, lumbering Screaming Trees, and the noise they make is equally unpretentious, a loud moan of anguish, a lovely, hard wail. They go over well even before they play their 1992 hit "Nearly Lost You." After that, they have the audience in the palm of their hands.

Next up are the kung fu monks of ShaoLin, China, whose display of "nonaggressive" combat tactics—the live-action version of half the video games on the planet—lulls and fascinates the throng. The monks are followed, at around four o'clock, with about six more hours of nonstop killer rock: Rancid, the Ramones, Rage Against the Machine, Soundgarden, and Metallica. (In Los Angeles, Seattle, Phoenix, and San Francisco the Rage slot will be filled by Devo.)

No wonder Lollapalooza had to send the four carnival rides it had hired back after the fourth date. No one has time to ride them without missing some essential act. Even the second stage—actually, a second and third stage, which alternate throughout the day, encompassing some ten different acts—isn't drawing too well (although this tends to vary a lot, depending on the layout of the venue and whether Sponge, a huge draw, is on the bill).

V.

Tim Armstrong blows into the tour bus an hour later, still dressed overwarmly in skintight zip trousers and leather jacket, and a T-shirt on which he has handwritten the words "Disorder and Disarry" (sic), the misspelled title of one of his own songs. He's just finished worshiping at the altar of the Ramones, whom he watches faithfully every night. ("If it wasn't for the Ramones," he says, "we wouldn't be on this tour.") It's about a million degrees out and humid with it, but, like so many of the fans in the audience, Armstrong claims not to feel it.

Besides, the bus is air-conditioned, so Armstrong takes a pew. "There have been so many rock-star moments on this tour," he giggles. "This morning, we pulled up here around four A.M., and me and some of the others went walking in the field where everyone is camping out, and you wouldn't believe it: they were blasting Ted Nugent!"

Tim finds this funny, because Rancid was nurtured at punk rock mecca Gilman Street, a place where the Nuge is banned for life. But its members have taken to the stadium with the same aplomb as their hometown

friends Green Day. Two years ago, Green Day used nudity and rudity to capture this same constituency;
Rancid have been a bit more pragmatic, augmenting their natural energy with a three-piece horn section and a keyboard player.

True, they had to hire a whole extra tour bus to carry that big a band— but the extra space they farmed out, free of charge, to the Ramones' long-suffering road crew. No wonder Rancid are the darlings of Lollapalooza, both in front of the stage and behind it! No one has a bad word to say about Rancid since the date in Toronto when the band broke out their own blow-up swimming pool, placed it in the center of the backstage area, and invited everyone in for a swim; they have created an unlikely camara-derie almost out of whole cloth.

"But everyone here is so cool," protests Armstrong. "The Ramones! Psychotica! Even Metallica, they've been so nice to us. Jason from Metallica, he's traveling in his own bus with his own recording studio in it, and the other day he recorded us with it in his hotel."

As Armstrong has noted, Jason Newsted travels in an entire bus by himself, reportedly because he wants to get to hang out and be ordinary with the other bands. But Metallica's Learjet is rumored to have two stew-ardesses and a humidor full of hundred-dollar cigars. They use it on days off to go special places: to see Kiss in Charlotte after the Knoxville gig, for example; and to go to Las Vegas, while the other bands are slogging it out between Dallas and Phoenix.

The Ramones, on the other hand, are saving money by traveling by minivan—all except for C. J., who is getting to gigs via his Harley, escorted by a couple of Hell's Angel friends.

Once, C. J. was held up for two hours at the Canadian border, almost making him late for the Toronto gig. "Everyone was all worried, and then he roared up the center of backstage on his Harley just in time and we're all cheering, 'Yea, C. J.,'" relates Armstrong. "Another total rock 'n' roll mo-ment."

In truth, Rancid is barely breaking even on this tour—every band is taking a cut on its salary at venues where ticket sales are slow, and the cost of the buses and hotels makes it almost impossible for the early bands to turn a profit. But Rancid will profit by being here on record sales and merch. Their T-shirts—which they sell for twelve dollars, half the cost of the other main-stage acts—are selling like crazy.

Rancid's great popularity here also underscores the irony of this Lolla-palooza, which is that, although this is the tour's least successful year in terms of projected ticket sales, it is its best in terms of value and artistry. The final two acts on the bill, Soundgarden and Metallica, have both scored huge number-one LPs in the last few months; and no one on the bill— from Rancid to Rage Against the Machine to Steve Earle to the Ramones— is less than critically acclaimed.

Kids who come to this show are being nailed to the ground with every act. For seven straight hours, each succeeding act is topped by a band they like better—which is one reason this year's midway has been scaled down a lot from previous years' designs. Gone are the peripheral cyberspace displays and sideshows: this year's unmusical fare consists only of a couple of "freak" displays, the chill room, which is full of political activist literature and couches (and is air-conditioned for comfort), and the eight mist tents, which are so essential in the blistering midwestern heat.

There is also an Airwalk display, complete with skate ramp and skate and BMX bike pros. But in general the vibe here is much more music-based than it's been in the past. In New Orleans, for some reason, the ShaoLin monks are replaced for one date by Waylon Jennings, who goes over extremely well. (In Des Moines, he was booed until James Hetfield came on stage and bawled out the audience.)

In Dallas, however, Rage are off the bill, replaced by country rebel rocker Steve Earle, who is bottled by the rowdies up front. "Rage would have sold at least five thousand more tickets," a promoter says bitterly as he watches.

Meanwhile, the big joke backstage—and probably in front of the stage as well—has to do with Metallica's new look: neat jeans and muscle shirts, clipped facial hair, makeup, and piercings. Despite the fact that one of Metallica's guitar techs has a case full of pro-gun, pro-redneck, antiliberal, antigay bumper stickers, several of the band members look like nothing so much as a typical gay man, circa 1978.

The band's motto this summer is "We Don't Give a Shit," which is plastered across their special laminates. Also, after the third or fourth song, singer James Hetfield habitually announces to the crowd that Metallica doesn't give a shit.

"We don't give a shit!" he yells.

"But what does he mean?" I say wonderingly after hearing it for the fourth time.

"He means that they don't give a shit that everyone thinks they're queer now," a singer for one of the other bands on the bill butts in. Huge titters all around.

Judging by the number of stripper types around the band, Metallica are not, in fact, gay. Not yet, anyway. But one can't help but wonder if their "real" constituency—all the ones who aren't here, that is—are indeed staying away merely because they are disappointed by Metallica's new look—particularly Kirk Hammett's chin stud. Maybe that, more than price resistance or fear of palooza, is what's keeping them away.

Poor ticket sales notwithstanding, Metallica are not about to fade away: *Load* was number one for three weeks. But if this Lollapalooza has taught the record business one thing, it is that punk rock has more of an ability to assimilate with the mainstream than anyone ever thought . . . more ability then metal.

Joey Ramone: "There's a much healthier attitude in music right now than some years. Everything's a lot better now . . . and I feel like rock 'n' roll's better because of the Ramones. I mean I don't want to sound all full of myself, but I know how things were before, back in the dark ages, and now everything's opened up. Everything's open for business now."

vi.

At six o clock every Lollapalooza morning, a little village is erected in the dust. It's a village that includes three stages, three sound booths, an entrance, an exit, a bunch of food stands, toilets, showers, and miles and miles and miles of fence, not to mention several large inflatables—a gorilla, an elephant, and a clown—which are unleashed and inflated each day by one Chris Althoff, Lollapalooza's gorilla wrangler. At seven o'clock, he kills the beasts by unzipping a flap on their legs. "If you ever see a wild gorilla," he jokes, "you can subdue them by finding the zippers on their calves."

Wiley Dailey is the tour plumber. He erects and maintains the eight mist tents, as well as the hoses at the front of the house that hose down the sweating crowd. Then there's catering. Caterers, who are contracted separately in each city, feed three meals to the army of workers. Alas, the quality of the meals differs from place to place, and tends to be the one thing that people on tour remember about a gig. The food can make or break the backstage atmosphere, and thus, the entire show.

These are just a few of the hundreds of specialized workers who are needed to make Lollapalooza happen—and besides them, there are the seven main-stage bands, ten indie-stage bands, and their separate crews and management. It's an incredible thing to see in action—this mobile village, this lumbering circus—but one wonders if it's worth it. Do kids need to see seventeen bands in one day, to come out to a field in the blistering heat and bond with their own kind?

Ross, who has been involved with Lollapalooza since its inception, thinks so. "There's a lot of great music here. The problem is that the press, for whatever reason, takes Lollapalooza from rock concert status to lifestyle status, and assumes that we have an agenda and criticizes us for our wavering from that agenda.

"The fact is, we don't have an agenda. We produce the best rock show we can. We try to give people a lot of things to do. They can see a wide variety of music, they can get political information, they can shop the little stands that are out there, and at the end of the day they can say, 'I had a good time, I was treated well, it was safe, I'll come back next year.' That's really our agenda."

That being said, there is a sense, here in 1996, that Lollapalooza has lost its constituency; that by combinining punk and metal, Lollapalooza has allowed the H.O.R.D.E. tour—which stands for Horizons of Roll Developing Everywhere—with its raft of sixties impersonators (the faux Janis, the faux Stones, and this year the faux Jimi) to take over the zeitgeist. On the Coasts, Lollapalooza is oft-criticized for providing just as fake an "alternative."

But in New Orleans, the Times-Picayune still covered it as if it were novel and weird, sending a reporter into the crowd to make snide remarks about piercings and bizarre clothes. And in Texas, the local paper of Ferris called its arrival an influx of a nest of Satan worshipers.

Ross: "A reporter asked me about the Satan worship this morning and I said, 'It's true. What we do is, as soon as the kids walk through the gate, we have people who take them aside and implore them to give up all Judeo-Christian values."

Articles like those are why it's in places like Ferris and Newport that one is better able to see the necessity of Lollapalooza. To kids who live among people who think that rock is the devil's music, the opportunity to see bands like the Ramones is still really special. Respect is due to the fans of New Orleans, who moshed to Waylon Jennings as well as to the Ramones; to the fans in Ferris, Texas, who came out at 11 A.M. in hundred-plus-degree heat and sang every word of "Psychotherapy" and "Sheena Is..."; to the fans in Newport, Tennessee, who camped out all night playing Nugent and were immediately confronted with Psychotica—and clapped.

Even the artists are having their eyes opened by some bands. "I was with some friends," says Joey Ramone, "and we were watching Soundgarden and Rancid and Metallica, and they kept saying, 'Oh! I didn't know Soundgarden were like that.' Seeing 'em live kinda turned them onto it."

Singer Patrick Briggs, leader of Psychotica, is also no stranger to the sense of having his eyes opened by Lollapalooza. Briggs is going on his third year as a Lollapalooza performer. In 1994, he was on the third stage doing spoken word. Last year, he emceed the second stage in drag. ("Next year," he jokes, "I'll own it.")

Briggs's experience in the pit—he calls it his "field research"—with the kids is, he says now, what led him to form Psychotica. "When I went out that first year, I realized that contrary to what I had been told on the East Coast and in New York—that the Midwest was very close-minded and stuff—I came to find that wasn't true at all . . . that we were really making rash judgments about the Midwest, that we had no idea what we were talking about.

"You know," he continues, "these kids pay forty dollars to come and be entertained, and if you provide them with that, then they're pleased. It's a very simple arrangement, really. I mean, the kids this year may not be as obviously creepy-looking as other years, but they want the same thing. Even a staunch Metallica fan just wants to be entertained."

Briggs's words are an important reminder of what's good about Lollapalooza: whether you're a Smashing Pumpkins fan watching Jesus Lizard for the first time, or a friend of Joey Ramone being unwillingly confronted by Soundgarden, it is a festival best attended in a nonjudgmental frame of mind. Questions about what constitutes "alternative" have been moot for many years, but now that Metallica is sporting eye makeup and facial piercings and the Ramones are considered part of the Monsters of Rock, they are less than relevant, they are positively retarded. There are no monsters anymore—only people, hardworking people, undisguised, undistinguished, playing their workmanlike songs, doing a job, and doing it well.

vii.

One night in Ferris, Texas, just as Soundgarden takes the stage, Tim from Rancid decides to take a bike ride through the fields of goldenrod and bluebonnets that surround the venue. The song "Outshined" is filling the sky all around us, and, as we look back at the arena, glowing in the distance, Tim is silent for a sec. "You know what? Once in 1986, when I worked at La Vals pizza, James Hetfield came in with some friends and ordered a pizza from me," he says reflectively. "And the next night, I saw him at the Berkeley Square, and he yelled out, 'Hey pizza boy!' 'Pizza boy': that's an insult, right?"

Tim pauses. The light from the sky has suddenly become achingly beautiful, and sonically, Soundgarden is peaking. "Back then," he goes on, "I wasn't even in Op Ivy; I never thought I'd ever go to a concert like this, much less be onstage and be like . . . popular."

Tim ducks his head shyly, a characteristic gesture. "You know, in a way I feel like this sort of my revenge. Revenge of Pizza Boy!" he laughs. Then he stands up on his little bike's haunches and screeches off into the dust, back into the arena, and the belly of the beast.

Chapter 3
hippiesomething

I live near Haight Street. Well, somebody has to. It used to be such a lovely place: in the mornings when the fog was lifting off the park, the walk across the Panhandle to, say, the post office on Clayton Street was endlessly entertaining, utterly full of charm. One tripped gaily past all the gaily painted three-story Victorians with complicated scrollwork and thought about the neighborhood's history: once a black ghetto turned tourist mecca, the Haight spent the eighties—my first ten years there—as the forerunner of Alternative Nation. I used to walk the street and feel like I was literally traversing the edge of American pop culture.

But as the Verlaines once said so truly, it's hard living your life on a knife-edge, and after the dwindling line of desiccated hippie chicks selling pot and crappy love beads gave way to groovy grungers in torn dresses and old sweaters, the Haight suffered a bizarre explosion in radical chic that's left it raddled and disgusting, a marketplace of cheap ideas whose only purpose is to expose how meaningless each meager musical move-ment becomes when it is ravaged by capitalism. Whether you're talking about body piercings or heroin, espresso drinks or tie-dye, used jeans, combat boots, D.R.I. T-shirts, ecstasy, smoothies, vegetarian burritos, you name it—nothing is worthy of one's undying devotion once it's become readily available to the masses.

Now why is that, I wonder?

Nowadays, on a sunny Saturday, Haight Street is a riot of ridiculous trends made even more so by the archaic nature of their adherents. You see them all lined up on the pavement going, "Spare change? Spare change? Spare change?" and you have to laugh. At this point in the millennium, it's hard to know what any of these people think they represent. Homeless bums (with their red-rimmed eyes and skin diseases) or equally skanky-looking youngish hippies; cleverly clad punk rockers and the groovy, well-coiffed, suburbanoid pierced people...they're all poseurs, every last one of them, fooled by their youth and idealism into thinking that they're counter-cultural.

And it's not just the hippies whose dream turned out to be a lie—though they are now the main offenders. The indie world that spawned alternative is now equally suspect, exploited from within by its very own heroes. "Selling kids to other kids," to quote the band Jawbreaker—itself a victim of co-option (as will be seen in another chapter).

Take, for example, the store X-Large. X-Large was founded in 1991 by Eli Bonerz and Adam Silverman, with the help of an investment by co-owner Mike Diamond of the Beastie Boys. Like the Boys' music, the store markets an expensive white take on hip-hop culture by providing designer T-shirts in primary colors, baggy jeans and hats with logos, and other such necessary accoutrements of cool. It is aided and abetted by a line of clothing for extremely skinny women called X-Girl, which is designed by Sonic Youth's Kim Gordon (despite the fact that Sonic Youth, far more than the Beebs, have always claimed to disown the mainstreamization of rock, and Gordon's supposed text is supposed to be feminist); and both lines are quite successful: X-Large has sixteen retail stores (eight of them based internationally) and plans on expanding. On Haight Street, the X-Large store is locked between the indie record store (Reckless of London), a salad place called the People's Cafe, an upscale furniture emporium, and the Gap.

X-Large is a constant reminder to me of the true meaning of the term "selling out." Selling out is not, as so many rock fans think, the automatic result of a band suddenly making some money; it is a much bigger and more insidious concept indeed. People often say that selling out is inevitable when it comes to rock music—inevitable because we live in a capitalist society, rather than a socialist or communist one. (And rock 'n' roll has not exactly thriven in those societies, for whatever reason.) Also, Elvis Presley sold out, did he not, right at the start—circa 1956. That is part of his paradigm: poor cracker kid makes good via music, enriching himself beyond his wildest dreams, and damning himself at the same time.

But history does not exactly bear out the idea that rock 'n' roll is damned by its own nature. True, the Beatles begat the Monkees, and Led Zeppelin and the Rolling Stones became circus acts. But it doesn't quite follow that massive success degrades its object. The Beatles' history is relatively pristine, and Dylan was only co-opted by hobbits recently, through no real fault of his own, so that what was once difficult, verbose, dense, even spiritual, is now reduced to sing-alongs wherein swirly crusties sway back and forth chanting "Everybody must get stoned!" like so many Jimmy Buffett fans.

Dylan notwithstanding, lots of other great movements in art—from impressionism to Bauhaus, from glam rock to jazz—have evolved over time without denigrating themselves into meaningless oblivion. Hip-hop and country have retained an edgy aspect (though their mainstream incar nations wouldn't lead you to think that). In fact, only two rock movements have destroyed themselves for filthy lucre, and both, alas, are the ones that swore they never would: the hippies and the punks. Idealistic, angry, completely opposed to mainstream values—they are now besmirched beyond recognition by their dull and stupid associations.

But the hippies have more to answer for than the punks. They did it first, and they did it worst—as evidenced by the sentimentalization that surrounds Woodstock. (Contrary to popular belief, Woodstock, *The New Yorker*'s Hal Espen points out, wasn't intended to be a free concert; it just turned into one, so that "incompetence came to be represented as purity, and a foul-up raised to a principle, as if socialism were merely inept capitalism.") The Dead have been similarly debased. And in the end, Haight Street was ruined by Jerry's deluded children and no one else.

That's why the day Jerry Garcia died of natural causes at a rehab center in Marin, a former roommate who currently lives in LA called me up at 7:30 in order to gloat about it.

"Ha ha ha!" she jeered, jubilantly. "I bet you they're parading up Haight Street right this minute. I bet you They drum annoyingly all day long. I bet Ben & Jerry's [the tie-dye-friendly ice-cream parlor on the corner of Haight and Ashbury] is mobbed. I bet CBS News calls you up for a quote any minute.

"Better quick think of something gracious," she added. "Or else you'll need to go in a witness protection program by nightfall."

We hung up, and the phone rang instantly. It was the local CBS-affiliate asking for a quote. Luckily, I'd come up with something. "I just wish," I said, as carefully as I could, "that Kurt Cobain could have lived so long."

CBS didn't use my quote. They said it was "too negative." And when I ran up to Haight Street, there were legions of television and radio remote trucks, but no mourning Jerry fans in Jerry-wear and flowered hair. Those people didn't arrive for hours; not till the broadcasting networks told them right where to meet them.

ii.

Of course it's sad that Jerry's dead, at least when you consider him as a human being as opposed to an icon. I feel sorry for his family—his three wives, four kids, and the bandmates whose gravy train will now grind to a halt without him. But as a Bay Area native who's lived two blocks from Haight Street for over a decade, it's difficult for me to think of him as human.

This was life on Haight Street, B.J.D. (before Jerry's death). At any time the Dead were coming to town—or Jerry was playing solo with the Jerry Garcia Band—for a week before and after the gig, legions of stringy-haired girls would sit cross-legged at every corner, asking if you want them to wrap your hair for ten dollars. Equally hairy guys, the owners of sad-faced, poorly groomed, probably hungry dogs, wandered about asking if you want to buy some (really bad) bud. All of them blocking the pavement, twenty-four hours a day, going, "Spare some change, spare some change, spare some change? We need gas to go to Vegas. A ride to the Oakland Coliseum. Tickets for Sunday's show."

Need, need, need. Give, give, give. What did these Deadheads give back to my community? Mess. Noise. Traffic. Bad LSD, overpriced bracelets, and an atmosphere of fuzzy-headed dissipation diffusing itself throughout the land. Just the sight of them makes me want to yell, "Get a fucking job, or go back home to your rich white Marin County parents." That's how my life as a nihilistic punk rocker now manifests itself: in judgmentality and negativity; in meanness to bums and hobos.

But my real objection to the Grateful Dead? The drugs and violence that surround their milieu. True, much of this grime is manifested well outside the band's own sphere, but even inside their little world has been none too clean and safe: the Dead have sustained four band members' deaths in the past twenty years, and three of those—Pigpen, Brent Mydland, and Jerry Garcia—were drug- or alcohol-related.

And then there are countless other druggy rumors, episodes, and stories that swirl around the band's ethos, positively glorifying the out-of-control atmosphere that surrounds the band's self-proclaimed "long strange trip." At least grunge stars like Layne Staley, Scott Weiland, and of course Kurt Cobain have been held accountable by the media for their drug use. When Jerry died he was lauded by mainstream news outlets like *Newsweek*, even by President Clinton.

iii.

Smelly and passé though their followers undoubtedly were, the Grateful Dead provided a ready-made identity for young people searching for one. And that, after all, is the role of punk, goth, rockabilly, and every other form of music. But the ready-made identity that the Dead provided to its minions was illusory, conservative, out of touch, and—this is the real rub—aesthetically unpleasing. (Think, if you will, of R. Crumb, Kelley Mouse, and Jerry's line of ties.) They are not artistic, but ugly, Hallmarky, sentimental slosh.

What on earth was its appeal? Musically speaking, minus the "scene," the Dead were merely a competent cover band that played meandering white folk-blues. And yet, when they began, there must have been just as much true exuberance and excitement, that wondrous sense of discovery and rediscovery, of hail-fellow-well-met-ness that made punk so attractive in 1978. I imagine that hearing the Dead in 1966 was probably a lot like how hearing R.E.M. was in 1983. Like seeing the American landscape through new and pale blue eyes.

The Dead were also supposed to represent some harkening back to the ideological sixties. But the eighties and nineties were such a politically different landscape, it's impossible to see how. Somehow, all that Peace and Love and Save the World shit boiled down to in 1990 was support for saving the rain forest and blind children in Tibet, two worthy issues that are, nonetheless, totally irrelevant to modern life in America. I guess people who live in glass houses don't see the crackheads and AIDS victims and battered women and abandoned pets who litter the streets of our towns.

iv.

The Dead have a lot to answer for, culturewise in America, but they were not always the travesty that they seem now. Formed in 1965 by a bluegrass banjo player named Jerry Garcia in conjunction with Bob Weir, Pigpen, and electronic music composer Phil Lesh, their initial work must have seemed very cutting edge indeed, mixing, as it did, traditional folk and country songs with electric blues and rock at a time when most rock music was mere "pop."

The Dead were the house band for Ken Kesey's Acid Tests and integral to the mythologizing of the Fillmore, the Haight-Ashbury, and the Summer of Love—but those things occurred before their recording career even began. Most of the songs people associate with the Dead—like "Truckin',"

"Casey Jones," and "Dark Star"—were all written and recorded in the early seventies, hardly the most culturally romantic era, but the time that most Deadheads mistakenly ape, stylistically. They imagine the Dead living communally in their house at 710 Ashbury, grooving with their chicks, dropping acid, "balling," and noodling, all in the name of Free Love or something. In fact, that era ended in 1968.

Besides, the reality behind the Dead's post-60s scene was exposed in Robert Greenfield's oral biography of Garcia, *The Secret Life of Jerry Garcia,* in which various people who worked around Jerry speak chillingly about his huge need for drugs, his personal reclusiveness, his "fucked scene with chicks," even the Dead organization's need to keep him isolated, on the road, and happy, at the expense of his health, his home life, and his inner peace.

The picture that emerges from Greenfield's book is of a sick, isolated man with sores all over his body, completely at the mercy of various women and the machine that was his band's organization. For example, when Jerry, worried at last that the audience's ridiculously iconic behavior toward him was out of hand, suggested that the band not do stadium shows, he was shut down by management. Why? According to John Perry Barlow, "Because [we] had this nut to pay . . . fifty employees."

In short, he was a prisoner of the his own myth, and eventually it killed him—and not without the help of the fans who made the myth so powerful. In the end Barlow describes the Dead organization as "a beast. A cranky, hard, crusty old dragon that knew how to survive."

At least, until Jerry died—and after all, rock 'n' roll and death do have some kind of bizarre attraction. For all its apparent energy, the medium does not seem to be a life force for its practitioners.

That would be okay—die young and stay pretty being an understandable, if not a very brave or admirable, motto—if it weren't that rock 'n' roll deaths tend to be so very ignoble. Elvis dying on a toilet while trying to move his bowels; Bobby Fuller, beaten and forced to drink gasoline by mobsters; John Lennon, killed by a fan; Tupac Shakur being gunned down by some unnamed OGs; Kurt Cobain's ashes reportedly being hauled around in a teddy bear and made a show of by his widow . . . the list of indignities that dead rock stars have had to suffer is endless—not to mention endlessly depressing.

The depressingness of rock deaths becomes immediately apparent to anyone who has visited Jim Morrison's grave at Père Lachaise cemetery in Paris, which also houses the graves of luminaries like Edith Piaf and Oscar Wilde. Jim's grave could hardly be called a place of repose, surrounded as it is by scraggly-haired kids of all nations who haunt it unscrupulously at all hours of the day and night. Not just his gravestone, but also everything in its immediate vicinity is covered in ugly graffiti and messages and pictures.

Père Lachaise is an inherently beautiful spot, high on a quiet, leafy hillside in the Fifteenth Arrondissement, but if the soul turns out to be immortal and it ever lingers near its body's place of rest, then Morrison must feel eternally trapped at a boring bong party full of of morons who worship him—a terrible prospect. See, once a rock star, always a rock star—the crowds will hound you after your death.

But worse than crowds is the way people will do whatever they can to exploit their own community. Woodstock '94—sponsored by Pepsi, Häagen-Dazs, and Nobody Beats the Wiz—was a grotesque attempt to exploit the nuevo hippie gen's warm feelings of nostalgia for Woodstock I ("nostalgia generation without memory," one pundit called it). And one year exactly after the death of Jerry Garcia, the Furthur Festival—a conglomerate formed by Dead associates and featuring Dead spinoff acts like the Rat Dog Revue, Mickey Hart's Mystery Box, Hot Tuna, etc.—is also attempting to hold on to the Dead's huge audience.

Furthur was inspired by the H.O.R.D.E. Festival, which was inspired by Lollapalooza, and you can look at that two ways, depending on your attitude: You could say the tour is trying to keep a precious underground community cohesive in the face of the death of its icon, or you could, more cynically, say it is trying to make Deadheads keep on coughing up their dough.

Having sat through a portion of the festival in 1996, I can't say I was any more charmed by the post-Jerry Dead world than I was by the real thing. Rather less so, in fact: from my vantage point, the whole thing looked like a greedy corporation hiding behind a phony attitude in a last-ditch attempt to part a special population from its money.

Interestingly, some critics have propounded a similar argument about Lollapalooza, suggesting that its promoters don't see the alternative world as a subculture, but as just another market. That may be so, but when it comes to marketing, the Furthur Festival had Lollapalooza beat hands down. The whole place—both outside and in—was one long endless vista of merch booths. Dye in the Sky, Liquid Blue, Not Fade Away USA, Wheel of Life Importers of Embroidered Nepali Handcrafts, Avatar: Tapestries for a Groovy Planet; the list goes on and on, and the stuff they were selling was expensive, from $50 velvet dresses to T-shirts with slogans like "Users Don't Lose Drugs." Baby clothes, photographs, tapes, hemp products ... you could even get $150 "Dark Star" sunglasses at the booth marked "Grateful Dead Mercantile Co."

The amazing thing is that almost everything else there—including the booth which sells T-shirts combining the logo of every university in America with little trademark Grateful Dead bears—must be licensed from the Dead. No wonder BGP thought to take out a trademark on the term "Summer of Love."

Unlike H.O.R.D.E., the Furthur Festival has little hope of surviving another year—unless Los Lobos' David Hidalgo agrees to join the Grateful Dead as desired by the band, and that's not very likely. The Ratdog Band isn't good enough to support the situation as it is, but no doubt the Dead Organization will find another way to use its constituency, Deadheads, who, in their innocence, are being used, just as they've always been used; exploited for their love of and loyalty to a scene that has been nothing but a cruel and twisted myth for years.

V.

These days, my hatred of the Dead phenomenon has become so intense and profound that I sometimes think I must secretly love them. You know how the things one hates about oneself are always the most repellent when viewed in other people? Clearly the Deadheads' cult-like attitude toward their beloved band strikes a chord of fear in my heart. When I was living right off Haight Street in the mid-eighties, living my most underground, countercultural, junk-store-clothed, punk rock life, I thought I was as far removed from Deadheads as it was possible to be. My friends and I abhorred the Deadheads who plagued Haight Street, but to outsiders, we probably looked exactly alike.

And it's true: there was a similarity of purpose between the grunge and the hippie scenes which even now I am loath to acknowledge. *Our little group has always been and always will until the end....*" Come off it, Gina, who are you kidding? You and your punk rock pals were rich white countercultural types, looking for a community to belong to also. Minus the negativity—and the fact that we didn't panhandle—there wasn't that much difference.

The truth is, all joking aside, I feel sorry for Deadheads. I know what it's like to lose the center of your scene, to watch it implode under the weight of its own myth, to commercialize itself into oblivion, and regardless of the object of the myth, that's a sad thing, because heroes are hard to find. The death of Jerry is the end of an era, and and you know what that means? It means that today is the first day of the rest of our lives.

Austin, 1996. Seen from the rooftop of the seventeen-story Omni Hotel, the town of Austin looks somnambulant; a quiet old Texas town on the vast Edwards Plateau, basking under the big black sun. But during the four days of SXSW—the South by Southwest Music and Media Conference, an annual conclave of some six thousand music bizzers and six hundred bands that happens every March—the six-block stretch of Sixth Street known to all and sundry as "the Drag" is something else entirely. During the convention, a bizarre medley of every type of electrified rock blasts out of the wooden warehouses and square stone buildings for ninety-six solid hours straight. And whether you're standing on a bridge over-Town Lake outside of the Liberty Lunch, or walking away from it, in Austin music follows you down the street, as one critic put it, "like perfume in the night."

To the thousands of music business associates who gather here every spring, the town of Austin has long felt like the historical vortex of American rock music. It is perceived as having been a vibrant live music center since the year 1881, when a then-unknown writer named O. Henry used to eke out a living playing fiddle for the locals in a rowdy Austin bar; later, he started a magazine presciently entitled *The Rolling Stone*.

But in actuality, Austin hasn't always been like this. According to Austin singer/songwriter Kathy McCarty, who moved to Austin in 1979 to attend UT and immediately started a band, downtown used to be a burned-out, scary old place. In 1979, most of the shops were dusty drugstores or boarded up; you could buy any building on Sixth Street for five thousand dollars, straight up.

Places like that are ripe for punk rock: after all, large cheap warehouses with no running water are punk rock's spiritual home. And indeed, Sixth Street soon abounded with bands like Kathy's and others. Now, from the roof of the seventeen-story black glass Omni Hotel, she points out the local landmarks. "See that building with the mural down there?" she says, pointing to a place that now houses an elegant French restaurant. "In 1980, I lived there with my band the Buffalo Gals, and we each paid eighty-five dollars a month rent."

Austin began to change in the early eighties, when some proto-yuppies took a hundred-year lease on the building that now houses the Pecan Street Cafe. A quick tide of urban renewal and gentrification—similar to the tide that created Horton Plaza and the Gaslamp District in San Diego, revamped Pioneer Square in Seattle, created the South Street Seaport in Manhattan, and was responsible for the Soma District in San Francisco—then swept downtown Austin, just as it was sweeping the rest of the country.

But the real change to Austin came via a massively successful campaign, conceived of by the city council and chamber of commerce, to market Austin as "the live music capital of the world." Austin already had a certain amount of street cred, thanks to artists like Janis Joplin and Roky Erikson, who got their start there in the sixties, not to mention Willie and Waylon, who based themselves there in the early seventies, and famed clubs like Armadillo World HQ and Antone's (neither of which is on the Sixth Street drag).

In the early eighties, bands like Kathy's own Glass Eye, Doctor's Mob, the Big Boys, the Reivers, the True Believers, the Butthole Surfers, and Timbuk 3 came into being; but it wasn't until 1986, when Austin city planners invented SXSW to draw outsiders into the joys of the Lone Star State, that Austin—and Sixth Street—really took off.

The rest is pretty much history. Austin has receded as a punk rock mecca since the days when the Big Boys and the Butthole Surfers terrorized its clubs, and real estate–wise, Sixth Street's on a downhill slide as well. But SXSW has—like the alternative music business itself—grown and grown and grown, mimicking in its economic expansion the exact same pattern that has seen the music business as a whole go from annual sales of $4 billion to $12 billion in the course of the last decade. Nineteen ninety-six's event—the tenth—drew 5,500 registrants, 600 (official) band showcases, and 12,000 wristband holders (for $40, wristband holders can attend any showcase that isn't already full of badge holders).

Now when you walk down the street on a weekend—or during SXSW—Sixth Street is awash with noise: cover bands, blues bands, country bands, funk. There is a disco, a three-tiered madhouse called Maggie

Mae's, where bands play on each floor and bleed into one another's sets, and the bright purple warehouse known as Emos, a bar so infamous that one of Austin's most popular hardcore bands, the Fuckemos, is named for it.

ii.

John Cougar Mellencamp—of all the inappropriate people—said it first, and in some ways he said it best. "Money," he said, "money changes everything." After Nirvana released *Nevermind* in the fall of 1991, money did indeed change everything in rock, and it changed it swiftly, and irrevocably.

Before that moment, bands who struggled to make a living in cheap towns like Austin were happy to sell forty thousand copies of their independently released LPs. After *Nevermind* went platinum the first week of '92, there was money coursing through the system, great gobs of money, oozing down rivers and streams cut out of the independent label system. It was the trickle-down theory of economics seen in triple-fast action, as bands, managers, journalists, drug dealers, and people who had good dirt on Courtney Love started to command huge prices for their wares and services.

As usual, the largest hunks of money came from record companies, and were given out to bands who were deemed by the pundits to be "the next Nirvana." (In fact, more cities were deemed the "next Seattle" than bands were dubbed "next Nirvana," but that's another story entirely.)

Some of the bands who benefited immediately from the windfall included Hole, Rocket from the Crypt, Smashing Pumpkins, Helmet, and Kansas City's little-known Paw, who somehow fired up a bidding war at SXSW '92 based on a vague resemblance to Nirvana's sound. So, too, did bands like Babes in Toyland, and All.

Helmet, who scored a reputed million-and-a-half record deal with the newly minted label Interscope, were another odd choice for "next Nirvana." The New York City arty-hardcore act led by guitarist Page Hamilton had sold some thirty thousand copies of their first record, *Strap It On*, on the Amphetamine Reptile label when a bidding war suddenly flared up over them in the fall of '91.

Tom Hazelmyer, who runs Am-Rep, still doesn't recall how it began. "It came straight from major labels," says Hazelmyer now. "I really don't remember anyone in the indie or zine world calling Helmet the next Nirvana.

They would have been embarrassed to say that. At the time, there was all this gold-chain-wearing seventies refuse at labels who wouldn't know the next Nirvana if you stuffed all four members up their ass. They were like, 'It's loud and obnoxious, it's the next Nirvana!' "

In the fullness of time, Helmet signed to Interscope, while Am-Rep scored a bunch of cash for back-catalog and such like—they won't say how much, but enough to buy their own building.

Of course, Hazelmyer points out that property in Minneapolis is cheap, and that the building—an abandoned doctor's office—had been empty for three years before he bought it.

Helmet's record *Meantime* sold some half-million copies and was certified gold. The 1994 follow-up, *Betty*, did less well, selling some three hundred thousand domestically (with another quarter-million abroad). For some reason Paw, the Lawrence, Kansas, band that was next up for next-Nirvana-hood, wasn't half as successful in its quest for fame, although *Dragline*, its A&M debut, certainly had as many likably grunge elements as, do, say, Everclear or Bush.

The point, however, isn't that Helmet and Paw were bad guesses on the industry's part. After all, Stone Temple Pilots, Candlebox, and Silverchair (who, incidentally, claim Helmet as their biggest influence) proved that there was a gaping maw in the public just waiting to be stuffed to the brim with Pearl Jam and Nirvana-be bands.

No, the point is that just after Nirvana broke, there was a moment in time when it seemed like everything—radio, MTV, the music industry in general—would change. The music business was like a governmental cabinet changing ministers and parties; younger people started getting better jobs in it in A&R and management. Good bands—like Ministry and the Butthole Surfers and Soundgarden—could suddenly be heard on radio and MTV; unusual bands, like Rocket from the Crypt and Shonen Knife, were being treated with respect.

It was such a strange time that even the Melvins, a turgidly slow band whose leader Buzz Osborne had taught Kurt Cobain to play guitar and was often referred to in a complimentary fashion by Cobain, was courted heavily by majors despite his band's rampant uncommerciality. At one point, Osborne was approached by T Bone Burnett, who said he desperately wanted to produce them. (Later, Osborne assumes, Burnett changed his mind.)

But five years after the revolution, those execs—bred in indie label hothouses—are buying homes in Silverlake, and little has changed in the trenches. It was as if a window opened briefly, then seemingly slammed shut. It's meet the new boss, same as the old boss in the boardrooms. And on radio?

On radio, it's even worse. Radio somehow missed the boat, and instead of Fugazi or Team Dresch, a slew of faceless bands with names like 1,000 Mona Lisas and Deep Blue Something reside there.

~ This, of course, was only to be expected. "Look at what happened in the Top 40 from 1967 to 1976," points out Hazelmyer. "Somehow, totally wild, psychedelic songs like 'Purple Haze' gradually turned into the Eagles. You watch, pretty soon there'll be some Seals and Crofts for the nose-ring set."

The Melvins' Osborne concurs with this theory. The Melvins sell some fifty thousand to one hundred thousand of each record they've released since 1992, and have gained a large touring following thanks to gigs opening for Primus and White Zombie. In 1996 the Melvins released an album, entitled *Stag,* and have a slot on the second stage at Lollapalooza. But they have seldom, if ever, been played on the radio.

"I'm not foolish enough to say that [the punk/grunge tag] hasn't helped," says Osborne now, "but radio and MTV, that's very arbitrary. Who says they can't play us on radio? Kids accept what they accept, because that's what they've been given. It's like our bass player, Mark, says: If you shove a bowl of Cheerios under the door of a prison once a day, the prisoner will come to like it. That's what radio is like.

"I have no idea how KROQ or MTV comes up with their playlists," adds Osborne. "Well, I have an illicit idea how worthless untalented crap gets played there, but... actually, I've lost faith."

So has Hazelmyer. "On the one hand," he says, "it's great that the Poisons and the Mötley Crües are being replaced. But [the money in the system] has skewed even the most pure people."

iii.

Time, of course, tends to date even the most forward-looking of cultural statements. Viewed in that dispassionate light, perhaps it's a good thing that grunge—a reaction to twelve years of repressive Republican rule and the concomitantly enforced cheery conventionality of radio and TV— has outlived its usefulness.

But in some ways, the Battle of Seattle was lost before it began, when it pinned half its zeitgeist onto the so-called glamorousness of heroin addiction. In a 1995 article in *Spin* magazine about Mia Zapata, a Seattle musician who was brutally murdered by an apparent drifter on her way home from band practice one night, a local musician said, "[that kind of incident] is the reason we do heroin." But that's a cop-out. People do heroin because their friends do heroin—just as people play grunge because their friends listen to grunge, and so on. And heroin kills.

You'd think, at this point in time, heroin would have lost its cachet, but no. In 1996, for example, Scott Weiland, lead singer for one of grunge's top acts, the Stone Temple Pilots, was convicted for the second time for possession of heroin and remitted for treatment, thus scotching plans for an STP summer tour in support of their then-new record *Tiny Music*.

And STP isn't the only big grunge band to be adversely affected by drugs. Alice in Chains singer Layne Staley has also been prevented from touring due to heroin problems, as have so many other bands.

And of course there's Kurt Cobain, the largest star of the idiom, who killed himself after escaping from a drug treatment center in 1994, setting off a slow chain reaction of rock 'n' roll suicides-as-a-coping-technique.

These days, the question of which grunge bands have been affected by heroin isn't really half as relevant as which bands *haven't*. It's no coincidence that the members of grunge music's two beloved, successful, and consistent acts, Pearl Jam and Soundgarden, are drug free, and anyone who thinks that doing heroin will add to their glamour, talent, or chances of making it in the music industry would do well to keep this fact firmly at the forefront of their brains.

iv.

Grunge has other problems as well. Although Weiland's trouble with drugs is symptomatic of its sickness, the genre as a whole is also suffering from a lack of inspiration within its flagship bands. It shows no spiritual, emotional, or musical growth—in fact, it shows the opposite. Grunge is now the soylent green of rock, an ultraprocessed and uninspired melee of sounds, created by eating its own words and noises.

Sadly, the results of the opening up of the airwaves has had just as many bad aspects as good ones. On the one hand, new bands have finally broken through the barrier raised by the clueless gatekeepers of the early and mid-eighties. On the other hand, despite the breakthroughs, a look at which acts are really succeeding still gives one pause. A world ruled by Hootie, Mariah, Live, and Boyz II Men is not one that is going to spawn a brave new cultural frontier.

These acts may well be the people's choice, but their heavy-handed mediocrity is bound to have a dampening effect on the future—and in fact it already has. Whereas 1994 was a banner year for record sales in general, with people flooding record stores to buy titles ranging from the Off-spring's *S.M.A.S.H* to the soundtrack of *The Lion King,* 1995 was an entirely different story, colored by the slow sales of acts previously considered sure-fire hits. *Lucy,* Candlebox's follow-up to its smash debut, bombed big-time, as did follow-up LPs to former hit acts like Blind Melon and the Spin Doctors. Even Green Day's *Insomniac* was nowhere near as big as *Dookie* was. And 1996 was a downright disaster, with growth in sales down to a minuscule 2 percent.

According to articles in *Rolling Stone, Billboard* magazine, and the *New York Times,* the industry believes that the year's big downturn in sales was due to a huge rise in CD-ROM and video game sales, as well as personal computer and Internet software. They believe that people's disposable income is now being stretched between an ever-increasing number of entertainment choices.

But another possibility is oversaturation. Too many records are being released, and too many of them sound like bands that came before them. Pearl Jam, Smashing Pumpkins, and Green Day sound-alikes abound, and although critics are loath to believe it, there is some justice in the marketplace. Most people don't like to throw bad money after good any more than they enjoy doing the opposite; and judging by the extreme blandness of bands like the Toadies and 1,000 Mona Lisas, the margins—once so vital—have been swallowed up. Alternative rock is a wasteland of nobodies, and all of them are Better Than Ezra.

And yet, there seems to be a perception that the music business is booming right now, because there are simply so many bands being signed and so many records on the shelves—a flood of product in the system. The truth is that, ever since 1994—the year that the Eagles dared to charge over one hundred dollars per ticket in some markets, and Woodstock '94 drew some 250,000 people (all of whom probably had a pretty bad time there), the rock market has been less easily led and more judgmental, more careful with its money . . . or something.

That's why record sales and concert revenues are down by a lot. And none of the bands that are now out there are really able to break through on the huge level that Nirvana's sudden success seemed to promise. Only one band has made a run for such a thing, and that band is Green Day, a Berkeley-based trio who reclaimed punk soil for their generation at an all-ages club called 924 Gilman Street. When *Dookie* went platinum in 1994, people took that as a sign that punk—brought to the masses' attention by the concerted championing of bands like Pearl Jam and Nirvana, who talked about their influences incessantly—really had finally broken.

Unfortunately, their success has merely ensured a devastation of their scene and others like it, as it, like grunge before it, has been co-opted by the industry—often with disastrous results. Consider the unfortunate case history of the Berkeley band Jawbreaker, who signed to Geffen for six figures in 1994.

From the start, it was a transaction that surprised many a longtime Jawbreaker fan, since Jawbreaker had long been one of Gilman Street's most popular, but one of its most vocally anticorporate, acts, thanks to three independently released LPs, *Unfun,* (1989, Shredder) *Bivouac,* (1991, Tupelo/Communion), and *24-Hour Revenge Therapy,* (1993, Tupelo/Communion).

Jawbreaker formed at New York University in the late eighties, when singer Blake Schwarzenbach and his high school buddy Adam Pfahler, also a student at NYU, answered an ad they saw in the dorms placed by soon-to-be bassist Chris Bauermeister. After releasing *Unfun* on Berkeley's Shredder Records, Schwarzenbach booked a two-month tour of the United States by calling all his favorite clubs with the help of his father's phone card. In 1991, the band relocated to San Francisco; by 1992, they were selling out clubs in Berkeley, Seattle, and LA. After three U.S. tours and two European ones, each of Jawbreaker's three independent records sold upwards of twenty thousand copies with no press or radio play.

By contrast, in the year since its release, *Dear You,* with all Geffen's backing, has sold far fewer copies.

How could this happen? Well, for one thing, *Dear You,* produced by Rob Cavallo (who also did Green Day's smash *Dookie*) sounds quite a bit different from previous Jawbreaker releases: it exchanges the raw and vicious sonics of previous LPs for a smoother, richer, and a lot more radio-friendly sound—a sound some people have characterized as reminiscent of the Smiths. (*Dookie,* by contrast, sounds remarkably like Green Day's previous Lookout! releases.)

This could be interpreted by former fans as a "sellout" move, but Schwarzenbach vehemently denies that this was his intention. "I got a lot of letters to that effect, like, 'Rumors say that they made you do this,' or, 'On the Internet it says they made you remix it,' and it's just not at all true. In the studio, we were basically unsupervised. Part of it [the sound change] was just that this record took a longer time to make—six weeks—and our other records took three days, literally. Also, I wrote this one differently, in a key I could sing and not have to yell this time. As for our sound, we'd already changed it, before we signed."

But another reason for Jawbreaker's downfall could be that it lost its entire fan base without—as Green Day did—picking up a new one. Before signing to Geffen, they had been more outspoken against major label deals than Green Day or the Offspring ever were.

"[Before we signed the deal] I really didn't know that much about [major labels]," admitted Schwarzenbach a few months after the switch. "And I'd seen plenty of bad models. But once we checked it out more . . . it was like, well, we could do another indie record; or we could do this. It wasn't a hungry thing, that's where some bands shoot themselves in the foot and get into bunk deals.

"We didn't just jump into the Geffen deal," he added, "like, this is our shot, let's go for it! We got a good deal because we didn't need it. But it was a really big thing for us, we agonized over it, and we all got really paranoid after we did it."

Jawbreaker took a risk by signing to a major label after so much caviling against it. Sure, other bands had done the same thing—Sonic Youth, for example, and Husker Du. But those bands survived in part because, however much their original fan base kicked against them, the records they released on major labels sold more than the records they released on indies. Not so Jawbreaker's, and less than a year after the release of *Dear You,* Jawbreaker broke up.

Among other things, Jawbreaker's failure indicates a terrible crossroads that faces indie bands—and their labels. At the indie trends panel at the North by Northwest Music and Media Conference in Portland in the fall of 1996, for example, indie record label owners discussed the near impossibility of breaking an indie band today—an impossibility that's based in part on the oversaturation of the marketplace, the wide availability of major label deals to bands (like Jawbreaker) who aren't really mainstream material, and finally, the shrinking of media and college radio interest in indie label product.

"There are now only three ways to make money as an indie label," Mike Jones, owner of Schizophonic Records told a panel of label owners in late 1996. "One, to sell a million records by one band; two, to take money from a benefactor; and three, to let a band go and get money for them from a bigger company."

The last way is the one most indie labels take—partly because bands are often so eager to jump ship that they get on a major label before they're ready to go. The problem, of course, is expectations. In 1985, bands like the Replacements had none whatsoever. Nowadays, even the smallest band has the sense that they could make some cash. "I don't want bands [on my label] that expect me to sit around and write checks to turn them into celebrity monsters," sighs Candyass Records owner Jody Bleyle. "But that's what I have."

What emerged from the discussion in Portland is the fact that indie labels are trying to figure out a way to streamline who will hear their records. If they attempted to service (i.e., provide product) to everyone interested in "alternarock," they'd go broke. The thing these labels need to do is narrow their databases down a bit, but that just begs the question. There are still the vast numbers of great, unknown bands who desperately need the indie label network in order to be heard at all.

V.

To date, rock 'n' roll has been cyclical—sometimes exciting and sometimes very dull—and unfortunately, this is an extremely fallow period in its history. Moreover, it'll continue this way until kids stop forming bands in the hopes of getting popular and rich. Only when people return to being hopelessly creative will a new set of subversive icons emerge, who will in turn influence the mainstream as did Public Enemy, the Talking Heads, and the MC5 before them.

Some people, however, contend that this is a better time for bands to be signed than just after Nirvana broke, because there's more uncertainty in the industry right now. At the moment, A&R people are looking not for the next Nirvana or even the next Green Day, but the next... something else.

Rob Cavallo is the man who signed Green Day to Warner Brothers (and who produced Jawbreaker's last LP). "Right now, there is no one strong sound on radio," he says. "So there is more of a window of opportunity for new bands. From my point of view, it's a more dangerous time to sign bands.

"As an A&R guy," says Cavallo, "the easiest thing in the world to do is to sign a band that sort of sounds like someone else, take it to a producer who did a band that sounds like that, and deliver it to your company and say, 'This sounds like so-and-so.' And that totally sucks, and what's more, most of the time it doesn't work. I think greatness in A&R is recognizing the quality of music that has nothing to do with a time and a place—that has merits outside of trends."

Cavallo says he's committed to finding a band that sounds like nobody else, but adds that it's a hard road. "Right now there's no real scene, just England, and none of those bands are even close to doing great here. We get a lot of tapes that sound like the Gin Blossoms, and a lot that sound like—what's that band that does 'Breakfast at Tiffany's'? Whoever they are."

Even on an indie level, the creativity seems stagnant. "I used to hear one good band out of every five hundred I listened to," says Hazelmyer. "Now I'm down to one in two thousand. No one's rising up anymore. A band like Brainiac," he adds, "ten years ago would have had the impact of a Sonic Youth. Now they're lost in the shuffle. There's just too many bands in the system."

Most people agree that what we are waiting for is a new catharsis; that it is up to the artists—the kids themselves—to come up with something salable, and meaningful, and righteous, and good. But be that as it may, what really needs to change in the industry isn't the labels or the music itself (which is cyclical) but the medium of dissemination itself. Technological changes, such as the invention of the CD and synthesizers, have helped other aspects of the industry improve; perhaps another such change will come along affecting communication. If, for example, a person could pick up every station in America, stations might actually have to compete with one another in a real way—become different from one another, rather than more similar.

vi.

And so rock 'n' roll ebbs and flows and is regenerated, usually by a band that takes as its inspiration some earlier act, like the Beatles. And yet, you can take that model too far. In 1988, the *Los Angeles Times* ran a piece on a little-known Orange County band called Dexter, which had won *Musician* magazine's "Best Unsigned Band in America" contest in 1985 . . . and two years later was still unsigned.

The reason? Dexter sounded like the Fixx at a time when A&R people were searching for Whitesnake clones. At the moment, the industry is looking for Nine Inch Nails and Green Day clones. But Green Day's last LP, *Insomniac,* tapped out at 2 million—8 million copies short of *Dookie.* Clearly, nuevo-punk's days are numbered.

And is the window shut for grunge as well? "I wouldn't sign anything grunge," says Cavallo, who just inked a deal with a band called Kara's Flowers, who he says sound "like the Beatles but not Oasis." He adds, "I wouldn't even sign anything punk right now."

Cavallo thinks there's a possibility that metal may make a comeback. "There's definitely room for something heavier on radio," he says; and others agree. (Osborne: "Whenever I see Weezer on TV I wish that Slayer would come out and slit their throats.")

Hazelmyer: "Somewhere, some kid is rebelling against this stuff. True, it's a weird time right now because the high school mutants can go pick up a Melvins record at the Wal-Mart, whereas you used to have to search it out. But whenever shitty music is predominant, you'll get a handful of mutants in suburban USA who fight back."

And then the cycle will start all over again. Will the industry have learned anything this time? Unlikely. As Marx once said, "History repeats itself—the first time as tragedy, the second time as farce."

Chapter 5
The Rot Sets In

It's rush week at Chico State and the frat houses are surrounded. Cops line the fences, checking the wristbands of the pledges as they wander down oak-lined Fifth Street in search of the perfect beer bash. It's like *Animal House* only updated for the nineties: loud music blares out of the backyard "beaches," and from the roof of every one of these lovely old houses, a giant vinyl banner with a logo proclaims with pride what company provided the free beer.

These days, frat parties are considered almost as good a product endorsement opportunity as the Olympics, albeit on a smaller scale. In the backyard of the Phi Kappa Tau house, for example, a mini–rock concert is under way, featuring the bands Red Sunset, Munkafest, and Bullet Proof Buddha, a five-piece from San Diego who sing songs that sound uncannily like songs by the Stone Temple Pilots. Singer Chad Crites even looks like Weiland, puffy face, bright red hair, goatee and all. Every few songs he looks out at the crowd—boisterous, large, loud, and drunk—and attempts to make eye contact among a host of wasted, white-shirted nineteen-year-olds.

Once he mentions the rival TKE house, in the hopes there'll be a rousing boo. Twice he tells the crowd the band's name, adding that they'll be back in Chico in a month with freshly pressed CDs to sell. And three times he makes a pitch for his band's kind sponsor, the product that brought them up here in the first place, and whose banner hangs cheerfully on the roof behind the stage. "Hey, check out the booth at the back," says Crites, "there's free samples and stuff, it's pretty cool."

The product in question is Skoal chewing tobacco. As the band charges through originals as well as covers of "Ziggy Stardust" and "Warpigs," the company minions are passing out little packets of their wares to anyone who can prove they're eighteen or over.

ii.

Once upon a time, rock bands looked askance at product associations, however tame the product in question. But today, being sponsored is no big deal, whatever type of music you play. Epitaph Records has a connection with Airwalk shoes. Molson Ale sent Hole and Metallica to the North Pole. Even the Sex Pistols' "Filthy Lucre" tour was "brought to you," according to the ticket stub, by Apple computers.

Tobacco, however, is currently under fire from the FDA and the U.S. Congress, making it a slightly less appealing sponsor to a young band that describes itself as alternative.

Or so you'd think. Bullet Proof Buddha has no problems with the association. "We're not obligated to affiliate ourselves with the actual product at all," says guitarist Gabe Cateres. "We just go out and work together as a team, have fun, enjoy travel, entertain. We're fortunate enough to have some financial backing; if we can help them and they can help us, it's just a mutual relationship.

"We're just providing a service of entertainment, that's as far as that goes," adds Crites. "I don't think having a corporate sponsor is a negative thing."

Bullet Proof Buddha say that they're not being sponsored by U.S. Tobacco, although U.S. Tobacco owns and operates the Skoal Corporation. "Skoal Music is different from U.S. Tobacco," explains Bill Berman, formerly a San Diego law clerk who is now president of Impact Entertainment. He is also the band's business manager and the one who got them the deal with Skoal in the first place. "It's like the service branch of their organization. We're not really promoting their product—we're just getting our music out there, and they're helping us create the buzz that the business is looking for."

The point of the deal, according to Berman, is exposure. "Major labels," he says cannily, "are only going to put their money into a band with a following, which Skoal is helping us to get. They [Skoal Music] are paying for everything—staging, sound equipment, staying at motels, strings, picks, clothes, food, phone calls, gas."

It's an arrangement which Skoal is perfectly happy with. "Skoal is kind of a grassroots company," says Skoal Music's Allen Martindale, "and this is kind of a grassroots band. We have no expectations that they're going to get rich and famous with our logo all over them, that's not real world, but it feels natural to us to sponsor an up-and-coming band."

iii.

The name of the game is name recognition, of course, combined with the vague free association of ideas that the entire industry of advertising is based on—i.e., that if you thrust a product—any product—on top of something desirable, human beings will believe that the product is desirable, too.

A corollary of this theory has to do with appealing to niche markets— subsets of people whose similarity in race, class, and gender makes their ideas as to what is desirable easier to pinpoint, and thus, manipulate. The beer industry in particular has always relied on the creation of niche markets, and never more so than today, when a surge in microbreweries has glutted the market with so-called local beers. That's one reason why the beer industry is the leader in co-opting rock 'n' roll for its own fell purposes, via massive promotional campaigns that prey on local bands.

Take, for example, the "Bud Family in Concert" program, a deal whereby the giant St. Louis–based Anheuser-Busch Corporation agrees to sponsor various unsigned local bands, by giving them cash and prizes in exchange for a few minutes of that band's time each night that they perform.

To wit: for a base fee of six thousand dollars a year, plus some free equipment from cosponsors (Zildjian cymbals, Dunlop picks, GHS strings, and Yamaha drums, guitars, and synthesizers), the band in question must hang a giant Budweiser sign up behind its stage, announce that it's sponsored by Budweiser once during the evening, and play at least one song on a customized Fender guitar that lights up and says "Bud."

According to Sarah Palmer of Entertainment Marketing, the corporation that A-B hires to implement this program, the point of the Bud Family in Concert program is to infiltrate places that serve beer to five thousand to six thousand people a night. "Anheuser-Busch bands are ambassadors to the club when our wholesalers can't be there at two A.M.," she explains. "They make our presence known."

Palmer is herself one of the people responsible for choosing Bud's bands. The way she finds bands, she says, is by talking to local radio stations and newspapers, and to Anheuser-Busch accounts and wholesalers in the area she's scouting.

Palmer says there's no such thing as a Bud "sound" per se, but that the company is primarily interested in bar bands. They won't consider "performance art and classical music.

"We don't scout bands based on their own merit," adds Palmer pragmatically. "It's just what market they play in that interests us. We don't want to work with bad musicians, but I'm not looking for the next U2, either."

Palmer's words ought to be a warning to potential Bud bands, but there's no doubt that Bud is a route to free money. Last year, Budweiser spent $1.6 million on its program, sponsoring forty bands around the country. Of course, at corporations like Budweiser, says one advertising executive who's worked with many of them, the budgets for ad campaigns are "rounded off to the million." So sponsoring local bands is a puny expense in comparison.

In order to qualify to be a Bud band, the program specifies that each of its bands play at least one hundred gigs a year. That means Bud signs appeared in at least four thousand gigs nationwide, so Budweiser is definitely getting what it pays for—if not a lot more than what it's paying for, since, as any student of marketing, business administration, or communications knows, advertising is a crucial part of any market economy. Where competition exists, so too will billboards, print ads, posters, and so forth, anything and everything to brand your gray matter with a product's logo, in the hopes that this will cause you to order it prereflexively when next you're standing belly up to the bar.

That's the American way. Donald Barthelmy is the songwriter and guitarist for the band Fastgun, which is sponsored by Bud Light. "We're glad to be sponsored by Budweiser," says Barthelmy. "We've been drinking beer forever. Of course [being sponsored by Budweiser is] a positive thing. How could it not be? Heck, everybody I know drinks beer. Beer don't hurt nobody."

iv.

Like gangs and animals, beer companies like to stake out their turf. Upscale microbreweries go for yuppies, via neato packaging, flavorful gourmet additives, and an emphasis on "taste." The lower-priced beers have a harder row to hoe, attempting to distinguish between white-, blue-, and pink-collar drinkers, between rural and urban markets, and between young and old.

But attempting to hack some consumer loyalty from groups of American beer drinkers is a rough-and-tumble game, particularly given the weak and indistinguishable nature of most brands of cheap beer. That's where promotions and marketing come in—the step beyond mere glitzy advertising into the hazy world of psychological warfare.

Beer manufacturers like to advertise in crowded rooms—at ball games, at frat parties, at the beach. But one of the main places they like to infiltrate is rock concerts. The reasons are pretty obvious: rock concerts contain a high percentage of heavy-duty beer drinkers—no matter who the artist is, what the style of music, or where the venue. Moreover, they are invariably infested with the beer company's favorite demographic, the twenty-one to thirty-four-year-old male.

But most important of all, rock bands themselves provide a link to that ill-defined virtue "coolness"—an attribute that companies will go to great lengths to acquire. On Labor Day weekend of 1995, for example, Molson Ice held a rock concert in Tuktoyaktuk, Canada, as close to the North Pole as they could get. The concert featured performances by the bands Metallica, Hole, Veruca Salt, and Moist, its attendees were not the local Inuit population, but five hundred lucky winners of a beer-sponsored contest.

Hole later alleged that it was paid four hundred thousand dollars to play this rather specious rock concert; if you add in the salaries of the other three bands, plus the transport of equipment, the cost of advertising it, and so on, you'll get an idea of the lengths that beer companies will go in order to seem exotic, desirable, special. In comparison, Budweiser's local band program seems downright cheap and homely.

Just when rock 'n' roll started to seem "cool" to the common man, rather than cultish, fringy, and rebellious, is another question. In the sixties, the Who did a cereal commercial, but it wasn't until the early eighties that companies really began using rock stars as spokespeople—Michael Jackson and Pepsi pop to mind—and purchasing the rights to rock songs and attaching them to products. (The Beatles' "Revolution" was bought by Nike, Carly Simon's "Anticipation" by Heinz ketchup, and so on.) This caused some concern among media pundits—critics who declared that the artists who sold their songs thusly were destroying the song's impact by turning it into a jingle—but it hasn't stopped the number of songs that have been used in this way, by artists of all stripes.

In the middle of the eighties, Miller beer used to sponsor indie rock bands, in a program that failed in part because the bands it chose, though critically acclaimed, were denounced by their peers for shilling for the Man. The Long Ryders and the Del Fuegos were two up-and-coming bands who appeared in Miller commercials; neither band was subsequently heard from again.

In recent years, however, Budweiser has gotten smarter. The "Bud Light Network" on radio—which is just an advertisement meant to sound like a news show—plays and reviews up-and-coming bands who have no say regarding their participation. Budweiser also sponsored the Rolling Stones "VooDoo Lounge" tour. Sponsoring a high-profile tour like the Rolling Stones' makes a lot of obvious sense: millions of consumers will see the giant Bud signs at every venue, plus, the beer gets associated with a glamorous band. Also, high-level executives get free tickets to the gigs, and most important, to shake the hands of band members at a "meet and greet" beforehand.

V.

In the case of products like Skoal, however, glamour is never going to be achieved. But given the inherent yuckiness of chew, just making their product familiar to kids, undemonizing it, and associating it with a respectable entity like a fraternity house is almost as good as gold.

And like Budweiser, Skoal is willing to pay up for the service—a fact that Berman has exploited to the advantage of Bullet Proof Buddha. Ultimately, of course, Berman wants Buddha to sign a deal not with a Fortune 500 company, but with a record label. "I could tell you right now who all the best A&R people in LA are," he says, "but there's no need for me to put our tape on their tables until, ideally, it would be a lost opportunity on their part not to sign us."

When that tape does get on the table, Bullet Proof Buddha and Berman don't believe that being sponsored by a product—even a product with a negative reputation—will hurt them one bit. Are they correct in their surmise? Geoff Weiss is an A&R person at Warner Brothers Records whose last signing was college rock up-and-comers Schleprock, and he admits that corporate sponsorship is not necessarily prohibitive to being signed.

"There's nothing you can tell me about a band that would make me say 'forget it' about them," he says. "I've signed bands with every kind of liability—drug problems, personality disorders, lead singers who are hideously ugly—and believe me, *that's* a liability.

"Whatever the negatives are, they can be overcome if a band really has killer songs. But I would be very, very skeptical of a band [that's sponsored by anybody]. I wouldn't say I wouldn't go see them, but first off, I'm always skeptical of bands with a strong business sense right off the bat. Unless they learned it from the bottom up, like Girls Against Boys or something, any band with a hotshot lawyer or business manager is immediately a red flag."

Another red flag may be the band's sound itself. Although they've only been together six months, Bullet Proof Buddha are an accomplished grunge band whose set relies heavily on riffs and attitude copped from bands like Soundgarden, Rage Against the Machine, and Bush. Berman goes so far as to describe them as "a cross between Alice in Chains, Pearl Jam, and Stone Temple Pilots," and he's not far off. But is grunge still viable in 1996, or has it been usurped by punk?

Weiss: "It depends on the marketplace you're in. A brand-new grunge band is definitely a suburban rock market, as opposed to the Telegraph Avenue crowd, but obviously, there's a huge market of people who like that kind of music, even if it's music that's a derivative, watered-down, second-, third-, fourth-, or fifth-generation version of it."

What's interesting about Bullet Proof Buddha is Skoal's belief—probably not erroneous—that the grunge audience is a possible new market for chew.

One obvious reason for such a belief is that the audience is predominantly male. Another reason might be that the grunge audience is inured to—and indeed, seems to thrive on—perceived grossness. Tattoos, piercings, drugs, cigars...why should an audience that apparently admires junkies fear discolored and rotten teeth, stinky breath, and the possibility of throat and mouth cancer?

Asked if Skoal Music feels there may be an ethical problem with allying itself to the distinctly youth-oriented rock market, Skoal Music events promotions director Frank Piscani says, "Absolutely not. The tour is geared to an eighteen years old or over crowd. We're not targeting anyone under eighteen years of age. Kids in college are all at least eighteen."

Until recently, Skoal Music contented itself with sponsoring and promoting rodeo and NASCAR racing events, as well as the occasional country-and-western gigs, like the "Rockin' the Smokies" concert in Tennessee last July, and an entire Charlie Daniels Band tour.

Given the known geographic and economic conditions of users of chewing tobacco, there were sound reasons for this. But according to the U.S. Department of Agriculture, the use of smokeless chewing tobacco is on the rise. In 1993, Americans chewed or dipped 60 million pounds of products—up from 53 million pounds in 1990. There are also about thirty thousand cases of oral (mouth) cancer diagnosed each year, the primary cause of which is chewing tobacco. And most of the new users are under the age of twenty-one.

Skoal has reacted to this rise with an attempt to move into a more youthful, and more western market; one of the first steps has been this deal with Bullet Proof Buddha. "Basically, we were involved in a lot of music promotions in the mid-eighties, like the Charlie Daniels Band," says Piscani. "But if you get involved with a top-name band, it's a lot of money, a big investment, so we got out of it. We're getting back into it now, and this is the type of music that's popular. I don't think [the fact that they're a grunge band] came into it: it's just, we had a personal connection to this band, and they're popular in San Diego. It was an avenue for us to get back into music promotion . . . a natural fit."

As Piscani says, it's also "a dream come true for a band of this level." Bullet Proof Buddha used to play local gigs at beach clubs like Blind Melon's and Hurricanes (which was formerly a daiquiri bar). Skoal Music, however, has given them a leg up the ladder, helping to pay for the recording of a demo, which the band has just released as a CD and they plan on selling at gigs, and booking them on a two-month tour of college campuses around the western United States—gigs like an outdoor music festival on the beach near Camp Pendleton, which played to eight thousand jarheads, and the Chico State one—which are sponsored by Skoal. All the band has to do in return is hang Skoal's banner behind the stage.

Like many corporations with ties to the rock concert circuit—Bud Light, for example—Skoal is pretty smart to court unsigned bands. In general, those bands are cheaper, needier, and not as smart. But it's partly a personal decision. Some bands can live with it, some can't. Asked if Rocket from the Crypt would have signed a deal with Bud Light (in the lean years before signing to Interscope), manager Greg Jacobs laughs. "No way in hell!" he says off the top of his head. "Rocket is a band, not an advertisement."

Rocket does endorse certain products, Jacobs adds—but they are band-related products, like guitar strings, and the band hasn't signed any contracts. "They [companies] don't give us money, just free stuff," he explains. "[But] it's not potentially harmful to your audience to endorse a certain kind of instrument."

To Bullet Proof Buddha, however, the benefits of Skoal's help definitely outweigh the negatives. In fact, they can't think of any negatives. "For us to get a chance to go play our music to people and have someone help us out, well—we thought it was great," says Cateres. "Ultimately that's our main goal—to play for people, get exposure, go on the road."

This may be a sound strategy. It may, however, not be. Trouz Cuevas, who has worked with Primus and Metallica and is currently managing bands like the Charlie Hunter Quartet, Crumb, and Blinker the Star, says that if one of his bands was offered a similar deal with Skoal, "I'd sit them down and advise them not to do it. On the one hand, it's a dilemma—I mean, these guys could take the money and it could break them—get them signed, help them buy gear. On the other hand...chewing tobacco? It's kind of like Smith & Wesson."

Weiss doesn't exactly agree. "The nature of the product wouldn't be that significant to me—even if was Ben & Jerry's or something PC like that. To me it's just that—the music business is the merging of art and commerce, but I at least like to *think* a band's closer to the art part than the commerce; that the artist's acting out of a pure motive. I'm uncomfortable with that kind of crassly obvious association. I mean, we [at Warner Brothers] recognize that it's financially very difficult to be in a young, up-and-coming band, but there's nothing like honestly working your way out of that hole for credibility's sake alone."

To date, there's no concrete proof, of course, that selling your image to a Fortune 500 company devolves poorly on one's band profile. But the consequences may be deeper than they know. Dave Marsh, author of numerous books on rock 'n' roll (*Born to Run, Louie Louie,* and *Fortunate Son* among them) is a longtime critic of corporate sponsorship, and he has this message for bands who are considering corporate sponsors: "They shouldn't debase their art in the service of economic institutions that continually display contempt for the rock audience and for the best aspects of what music stands for."

Former *Creem* editor Robert Duncan, who now heads his own advertising company, concurs. "Whether it's wrong or not, it's a bad decision from a marketing point of view. It's ringing your own death knell. Promote their product; kill your own chances of marketing yourself effectively."

One thing is certain. Somehow, in the four years since Nirvana jokingly made T-shirts with the words "flower sniffin', kitty pettin', baby kissin', corporate rock whores" on the back, the precepts of grunge—and punk, which they were derived from—has degenerated into all the things it originally decried. Clearly, to the kids who'll mosh to Bullet Proof Buddha, Kurt

Cobain's "Corporate Rock Still Sucks" gestures are not just forgotten—
they were entirely meaningless to begin with.

Right now, Bullet Proof Buddha feel pretty confident that they are on
the right track to getting signed. Asked whether he has a feeling about signing to an indie label or a major label, singer Chad Crites shrugs.

"I think it depends on the deal, what they have to offer. We haven't
been down that avenue yet, so I don't really think about it.... If the deals
start coming in, whatever. It's kind of like, do you like the Ford or the
Bronco, or the Chevy—ultimately it's the one with the right price."

Chapter 6
Know Your Product? No, You're Product

Well, it isn't a pleasant pass when grunge and/or punk fans have come to represent the perfect target market for anything, be it computers, beer, or chewing tobacco. It is, in fact, perhaps the one thing above all others to be avoided, since to be co-opted is to go from being a consumer to being the thing consumed.

But if products can co-opt music and, by proxy, its audience, so too can music co-opt products for their own fell purposes as well. The genius of nuevo punk—punk of the nineties—is that it has taken an active role in the process of co-option. Instead of simply thoughtlessly allowing a product to use its music to sell its wares, it found a whole hidden market of its own, upon which it imposed an entire musical aesthetic.

The perfection of the plan is indubitable, especially given the upscaleness and the newness of the product in question. Snowboarding was only invented in the early eighties, almost on the heels of punk, but in the last five years, participation in it has increased 165 percent, making it, according to a study conducted by American Sports Data, one of the top growth sports in the world. A cross between surfing and skiing, it's already an Olympic sport, huge not only in America and Canada, but in Finland, Scotland, Japan, and the Czech Republic. By the year 2000, it is estimated that in America alone there will be 5 million snowboarders.

The link between punk rock and snowboarding is one that has been fostered and nurtured by both record companies and snowboard companies, as well as by actual snowboarding band members themselves, for several years. In fact, the chronological growth chart of boarding as a business almost exactly mimics that of nuevo punk rock—beginning in 1992, when ski filmmaker Taylor Steele used the music of his friends' band Pennywise in the background of one of his first boarding videos.

Now the image of snowboarders as young, white, and gnarly teenagers, slamming down mountainsides to music like that by Bad Religion and their co-labelmates Pennywise and Offspring, as well as similarly loud-fast bands like Lagwagon, the Supersuckers, Rage Against the Machine, and Rocket from the Crypt, is one that is firmly implanted in every teenager's brain. In olden days, punk rock was patently anti-athleticism, but nowadays no self-respecting punk fan would let a winter pass without at least one run to the mountains, board in hand.

ii.

A glimpse of the slope at the Big Bear ski resort near Lake Arrowhead, on Valentine's Day 1996, merely confirms this impression. As is often the case at this beautiful but often dry ski resort two hours east of Los Angeles in the Angeles National Forest, the sun is out, the sky is blue, and it hasn't snowed in about four weeks. It's also a school day—but the place is packed. Only instead of its usual network of antlike snowboarders carving the slopes, some three thousand kids are sitting down flat on their butts in the snow, watching the hardcore band Bad Religion perform on a stage that has been set up at the foot of the ski runs.

All day long the air has been full of various forms of punk rock—music made by bands like Seattle's Seven Year Bitch, Long Beach's Sublime, and San Diego's Unwritten Law. There have also been speeches from various celebrities and AIDS activists who are taking this opportunity to educate young people on AIDS prevention. Today Big Bear is the background for Board-Aid, a benefit concert sponsored by the Oceanside-based skate-boarding magazine *WARP*, in conjunction with Lifebeat, a music-industry-sponsored AIDS organization.

In the past two years, Board-Aid has raised over $100,000 for youth-oriented community AIDS organizations, and this year will prove no exception. At the end of the day, the concert will have attracted four thousand kids and raised approximately $160,000 for various AIDS organizations.

Board-Aid's success can be attributed in part to massive mobilization on the part of *WARP* magazine's staff with Lifebeat, MTV, and the thirty-five corporations who, according to event coordinator Mark Spirling, have "recognized this as a legitimate event and cause, and a great opportunity for product exposure."

But it's also a tribute to the success the Transworld organization has had in linking up the record industry, the snowboarding industry, and kids. At Board-Aid, there are numerous tables set up, some dispensing AIDS prevention information, some advertising boarding equipment, and others—funded by record labels—promoting various rock bands who are perceived as appealing to snowboarders.

That means punk bands. Why the link? According to former Circle Jerk and current Bad Religion guitarist Greg Hetson, punk rock and snowboarding share a common attitude. "They're both about letting yourself go and losing your inhibitions, and getting crazy. Snowboarding has a total punk attitude, it's a do-it-yourself kind of thing. Boarding," he adds finally, "is like being in a mosh pit—if you're not alert, you get hurt."

Selene Vigil, of Board-Aid opening act Seven Year Bitch, has another take on the connection between punk and snowboarding, however. "Sixteen-year-old boys," she said succinctly. "They love to snowboard and they love punk rock."

Vigil's response really gets to the crux of the question: as a marketing strategy, linking snowboarding to punk is pure genius, because it targets the single most desirable advertising demographic, the eighteen-to-thirty-four-year-old white male. And it's a strategy that's worked brilliantly, particularly for the artists on Epitaph Records, whose artists are more linked to snowboarding than any other, although, according to Melissa Boag, "the link is organic. The initial connection [between boarders and Epitaph fans] was already there, and not the other way around."

To a certain extent, Epitaph's Jeff Abarta confirms this, although he doesn't deny a degree of fortuitous recognition of a trend. "In ninety-two, when Taylor Steele asked Pennywise for some music for his films, they hooked him up with us—and we loaded him down.

"Then," he adds, "we actively started searching for marketing opportunities to do with boarding."

How influential has the connection been to the company? "Extremely crucial," says Abarta. "When Pennywise's first LP came out, in its first year it sold twelve thousand copies. Then they did the snowboarding films and it jumped to fifty thousand or sixty thousand immediately. That's a pretty significant jump."

Certainly the Offspring, who also first came to prominence via snowboarding videos like "Totally Board" (TB1) and "Stomping Groungs," and whose 1994 LP S.M.A.S.H. went on to sell 10 million copies, proves that the snowboarding connection can initiate a sales buzz. But there's no question that the opposite is now true as well. Just as the Beach Boys glamorized surfing, bands like Bad Religion, Biohazard, and the Beastie Boys are currently crucial elements in the glamorization of boarding. Seldom an hour goes by on MTV in the wintertime when the cameras aren't somehow alluding to boarding, whether it's via board-happy T-shirts on artists like Megadeth's Dave Mustaine and Anthrax's Scott Ian, or by events like Board-Aid and the WARP Tour. In fact, few national or international snowboarding events are complete without a big-name band headlining a rock concert after the day's events.

And the merch connection is getting bigger every day as well. For example, the San Diego–based company Airwalk, which manufactures shoes, says it gives away up to four hundred pairs of free shoes a month to band members and other celebrities. Airwalk provides freebies to big acts like Nine Inch Nails, the Chili Peppers, Duran Duran, k. d. lang, the Beastie Boys, and Gwar, but they're also big supporters of smaller, local San Diego bands, giving free shoes to members of Tiltwheel, Blink 182, Unwritten Law, and Fluf.

"It's totally justifiable from a product-recognition point of view," says Airwalk spokesperson and skateboard team manager Rob Dotson. "It makes kids feel like they can become more part of a group they already admire if they see them endorsing a product they like. Plus, we give bands stickers to give away; and the kids get stoked. It's a really great investment for us. If just one kid sees some musician they really like in our product and is influenced to buy it, it's been worth it for us."

iii.

Airwalk is one of the larger independently owned companies that has cashed in on the growing sport of snowboarding; another business, located in San Diego, is Transworld, which employs sixty-five people in its warehouses in Oceanside.

WARP, and its sister magazines *Transworld Skateboarding, Transworld Snowboarding,* and *Snowboard Life,* are all part of the Transworld empire, which includes six in-house magazines (the other two are trade journals), some in-house merchandising, and various projects like last year's WARP tour (featuring L7 and Sublime) and Board-Aid. According to Clark Staub, senior executive in charge of marketing at Capitol Records, "what Transworld does so well is really take the individuality of snowboarding, and then use all the marketing available today—not just put its nose up in the air about the money issue like an ignorant scenester would."

Staub, however, denies that either snowboarding or punk helped each other to the top of the heap, despite the coinciding time lines. "It's true that when bands like the Offspring and Green Day became big, they blew up a lifestyle, and that lifestyle became mainstream," says Staub. "But the growth of snowboarding as a marketing tool isn't only about the growth of commercial punk rock. It's partly due to the growth of what's possible in boarding due to design developments in the boards, and partly due to media images."

The success of Transworld publications—the biggest, *Transworld Skateboarding*, has a monthly circulation of 350,000—is due in part to its recognition of the merch link between skateboarding, snowboarding, and surfing. This is sometimes called "sideways culture"—in other words, sports where you're standing sideways.

Transworld Skateboarding is a fourteen-year-old magazine; *Transworld Snowboarding* is nine years old. But in the past five years, snowboarding has superseded skateboarding as a pastime, particularly in San Diego County. Why San Diego, a place not known for its snowy mountain vistas?

"There's a lot of crossover potential between surfing and snowboarding," explains *WARP* editor Mark Woodlief. "Snowboarding is essentially surfing; the same terms apply, like carving the water or carving the mountain, but snowboarding is easier than surfing. The learning curve is a lot briefer."

WARP is a Transworld magazine that by definition explores the implicit link between sideways culture and sound. Surfers have always listened to music to get pumped up to surf. "It's a big part of their scene, there's a sort of sound track that goes with it," explains Woodlief. "For the most part it's punk rock, but hip-hop figures in, and so does indie rock. . . . Anyway, it's safe to assume they—surfers—aren't listening to the Wave [an easy listening station in San Diego]."

Woodlief agrees, however, that in recent years, snowboarding and punk have become artificially linked by advertisers. "Totally," he says. "Companies give snowboards to musicians; the Beastie Boys are always wearing Airwalk shoes, and so on. [Snowboarding] is maybe at that awkward age, being filtered through media images that are shaping its future."

Dotson, a professional skateboarder for eleven years, agrees. "Rap and gnarly punk rock, sure, that matches the fast pace of snowboarding. But I have friends who are professional boarders and all they'll listen to is jazz and classical. It's whatever you're into, really."

In fact, the link between punk and boarding, although it is also partly rooted in snowboarding history, is at least partly bogus. Skateboarding, from which boarding takes it self-image, is punk because it is truly DIY: you buy a board and just do it. Snowboarding mimics the style and 'tude of skateboarding, but it involves a more serious investment just to get started, not to mention the fixed and constant expense of lift tickets, which cost upwards of thirty-five dollars a day, approaching the cost of heroin addiction. According to ADS, 65 percent of all snowboarders have a household income of thirty-five thousand dollars or over. A whopping 31 percent have incomes over seventy-five thousand dollars.

It's not like you're seeing any real lowlife—tattooed love guys with tracks on their arms and electric guitars in their closets—on the mountains. That said, the "punk" label does have real roots. California's surfers and skateboarders were snowboarding's first aficionados, and they are traditionally an integral part of the punk scene. Those original snowboarders weren't allowed on ski resort slopes, so they cut their own trails—an exercise called "backroading," which certainly has its punk aspect.

Most importantly, initially, there was a lot of tension between skiers and snowboarders who shared slopes. Because of their sideways stance on the board, boarders have a built-in blind spot that sometimes interferes with skiers coming down behind them. This combined with the perception of snowboarders as gnarly, radical, tattooed punk rockers give the sport a bad reputation at ski resorts and among skiers.

As is often the case with misconceptions, however, one can't help but think that the more those board jockeys got called "punks," the more they conformed to the accusation. Perhaps it took some snotty old ski dude calling a brash young boarder a "punk" for him to want to listen to tracks by Black Flag or Bad Religion. It's been a self-fulfilling tag.

Staub, a snowboarder himself, disagrees, however. He sees the link between boarding and punk as being one that's essentially of the spirit. "The rush I get out of snowboarding is very similar to punk—to being in a punk band and beating the shit out of the drums. Riding the back country, it's fucking awesome—it's like making music, when you walk in a room and it's utterly silent, and then you come up with something loud and wonderful, or even cranking up a CD that speaks to you."

And Staub should know: in 1978, when he was fourteen and worked at an LA-area skate park, some older employees took him to San Francisco to see the Sex Pistols at Winterland, also shows by Black Flag, Circle Jerks, Germs, DOA, the Subhumans, and others. He was still underage. Staub eventually switched from skateboarding to snowboarding—and from being in a punk band to marketing them.

But he claims to still have the fire inside. "Punk rock," he says passionately, "is about personal evolvement. "Yeah, fuck the system—because the system is everything outside of you. Punk—and boarding—is about raging individualism, it's about doing something for yourself. That's the connection between the two things."

Those are beautiful words, and if you think of boarding as something that takes place outside of resorts, on lost and empty mountainsides, then it might very well be true—it may be a sort of personal art form. But the perception of boarding as being "alternative"—or at least low-end, populist, and counterculture—is growing ever falser as the business of snowboarding takes off.

Woodlief points out that snowboarding, like punk, has radically altered the entire winter sports industry, infusing it with a much-needed jolt of both energy and cash. Skiing is still the world's most dominant winter sport, but snowboarding's market share is growing so fast that these days, he points out, boarding's pioneers probably feel as alienated by the crowds of jocks on the lifts up the mountains as the original Nirvana felt by boneheads who rushed the pit.

Now, agrees Staub, boarding is "hipper and trendier and younger than skiing—and it's not as rigid as a sport. Moreover, the snowboard population is growing by leaps and bounds. The result is that outside sources look at it as this great marketing tool. They want more thirteen-to-sixteen-year-olds; they see snowboarding as having them. Then you get some idiot at Taco Bell saying, 'Let's do an Extreme campaign,' and voilà: the 'Extreme Meal Deal' is born."

Actually, Staub himself looks at boarding as a great marketing tool. Three years ago, when he first came to Capitol Records, he was assigned to work a record by the excellent band Spearhead. But when the LP came out, it was rejected by the black community. "[Spearhead leader] Michael Franti had been on tour with U2, was friends with Michael Stipe.... The urban world knew that and wrote him off as wanting to be white. We found we couldn't make any headway in the rap community, and we noticed that the majority of the live audience was white alternative kids. So we began building a campaign that was geared toward them."

Capitol Records worked hard to get Spearhead put into MTVs Buzzbin—which took four months. The eventual result was that the video for the track "Hole in the Bucket" became a minor sort of hit. Then Staub took it one step further, and began marketing Spearhead to snowboarders—inventing a connection between the two items. Presently, he took Spearhead to the Transworld-wide Convention in Wyoming, where they played in front of a thousand people from the snowboarding community and, Staub adds now, "slaughtered them.

"It seemed kind of iffy, but Spearhead kicked their asses. So this year, we came up with the idea to do a regional tour of Colorado in a bunch of snooty ski resorts. I think having an all-black urban hip-hop band play honky-tonks in all-white Colorado is *very* fucking punk rock."

iv.

I went snowboarding once: I was carried all the way up the pristine mountain on a lift, and then all the way downward on the flat of my butt. Green trees, blue sky, white snow, golden sun: it was great—involving that kind of extreme physical effort that wipes out every thought in your head. I enjoyed every minute of it, but to me it was the antithesis of punk rock; everything that punk rock wasn't. It wasn't about art and togetherness and community and nonconformism; it was about personal, physical fulfillment and the hedonistic rush one gets from showing off.

Perhaps if I practiced enough, I too could go backroading—and carve a mountain that was the equivalent of some secret punk club, and like Staub, I could make it all my own. But it would take a huge investment—of time and cash, and that, in the end, is the point. As a marketing tool, snowboarding beats skateboarding cold because its potential field of consumers is not limited to fearless twelve-year-old boys; unlike skateboarding, it has attracted skiers, surfers, and even many young women into its fold. This can only be considered a good thing—but it's also a remunerative one. The amount of merch the sport has generated in the past five years—from equipment to specialized clothes—is phenomenal: according to *Snowboarding Business,* in 1995, Americans spent an estimated $675 million on snowboarding equipment, and projected figures for the 1996 season are over $800 million.

True, many of the over three hundred companies currently supplying clothing and boards are independently owned. But capitalism is capitalism. And in the end, the selling of snowboarding highlights the difference between '77 punk rock and the nuevo punk of Epitaph bands like Bad Religion and Pennywise. Punk rock used to be made by seedy, unhealthy, pale-skinned antijock types, expressly for people like themselves. Now it's the province of beefy, healthy jock types—the very same types who ruined punk rock to begin with when they first invaded mosh pits.

But maybe that's just to be expected. "It's growing pains," says *WARP*'s

Woodlief, "just like punk rock went from being about British kids on the dole to being suburban, SoCal punks."

But there's always been this myth that garage rock—punk rock, whatever—is the bastion of struggling blue-collar kids who see no other way out of a dead-end future. In fact, that myth was outmoded with the Reagan administration, when the bottom fell out of the housing market. Nowadays, to form a real garage band you gotta have a garage, and in America, that already implies middle classdom.

In short, neither snowboarding nor punk rock is the stronghold of cultural opposition, as they once were, and as their adherents—or rather, their salespeople—would have you believe; both are now luxuries, purchased at the cost of being a raging individualist. That doesn't make either thing bad or wrong—it just makes them status quo.

PART 2

THE PUNK PREDICA-MENT

Chapter 7

Millions Like Us

To understand how all things punk became so status quo, though, one first has to recall the days when they weren't. One has to set the way-back machine to 1985, to the days when Ronald Reagan was president, the Berlin Wall was still standing, Yugoslavia was one country, and nobody owned a single CD. Nineteen eighty-five was the year of "Live AID" and "We Are the World," and the year that Tupac Shakur turned twelve years old. In 1985, there was no *Simpsons*. No *Roseanne*. No Smashing Pumpkins. No Sharon Stone. And bands like the Replacements, Sonic Youth, the Minutemen, and Husker Du were all on independent labels.

Oh, those nights spent in their presence! I saw you standing there next to me: at some hole-in-the-wall like Raji's. T T's. The I Beam. The Uptown, the Central, Maxwell's, or the Continental. We were not in hiding from the mainstream in the confines of that night. Are you kidding? No one was looking for us or at us . . . no one was listening to a single word we said. We were like little teeny bands of marauders, clad in junk-store dresses and combat boots, embattled against a cacophony of bad music and bad haircuts that we wanted to have no part of. We were a tiny little community, all of us together, us against the world. It was a different era entirely.

Since those days, countless new countries have been invented and countless new children have been born. Hardly any bands have broken up, but more have been formed than you can count on all the hands in China. And yet, though one acknowledges the futility of judging, say, new Supreme Court decisions, various passages in the Bible, and the efficacy of current U.S. AIDS policies by the standards of a bygone era, many independent rock fans persist in upholding the standards of the 1985 era on behalf of a host of new young bands whose goals, priorities, and, most importantly, temptations are entirely different from the ones faced back then.

Accustomed as many of us have been over the past decade to think of major labels as the Corporate Ogre, the time has come for bands and fans alike to acknowledge that things are not the same as they were eleven years ago, when Warner Brothers Records first signed Husker Du.

Heck, things are not even the same as they were seven years ago, when Slash Records signed a punk/pop band called Sweet Baby. At the time, Sweet Baby had contributed one track to a compilation of Gilman Street bands called "Turnaround" on the Lookout! label, which documented the work of a tiny group of bands that congregated around a punk rock collective located at 924 Gilman Street in Berkeley.

In 1990, Sweet Baby, championed by then-Slash producer and A&R person Matt Wallace (who left the label soon after signing them to it), were given ten thousand dollars to make their self-titled record. There was no advertising budget for the record, because Slash felt that advertising would ruin the band's punk rock credibility. They didn't release the record on CD (it was vinyl and cassette only). They sent the band out on a little tour, which fell apart halfway through due to a series of gigs booked on nights when the club in question was generally closed. After returns, Sweet Baby's record sold approximately two thousand copies.

The same year that Sweet Baby recorded *Sweet Baby*, another Gilman Street band, this one called Green Day, was recording its first seven-inch single for Lookout! Three years later, Warner Brothers Records signed Green Day. They gave the trio a deal worth three hundred thousand dollars, not including money for video and tour support. A few weeks before the band's major label debut, *Dookie*, was released, Warner Brothers bought the back-page ad in *Billboard* for fifteen thousand dollars—five thousand more than Sweet Baby's whole budget.

The week *Dookie* came out, the marquee outside of Tower Records in San Diego screamed "Green Day Record Finally in Stock!" The very next week, February 19, 1994, *Dookie* entered the *Billboard* charts at number 127, selling nine thousand copies its first week.

ii.

October 1993. It's midway through Green Day's set at the 2,500-seat Warfield Theater. Not only is it the biggest venue the band has ever played, and the first time they've cracked the Bay Area's BGP curtain (meaning clubs owned or operated by the Bill Graham Presents organization), but it is only the second time in their five-year existence that they have played San Francisco.

This is the equivalent of a band from Hoboken never having played Manhattan, or a band from Anaheim never playing LA. Berkeley, the band's hometown, is about five miles east across the Bay Bridge. Tonight, Green Day are opening for the band Bad Religion.

Green Day are clearly not well known by the majority of the crowd, but their tight poppy punk rock is winning the audience over. The kids—it's a rare all-ages show at the Warfield this night—crush the stage and pogo to songs that sound like what the Ramones would sound like if they were shorter, cuter, more earnest, more energetic, and a hell of a lot younger.

After a rousing version of "Don't Leave Me," from the band's Lookout! LP *39/Smooth,* during which singer Billie Joe Armstrong and bassist Mike Dirnt trade supercharged antics running back and forth cross the stage, the bands stops for a brief breather.

"Hey," says Billie Joe, who is performing here tonight clad in a fetching white lady's slip, sans underpants. "I thought they only let old hippies play this joint."

The crowd cheers. "This," he continues, "is a song off our upcoming album."

This time, the crowd jeers. Or at least, one member of it does: "Green Day sucks!" yells a lone voice up front. "Sell outs!"

"Takes one to know one!" ripostes Dirnt.

"Ah ha ha . . . this is about you, buddy," butts in Billie Joe. The band rips into "Chump," which segues neatly into the song "Longview." Halfway through, the band stops dead, hits three power chords, and bursts suddenly into "Eye of the Tiger," the theme from *Rocky II* by Frank Stallone. Or was it the theme to *Rambo*? Whatever: the audience goes fucking insane. Green Day has them in the palm of their hands.

They finish up with a couple more numbers, then invite their friends Rancid on stage to sing the old Operation Ivy song "Knowledge": "I know that things are getting tougher / when you can't get the top off the bottom of the barrel / Wide open the road of my future now—it's looking fucking narrow!"

That song—the unofficial anthem for the Gilman Street punk rock scene that has helped Green Day get where they are today—has never sounded less than jubilant, but tonight, as they face down the largest crowd in their life, in the city they couldn't crack, "triumphant" would be too mild

■ Green Day, 1991
Murray Bowles

a word for the atmosphere they're exuding. Tonight, the road to Green Day's future is about as wide as the eye can see.

iii.

"The one thing that gives music its potency," said Sub Pop's Bruce Pavitt in 1993, "is its context. You have to look at the artists' community at large, where they're coming from, who they were speaking to in the first place. Look at San Francisco in the sixties: Haight-Ashbury, Owlsley, Ginsberg. That was what made the Grateful Dead and the Jefferson Airplane more than just bands, what made them resonant and important. A better example is Dischord Records in D.C.: teenagers making records, and their whole antidrug philosophy, putting huge Xs on their hands to mark their solidarity with people underage. The context is the whole story."

What Green Day have that many other bands on the market today lack is context. Green Day's roots are real, and they lie on the corner of Eighth Avenue and Gilman Street, four blocks shy of Highway 80 in Berkeley. That's where a collective of teenage punk rockers led by *Maximum Rock 'n' Roll* founder Tim Yohannan started 924 Gilman, an all-ages punk rock clubhouse, in 1987.

The clubhouse, an old cane shop decorated with a lot of graffiti and a couple of basketball hoops, is run on a strict percentage basis by volunteers. The stage cuts off one corner of the room; the tiny "bar" area, flyered with notices for upcoming riot grrrl meetings, band-member wanted posters, and flyers of old shows, serves only Hansen's soda and a variety of candy.

But the club has, since its start, flourished in the hearts and minds of Berkeley teens, providing a safe haven—a community—for runaways, misfits, and putative punk rockers. Waiflike girls in junk-store dress, guys in dumpers and dyed hair, Jawbreaker, Samiam, Blatz, Fifteen. A romantic world, where, to quote Billie Joe, "It was even kind of neat when our van's transmission blew out and stuff. It was cool that we were in the hole, because all we cared about was that we were really tight as a band and we got to play a lot of basements and rec halls and squats for beer, and kids would get together in their kitchens and the minute you mentioned Gilman Street or Lookout! you'd have this total connection."

Like many a revolutionary concept, however, Gilman Street's first year was its headiest time. In its earliest incarnation, it flourished with the help of a host of bands, including Isocracy, Sweet Baby, Crimpshrine, the Look-

■ **Operation Ivy at Gilman Street 1988**
Murray Bowles

outs, and of course Operation Ivy, the latter being the cornerstone band of Gilman Street legend.

And legend is the right word: in underground circles fueled by articles in fanzines like *Maximum Rock 'n' Roll* and *Flipside,* the club has served as a model to punk rock communities ever since. Sweet Baby's Dallas Denery recalls playing similar clubs around the country on Sweet Baby's one tour: "The kids would always say, 'Is this anything like Gilman Street,' and we'd always tell them, 'Hell, this is better!' "

Operation Ivy was Lookout! Records' breakout band, and thus, the one who funded Green Day's initial pressings. If you think GD's sales are phenomenal, check this out: after a ten-month, one-tour existence, Operation Ivy sold almost twice as many records as Green Day did up till *Dookie,* all by word of mouth. The band's history is, according to label owner Lawrence Livermore, "almost magic." In January of '89, Op Ivy played their record-release party at 924 Gilman. Green Day was one of the openers. "It was magic," Livermore recalls. "It exceeded all expectations, and everyone had this dazed, happy look on their face. . . . There were millions of kids here, singing all the choruses, and we couldn't figure out where they'd come from. It was like a punk Woodstock—and I was at the real Woodstock, so I should know. But it was also like Woodstock in that Woodstock was supposed to be a celebration of hippiedom, and in actuality it was a big wake."

This, then, is the scene from which Green Day emerged—albeit in the second generation of bands to take the stage there. Op Ivy broke up soon after that last transcendent Gilman Street gig, but their record has gone on to sell over one hundred thousand copies for Lookout!—financing in part the records of Green Day, whom Livermore signed soon after Op Ivy's demise.

They were signed, Livermore recalls, as much for being good sports as for their music. Then called Sweet Children, they had driven 180 miles in the snow to play a show at someone's house in Willits that was an utter fiasco—only five people showed up, there was no ceiling to the cabin, it was raining, and they had to start up a generator for electricity, so they played lit up by candles.

"And instead of being bummed out, they played like it was the Oakland Coliseum," Livermore recalls. "They didn't sound punky, more poppy and sixties-ish. After two songs I said, 'You can make a record on my label anytime.' "

At the time, Green Day's members were seventeen years old. Subsequently—beginning in 1990—Livermore helped Green Day release a seven-inch, called "1,000 Hours." Then he sent them on tour. Four years, two records, seven U.S. circuits, three European tours, and seventy thousand copies of 39/Smooth and Kerplunk later, serious major label interest in Green Day was assured, despite their distinct lack of mainstream profile. Frankly, with stats like that, they could have sounded like the GG Allin and they'd still have been signed.

Consider this: in 1987, four years after its release, the Meat Puppets' Up on the Sun LP had sold only thirty-three thousand copies. Given this fact, it is not surprising that, when manager Elliott Cahn, a former member of Sha Na Na who'd played with Henry Gross (remember the song "Shannon"?) and, more recently, been lawyer for bands like Testament, Mudhoney, and the Melvins, started playing Green Day demo tapes to A&R people in the early spring of '93 (accompanied, of course, by proof of the aforementioned statistics), every one of them bit hard. Cahn was in a position to dictate his terms, which were relatively modest. Three hundred thousand dollars is, after all, seventy-five thousand less than Nirvana got three years earlier from Geffen and considerably less than bands like AMC, Helmet, and Rocket from the Crypt have received subsequent to Nirvana's success.

That Cahn and Green Day got what they asked for was not even an issue. What was surprising to East Bay onlookers was that Green Day wanted to be on a major label at all. Green Day's deal with Lookout! stipulated that they receive 60 percent of the profits from their records sales. If you calculate the average profit on an indie CD—which retails at $9.29, minus 20 percent distribution and $1.50 per disc for production—as being about $5 per CD, that means Green Day received approximately 60 percent of $350,000 over four years' time. "They are," one interested industry onlooker (who was interested in signing them himself) has said, "without a doubt the only band I've ever met who had a good experience on an independent label."

Nevertheless, Green Day decided to go major, thus setting themselves up to be the scapegoats of the indie world, the final proof that the Nirvana record world is a whole different ball game than the one that dealt previously with Sweet Baby, Husker Du, and so many other long-forgotten bands.

Since then, they have, to quote Billie Joe via Paul Westerberg, been allowed to step on the ladder of success and miss the whole first rung.

iv.

And so the limousines rolled up Ashby Avenue, including one containing Interscope's Tom Whally, who, according to Billie Joe, "seemed real nervous about our neighborhood and kept looking at his really expensive watch." Sony and Geffen people came, too, invited, like everyone else, to hear them play in Green Day's postage-stamp-sized practice room in the basement of their run-down house.

In the end, it came down to Sony and Warner Brothers. (Interscope had axed itself with the limo performance; Geffen's Gary Gersh was already rumored to be jumping ship to Atlantic.) Sony, whose A&R guy Benji Gordon (he was responsible for Soul Asylum's success) was actually on the Green Day tip well before Cahn came into the picture, came close to nailing the deal shut. But in the end, Green Day went with Warner Brothers and Rob Cavallo, a thirty-year-old protégé of Michael Ostin, whose last two projects were the Muffs and the Goo Goo Dolls, and whose own father had managed the Lovin' Spoonful, Little Feat, and Earth, Wind and Fire. He came to Green Day's house carrying a guitar case, jammed on some Beatles tunes with them, smoked some pot, and took them and their girlfriends out for Indian food on Shattuck Avenue. He signed them long before he'd ever seen them play live.

In some ways Cavallo, a graduate of USC, was an unlikely choice for Green Day to choose as mentor, but Billie Joe and his friends somehow found some common ground to share with him. "He's from LA and stuff, but he's married and thinking about having kids," commented Billie Joe at the time. "And that made him seem like more of a genuine person, whereas a lot of those fuckers are just like hipsters. Some of them just seemed to want to get laid, to tell you the truth."

In addition to signing Green Day, Cavallo also produced the project, a fact that some industry insiders decry as a conflict of interest. One source claims that Cavallo told a producer's agent not to let Green Day meet any other producers, so they wouldn't know they had other options. Green Day were enthusiastic about the Muffs album, which Cavallo also produced, however. Cavallo, for his part, says, "I did mention to them before I signed them that I would be thrilled to produce, but it wasn't part of the deal. It just signified how interested in the project I was: I considered it a gift to spend time in the studio with them."

Warner Brothers may not have been an ideal choice for a punk band to sign with for other reasons as well. Their track record for alternative bands had been a poor one. "They never push the right buttons and there's too many managers there," says one industry onlooker. "Even sure things like Paul Westerberg do bad there. It's a really comfy, happy, jolly place to work, but they have nothing in the charts."

Dookie changed all that. Cavallo and Green Day took to the studio to record it in the summer of '93. At first, Green Day managed to keep a fairly low profile despite their label deal, deflecting anger from their close friends by continuing to be just regular guys. They continued to play gigs at Gilman Street and the Berkeley Square (since drummer Tre had just tur ned twenty-one, this was made easier than it had been before). They ar ranged to give their former label Lookout! excellent terms for the back catalog. And they insisted that they record in a studio—Fantasy—they could bike to. None of this saved them from getting shit from their audience, however: At a gig midsummer at the Phoenix Theater in Petaluma (along with the city of Benecia, a teenage Green Day stronghold), there was a picket line outside made up of punks who passed out literature urging fans to boycott Green Day's upcoming record.

In part the shit storm was due to the world they came from: Gilman Street and *Maxi* (a magazine which Green Day insist has never supported them). In part, it was the inevitable jealousy of other bands—human nature, perhaps. Mostly, however, it was a holdover from attitudes formed around the results of decade-old deals.

Green Day themselves were still a bit unsure about their decision. "Sometimes," guitarist/frontperson Billie Joe said bemusedly, "people ask us, you know, 'Why did you do it?' and I'm still like..." Billie shakes his head, eyes open wider and wider. "I don't know! I just don't know!"

V.

In some ways the story of Green Day's rampant success is simple, indicative of nothing except the usual way record companies work. It is the logical end to a tale of talent, which would have occurred to any band with the same set of songs.

At least, that's the contention of Cavallo. "If I got the demo tape five years ago? I think it would have interested us. Let's face it, this record is not the most radio-friendly in the world based on airplay, but the songs themselves would have interested us, plain and simple."

At the time, I asked an industry player if Green Day's signage was a direct result of Nirvana's success, and he said, "No, of course not. This is the start of a whole new bandwagon."

But that, I think, is a disingenuous response (as, in fact, is Billie Joe's). Green Day don't sound anything like grunge rock—they sound, briefly, like the Ramones would if they were earnest teenagers instead of a group of jolly, monster-obsessed cartoon characters—but their story is still a direct repercussion of *Nevermind,* in particular, of Nirvana's punk rock associations. One way or another, Nirvana accidentally brought certain punk rock subcultures, such as *Maximum Rock 'n' Roll,* in the strong light of day, which has in turn spotlighted the Green Days of the world.

Nirvana's success benefited sidelights and antecedents including K Records, the riot grrrls, and the Vaselines. Similarly, Green Day's success has its roots in the success of Gilman Street, *Maximum Rock 'n' Roll,* and Operation Ivy. But Green Day's success has already called down a holocaust of sorts on the Gilman Street scene of old in the form of a pride of A&R people on the prowl for fresh talent.

Livermore, for one, already started thinking about getting out. "It's sad because this thing we've been involved with is going away from me, but I can't get bent out of shape about it. For years we specialized in East Bay bands, but the chemistry has changed radically. Now as soon as a band gets two hundred people to show, they want tour support, a bigger recording budget. . . . They're like, 'If Green Day can do it we can,' totally forgetting the five years of hard work Green Day logged."

Brian Zero is a member of the Gilman Street band Siren and the ringleader of the anti–Green Day movement that picketed the Petaluma concert in 1993. His objection to Green Day, he says, is not personal or musical, but philosophical. His points are exactly the same that existed ten, fifteen, even thirty years ago. He is against, he says, the fact that "big record companies are coming in and marketing our music. What I really object to is them polluting the strength and integrity of the independent scene."

Zero's zeal is naive, perhaps: he reminds one of a hippie preaching peace and love well into the nineties. But his idealism is nonetheless vitally important to the health of the independent music scene, in that it harkens back to long-forgotten, and perhaps best resurrected, ideals. He believes, for example, in an underground resurgence of sorts; that an independent network will rise up in defiance of the corporate structure. And he was actually shocked, upon meeting Green Day's Tre Cool, to discover that

Green Day resented his protest of their gigs, to the point of threatening him with bodily harm. "If they had their shit together they'd see that it was *positive* and *educational,*" says Zero, wide-eyed.

"The thing is," he adds sadly, "this society is so cultureless. It has no identity of its own. The punk scene not only helped make me a person, but it gave me a community. It's not Utopian, but it is my tribe. And I think that sense of identity is being completely decimated by major labels. This is kind of an ironic comparison, but it's like indigenous peoples working with Hollywood and then seeing this totally phony result on-screen. People aren't receiving what it's all about, they're just receiving a product."

But whether the product that people received, *Dookie,* is Warner Brothers' idea of slacker-generation antiheroes, what Cavallo calls "meaningful aggressive punk pop," or, to quote Billie Joe, "songs about yet another generation falling down the chutes; songs for people who have the same ideas as I do that will maybe help some of them get up off their asses and show them another world" is another question entirely. I myself think it's pretty much all three. Is that co-option or conversion? You be the judge. If, as Robert Christgau once said, the compulsion to great refusals is a mark of virtue, oppression, neurosis, or all three, then Green Day's Great Big Yes means that, given the constraints of today's music industry, they are liberated, sane, and utterly immoral.

Brian Zero would have it so, but then Zero's philosophy doesn't take into account the inevitable pull that modern American life makes toward cultural hegemony: the unassailable reality that most people—I would almost even say *all* people—will, merely by virtue of their fallible humanity, always end up gravitating toward fame, adulation, validation by the mainstream . . . and large lump sums of cash.

And there's nothing wrong with that, because in the final analysis, the tension between major labels and independents is, as it has been since the times of Muddy Waters and Elvis Presley, a simple class issue. Blue, that is, versus white. Worker versus management. Billie Joe is the youngest of six children whose father (who was a jazz drummer) died when he was ten. His mother supported all six kids on her salary as a waitress. Mike Dirnt also comes from a single-parent home; at times he has supported his mother, who had been on welfare.

The fact that kids from this background would choose the security of a major label future over the more romantic and more Marxist, but far less secure, life of selling records out of the metaphorical equivalent of the back of a van, is hardly surprising.

"I," Billie Joe says stubbornly, "am exploiting myself. One thing that really bugs me is all the rich snobby kids who claim all this punk rockness coming out and saying, 'You can't make money' and stuff. How can they even say that to me? They already have money. They live punky now, but in twenty years their parents will keel over and they'll get everything."

This is not to say that Billie Joe was uncomfortable on Lookout! or in punk rock houses. "I've been really fortunate to be part of the punk rock scene... 'cause I see my friends back in Pinole that are stuck in a rut. An alternative lifestyle is a lot more fulfilling, sometimes just because you don't have money," Billie says.

"My situation," he continues, "was I could care less about which way I go [indie or major] as long as I can keep playing music. But I noticed that something needed to change. If we wanted to stay together, something was going to have to happen that would fuck us up a little bit but at the same time... it wasn't anything to do with the music or even money, it was a career thing."

Green Day are highly wary of talking about Gilman—in part because their friends still hang out there and they respect those people's decisions. "There are people like Philth and Blatz [at Gilman] that really do want to stay underground and I think that's neat. Good for them. That's really important, that they exist for people.... But one reason we don't want to sound too much like we come from a super punk rock background and stuff is because the one thing we do know is that we still are a bunch of geeks from the suburbs, and that's how our music comes across. That's what I write songs about. See, I write about life. And that's why we signed to a major label... life. It was just another demand life made that we had to fulfill."

Or to put it another way, when I was a child, I spake as I child, but now I'm a man, and I no longer frequent 924 Gilman Street. Billie Joe sighs. "You know, home is just wherever you hang your hat. And I'm gonna make sure I keep my hat on when I get 'round the Warners building."

Chapter 8
Roots Radicals

Berkeley, 1995. On most topics you could name, Tim Armstrong and Matt Freeman are two minds with but a single thought. The joint product of the Albany kindergarten, elementary, junior, and high school system, the two thirty-year-olds have, like Mick and Keith before them, been friends since the age of five. Once, a couple years ago, Tim and Matt had no trouble agreeing to tear up a check for $1.5 million made out to their band, Rancid, but there is still one argument that they simply cannot resolve, however long they argue about it.

"The Clash," says Tim, "blew the fucking Who away at Day on the Green at the Oakland Coliseum in 1982."

"I'm sorry," interrupts Matt. "You can call me un-PC or totally uncool or whatever, but I still say the Who kicked the Clash's ass."

"No way!" squeals Tim from the backseat of Matt's cherry 1965 Chevy Nova, but before he can begin what is doubtless an oft-heard tirade, he's interrupted by Lars Frederiksen, Rancid's good-natured twenty-five-year-old guitarist. "Will you guys stop already? It's been twelve years now, don't you think it's time to move on?"

Tim and Matt bust up laughing. Move on? In one sense, Rancid are as close to the Clash as they were that day in 1982. Their music is entirely informed by that band's oeuvre: rollicking punk rock, varied on some songs by a reggae downbeat sped up to ska proportions. Tim and Lars even wear Mohawks, out of loyalty to an era when rock bands really mattered.

But in another way, the two friends are further from the Clash's world— Thatcher's mean-spirited, dole-ridden England of 1977—than the hard-edged punks of King's Road could ever have dreamed of at the time. An edgy American mixture of blue-collar suburban upbringings and imperfectly expressed anticapitalist beliefs that the punk rock underground champions via its fanzines, bands, and lifestyles, Rancid are the inevitable progeny of

"White Riot" and "Janie Jones." These are people who do not take part in American society as we know it: they've never been to Nordstroms in Walnut Creek; *Melrose Place* is like watching a documentary on Mongolia.

Rancid wrap the good things about the city of Berkeley around them like a cloak or a suit of armor. It is their impenetrable fortress, a place where they can walk down the street and barely draw a second glance, despite their blue Mohawks and clanky chains. When Rancid are at home, their universe is bordered by Gilman Street to the north and the Ashby BART station to the south; they made their latest record in the far west, at Fantasy Studios, so that Tim, who doesn't drive, could ride his bike to work.

Really, these guys are so deeply ensconced in the East Bay that even Oakland strikes them as far away: Matt, who lives near University Avenue, describes Tim and drummer Brett Reed's place off Ashby as "far away." And you can forget San Francisco: Tim stopped going there to hang out in about 1987.

"I grew up in a real cool, cultural area," he says. "But I sometimes wonder what I'd be like if I grew up in Crockett."

ii.

Tim Armstrong loves the East Bay. He credits it with giving him his roots, his perspective, and, as he sings on one song on Rancid's latest LP *...And Out Come the Wolves*, a place to belong. But once upon a time, Tim was just another fucked-up kid on Telegraph Avenue. He used to hang out wherever beer could be found, whether that meant at parties full of rich kids who went to Royce-Head, or on the Avenue with dropouts who used to go to Berkeley High. One time Tim got drunk with a bunch of Deadheads in the parking lot of the Greek. Another time he woke up after a party inside rock critic Greil Marcus's house, where he proceeded to rid the fridge of some of his Anchor Steam.

Then he saw the bands the Exploited and later, Fang—a local outfit led by a crazy dude named Sam McBride, later famed for two things, killing his girlfriend and writing a song called "Money Will Roll Right In," often covered by Mudhoney, Nirvana, and the Butthole Surfers—and the experience changed his life.

Another band that inspired Tim was the Uptones, a ska-ish band out of Berkeley High students led by Eric Rader and Eric Dinwiddie. "They were opening for Bonnie Hayes and the Wild Combo and they were totally rad! They were like, 'Fuck Bill Graham!' and were talking shit," recalls Tim. "They really made a huge impression on me."

For much of the 1980s Tim wandered about the streets of the East Bay, leading the generically nomadic life of your average alienated teen. Then, on December 31, 1986, when they were twenty-one years old, Tim and Matt attended the opening of 924 Gilman Street, the seminal all-ages club.

For the next seven years, Tim went there about three times a week. "I was so hungry for something like that.... I really needed a community, because I'd never felt a part of anything in my life."

In 1988, Tim formed the ska-inspired outfit Operation Ivy with Matt and their friends Jesse and Greg. (At the same time, he formed another band called Dance Hall Crashers, which has since gone on without his membership.) Operation Ivy released one single and one record on Lookout! Records, a label formed by local entrepreneur Lawrence Livermore, and for a short while they ruled the roost at 924 Gilman Street. No band before or since has approached the kind of rabid fan loyalty they inspired— not even Green Day, a band formed three years later whose members once worshiped at Gilman, at Operation Ivy's feet.

Operation Ivy was the first band to sell out Gilman Street, the first to have a mosh pit spontaneously generate beneath them, and the first to tour the United States—"thirty-two dates in six weeks, and we lived totally on cheese sandwiches," recalls Tim, fondly. Alas, Op Ivy were also the first to break up, forced to by some mysterious internal pressure created by too much small-town fame. "Jealousy," sighs Tim, recalling the end of Op Ivy. "It was weird, you would have thought that we were superstars, and people got really mean."

Ironically, Op Ivy broke up right after their record-release party, in early 1989—a show that was opened by a band called Green Day, whose first record would be funded by the profits from Op Ivy's release.

Op Ivy's untimely demise also coincided, more or less, with Gilman being divested by Yohannan and *Maxi*. Since then, the club has thriven under the auspices of other patrons and punks; waves of new ones arrive every year. But Op Ivy's heyday is looked back on as Gilman's golden era, an almost hippie-ish time when everybody at Gilman was friends and nobody ever fought...the time when Gilman really was the "punk rock mecca" it is celebrated as in underground rock circles around the country.

Tim points out proudly that the Operation Ivy record is currently one of the few things that punk's many factions can agree upon. It has sold

175,000 copies since its release—not bad for a record you probably never heard on the radio.

iii.

The Gilman Street world has changed a lot since those days, but it's still all-ages—a fact that distinguishes it from San Francisco's more arty, bar-oriented, postcollegiate underground rock scene. Gilman Street is the crucial aspect of the Rancid story, since, as Bruce Pavitt pointed out earlier, music is invariably more resonant and meaningful if it has contextuality. Unlike the legions of white indie rock college bands that line the streets of Chapel Hill and Chicago, Rancid come from a specific time and place; they have stories to tell and a message to deliver. The tales are of down-and-outers, drug addicts, and dirtbags, but the anthemic message, delivered time and again, is "Don't give up hope." It rings out of every beat and chord change, from the depths of its happy ska tempos, welling up from Armstrong's intense and raspy voice, and out of songs like the strangely confessional "Journey to the End of the East Bay": "For me, there wasn't always a place, but there was always an urgent need to belong."

That, in itself, is Rancid's manifesto: the almost heartbreakingly frank admission of what being a punk rocker is all about . . . belonging. It's a funny comparison to make and one that band members themselves would doubtless deny, but Rancid really fit right into the Bruce Springsteen tradition. Rancid aren't as corny as Bruce, but spiritually speaking, "Junkie Man" isn't that far removed from "Jungleland," and the band's message, "Rock 'n' roll saves lives, it fucking well saved ours," is all too convincingly delivered.

Oscar Wilde once said we are all of us in the gutter, only some of us are looking at the stars. For Tim Armstrong, the gutter and the stars almost overlap in proximity. In 1993 Tim was living on the street and drinking so bad that he hit detox clinics five times and the emergency ward at Alta Bates thrice. If it hadn't been for Matt, who picked him up off the street countless times, dragging him to a hospital or a halfway house, Tim could easily be dead.

Tim's heavy drinking began when Op Ivy broke up. Matt had joined MDC (Millions of Dead Cops) as bassist for a while; Tim worked for them as a roadie before dropping out completely. "It was a kind of fucked-up time for me," Tim recalls, "because I couldn't get in a band that lasted anything more than a couple practices. It was really a painful time, too, because I had loved Op Ivy so much and all I ever wanted to do was to play music, and I couldn't. I couldn't just be a roadie, that was lame, to be a roadie! All I wanted to do was be playing every night. And so I was drinking so heavy and taking pills and everything."

Tim's drinking quickly degenerated into serious business. "I think I was drinking because I had no hope, no vision of the future," he adds. "It was like what the fuck, what am I gonna do, I'm dyslexic, I can barely read or write, I hate school, I don't have any talents except to play guitar. I mean, what am I gonna do—be a construction worker? Join the army like my brother Greg? Am I gonna be a janitor like my dad? I didn't want to be any of these things so of course I was like fucking drinking myself to death. It was lame. It was fucking not rad.

"Sometimes," confides Tim, "I'd go over to Matt's and say, give me money for food, but he wouldn't give it to me, he'd take me out and buy food instead."

"It really sucked for me," rejoins Matt, "because here I've known this guy forever and I see him get worse and worse and worse. It's a really powerless feeling, because there's really nothing you can do. I didn't know if he'd even survive."

He nearly didn't. "There's this fucked-up detox house that I'd go to," says Tim. "I'd drink until I had no money, Matt would drop me off there, I'd stay there for three days and Matt would pick me up and I'd be clean for about a day."

"I coulda got a job as a shuttle driver to and from there," laughs Matt.

"He could drive me there in his sleep," agrees Tim. "Anyway," he continues, "you go there, and they give you a bed, and you sit around the house and watch HBO all day. There's no, like, counseling or anything, and most of the people there go there at the end of the month after their check has run out...'cause they do feed you there. A lot of 'em smoke crack. But a lot are just drunks. Like this one guy named Linus—we were watching a Raiders game, and he just freaked out. He started having a seizure, and there was like two minutes left to the game, and the medics don't come till right after the game finishes, so we figured they were watching it and didn't leave till it ended.

"The Linus story doesn't have any relevance to me, except that, by that time I was realizing that okay, this is not the way to fucking do it, to keep ending up there. That was the last time I went there. The next time I ended up going to a Salvation Army shelter where you work all day and they give you a bed—and that was when I quit drinking. It was so fucking hardcore—a lot of guys come in out of prison, some of 'em are just fucking sad homeless vagrant types, and I was there for two weeks, and I've never drunk again. No Betty Ford Clinic, it was just fucking, 'I just don't want to deal with this bullshit anymore.' "

What finally pulled Tim out of the downward spiral, he adds, was writing songs with Matt in Matt's basement—was, in short, the nascent formation of Rancid. "The best thing he coulda done with me was what he did, was go write songs in the basement like he did. But sometimes it just was physically impossible. I had to get to that point where I knew it was over."

And Matt's role in all this? He shrugs. "I guess maybe it was an act of faith, but he's been my best friend for so long. He's the only best friend I ever had. And he really is the only one I wanted to play with. I've played in other bands and stuff, but it wasn't the same. And the thing about being in a band is, it's the kind of thing where, especially at this level, you love it or you don't. For me, being in a band is a feeling, and I never got that feeling from playing with anyone but Tim...and Lars and Brett."

Brett was recruited straight off Telegraph. "He was a skater kid who could barely play drums," says Tim, "but he was a homeboy, he was a cool kid, and Matt's a great bass player, he can teach people to play drums, so Brett got real good. At first he kinda sucked but now he's a hell of a good drummer!"

"He worked hard," comments Matt. "His attitude was the right thing, and that's the thing with musicians that we've found, if they have the right attitude, anyone can learn to play. I've played with some hot drummers who are the biggest fucking dicks—and that's not what it's about, you know?" (Lars, a Campbell native who played with the UK Subs, joined the band a year after Brett, in time to help record *Let's Go*.)

Presently, Rancid started playing out again, at crazy keg parties in West Oakland, like Genoa House in West Oakland and Fraggle's house on Pill Hill. "Not even Gilman," laughs Tim. "It was a year before we got paid one hundred dollars! That's how you got to do it in the East Bay, you can't come out trying to be a rock star....I've seen bands try that and fuck them, they don't matter."

But what about Op Ivy?

Tim shrugs. "The East Bay punks didn't go, 'Yea! They're back, everybody show up, Op Ivy's back,' it wasn't like that at all. But for me it *was* like that, like 'I'm back!' I could wake up in the morning like, with ideas and creative thoughts and write a lot of songs and I had a focus again, even how feeble it was at first just to jam in his basement, to me, it was like..." Tim starts to mutter. "It was like I had a reason to live again."

■ Rancid, 1995

Lori Eanes

From that moment on Rancid's career turned into a fucking fairy story. Rock bands are like love affairs: they tend to have their own momentums. For some bands, even great ones, everything goes wrong from the start. They sign to a label that busts up the next day; they arrive in every town their first tour on the same night that Nirvana's playing; in short, everything falls apart.

But since the day they formed in Matt's basement, Rancid has been in the opposite situation. They are juggernauts of good fortune, rolling over every potential obstacle, plowing up the landscape with a ridiculous roll of sheer good luck. Rancid would probably have done just fine whatever the circumstances of their existence—MTV played the "Salvation" video, directed by Tim, quite a bit; "Roots Radical," a song from *Wolves,* was a pre-release hit on Live 105; and the ska sound itself looks like it's making a mighty, mighty comeback—but in 1995, just prior to the release of their second record, *Let's Go,* two things happened that ensured that Rancid would be paid serious attention to by the notoriously fickle record industry.

The first was when Rancid's peers, friends, and neighbors Green Day released *Dookie,* thus turning the eyes of the record industry toward Berkeley. The second, more important event was when Rancid's LA-based labelmates the Offspring released "S.M.A.S.H." Green Day's record sold 10 million copies with Warner Brothers' help; but the Offspring were the first band on an independent label to go platinum. Both bands signified a renewed interest in punk rock bands; and the combination of circumstances—hometown colleagues and labelmate superstars—plopped Rancid in a position of enormous power.

Thus began a bidding war of seriously mammoth proportions. Rancid were, as Armstrong puts it now, "practically being stalked. Before last fall, I didn't even know what an A&R person was, I had no idea, and here they were, turning up at our shows, at our hotels. . . . It was really crazy and overwhelming."

In the end, after weeding out the jerks, Rancid was offered $1.5 million to sign to Epic Records. But at the very last minute the band chose to stay with Epitaph Records, the label run by former Circle Jerk and Bad Religion member Brett Gurewitz, which had released their first two records, *Rancid* and *Let's Go.*

In so doing, Tim says, the band took a lot less money. (They won't say how much they got, but the band scoffs at the idea that Epitaph's deal neared Epic's offer. "If they could have offered that, they didn't.")

But Armstrong denies this seemingly self-sacrificial gesture had anything to do with remaining true to their punk roots. "We don't give a shit about that—that wasn't it *at all*. We don't give a fuck about being PC; I mean, half the PC bands you see at Gilman or wherever are total dicks, they just want to fuck girls and watch football on TV, just like un-PC bands. . . .

"It really had to do with, I felt like Brett cared the most about us, he really did, he'd been with us from the start."

And in fact, Tim's decision, which sounds so naive in black and white, may not have been quite so dumb. For that kind of money, there are usually hidden pitfalls or obligations or encumbrances that reduce the goodness of the price. Also, Epic's deal was for seven albums, while Gurewitz does all his deals as one-offs. "Seven years is kind of scary," says Lars.

Rancid may also have hoped that their one great refusal would spare them some of the pain of leaving their contextuality—i.e., Gilman Street—behind. If so, they were wrong. Jealousy and meanness lurk in every corner; fame is a fucking bitch to negotiate. A year after the release of . . . *And Out Come the Wolves,* almost every smaller band in Berkeley is casing on Rancid in print. The worst case is the Mr. T Experience—a band one year younger than Rancid, whose first LP was financed by the proceeds of Op Ivy, and whose singer, Dr. Frank, called them "posers" in the pages of *Guitar Player* magazine, and accused Lars of "changing their punk rock clothes" three times on *Saturday Night Live.*

"If he'd ever been on live TV," snaps Tim when he reads this, "he'd know the lights are so goddamned hot you *have* to change your clothes after each take."

iv.

It's a warm night in August, two weeks before the release of Rancid's third record, . . . *And Out Come the Wolves,* and the three members of Rancid are tooling up Shattuck in Matt's Chevy Nova. (Brett has stayed at home to pack: in twelve hours, the band is flying to Hawaii to play a one-day outdoor punk rock festival somewhere near Waimea Bay.)

At most times, Rancid are a friendly band, cheerfully acceding to the demands of being in a band. But tonight they are like babies with a bad case of the colic. As long as the car keeps moving, they're happy: staring straight ahead of them, looking at the future rather than the past. But as soon as the car slows down or stops, they fall silent, reflecting, perhaps, on a present whose strangeness is daunting to contemplate. Tim hasn't been to Gilman Street in quite some time now—too busy touring, and mixing his record, and shooting videos, and so forth.

Rancid twist through the hills of Berkeley and Kensington, past the East Bay's only rotary, all along the road to Tilden. Finally, Freeman alights at Indian Rock, and the band clambers up to the top. Spread out below them, muted by summer fog, is the band's little kingdom, an area ceded to them by Green Day, who recently retreated, mortally wounded by success. Unlike the Counting Crows' Adam Duritz, who moved to L.A. when fame in Berkeley became too weird, Green Day still live here, but it seems like it's more than their lives are worth to appear in public at Gilman Street these days.

Green Day's long-awaited follow-up to *Dookie*—called *Insomniac*—is due out in October, but the band's three members have become more and more removed from the scene they once held so dear. In a few weeks, it seems likely that Rancid, now poised on the brink of massiveness, will be following Green Day's path to stardom. The single from *Wolves* (called "Time Bomb") is already huge on KROQ and Tim's pretty face has already graced the cover of *Details* magazine.

Soon the money will roll right in, and a person has to wonder: Is there any way that they can escape the disillusionment and pain success has brought to Sam McBride and Eddie Vedder and Kurt Cobain and Billie Joe? A year from now, will Tim Armstrong still live with nine roommates and ride his little bike around? Will he still be straight?

Tim thinks so. "I went down so far, I never wanna go back there. It's like it's not even an option for me. You know, all the time I was drinking, it wasn't like, 'Oh, I'm going through this little phase now,' like maybe I was a frat boy who drinks too much at parties but one day I'll go have a career. I didn't know Rancid would happen. I had no idea there'd be a happy ending."

Presently, a cop appears on Indian Rock, telling us it's time to go. All rise, clanking, clamber down, and hop back in the car. Then we whiz downhill, back to the real world, where, at the corner of University and San Pablo, I spy a number of peach-fuzz-heads on their way to see Skankin' Pickle. Pretty soon, the world will be full of punks like these, and Mohawks will have lost their meaning: Cindy Crawford will appear with one, and David Letterman, and Dan Rather, and they, like everyone else, will be meeting Rancid in the pit. Is that a happy ending?

Chapter 9

(How to) S.M.A.S.H. the Bourgeoisie

L.A., 1996. The history of Green Day, Rancid, and 924 Gilman Street is an object lesson in punk rock's purpose: it is to engender communities in this soulless and spiritless age. Punk rock's minions build their own churches, where the faithful gather and sing, and within those sullen edifices, its rituals are as primitive—and yet, as personally uplifting—as any caveman's conclave or medieval religious rite.

But if clubs like Gilman Street are the temples, then indie labels are the palaces, the place where the head of state resides and hands down its edicts to the masses. Labels disseminate the music, which in turn gives them economic power. That makes them the government, in charge of exactly who are the haves and the have-nots.

Over the years, there have been several key indie punk labels (SST, Dischord, Rough Trade, Lookout!, Sub Pop, etc.), each with its own constitution and congregation, its own code of ethics, and even its own recognizable musical sound. They differ in some ways, but all of them are punk in that their personal codices were learned at punk's altar. Rule 1 is "Loud fast rules." Rule 2 is DIY. And rule 3: "Don't suck corporate cock," the slogan invented by LA label SST.

Alas, seminal punk rockers haven't always obeyed these commandments to the letter, which is why until recently, punk rock's economic power was minimal. Instead, many indie bands wound up ceding their financial clout to corporations in order to maximize their audiences and supposedly their profits (hence the term "selling out").

For example, Nirvana began its career on Sub Pop, but went to Geffen in 1992, where it sold 10 million copies of *Nevermind* (10 million CDs equals a gross profit of about $100 million, about $90 million of which goes into Geffen's, not Nirvana's, pocket). The next year, Green Day had the same kind of success on Warner Brothers (rather than on Lookout!, the label that gave them their start). Sub Pop and Lookout! both profited from these deals—but only in the way that children profit by their parents' handouts. Indeed, Sub Pop has since sold 49 percent of its stock to Sony, thus wiping out any possibility of an autonomous power structure in the future.

Thus, it wasn't until 1994, when a small indie label unaffiliated with any major corporate ogre sold a similar amount of records—8.5 million, to be exact—that punk rock gained the kind of economic power that really starts to mean something in the marketplace. The record was called *S.M.A.S.H.*, the band was called the Offspring, and the label in question was Epitaph.

Now Epitaph resides in the center of the storm of controversy surrounding the very meaning of punk. According to some pundits of punk theory, profit and popularity somehow negate the music's inherent edginess and its practitioners' credibility. But Brett Gurewitz, who started Epitaph in 1980 in order to release one single by his band, Bad Religion, disagrees. Sitting in his well-appointed office on Sunset Boulevard on a hot October afternoon in late 1996, Gurewitz reflects somewhat truculently on the recent past and his company's charmed history.

Gurewitz formed Bad Religion and Epitaph with two of his fifteen-year-old friends, Jay Bentley and Greg Graffin, at El Camino High School in Woodland Hills, California. In 1980, his dad lent him the $1,500 he needed to do it; the three of them made 1,500 copies and assembled them by hand.

Greg paid his dad back and made a record called *How Could Hell Be Any Worse?* He also released *Peace through Vandalism* for a group called the Vandals. "But it wasn't a serious endeavor," says Brett now. "It was me and my two fifteen-year-old friends being punk. We wanted to make our records so our friends could hear us. Also, to us, an important element of punk rock culture was making your own records and singles. Everyone was doing it."

Bad Religion wasn't ambitious, but that first LP sold ten thousand copies, which was typical for that era: the early eighties was a time when radio and other music outlets were so close-minded toward exciting—hell, even just guitar-based—music that the spillover potential of underground records into the hands of the consumer was higher than it is now, when everything is available to everybody, everywhere.

How Could Hell and *Peace* both said "Epitaph" on them, but according to Brett, there wasn't a label. "There was no phone number, there was no fax machine. There was a PO box on Ventura Boulevard, and there was a logo. In punk rock, everything has a logo... your band, everything. So I had a logo, but not a label."

ii.

Those were the days when LA punk, led by bands like Black Flag, the Circle Jerks, TSOL, and X, was thriving. But the brilliance faded as the decade progressed, and one thing led to another. One by one, LA punk bands were either signed to majors or disintegrated due to drugs or adulthood. It didn't help that violence at punk shows increased drastically, that Reagan's election signified middle America at its most frightened and repressive, or that mainstream rock 'n' roll was going through a techno period exemplified by meaningless bands like Human League, Duran Duran, and Missing Persons.

During that exciting time, Gurewitz himself dropped out of high school, and had a number of odd jobs in the music business. His parents sent him to a six-week course at a vocational school for sound engineering and he got a job at a recording studio scrubbing toilets.

Meanwhile, Bad Religion played around LA, and, according to Gurewitz, "anywhere you could drive in one day from LA: the Mabuhay Gardens and On Broadway in SF, and with the Dead Kennedys in a hall in San Diego."

By 1983, however, Gurewitz had stopped playing with Bad Religion. "I had," he says frankly, "a bout with serious drug addiction for a number of years. And in that time, I did manage to carry a number of odd jobs in the music business. I worked in a recording studio, I worked in sales at a record distributor, I helped out at an independent label called Bomp, and they taught me a lot of stuff.

"But by April 14, 1987, my drug habit had gotten to the point where I found myself in the hospital and I stayed there and detoxified and then went into a rehab program, and I managed to rise above the drug addiction, and a year after that, in 1988, that's when I decided that what I wanted to do in my life was have a record company."

Gurewitz had about fourteen thousand dollars, culled from the five thousand shares of AT&T stock his dad bought him when he was thirteen, and this time, he decided, it *was* going to be a serious endeavor. "Fortunately for me, these three records I'd made when I was eighteen, seven years before, had kind of become noteworthy records in the interim—they had some significance. And when I started the label, I signed two bands: one was L7 and one was Bad Religion, whom I rejoined.

"So at the end of 1987, I officially started Epitaph Records. And the record that put us on the map was Bad Religion's *Suffer*. It came out, and punk rockers across America and across Europe unanimously loved it. *Maximum R 'n' R* and *Flipside*, who don't agree on anything, both voted it record of the year... and we sold twelve thousand copies pretty fast. It was a modest beginning, but I had a record to start my record company with."

The next band he signed was an Orange County outfit called NOFX. The group after that was Pennywise. And pretty soon, through these groups and others like them making records and touring, punk rock started to burgeon. "Before you knew it," says Gurewitz, "Bad Religion was playing in front of a thousand people every night, across the country, and across Europe, and shortly after that NOFX and Pennywise were too."

Of course, Gurewitz can't take sole credit for this resurgence. At the time that he is talking about, other bands were reigniting as well. In D.C., Dischord, which had suffered a huge dimunation in popularity when Minor Threat broke up in about 1984, came back wailing in '87 with a band called Fugazi. In Minneapolis, Amphetamine Reptile was putting out loud-fast albums by acts like Helmet and Killdozer. New York City had a huge hardcore scene led by Agnostic Front and Reagan Youth. And 1987 was also the year that *Maximum Rock 'n' Roll*, a fanzine based in San Francisco, opened 924 Gilman Street in Berkeley, which would later nurture and spawn bands like Green Day and Epitaph's own Rancid.

But despite these small developments, Gurewitz points out, no one was noticing much. "People used to say to me, 'What do you do for a living?' and I'd say, 'I have a punk rock record company,' and they would laugh at me and go, 'Punk rock is not around anymore,' and I'd be like, 'Uh...I beg to differ.'

"Subcultures don't go away," he adds, "especially if they're relevant. All I did was realize that there were great bands that existed and if the records were made and made properly and made available, the rest would take care of itself.

"My belief is, cream rises to the top. And if someone makes good music, someone will appreciate it. Regardless of the genre or anything else. I never felt that punk rock had reached its potential; I always thought it was the rock 'n' roll of my youth. Punk rock was rock 'n' roll, and rock 'n' roll hadn't been around for a while. Not on the radio, not anywhere . . . and yet there was this subculture of kids who liked it. It never did go away, it never *will* go away."

iii.

In 1987 the punk scene in America was less than vital, says Gurewitz. "But there was still an interest in it, there was still a punk rock subculture. It still existed, but it wasn't a healthy, vibrant, vital scene like it had been in 1980. . . . It wasn't the threat to the American value system that it had been. It was petering out. There were no good punk rock records coming out anymore, but there were kids who wanted this kind of music, and they were listening to records that were ten years old or eight years old."

Gurewitz set out to change that, and by 1990, Epitaph was doing well with Orange County bands like NOFX, Pennywise, and the Offspring. One reason they were doing so well was an unspoken marketing merger between the relatively new sport of snowboarding and this new take on punk. The two subcultures found they had an emotional affinity for one another, and often cross-promoted things.

In 1992, Epitaph lent a number of their artists' songs to various promotional videos for snowboard companies. Chief among these was music by the Offspring, from their Epitaph debut, *Ignition*. In a matter of four months, the first record's sales shot from sixteen thousand to forty-six thousand.

Although the Offspring are often referred to as a new band and lumped with younger outfits like Green Day and labelmates Pennywise and Rancid, in fact, at the time they signed to Epitaph, they were nearly a decade old.

The band was formed in Orange County by Bryan Holland and his high school buddy Greg Kriesel, but seldom played out live, since many Orange County nightclubs—frightened by the violence that flurried around early-eighties OC bands like TSOL and the Adolescents—had a prejudice against presenting punk bands. One time, Holland recalls, he recorded a tape of himself playing acoustic to give to a promoter, in order to fool the club into thinking the Offspring were a mellow folk band. "We didn't get to play very often for years," Holland says, "but we were always a band in spirit."

Perhaps because of their maturity—in his off hours, Holland was studying for his Ph.D. in microbiology at USC—the Offspring's music is much less angry than your usual punk rock band's.

"We never did PC stuff," explains Holland. "We just like to drink beer and play music. We're more about entertainment than having a message or content. Most of our songs are just about feeling like an outsider. That's how I've always felt. Punk draws people together, that's what I always related to about it, and that's what I sing about."

By 1987, the Offspring had finalized their lineup with guitarist Kevin Wasserman and drummer Ron Welty (then only sixteen years old). But it wasn't until 1990 that the Offspring got it together to pay for the production of its first, self-titled release.

That caught the attention of Gurewitz, who signed them in 1992, releasing their first record and funding them on a constant tour. In early 1994, the Offspring were departing from a show at Berkeley punk club 924 Gilman when their van—a decaying Holiday Inn shuttle bus spray-painted green—died on the highway. "Its second engine just ceased," recalls Holland. "We had to leave it somewhere near Livermore."

Although they didn't know it at the time, the band was also leaving behind all hope of ever playing at Gilman Street again. Although the all-ages collective was one of the clubs that gave the band its start, its strict "no mainstream bands" policy means that the Offspring have more hope of headlining Madison Square Garden than of ever darkening Gilman's door again.

Much more. In April of 1994, the single "Come Out and Play (Keep 'Em Separated)" quickly became the most requested song on KROQ after only a couple of late-night airings. MTV followed radio's lead by adding the band's low-budget video for the song to its buzz bin, and—voilà!—a chart monster was born.

By June, the album it came from, S.M.A.S.H., had gone double platinum. The Offspring began touring for S.M.A.S.H. in May of 1994, beginning with a gig for three hundred people in the town hall of Valdez, Alaska, during a skate- and snowboarding championship, and they immediately found they had an entirely new audience from the one they had in Gilman days—newer, and much larger.

But there was a downside to its newfound success—the attitude of former fans like those at Gilman Street who believe that by becoming popular, the Offspring have sold out. "They embraced us and made us what we are, so to be rejected by them feels really bad," says Holland. "I kind of understand though—they have a different agenda. And it is very, very long."

The effect of the Offspring's hit still cannot be overstated. Other independently labeled bands have charted higher than the Offspring—most notably N.W.A., Ice Cube, and Run DMC—but the Offspring's was the first entirely independent punk rock release to do that kind of business. The most immediate result was that the mainstream music industry began madly seeking out punk bands, including All, Schleprock, Blink 182, and Screeching Weasel, and signing them to major labels; one can hardly remember the time, less than five years ago, when metal and glam acts like Guns 'N' Roses, Metallica, Aerosmith, and Poison ruled the charts and the airwaves.

Nevertheless, Epitaph has its detractors, people who say it diversified too fast, and people who say it's sold out punk. In 1995, the Offspring defected to Sony. But Rancid, Epitaph's next biggest band and another graduate of 924 Gilman Street, had another take on the topic. In 1994, when the Offspring record was at its peak, a wild bidding war broke out over Rancid, who had (like all Epitaph bands) only signed an album-by-album contract.

At the time, Rancid had its qualms about Epitaph—their 1994 LP *Let's Go* seemed to have gotten lost in the shuffle of the Offspring's wild success. But after *S.M.A.S.H.,* A&R people began following them around—going so far as to book themselves onto the same flights and bullying flight attendants to seat them next to the band members. Madonna pursued them for her label Maverick, meeting with the band three times (Tim: "She was cool as shit!"). One executive reportedly shaved up a Mohawk and dyed his hair blue, to prematurely celebrate a signing that eventually didn't take place.

For a couple of days in December, industry dirt boards on the Internet breathlessly reported that Rancid actually *had* signed to Epic for seven figures—a rumor that eventually caused much consternation when it had to be denied by Rancid's lawyers. But in the end, Rancid stuck with Epitaph.

But Armstrong denies this seemingly self-sacrificial gesture had anything to do with remaining true to their punk roots. "Why would we even have talked to all those people if that was our beef? I really didn't give a fuck [about punkness] but I needed to make sure that we'd be okay. When the Offspring record first came out, we felt we were kind of being ignored [by Epitaph] . . . but that was just a misunderstanding."

The reason they finally stayed with Epitaph, Tim says now, is because "Brett loves us. He really, truly fucking loves us."

But didn't Madonna love them? "She said she loved the way we performed, and that we were really entertaining. She *said* she loved us, but Brett, the music we play is the music he grew up with. He's like madly in love with us. I think Madonna really likes us. But Brett, when we sent him the first demo of us, when we first started, the one that become the Lookout! single, he said it was the best thing he'd heard in three years. It really had to do with, I felt like Brett cared the most about us, he really did, he'd been with us from the start."

iv.

In 1995, thanks mostly to the combined sales of the Offspring and Rancid, Epitaph moved to a brand-new three-story building on Sunset Boulevard in Silverlake that includes landscaped gardens and security parking and a customized receptionist's desk made out of the engine of a '56 Chevy. The sight of it makes a person wonder if this is a case of meet the new boss, same as the old boss, or if, conversely, the old order changeth, and giveth way to the new.

One would of course like to believe it's the latter, and there is some evidence for it. For one thing, in addition to searching out new talent, Epitaph has been busy signing and resuscitating punk rock heroes like Wayne Kramer of the MC5, and the Cramps.

Epitaph has also released a new record by the Descendents, a ten-year-old band formerly on SST whose *Everything Sucks* is one of the best punk records of the year.

The Descendents are actually the perfect paradigm to explain the difference between punk circa 1985 and punk circa 1995. In the late eighties, the band was a relatively unpopular act who recorded for the insular LA label SST. They had a small following of rabid fans, but one could hardly call them thriving. In 1987, lead singer Milo Aukerman left the band (like Holland, to pursue his Ph.D. in microbiology at the University of Wisconsin). The Descendents became All and struggled on throughout the decade, releasing LPs on SST and touring incessantly.

In those days, the Descendents were lucky to sell out Raji's. But in October of 1996, a few weeks after the release of *Sucks,* a reunited Descendents instantly sold out seven straight nights at the Whiskey on the Sunset Strip. On the last day of these shows, drummer Bill Stevenson and Milo Aukerman (Ph.D.) stopped by the Epitaph offices to chat about the difference between their early years and now.

"Probably the easiest way to illustrate the essential difference is, say you have a club and you have a Descendents show and there's fifteen hundred or twelve hundred people in there," says Stevenson. "It's like you've got the army—which is the two hundred people in the front who know every word to every song and they have 'All' tattooed down their arm and 'Milo' tattooed down their face, and they have like a hundred CDs and every-T-shirt we had, and if someone even tries to slam while we're playing them they'll start hitting 'em, like, 'You're destroying my concentration!' They're total trollboys, like us, total nerds. And then, behind them, is—"

Milo: "Jocko Homo."

"—eight hundred punkers who are there because it's a punk rocky thing. That's how it is now. Before, it was just the two hundred. So it's like it's got this core, and then this fairly big layer of fat around it which, for better or worse, has made our thing a bit more eventful, shall we say. But I don't think it's really changed the essence of the art any."

But the art, as he calls it, is really at the crux of the question. Do the Descendents, who were doing the Green Day thing ten years ago, ever feel robbed of their due?

"Well, how I feel is, those bands brought London and Paris fashion and dressed-up Descendents and put it on parade on MTV," explains Stevenson. "But what people were buying was not Descendents, it was fashion. So that doesn't mean that we deserved to sell any more, because we are, were, and always will be the people that aren't cool. We weren't cool in high school, and those people on MTV were like the people who were throwing the last bite of their hot dog in my hair when I was in high school, and they still are. Those things don't change.

"But the thing to remember is, it's not the music, it's the fashion. Our music is still our music, they can't take that away from us. And what can you do? You can't hate them for being popular. You always got the ice cutters and then the cleanup act behind it, that's normal."

Stevenson's equanimity may be explained by one simple fact. In 1993, All—which is the Descendents without Milo—was given $1 million to sign to Interscope Records. "It was the most one-sided deal ever, in history," laughs Stevenson. "[After the Offspring hit] the major labels started beating our doors down, they just came after us! Dude, they paid us a *million* bucks to make one record, and then when we walked we took the record with us! They bought us a whole recording studio, and they gave us almost a million dollars for one record, and then we walked and took the tapes."

The All record in question was called *Pummell*. It was released in 1994, and sold like shit. Was this bad judgment on Interscope's part, or just stupidity?

Stevenson shrugs. "They could have made it stickier [for us to leave]. If they thought they were sitting on a gold mine, they could have probably kept us around a little longer. But they just didn't focus any energy on us, although at the same time they were doing really well with Bush, and also with a lot of those criminals that they bail out of jail and make CDs with. So we bailed from Interscope, and then we talked to Brett and he was like, 'It'll be cool.' "

But this interesting look at major label antics still begs the question as to why Green Day were big and All weren't. Why 1994, and not 1986?

"I don't know," says Stevenson with a shrug. "At the time, I thought, 'Everyone will always hate this, I'm just always going to suck, and everyone's always going to hate me and I'm never gonna get laid.'

"But I think that punk rock has finally taken its place as legitimate rock 'n' roll," he adds. "And I think that's because of the lyrics [of the newer songs]. They align really closely with the kind of skateboarder, slacker, hippie-yuppie-punker fashion that's what all the kids are into these days, whereas a song like 'Silly Girl' did not. It was at the wrong time, it didn't line up with anything."

Milo: "Dude, look what Billy's doing, he's putting the Black Flag bars on the carpet."

And indeed, Stevenson has, while talking, been idly scratching the Blag Flag logo into Epitaph's plush blue carpet with some pointed object he found under the couch. "I'm not ruining it, though," he says defensively. "I can brush it right out."

The gesture inevitably brings up the Descendents' old label, SST. My question is, Is being a punk rock band the same as in those days? Stevenson sort of sighs. "That definitely was a fond memory for me, going out to see bands or playing a show and having everybody on the bill be your friend, and all utilizing the same practice facilities, and watching D Boon fall through the stage.

"That's part of what Epitaph has. . . . I do get a real camaraderie sense from the bands here. But a large part of it is missing, not from the label, from music. We're real optimistic about Epitaph, and we're developing a real good friendship with Brett, and everything here feels really comfortable and warm over here, but . . ."

"It seems like seeing bands back in seventy-nine, eighty, eighty-one, there was an element of—I'm not sure if 'danger' is the right word—but an element of discovery, that you just don't get now," continues Milo. "I mean, you're not going to have that element of discovery or danger down at the mall."

This is the heart of the punk rock debate. To today's sixteen-year-olds, can the experience of seeing the Offspring at the Blockbuster Arena in 1996 really be the same as seeing the Circle Jerks at the Masque was in 1981?

I personally have my doubts, but Gurewitz says emphatically that it is. "You don't have to have a unique set of qualities to like punk rock music," explains Gurewitz. "Punk rock music is rock 'n' roll, and rock 'n' roll is rebellion. What the fuck was Beatlemania? Those fucking kids, that fucking music spoke to them because it brought out the rebelliousness in it. All the better if everyone else around you is feeling it, too.... Then it becomes a spiritual experience. It's visceral, it's sexual, it's primal, it's rock 'n' roll.

"[So] whether it's the Offspring or Little Richard, punk is the pure boiled-down essence of what rock 'n' roll makes you feel.... That's what punk rock is, it's the stripping off of the pretension and rocking. Yeah, people put politics in it, and yeah, they talk about breaking down the barrier between the star and the fan, and yeah, they talk about personal issues and issues in their community, and yeah, they talk about how punk rock is different because it strives to have relevant lyrics, and all of that's good, but that's just the frosting, that's not the cake.

"When the bohemian cognoscenti reflect on 'what punk rock means,' that's bullshit. It's a fucking visceral experience.

"The thing is, it doesn't matter how many kids can relate to you as a band," he adds wearily. "It doesn't make you any less valid. I just don't think rock 'n' roll was meant to be elitist, not any genre of it, and punk rock most of all. Punk rock claims to be a populist movement, and if it's a populist movement, then let's put it on every radio station. The 'punk rock is sacred' thing is dangerous, because punk rock cannot be about elitism. Elitism is bad, it's everything we hate as liberals, and so we can't go that way, or you're actually swinging so far to the left that you're right, and fascist or whatever. It's what's gone wrong in politics; and if our politics are liberal and populist, then we can't be elitist.

"Punk rock," he adds, "has this built-in paradox, a built-in duality, and if you understand it, you're okay. The duality is this: There's all these punks who say, 'Perhaps I'm so committed to being on the fringe of society, to only living a counterculture lifestyle, that I will go to any lengths to preserve that.'

"Now, that's a personal life choice, that's possible for a person to make. But if that's the case, then you have to also say, 'I can therefore only enjoy portions of our culture that are not widely enjoyed, because I'm committed to not getting into cultural norms.'

"Well, if that's your life choice, you can like a band when it sells ten thousand records and you can't when it sells ten million, and you're setting an arbitrary distinction, because it's not that the band's music changed in any way. The reason you're deciding you don't like them anymore is because that would change your lifestyle into one you're not choosing for yourself.

"But me, I love music too much to give a shit about that. And yet, for people who choose that, for themselves, you have to respect that. As long as they don't put it on you, you can respect it. But they always do put it on you. They put it on Kurt, they put it on Billie Joe, and they put it on Brett Gurewitz, for ruining punk rock. As if I had that power!

"So I really am at the center of this debate, and I understand it for what it is, and you know what? Fanaticism has nothing to do with rock 'n' roll. I'm as liberal a fucking person as you're going to find, when the next cultural revolution comes, I'm on the side of the freaks, 'cause that's what I am. But I'm not a fanatic. I've never liked fanatics. When I had a purple Mohawk, and all my punk rock gear, and I was screaming through the streets on black beauties, I wasn't fanatical then. I always had a head on my shoulders, and I knew what I was doing and I was reveling in what I was, but I wasn't fanatical.

"I respect MRR [*Maximum Rock 'n' Roll*]—Tim Yohannan and I have known each other for a long time, and he's a Communist. I'm a liberal social democrat, but he's a Communist, and if you're a Communist, you don't make a profit. The ideal to a Communist is to give records away. It's to play shows for free, if at all possible.

"But I've thought about this so much, and I've figured out, if you cut to the chase, and you throw yourself back forty years ago to a Jerry Lee Lewis show with black kids and white kids losing their gourds, it's very simple, and it has nothing to do with Communism.

"You know what? The fucking Communist, Eastern European countries have never come up with a good punk rock group. Couldn't do it to save their lives. They may have come up with Karl Marx, and they may have come up with Trotsky, but they'll never come up with Chuck Berry.

"Rock 'n' roll is about rock 'n' roll, and all the bells and whistles and frosting and politics ... it all just detracts from what it's about. If rock 'n' roll can precipitate a cultural revolution, like in the sixties, and like punk rock failed to do in the eighties...all the better. But it's not a necessary ingredi-ent! It's really not.

"But punk rock does kind of affect a person's code of ethics," Gure-witz adds. "For me, there is a kind of liberalism and populism that comes directly from punk. As you might have noticed, for the last fifty years, mu-sicians have been shit upon by businessmen. Whether it was an R&B mu-sician getting a car instead of royalties, or some artist in the seventies not getting creative control, whatever. So I decided that we were going to make a record company that's fair to musicians. And what that means is to redefine the role of record company to that of service provider and redefine the role of artist to that of principal director, because the re-cording artists are the ones that provide intellectual property to the part-nership.

"Without artists, there are no record companies. We recognize that the artists bring in the value to the partnership, and what we provide to them is a service that fifty other companies in the world could provide them with, so we want to do it in a more customized way, in a way that suits them better.

"We consider the artists our employers and they really are, in the true sense of the word: we're a service company, and they're not going to re-hire us unless we do a good job. And that's why I'm committed to short-term record deals as well.

"I think the ethics of this business are abominable. I think tying up a person to a seven-year personal-services contract is highly unethical. And that's the norm in this business! And I mean, what is a personal-services contract? Who provides me with personal services? I have a janitorial serv-ice here.... They didn't make me a sign a seven-year contract that says no one else can sweep my floor. They didn't!

"What does Capitol Records bring to the Beatles? They can put rec-ords in boxes and send 'em to the store.... This is the fuckin' nineties, and the record business is antiquated, and our culture thinks of artists as sec-ond-class citizens, and if I can make a small change in that, that's what I'm going to do, and that's what I'm committed to doing.

"And you know, maybe that's because I have punk rock ethics. I'm not saying that ethics are a vital ingredient to punk rock. I think a sociopath could make some excellent punk rock. In fact, I know a number who have! But this one has ethics, and that's what this company is dedicated and de-voted to doing."

V.

As befits its new role as punk rock palatial estate, Epitaph's new office on Sunset Boulevard in the Silverlake district of LA provides a good place for artists to gather. The day I was there, Brett kicked former Thelonious Monsterite Pete Weiss out of the room, only to usher in famed producer Geza X, while members of Pennywise and the Descendents all milled about the building throughout the day.

Midafternoon, the door to the lounge, a blue-and-purple idyll with a plush couch and a coffin-shaped coffee table, opens for the millionth time and Tim Armstrong peeps in. I haven't seen Tim for about a month—not since Lollapalooza ended—and he looks terrible, haggard and drawn. It emerges that he's spent the last month wandering aimlessly from place to place, pretty much in an attempt to make life imitate being on the road.

Tim just popped in because he wanted to nap here, but instead we go out for a Diet Coke. Tim tells me about the label imprint Brett's giving him: Hellcat, it's going to be called. He's going to look for bands to put on it, and produce them, but Brett (and Epitaph) will do the rest.

Then we talk about the Descendents, whom he has seen twice at the Whiskey this week. "You know how I feel about reunions," he says—Tim has strong feelings about not reuniting Operation Ivy, which he is often urged to do—"but this one was good, it was more like when Bad Religion came back in 1987 with *Suffer*. It's like they have something to say."

Presently we walk past a bunch of graffiti-covered storefronts that line up against the road there, and an airbrushed memorial wall mural depicting the death of some chola. "I like it here," says Tim. "It looks like Mexico. This could be Tijuana."

Then he suddenly adds that he's about to move down the street: "It'll be the first time I've paid like, legal rent," he says, laughing. But I can't help but feel shocked. Tim is the most East Bay–bound person I've ever met. Something must be wrong for him to move to LA, and something is: it seems that after Lollapalooza ended and Rancid dispersed for a six-month break, Tim had been at such a loose end, and so depressed, that he fell off the wagon for the first time in four years. "I drank five days straight," he says sadly. "I ended up in the gutter."

When he came to, however, Tim was surprised to find a hundred helping hands: not just those of Matt and his family, but also Brett's, and Social Distortion's Mike Ness's, and those of many other people involved in the Epitaph world of rock. "No one was mad at me, or anything," he says, as if surprised. "They were just . . . there."

Currently, Tim is living at Brett's house—Brett is sober, too, as are many of the Epitaph staffers—and going to two meetings a day. "In Silverlake, there's lots I can get to on my bike," he says. "And the latest one is at midnight. In the Bay Area, the latest I know of is at ten."

Back at Epi, Tim's minder comes around to take him to the gym, and then to a meeting, and then back to Brett's. And as he walks out the door, clanking as usual, it occurs to me how smart Tim Armstrong was to sign to this label. Epic would certainly have given them a million and a half bucks, but would they have helped him when he was down and out? That Gurewitz has done so is punk rock ethics in action, the final evidence needed to prove that punk is a positive thing.

Chapter 10

...And Out Come the Wolves

Pity the poor residents of the 1100 block of Keeler Street in Berkeley, California. One Monday night in 1995, they turned up in full force at the city of Berkeley's Zoning Adjustment Board hearing to dispute a neighbor's proposed construction of a carport.

Alas for Keeler Street, their dispute was item 14 on the zoning board's agenda for November 13. Item 13 was a hearing for a conditional use permit for the Seattle-based Hart's Brewing Company—the company that makes Pyramid Ale—to install a new microbrewery and ten-thousand-square-foot brew pub/restaurant at 901 Gilman Street. That site sits directly across the street from 924 Gilman Street, Berkeley's illustrious all-ages, all-volunteer punk rock collective. When completed, the Pyramid Alehouse will be the second largest restaurant in Berkeley.

Now Berkeley is a community where residents get vocally involved in every aspect of their government, but one glance into council chambers and it was clear that it was going to be an even longer night than usual. Old City Hall was chock-full of green-haired, nose-pierced, tatter-clothed sixteen-year-olds—all of them armed to the teeth with studies on increased traffic, lighting, and parking, a ten-point zone improvement plan, and a proposed draft absolving them of blame for any increase in calls to 911 that may ensue after the brewery's installation.

But these are all just smoke screens, formal shields against the real problem. Essentially, the kids at Gilman believe that Hart's will bring an undesirable element into their neighborhood—"the very element," says one scrawny Gilman Street punk, "which we're trying to avoid by going there."

That element? Yuppies, of course: thick-necked guys in polo shirts and women hideously coiffed like the chick on *Friends*.

As one Gilman Street defender tells the zoning board, "We don't want any incident on our corner reported to the police like, 'There's an incident at 924 Gilman and there's a guy with a Mohawk and a guy in a BMW,' and then—"

The kid is interrupted by Commissioner Poschman: "And then, the police will automatically arrest the guy in the BMW because we all know what troublemakers *they* are."

ii.

As that remark indicates, the atmosphere at the zoning board was not exactly pro-brewery—despite the fact that, ironically, Gilman Street's own zoning permit has been up before this same commission several times in the past eight years, answering to charges of a similar nature.

But this time, for the first time, Gilman's on the offensive. Years of fighting city hall has apprised them of their rights; moreover, in its ten-year existence, the club has learned from controversy.

To them, Pyramid represents the Corporate Ogre incarnate. They are convinced that the brew pub's proximity will bring a phalanx of evil drunks, who will imbibe masses of Pyramid wheat ale and then maraud on over to Gilman Street every Friday and Saturday night. Moreover, rents will go up, and residents will be driven out; and their anonymous little haven will have to find another, even more marginal, neighborhood to go to.

Now, it's not surprising the punks at Gilman Street feel that way. What is surprising is that the Berkeley zoning board pretty much agrees with them.

In fact, in retrospect, the hearing is a hilarious comment on the highly confusing state of society right now. When the Hart's issue finally comes up—at 10:15—precious minutes are wasted trying to decide how many people will be allowed to speak on the club's behalf. There are fifty-two requests, which dismays the commissioners. Ten is usually the outside limit of speakers—at three minutes each, that's a half hour of defense—but in the true spirit of Berkeley liberalism, they decide on this issue to be a little more generous. They tell the club representative that they can take their pick: fifteen kids can speak for two minutes, or ten kids can speak for three minutes. Also, kids under sixteen are requested to speak first, rather than stay up past their bedtime.

Before the debate begins, however, a representative from Hart's is allowed to speak. He is John Stoddard, president of Hart's Brewing Company, and the minute he rises he is quietly hissed by the assembled throng.

But if Stoddard expects to find his support from the other side of the podium, he's got a big surprise coming. He begins by saying his establish-

■ Pyramid Brewery, 1997

Christopher Arnold

ment is being miscast as some kind of yuppie hangout. "It's a family establishment, with diverse clientele," he says. "At our Seattle pub, you can find people from all walks of life."

Commissioner Poschman again, ironically: "[So] the family that drinks together, stays together?"

(Huge cheers.)

Poschman goes on to quiz Stoddard about the contents of the brew pub's menu.

Stoddard: "Salads, soups, sandwiches, burgers, pizzas, PBJs..."

The last-named item draws angry guffaws from the Gilman crowd, who see it as a transparent attempt to prove that tiny children frequent the brew pub. The head of the commission silences the crowd, but one can feel that Stoddard has done himself no good with the remark.

Soon it's Gilman's turn, and they present a united opposition, citing problems with increased traffic in the neighborhood, lax carding, and police and security-guard presence as reasons that the brew pub will be detrimental to their neighborhood.

"I'm not opposed to the brewery itself," says Matt Waxman, the first speaker on behalf of the club. "I think it's an addition to the community, but this West Berkeley neighborhood already has problems with crack and prostitution and the police. The zoning board hasn't taken into account our parking and needs. Also, there are going to be on-site beer sales, [so people] can buy a six-pack at the pub, so ... we're concerned with our future interaction between their patrons and our patrons. There's going to be lots of police calls and then *our* zoning permit will be up for review."

An ominous silence from the crowd greets his words, and even the commission looks taken aback: after all, it's already nearly midnight, and this issue is nowhere near being decided.

"We're unique in the community," continues Waxman. "We're an all-ages, all-volunteer punk club, much like a nonprofit organization or landmark which has been in the community a long time. So we'd like to have written into the zoning plan that we're unique and special, and we request that [their restaurant] be reduced from a three-hundred-fifty-seat capacity, that their zoning be reviewed, and lastly, that we get mediation."

Waxman has made his point, but the night is still young, and speaker after speaker stands up to reiterate it: green-haired girls with pierced lips who say "um" a lot; well-mannered boys with Mohawks; the occasional mom. Time drags on. In general, Gilman Street acquits itself admirably in front of the board, even presenting a petition to the board, signed by hundreds of people, including Billie Joe Armstrong of Green Day. (When asked, Billie Joe doesn't recall signing any such petition, but requests that his name be let stand anyway.)

The result is that the board meets most of their points halfway—stiffening up Hart's zoning requirements as well as insisting that better lighting be provided in the restaurant's design.

They also state that monthly meetings between a Hart's representative and a representative from Gilman must take place. But Gilman doesn't get it all its own way. At least one commissioner points out the irony of Gilman's attempts to block Hart's pub on the same grounds that their own club has faced in the past.

Poschman: "I was on the board in eighty-seven, when your club opened up, and people came to this meeting and said, 'This is our hood, and these kids will make this not an industrial neighborhood.'"

Waxman is defensive: "We feel we reflect the community. We're diverse. They're just a restaurant."

iii.

This last remark—indicating as it does an overconsciousness of ethnic and PC considerations—is very Berkeley. After all, Berkeley has always had the reputation for just these kinds of liberal/generational/cultural civic antics, and in the thirty years since the People's Park demonstration, Berkeley has worked hard to preserve its ideological reputation.

But despite the best efforts of Wavy Gravy, the Naked Guy, and Mimi Farina, the modern world has still encroached, and these days, if you walk down Telegraph Avenue just south of the Berkeley campus, you'll see nineties iconography—Starbucks, Noah's Bagels, Benetton, Tower Records—mingling uneasily with all that sixties flotsam and jetsam: head shops, dope dealers, stringy-haired chicks selling crystals and bead-and-feather earrings, and whole contingents of grotesque-looking homeless people with matted hair and bright red eyes and a truculent veneer.

Middle America may well still consider Telegraph Avenue wild and far out. But to a kid named Sunshine whose hippie mom probably shops there, it presents a far different spectacle. In fact, it's axiomatic that such a kid would want to hang out as far from the hippies—and maybe more importantly, the college kids—as it's possible to be. So ten years ago, a small contingent of them found just such a place in the hinterlands—an old cane shop on the corner of Ninth and Gilman, down by the waterfront in the industrial district, in which they could party pretty much in private.

At the beginning, 924 Gilman Street was led by an elder statesman of sorts, one Tim Yohannan, the founder of a zine called *Maximum Rock 'n' Roll*. Yohannan divested himself of the club in 1989—the politics of that are too byzantine to mention—but it was Yohannan's decree that the club be a collective. It books unknown punk acts from around the country on Fridays and Saturdays (and Sunday afternoons). And it is run by volunteers: generation upon generation of earnest fifteen- and sixteen-year-olds.

For many years, 924 Gilman was a secret place, known only to punky kids in Berkeley and the ones around the country who pored over copies of *MRR*. Since its inception, it has served as a deep wellspring of inspiration for every kid involved in the retropunk movement, but never as much as for that first generation, which included the members of Green Day.

By now, most people who care know Green Day's personal history: how they went from being virtually the house band at 924 Gilman Street to being the world's best-selling punk rock band, after bassist Mike Dirnt took a timely kick in the teeth at Woodstock '94 and the band got dubbed the official next Nirvana. But few people are informed about all the gory details: how, although the band's core members hail form various Bay Area suburbs (singer Billie Joe Armstrong and Dirnt are from Rodeo, a Stepford-like community of spanking-new tract homes; drummer Tre Cool is from the way Northern California hick town of Willits), they spent their formative teenage years in the People's Republic of Berkeley, worshiping at the People's Temple of 924 Gilman Street.

In 1994, Green Day's *Dookie* was widely released on Warner Brothers, and immediately its simple, tune-filled songs about suburban boredom—beautifully illustrated in Mark Kohl's pastel-colored videos—hit a chord with youth everywhere, as did singer Billie Joe's shit-pitching persona. Although one would hesitate to call them anything but derivative—Green Day's whole ethos is derived from the Jam and the Buzzcocks—the band does represent an entirely new generation's take on rock 'n' roll, uncluttered by classic rock, and no wonder: at age twenty-three, Billie Joe's own concertgoing experience is still limited to a single local gig by Bloodrage and Transgressor, at the On Broadway in San Francisco, above the Mabuhay Gardens, when it still held all-ages shows, plus a Replacements show his sister took him to soon after, plus a thousand nights at 924 Gilman Street, and his own self-created experiences onstage as a rock star. He still gets misty-eyed when he thinks of the Husker Du concert he missed, at age thirteen, because his sister couldn't get the car. . . .

Given the isolated nature of his experience, perhaps it's not surprising that Armstrong has managed to generate something that is totally meaningful to a new generation of rock fans. He has also, to his credit, seized the opportunity to raise the stakes that Nirvana laid down. Nirvana fought to have edgy opening acts, like Shonen Knife and the Butthole Surfers; Green Day was able to put a really edgy opening act on its entire fall tour—strident queercore activists Pansy Division, who play a forty-five-minute set entirely about buttfucking other boys. Whereas Pearl Jam fought Ticketmaster to make the service charge on ticket prices come down; Green Day just lowered the ticket price by taking a smaller cut.

Armstrong has also appeared nude on stage, told *The Advocate* he's bisexual, although mostly in his mind; married his girlfriend; and had a baby whose bedtime rituals sometimes interfere with what time the band takes the stage.

In short, there's not a lot bad you can say about Green Day, but some people—at least around Berkeley—persist in saying it anyway. The accusations range form the one that they "sold out" by signing to Warner Brothers, to—well, the one about how they "sold out" by signing to Warner Brothers in 1993. Had the band stayed on Lookout! Records, the tiny Berkeley label that signed them in 1989 (when the members were seventeen years old) and released the records *Kerplunk* and *1039 Smoothed Out Slappy Hours,* a compilation of its previous EPs, they might have avoided a certain amount of censure from their peers. But then again, they might not have. Prior to the band's signing to Warner Brothers, *Kerplunk* had sold some sixty thousand copies, and that kind of profit inevitably reaps jealousy and meanness.

"Its the nature of the beast, whenever you get popular, people want to tear you a new asshole," says Billie Joe with a shrug (speaking in December of 1995). "But I have no reason to justify myself," he adds stubbornly. "We didn't do anything wrong. I'm pretty happy and content with where I'm at now, and if someone doesn't like it, that's their problem. If I gave 'em something to bitch about, at least I gave them that."

At the time he made these comments, Green Day was on the road with the Riverdales (formerly Screeching Weasel), traveling between gigs with their former labelmates and sleeping—mostly—in the bus. Billie claims he chose the Riverdales to piss off *Maximum Rock 'n' Roll,* by co-opting their best writer. "Basically," he adds, "we just do the things we've always done. It's really easy. I mean, we've pretty much got the industry by the balls right now, so we can do whatever we want."

Those are brave words for a Berkeley punk, and on the surface, perfectly justified: *Insomniac,* released October 10, debuted at number two on *Billboard,* and the band's tour is one of the successful large arena tours of this fall. What Armstrong doesn't mention is that there's been a distinct downside to their success—a downside that has its basis in the band's very roots, and that has cropped up over and over again for the past two years. Even now, Green Day have to deal with questions about their credibility and their roots on a daily basis.

■ **Green Day**

Murray Bowles

Because Green Day happen to be an awesome band, they succeeded without benefit of the mighty underground punk rock community that spawned them: "Longview" is a song that was simply bound to succeed on any terms it wished to dictate. As it happens, those terms are relatively radical: Gilman Street may have rejected Green Day, but Green Day is still governed solely by Gilman Street's code of honor. For them, doing things like keeping ticket prices low, doing benefit concerts (the HJK—Oakland's Henry J. Kaiser Arena—gig was a benefit for the Berkeley Free and Haight-Ashbury Free Clinics; the band's only other Bay Area show was a benefit for the San Francisco Library), and taking friends' bands like Pansy Division on the road with them comes naturally: they were brought up in an environment where such gestures are de rigueur. Even now that they are yoked to Warner Brothers, the band retains the values it imbibed in its youth: keep things simple, and cheap, and thoughtful; stay true to your community and your friends.

And this is where they differ from every other band going today. Some critics—contemptuous of Green Day's obvious musical sources—still puzzle over Green Day's import in rock history, citing joie de vivre as its only tenuous hold on the popular imagination, and it's true that one could hardly call Green Day a deep or innovative band. Their music is a pastiche of much that has come before them, and Billie Joe is a little kid's icon, dabbling in antics that are bratty rather than bold.

But I think what Green Day secretly get at is something about class. Arriving in the middle of an era when fewer and fewer people can afford—or need—to go to college, but more and more bands are made up of upper-middle-class college kids, Green Day bypass the college rock ghetto completely, providing music—and a musical point of view—that's smart, and sassy, but entirely blue-collar. They come from the working-class world, and despite everything that has occurred between then and now, a working-class hero is still something to be.

This is what creates the tension that makes Green Day great—but it's also what causes tension between Green Day and Berkeley. Besides the band's yearlong avoidance of playing in its own hometown—an avoidance that Armstrong now writes off by saying, "We just couldn't find the right-sized place to play"—there has been other evidence of internal distress. When Armstrong's baby, Joey, was born last February, he refused to issue a statement to the press officially acknowledging it. When *People* magazine sent a reporter to cover the band, the band stonewalled and asked every one of their friends to stonewall also.

And for those HJK Arena shows, Green Day made a point of not issuing tickets to the press. "Basically," says Billie Joe, "our main thing was we didn't want to turn into a teen heartthrob thing. We wanted to walk away from everything and work on ourselves as people for a while, and not have to read all this bullshit that comes out. I personally make it a rule never to read anything about us anymore." To that end, GD made a brief attempt to bar all interviews, eventually making exceptions for *Rolling Stone, Spin,* and MTV News.

In August of 1995, the band left its original management firm, Jeff Saltzman and Elliott Cahn (who together make up Cahnman Management).

Green Day began being managed by their former road manager, Randy Steffes, because, according to Billie, "no one knows what we want more than us. We stuck to that a long time before *Dookie* came out, and we did pretty well. And we just want to get back to that way now, and do everything ourselves again."

That's a great idea in theory, but can it work in practice? Efforts to remain a low-key outfit are somewhat futile at this point: however hard they fight the Corporate Ogre in theory, Green Day are already truly ensconced well within the machine. And even if they could go backward, everything is already entirely different—thanks to the kind of emotional turmoil that any sudden influx of money into a formerly static financial environment invariably plops onto a community.

Over at Lookout! Records, for example, the East Bay label where Green Day got their start, employees point out that there are almost as many negatives as there are positives to Green Day's success. "On the whole it's helped us more than it's hurt," says Lookout! publicist Molly Neuman. "We've probably sold twenty times as many copies of every record. We have more resources, a better financial situation, a better office, and that's all great. But there are complications and problems that go along with that, a lot of new issues to deal with. For one thing, all of a sudden you have to deal with bands saying, 'You have all this money, give it to us.' And you have these bands who are like, 'We're older than them, we've been doing this longer, why isn't that us?' And as their label, we have to explain, well, partly it's promotion, and partly it's just been this weird fluke."

Neuman, a former member of Olympia-based band Bratmobile who is now in the PeeChees, has particular sympathy for East Bay band members who've watched Green Day turn into supernovas. "It happened in Olympia, too," she recalls. "For years you do these things because of the passion and emotion involved in making music the way you want to make it, and all of a sudden your friends are superstars, and you're like, 'But...my band's good, too!' "

Another issue that GD's success has forced Lookout! to confront is its own motivation in putting out records. Lookout! itself is content with moderate sales, but for the bands, it's a different matter altogether. "Like, the Mr. T Experience has just made their best record ever," says Neuman. "And that presents a big test for us: Can we make a record and break it on its own merits...and can we do this without losing our integrity and the fundamental ideology of why we do what we do?

"We go back and forth. Should we even be playing this game? Because the music business is *such* a game. And I guess [our attitude] is hard for our bands—particularly the Riverdales. It's hard for them to be on the road with Green Day and not get the attention—the difference in size is just so huge. It's not just an ego thing, it's an isolation thing. It's lonely for them out there.

"We have the money, we can hire people to push them, be more aggressive, do more promotion," adds Neuman. "But when it comes to bribing radio stations...we don't have the connections or the resources to schmooze people, and frankly, we don't even want to."

This is, of course, exactly the sort of prosocialist, anticapitalist, only-in-Berkeley mind-set that made Green Day what they are today—but it's also what has driven them from their haven. Billie Joe denies that this is a problem: "We're just like three kids in a candy store full of really golden opportunities to piss someone off," he says. "I mean, I don't have the same life I used to, it's hard to walk down the street and have a personal life and stuff like that, but we're still having fun. If it wasn't fun for us, we wouldn't be out there."

Billie Joe says that people have stopped giving him shit—"Now they pick on Rancid instead"—but last time he went to Gilman Street to see Dead Dawn and AFI—he wore a disguise. And one has to wonder what it feels like to be twenty-three years old and evicted from your spiritual home. And make no mistake about it, Green Day have been evicted, becoming as unwelcome at Gilman Street as those putative yuppies at the brew pub whom they, themselves, unwittingly ushered in. According to Charles Long, Gilman Street's current head coordinator of volunteers, Gilman Street's greatest fear—a fear that has been exacerbated more by the impending brew pub than by the release of *Dookie* or *Insomniac*—is that people who've seen Green Day on MTV will come over to Gilman Street and "be belligerent. You just get one guy who's drunk and, just because he's not a minor like most of the people here, a lot bigger than everybody else, going into the pit and not, you know, understanding anything about the punk rock community, and it wrecks everything.

"Up till now we've been really lucky," he adds, "because regardless of Green Day's success, we've remained relatively isolated. We're mentioned in *Rolling Stone* all the time, but people still don't really know where we are. We pretty much avoid the press; a lot of our shows are community-oriented, and we don't advertise.

"If anything," he continues, "[their success] has just more definitely defined our ideology: what we're about; what we're against. We're not in opposition to them at all, but they aren't really part of our world anymore."

iii.

A few months before the Hart's Brewery problem, in June of 1995 to be exact, Green Day played a two-night stand at Oakland's HJK Arena— their first on their home turf since well before the release of *Dookie*.

Those shows sold out in a record ten minutes, and pandemonium doesn't even begin to describe the epic explosion that occurred when this band hit the stage. "How ya fucking brats all doing?" intoned Billie Joe, and that was it: immediately, the arena floor looked like it had been hit with a fifty-thousand-watt jolt of electricity. Every single person standing on it shot straight into the air, arms flailing, legs pumping, torsos jutting forward, a veritable Hieronymus Bosch painting come frighteningly to life. Huge new pits were forming right and left, while the kids in the balcony practically fell down the stairwells, the better to throw themselves on top of the crowd, releasing high-pitched shrieks of idiot glee. Everyone in the arena was about fourteen years old.

And there you have it, in a nutshell. For the millionth or trillionth time this century, one is confronted with the same old rock cliché, that charismatic outsider giving credence to the unbeloved, and it's a sight that never fails to please. As the latest generation of rebellious youth greets its latest master, the old order changeth, it giveth way to the new. Meet the new boss, brasher than the old boss. I hate my dad. Someday I won't.

And someday soon, perhaps, Green Day will calcify into the staid old rock 'n' roll relic that the kids at Gilman Street already see it as. "But that doesn't matter," says Billie Joe with a shrug, "because there'll be another subcultural icon coming up from someplace...."

Chapter 11

Institutionalized

Songwriter Nick Lowe once said, "Writing about music is like dancing about architecture," and that may well be so. But gibes aside, music and architecture have more in common than one might think. The presence of music—live music; punk music—can affect a given neighborhood in a number of ways. And so, of course, do buildings.

In her highly influential book on city planning, *The Death and Life of Great American Cities,* architect Jane Jacobs argues that in order to be successful, a city or neighborhood has to be socially, economically, and even architecturally diverse—i.e., it ought to contain buildings of many different styles, sizes, and uses.

Once diversity has been blown, however—generally because a given neighborhood has become so popular and magnetic it drives out the lower-end and older aspects of it—Jacobs says the neighborhood will rapidly self-destruct. "Both visually and functionally, the place becomes monotonous," she writes. "In time, a place that was once successful and once the object of such ardent competition wanes and becomes marginal."

Jacobs was writing theoretically, about places like Greenwich Village and Boston's Northend, and she was writing in 1961. But she could just as well have been writing about the co-option of punk rock, circa 1996. Turn on MTV and you'll notice immediately that the genre has become both visually and functionally monotonous. Can marginality be far behind?

Not bloody likely—as a look at the Haight-Ashbury neighborhood in San Francisco indicates. In 1984, when I first moved to Haight Street, there was a huge campaign going to stop the Gap from occupying a storefront on the corner of Haight and Ashbury. A jillion flyers reading "Don't Mall the Haight!" didn't stop the chain store from moving on in; but a few years later, some more rabid antimallers burned down a nearly completed site for Long's Drugs—carelessly taking out several apartment blocks with them in the process, including the one that housed the Haight-Ashbury Free Clinic.

This little mistake eventually stopped the "Don't Mall the Haight" movement cold (and also kept Long's out). But despite housing both a Gap and a McDonald's, as well as many more mainstream businesses, the Haight has not exactly been malled as anticipated by the doomsdayers. But it's not a neighborhood that Jane Jacobs would approve of because, despite a thin veneer of dirty druggies who line its pavements, it is not economically diverse. It doesn't abide by one of Jacobs's main tenets of success, which is that there should be an even distribution of people throughout the day: Haight Street in the morning is dead-empty except for the bodies of the layabouts who sleep on it; while on weekends it's overrun with suburban shoppers, come to buy the coolest in punk and hippie wear, and whom no amount of homeless creeps and crime is going to stop.

More importantly, rents and housing prices in the neighborhood (and in San Francisco as a whole) are way up; poorer residents have been driven out, and food and clothing prices in the alarmingly hip boutiques there have risen sky high.

Gentrification like the type that's hit the Haight is something that affected every community in America throughout the eighties—from the Gaslamp District in San Diego to Pioneer Square in Seattle; from Sixth Street in Austin to the South Street Seaport in New York; and now, in a smaller way (which is much more evident about a mile to the west of Gilman Street, on Fourth Street and over in Emeryville), West Berkeley. It's been gentrified, pure and simple: enhanced economically and made desirable to a larger number of people than originally gave a damn.

ii.

Jacobs also said: "There is a tendency for outstanding success in cities to destroy itself—purely as the result of being successful."

This, then, is what Gilman Street is kicking against: not so much an influx of yuppies at their precious club, but the wider implications of urban renewal; the sad specter of a community explosion and eventually, its demise. In truth, the struggle between the Hart's Brewing Company—now officially renamed the Pyramid Brewing Company—and the punk club at 924 Gilman Street has wider implications than just little club meets Corporate Ogre (although, technically speaking, Pyramid is an owner-operated start-up, just like, say, Lookout! Records). The Pyramid Brew-haha is also about the implementation of the West Berkeley Plan, which is, in itself, an attempt by the city of Berkeley to deal with just the kind of shortsighted gentrification that has seen neighborhoods in other cities—SOMA, for example, in San Francisco—become one-dimensional and inhumane. Metaphorically, it is the city planning equivalent of a well-intentioned indie label that sells most of its stock to Sony and then attempts to mandate a DIY ethic.

According to one Berkeley city planner, the WBP is a confusing but well-intentioned document meant to somehow upgrade this rather unsightly corridor of Berkeley while simultaneously maintaining its low rents, its "industrial character," and, of course, its all-important ethnic diversity.

To that end, in 1993, after ten years of dispute, the Berkeley City Council finally voted to implement the highly ambitious plan, a 223-page document that seeks to "preserve the character of West Berkeley while still maintaining and expanding its manufacturing base."

It is, in short, afeared of the kind of destruction that Jacobs warns against; it is antigentrification. And at first glance, the Pyramid Brewing Company (which will be the largest manufacturer in Berkeley) is exactly the type of business that the WBP ought to encourage. The business will add thirty-six new jobs and ninety parking spaces to the area, as well as rehabilitating a building that has stood empty for nearly ten years.

But Berkeley being Berkeley, there is a lot of internal suspicion of Pyramid, a kind of unspoken feeling that the company is in fact a corporate hybrid, akin to the Starbucks chain, which will usurp and destroy the hood's natural demeanor. The kids who run 924 Gilman Street are certainly adamant in their belief that the advent of Pyramid will change the Gilman Street corridor into a more upscale haunt, like the Peets-and-Nature Company–ized strip on nearby Fourth Street. To them, Pyramid represents the Corporate Ogre incarnate. They are convinced its presence will cause trouble, if only by making it easier for the older elements of their own clientele to cross the street and get blasted before diving into the pit.

But there's not much they can do about it now. A year after the zoning adjustments board meeting, there is a mammoth, if empty, edifice taking up the entire 900 block of Gilman Street, directly across the street from the clubhouse. Pyramid had barely been slowed up by monthly meetings, beyond inviting members of Gilman Street up to Seattle for an all-expenses-paid trip to see the Pyramid Alehouse in operation.

Flying a bunch of punk rockers to Seattle may seem like rather a large step to take, but the new brewery and brew pub is rather important to

Pyramid's expansion plan. When complete, it will manufacture 80,000 barrels a year over and above the 125,000 barrels currently manufactured by Pyramid, and supply the whole Southwest. It will be a huge employer for the city of Berkeley, in both its plant and its restaurant capacity.

iii.

Eighteen months after the use permit for the new Pyramid Alehouse was issued and a scant six weeks before the brew pub's projected opening on December 2, Pyramid Brewing had to go before the city of Berkeley's Design Review Board—a subcommittee of the zoning board—to get one of its signs approved.

The restaurant had already run into problems with a smaller entrance sign, which was to read "Pyramid Alehouse," the name of the restaurant. According to the West Berkeley Plan, using the word "house" implies food—which would violate the city's sign ordinance for the area, which has to remain strictly industrial in nature. In order to sneak it up there, the brewery is going to have to go back to the ZAB and have their use permit altered.

But the sign in question at the September 30 DRB (Design Review Board) meeting is a different one entirely. This one is going to stretch across the length of the parking structure, directly facing 924 Gilman Street, and consist of sixteen five-foot-high letters made out of iron tubing and galvanized steel. It will be over one hundred feet long—making it the largest sign in Berkeley, larger even than the sign for Bayer Laboratories, which had been deemed "freeway art," by the DRB.

Needless to say, the members of the 924 Gilman Street collective are concerned about the sign. They too feel it would violate the spirit of the West Berkeley Plan—not to mention the anonymous, noncommercial nature of their turf.

"It's going to be like these huge letters looming up over us out of a mist," sighs Jesse Townley, Gilman's representative at the meeting, and he's sort of right: there's a huge difference between a dingy industrial street with no signage on it, and street with a gaping (if arty) advertisement blazing across its width.

Had the brewery's representatives heard his comment, they might have said, "Exactly." But the grounds on which they argue for its inclusion are more aesthetically oriented. To their mind, the sign is a subtle one, because it's not neon, or lit up from beneath.

"We tried to find something that would fit with the scale of the building," explains Derrick Chasan, vice president of marketing at Pyramid Brewing, "as well as with the architectural design of the building. It's designed to have a timeless feel, and I worry that a smaller sign won't deliver that."

Kava Massih, the architect for the brewery, argues that the nature of the sign's material gives it a more industrial look. "[And] the largeness becomes part of the structure," he explains. "The monumentality of it is sort of... industrial. It shows the optimism of the industrial age."

The Design Review Board agrees. After about a half hour of debate, the board votes four to one to allow the sign to go forward, essentially for artistic reasons.

The one dissenter is architect David Goldin, whose objections mirror Gilman Street members' contention that the sign—which is so large that it can't be seen in its entirety from one spot across the street—is commercial overkill.

"I would be happy if there was no sign whatsoever," says Goldin in the debate. "Everything about this building is already prominent and dynamic. It's a destination-specific place. If it was on a freeway, like the Bayer sign, I'd think differently, but as it is, it's complete and total overkill. I just don't think it needs a sign at all."

You have to wonder where Goldin thinks he is. After all, a place where a corporation like Pyramid Brewing puts up a 150,000-foot building without a sign advertising who it is is not a place in America, that's for sure.

The members of Gilman Street collective believe that the coming of the brewery will, among other things, make the land value of their club house site increase—thus driving them out, but John Stoddard, president of Pyramid Brewing, denies this. "Hey, if we wanted to see land values go through the roof, we would have done lofts!" he says, laughing. "Now, will [our presence on Ninth Street] drive up land prices? I don't know. Will it allow people to realize the value of their land? Yes. It legitimizes the address.

"But then, just the act of converting a vacant space into one that's occupied is going to do that."

iv.

Stoddard's words are small comfort for Gilman Street, who don't own their building. But one good thing did come from the meeting, from their point of view: not once but twice, board members urged the brewery not to try to go before the ZAB in an attempt to get their use permit altered so that the neon "Pyramid Alehouse" sign can go up. No doubt the board members remember the meeting eleven months ago, when City Hall was packed with irate punk rockers and the meeting lasted till 2 A.M.

Chasan admits that the brew pub had intended to take the use permit back to the ZAB. "You see, there's already other Pyramid Alehouses, one in Seattle and others in the planning stage," he explains. "We'd rather not put up anything than put up a sign which has the wrong name on it."

Nor does Chasan think the brewery could do without its brew pub: "That's the model of growth we've chosen instead of advertising," he says. "We've found that

■ **Gilman Street, 1988**
Murray Bowles

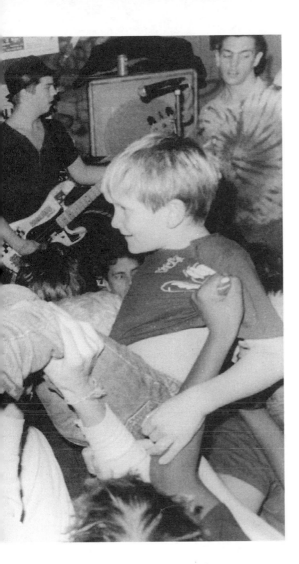

where there is a local brewery, there is a local following."

Stoddard characterizes the lack of a Pyramid Alehouse sign as "a pain-in-the-ass-type nuisance, but that's all it is.... It's certainly," he added somewhat wryly, "in keeping with [this] whole process so far."

What he's referring to isn't the punk rock opposition as much as the opposition of the Berkeley City Council, which in typical Berkeley fashion has made Pyramid's bid to be the largest manufacturer in the city quite difficult.

Pyramid is based in Washington State, and has been looking to expand into California for quite some time. "Berkeley," says Stoddard, "has always been our first choice [for expansion]. It's very unusual to get a building of that size in an urban setting like this, but that said, there was a threshold ... and we got very close to that threshold. We finally had to say to the council, "Hey! We have other options here!"

In short, facing down city hall, says Stoddard, was much more irritating than facing down Gilman Street—although Stoddard admits that when the punks showed up with their charter at the City Council meeting, Stoddard and his partners was taken totally by surprise.

Well—*almost* by surprise. "When I was coming down from Seattle for that first city council meeting," Stoddard recalls, "I was sitting next to two kids who ... well, I can't think how they got through the metal detectors, they had so much chain on their faces. We got to talking, and they said they were from Vancouver, and they were coming to the Bay Area to protest this threat to a great institution of theirs, because of this evil brewery that was moving in on it. And I was like, "Hi, I'm John, the Evil Brewer!'"

Stoddard laughs. "I tell ya," he says. "It [Gilman] is a great machine. But I have great respect for them," he adds. "They had a unified, articulate opposition to us, and they did a businesslike job of holding everyone to the agenda. As frustrating as it was, in the back of my mind, I was always kinda like, 'More power to 'em!'"

Stoddard adds that he's glad that the two organizations are already talking (prior to the opening of the pub). But Chasan confesses that he was taken by surprise at Gilman's continued objections, as evidenced by their presence at the Design Review Board meeting in September.

"I thought," he said, "they left Seattle reassured about our organization, that this isn't so much a brew pub as it is a full-functioning brewery. It's first and foremost a factory. So I don't really think this issue is about gentrification—that's such a loaded word—it's about local production."

At another public meeting a few months earlier, the club brought forth the argument that the mere sight of patrons drinking beer at the brew house would prove too great a temptation to Gilman's patrons. In order to rectify that—"to preserve the club's innocence," as Massih puts it—the committee caused Massih to change his design so that the wall around the patio was higher. ("People are always asking me about the height of that wall when they see the plans," sighs Massih. "And it's just part of the bizarreness of this whole assignment.")

There is, however, a level of disingenuousness about this argument: Gilman is an all-ages club, but that doesn't mean that the kids who go there aren't often drunk out of their mind. Stoddard sighs and quotes the nearby owner of a storage-unit facility on the same street as the brewery.

"He said, 'There's more booze served in my loading dock than you'll ever push out of that pub,' and I think that's probably true. But we chose to be responsive to the club's problems, and not drag it into the gutter and treat it on that level.

"I really think—I may be wrong—but I think the club has more issues with the zoning board than they have with us. I was watching one guy at the meeting and he was looking at the council, like, 'You guys put us here, and now you're doing *this* to us?' Their location was something they felt real comfortable with until we came in."

The brew pub is set on opening—sans sign—on January 10, 1997—somewhat ironically, one week after Gilman's official tenth-anniversary celebration. Gilman Street is still afraid of its yawning presence there, but Pyramid says it has no qualms about the hundreds of punks kids who hang about on the corner of Ninth and Gilman every Friday and Saturday night scaring off their own clientele.

"Well, of course not," says Massih. "They only look scary. When they open their mouths they sound like Tiffany. They're all totally nice kids from the suburbs who just happen to have bolts coming out of their necks."

Adds Stoddard, suddenly turning steely, "We've got a very significant asset, and we'll be protecting it. We're not going to be susceptible to vandalism, or anything like that. That's all controllable."

Do the kids really have a problem? "Sure," says architect Massih. "Are you kidding me? The lights are getting turned out on 'em."

In the next breath, however, Massih adds that he thinks there's a possibility it's all a tempest in a teapot. "The one place on earth where these two things could coexist side by side is Berkeley. It's not like Pyramid is a sports bar that draws Raiders fans; the frat-boy fear is a bit exaggerated. I just don't think World War III is going to break out."

And even if it does there are lots of other places in West Berkeley to which Gilman Street could relocate—marginal neighborhoods are a dime a dozen, not just in Berkeley, but in every community where gentrification is a fact of life.

V.

But urban gentrification isn't punk rock's only problem. In the past four years, the landscape of America has been marred by the completion of suburbia—hundred-mile-long cities in beige and neutral colors, examples of the so-called garden community which, according to Le Corbusier in *La Ville Radieuse,* "brings in its wake the destruction of the social spirit, the downfall of collective forces, the annihilation of the collective will."

And yet, the isolation of the individual spirit that Le Corbusier so rightly feared hasn't quite come to pass—not yet anyway—because inside those cold houses beats the warm heart of the opposition, beats and beats in ¼ time, beats along to the Ramones and Green Day and the Pistols. Listen next time, as you drive past, and you'll hear them muttering quietly, "a-one-two-three-fo!" The kids who live in those communities dream of blowing them all up and starting anew—and as long as they live there, they will sing of their frustration, and as long as they're singing there is hope.

At least, that's what the brew pub people think. "The whole idea of punk and kids and music on the edge and stuff...it always needs a little bit of a cause to keep it going," said Kava Massih, a few days prior to the pub's opening-night party. "Charles, over at Gilman Street, keeps saying that [Gilman Street] is an institution. But the minute punk becomes institutionalized, it's time to start poking it, make it a little bit agitated and ouncomfortable. So maybe this"—by which he means the brew pub—"is a blessing in disguise."

PART 3

STILL ROCKIN' IN THE FREE WORLD

Chapter 12

Kiss This

How sad is now? I'll tell you how sad. When the Sex Pistols finally made it to America, they chose to play the suburbs, the unnatural final repository of all their mythic sins. The Sex Pistols' U.S. tour began at the end of July in Boulder, Colorado, and by August, it hit the Bay Area— Mountain View to be exact, which is an ugly, tract-riddled commuter town about one hour south of San Francisco where the Bill Graham Presents organization co-owns a fourteen-thousand-seat shed called the Shoreline Amphitheater.

Like most of America's rock 'n' roll sheds, this amphitheater is large and sterile looking, a venue-cum–theme park full of designer beer booths, a wide-open lawn area, and a pleasant concourse where you can buy T-shirts, Thai food, and a bunch of hippie junk. It is a great place to see Whitney Houston or Celine Dion, but not a great place to rock out. Putting the Sex Pistols there was a piteous mistake, since most real punks don't have cars and won't pay twenty-five dollars for what they know for sure will be a forty-five-minute set.

And indeed, the show could hardly have been called an unqualified success. About 5,000 people attended it (4,280 paid), only a few hundred more than attended the original Winterland show in 1978, and unlike that show, the Shoreline house was papered.

Yup, by the night of the show, they were givin' tickets away—at record stores, on the radio, to volunteer organizations around the Bay Area, essentially to anyone who wanted them. The lawn, for example, was stacked with people who worked at the Haight-Ashbury Free Clinic. And that was the pattern around the United States.

There were exceptions, of course. The New York dates, played at Roseland, thrilled and chilled a critic-papered urban crowd. Seattle's was an okay date—but there, again, they played at Bumpershoot, on a bill with

. Johnny Rotten
of the Sex Pistols
AP/Wide World

every other band in Seattle; it mimicked the European festivals in that people hadn't paid just to see the Pistols.

But in outlying areas like Denver, Dallas, and San Francisco, they went for the suburban arenas, and this was a huge mistake. For as loudly as old punks like to bewail the pseudopunks' takeover of their genre, the Sex Pistols' U.S. tour proved that in fact, to the masses, punk rock has barely made a dent in their psyche. As it was, no punk was going to drive to Mountain View to see the Pistols play a giant outdoor fun park; and the result was empty arenas around the nation.

But "empty" is a relative term. The show would have looked full enough if it'd had been held at the Greek in Berkeley (an unseated venue that holds 8,000). And if they had played two shows at the Warfield (a 2,500-seat theater in downtown San Francisco), they could probably have sold out both.

Instead, this time out—just like last time—the Pistols were entirely relying on media hype to publicize this reunion tour; but unlike '78, it failed almost wholly to materialize. They never got a *Rolling Stone* cover—having refused to be interviewed by said magazine unless they were guaranteed one. Radio play wasn't exactly forthcoming (it never had been; why start now?). And their album, *Filthy Lucre Live,* released on July 30, the eve of the U.S. tour, sold dreadfully. It had moved only about fifteen thousand copies by the time of the Mountain View concert.

The Pistols were earning a million dollars up front to reunite; the tour's title, "Filthy Lucre," was merely an honest expression of their aims, rather than the ironic statement that some critics took it for. But clearly the band was asking for more than they were worth, and someone was taking a loss. In an eleven-show average, the Pistols earned $100,546 per night, and sold an average of 4,223 tickets. They sold out in LA (Universal Amphitheater, 6,251), New York (3,200 two nights), and Cleveland (Nautica Arena, 3,753). In Detroit, at the 6,500-seat Cobo Arena, they sold 5,372. Houston, International Ballroom, 2,578 (capacity 4,500).

Still, according to Gary Bongiovanni of *Pollstar,* "They didn't do badly considering they never got any airplay in the first place and only toured the U.S. once nineteen years ago. It's not logical to expect them to come back and step up to a full-size arena or amphitheater, not without a brand-new record being played on the radio. Now if they'd priced themselves to where promoters could have sold them, they may have done better. They also might have done better in the winter."

They also might have done better had America ever cared in the first place. In fact, if they had just put an okay and appropriate opening act on the bill—the Buzzcocks, for example, instead of Goldfinger—they could have done better than they did.

As it was, Shoreline looked emptier than I'd ever seen it, and every single person seated near me looked like a CPA.

That's not to say they didn't have a fabulous time, though. When the Pistols came on they went apeshit. The Pistols played the usual set—i.e., everything on *Filthy Lucre* except "No Fun" (which was replaced by "Problems"), and the audience knew every word to every song. Even the balding, bespectacled forty-five-year-old CPA behind me leaped to his feet and bellowed "*Bo-deees*" into my eardrum when the band burst into their opening number. The band looked disgusted throughout its fifty-minute set, but the audience—at least the parts up front in the seats—didn't seem disappointed at all.

ii.

When I was in high school, none of my clique of girlfriends liked the kind of music I liked. Hell, they barely like *music,* and no wonder: they listened to AM radio and sang along to the sound track to *Grease.* They grooved on Jackson Browne and James Taylor and Billy Joel and Loggins and Messina, while I wailed gently in the background about the poverty of their taste. Many's the time I've told the story about how we all went to see the Rolling Stones at the Oakland Coliseum and they wanted to leave after Eddie Money. And once I played them Blondie's *Plastic Letters*—thinking it was so poppy and cute—and they all went, "Ooh! But she's ugly!"

Eighteen years have passed since then and I've long since forgiven them their trespasses—or so I thought. In fact, I discovered a trace of ignoble enmity remaining in my bosom when I spied one of that crowd at the Sex Pistols concert at Shoreline. She came up to me at the bar before the band came on, laughing. "I bet you're surprised to see *me* here," she said. "Hey—am I going to hate it?"

Well, I thought back to the old days, when she made fun of my hair, when she took my Clash records off the stereo and made me listen to "House at Pooh Corner" instead, when she sang "Weekend in New England" on the way to swim practice every morning, and I thought, "Yes, Annette, you are." And even if she did like it—and there was a fat chance of that—it would bug me, just as it bugged me when she went to see Bruce Springsteen in 1984 and said how cute he was, entirely forgetting the time back in 1978 she told me that his singing sounded like he was barfing.

The Pistols and Bruce are different, though. I always thought my friends should like Bruce, since Billy Joel learned all he knew from him. But I never thought they should like the Pistols. That was my personal turf, get it? It was another planet, where everyone was mad like me. Annette and her ilk just weren't welcome there. Punk rockdom had no room for high school class presidents and "most likely to succeeds"; it was our little club of malcontents, and the contented could just stay away.

Of course, I took the opportunity to recap her sins at the bar during Goldfinger's dreadful set, but Annette just raised her eyes to heaven and giggled. "Oh, brother. Will ya get over it, already?"

But I don't think I will get over it. That was my most aesthetically formative experience, those long morning drives up to the Foothill College pool, suffering through "Your Mama Don't Dance and Your Daddy Don't Rock and Roll," listening to them all sing songs by Boz Scaggs and Billy Joel. I remember what punk was getting rid of, even if nobody else does. It was getting rid of wretched excess, of melodrama and foolishness and songs about getting laid, it was getting rid of Queen and Led Zeppelin and the Rolling Stones. . . . It was getting rid of Kiss.

Thus, the fact that the Pistols bombed in America in the summer of '96, while Kiss succeeded beyond their wildest dreams, proves once and for all that punk failed in the task it set for itself. And it proves another thing, also: nowhere in life is the truism "The more things change, the more they stay the same" as true as it is in rock 'n' roll.

iii.

In 1977, the year that the Sex Pistols were shocking London with their ribald antics, Kiss were huge in Middle America, while punk—the dangerous flipside of it—was buried and ridiculed by the powers that be.

A lot has happened since then—punk has permeated the very fabric of our lives, while Kiss have held conventions where they hawked lunch boxes and paraphernalia. Twenty years later, however, the same pattern persists. Kiss, who, after years of struggling solo careers, have reunited with the original members and original makeup, are tearing up concert attendance records all over the country, while the Pistols—also reunited, also trudging around the country wearing full body costumes and makeup—are not.

Perhaps it's not so strange that an unpopular band is unpopular now and a popular band is still popular. No, what's strange is the similarities between the two acts. Both were, of course, always more concept than band, but back then no two bands could have seemed more different. They were the rock 'n' roll dialectic in action, the thesis and the antithesis, the phone and the antiphone.

On the one hand, Kiss parodied rock 'n' roll by rendering it in its stupidest possible form: gestures, costumes, image, subject matter—all were clichéd banalities, ironic statements about the foolishness and childishness of rock 'n' roll. The Sex Pistols were—or so we believed—urgent and honest and unpretentious and political. Their music meant something... or so we all thought.

But here in 1996, the two bands are so similar you can barely tell them apart; so similar that the same band—Fluffy, a badly fashionable all-girl outfit from London—is able to open up for them both, for the Pistols in Finsbury Park in June, and for Kiss at the San Diego Sports Arena in October, two days before Halloween.

And indeed, that's not the only similarity between the two nights. The Sports Arena parking lot on October 29 is highly reminiscent of the Finsbury Park show four months earlier, from the balmy night air to the level of excitement wafting about in it, to the many parents with their little kids who've been made up to look like the band in question.

At Finsbury Park, babies had sweet little colored Mohawks, and the parents had donned their safety pins and torn shirts. In San Diego, children wore whiteface clown makeup with black-and-silver Ace Frehley—or Paul Stanley or Gene Simmons or Peter Criss—makeup on top of it.

Robert Munger, of Vista, California, is one such parent in attendance. He has brought his eleven-year-old son Ryan to see his first rock concert. The reason? "Kiss was my first rock concert too. I saw them at the San Diego Civic Center in 1975. Rush was the opening act."

Ryan has just had his face Gene Simmonized for free at a booth in the parking lot sponsored by a radio station. Now he's standing on the steps of the arena with 150 or so other Kiss impersonators, waiting to have his picture taken by the official photographer for station 105 FM.

"Okay now, all the Genes: stick out your tongues!" yells the photographer, and Ryan obligingly sticks out his tongue. Clearly, he has suddenly become a member of the Kiss Army, the official name for Kiss fans, circa 1976.

Tonight, the parking lot of the Sports Arena is more festive than downtown Tijuana on Cinco de Mayo. The place was full of the usual pre-show partyers in search of beer and bud, but mingling among them were people whose idea of a good time also included donning full Kiss makeup, black leotards, and platform boots.

We're not talking a few diehard dress-up fans here. We're talking one or two hundred of them, ranging from little boys in T-shirts and jeans whose Kiss faces have been badly drawn on with Mommy's lipstick to gorgeous girls in sexy black cat suits with their hair done up in ugly Gene Simmons topknots. We're talking about several gangs of four teenage friends whose faces are perfect Kabuki replicas of Gene, Paul, Peter, and Ace.

We're talking about a gray-haired lady, two kids in tow, whose spectacles sat on top of a Peter Criss makeup job; and several huge guys with beer guts wearing fake Gene Simmons tongues. We're talking about a big guy with a Bozo the Clown Afro who had his Paul Stanley star around the wrong eye.

Probably the lamest makeup job of all was on channel 8 newscaster Graham Ledger, who was broadcasting in front of a bunch of Kiss fans, in pink lipstick and an even more inexpertly applied Paul Stanley star. The best, by a long shot, were the costumes and makeup worn by four Kiss fans from LA: Leo Quinones, Chance Haas, Chris Malmin, and Jess Harnell.

Haas is a professional costume maker who designs duds for the store Medieval Times. He had sculpted and spray-painted silver huge leather breastplates for Gene (Jess) and Paul (Leo), complete with sharp points and wonderful details, as well as providing all four guys with foot-high platforms boots, complete with dragon faces on the toe tips.

When the four men—bewigged, made up, and, thanks to the platforms, all about six foot six—made their appearance in the parking lot, the whole place flocked around them. Kids asked for autographs. Ledger himself rushed up to interview them. So did I.

"What was the last concert you went to?" I asked Leo Quinones.

"Well, I had tickets to Hootie and the Blowfish. But we've been to see Kiss three times already and we're going on Halloween at the Forum also."

As Quinones's remark indicates, love of Kiss does not necessarily seem to be about love of Kiss's music: I overheard a hot conversation between a KIIS deejay and a lady fan about the unconscionable gloominess of Bruce Springsteen's most recent show there. ("*Serious* does not necessarily have to mean *boring!*" said the outraged deejay—a Peter-job; while his teased-hair lady friend, done up as Paul, nodded madly.)

But although the scene outside the Sports Arena was positively surreal, inside, it looked like any other giant rock concert. The mingled smell of vomit and beer, long lines at the ladies' bathroom, the Who blasting on the stereo between sets...the only difference was the $650 signed platinum record that's for sale at the T-shirt booth. (There's one at each concert, "but they don't exactly sell out every night," says the salesman.)

Once seated inside the giant arena, the number of Kiss-faced patrons diminishes: everyone looks more normal—at least until our pals Leo, Chance, Jess, and Company suddenly make an entrance at about 8:30, just after opening act Fluffy have left the stage. The four of them walk down the aisle of section 24 slowly, hamming it up on each step—sticking their platforms out at a ninety-degree angle, tossing their manes of hair back— and by about the second step, the entire Sports Arena, all fourteen thousand patrons, are on their feet cheering them.

Now you can see why these men went to the trouble (and expense) of doing this. It's not too much trouble to get cheered by the multitudes; not only that, but when they reach their seats, girls start flocking toward them, throwing themselves on their laps, asking to have their pictures taken. These guys are literally more popular than Kiss themselves would be, were Kiss to come on down right now. And it's not like these ladies don't know that Leo and Company aren't really Kiss. They know that perfectly well, but there seems to be something about masked men that intrigues them.

Presently, the lights dim. "Hello, San Diego!" says the disembodied and incredibly high-pitched voice of Paul Stanley...the curtain drops and the giant Kiss sign—a thousand lightbulbs arranged in the Kiss logo—flashes behind the stage. There's a huge explosion and Kiss appear, singing "Deuce."

At this point, the audience goes batshit, and stays that way for the full two hours of the show, through songs taken mostly from the band's first three LPs (1975–78), including "Dr. Love," "Love Gun," "Shock Me," "New York Blues," "God of Thunder," "Black Diamond," etc. Throughout these numbers, thousands of explosions went off. The stage rose and fell at will, and there were other—expected—special effects, like Ace Frehley's guitar, which shot so-called flames out of it, and which later caught fire during his "hot" solo, and then flew away; and of course Gene Simmons's famous vomiting-blood sequence, which wound up with him flying away on Peter Pan wires to the ceiling, his legs crooked perfectly like a fairy princess.

Meanwhile, the band's members are stalking around in their foot-high platforms while fondling their own metal-encased genitals, sucking on their fingers, humping their instruments, and rotating their pelvises. Stanley, in

Paul Stanley of Kiss, San Diego 1996

andy Hoffman

particular, is behaving in a manner that, were he not in full Kabuki makeup, would be called "flaming," flouncing and simpering and wiggling his behind.

True, in its over-the-top, mindless way, it was rather entertaining, but it wasn't quite entertaining enough. After all, Jon Bon Jovi's been known to fly all the way across the arena on wires. Pink Floyd have a giant pig. And at a Mötley Crüe's show, circa 1989, the entire drum kit was lifted up over the arena and spun around end over end, while a nearly nude Tommy Lee soloed. Surely Kiss could have come up with something equally scintillating: an alien landing, or the whole arena could have exploded or something.

Instead, come the exact two-hour mark, Stanley destroyed his guitar—yawn!—and the band were all hydraulically lifted on a riser to the edge of the audience, where they posed and preened in front of a flashing Kiss light, before returning to sing "Detroit Rock City."

For the second encore, Peter Criss came out and sang "Beth"—Kiss's biggest hit—solo, accompanied by a taped backing of strings and keyboards. Sadly, Criss is the only member of Kiss who doesn't quite pull off his role with the inherent dignity of the totally shameless. Perhaps because he's unable to don giant dragon-shaped platforms to drum, he can't help but look like what he is, a little, short, hairy-chested fat man wearing tights and kitty cat makeup; when he appears, all mystique (such as there was) vanishes, never to return.

The band may sense this, because when they come back for their final encore, Stanley suddenly breaks character to utter what almost amounts to an apologia. "Remember," he says (or rather, squeaks), "a lot of things in life may seem important, but every now and then it's time to put them all on the back burner and . . . rock and roll all night and party every day!"

At that, Kiss kicked into the song "Rock 'n' Roll All Night" and the audience, who'd been on their feet screaming nonstop for two straight hours, collectively rose up and figuratively levitated above the arena in a group. They were in heaven: howling and screaming and laughing fit to bust. Every one of them had gotten more than his or her money's worth—and it was fifty dollars for the expensive seats.

But all of this begs the question of what it all means. In 1996, Kiss's tour was the highest grossing of the year; and that's a scary thought. One has to ask oneself: What is it about 1996 that would make an incredibly stupid band of fifty-year-old has-beens who are wearing elf makeup and leotards the biggest band in America today?

Probably the same thing that made people reelect President Clinton five days later: self-satisfaction, a yen for safety, and a deep-seated sense that everything's pretty much going okay, so why rock the boat, or challenge oneself, or whine, or moan, or ask hard questions. "Put it on the back burner," said Stanley, and perhaps that is the moral of this entire book. Perhaps, as the success of Kiss indicates, rock, and punk, and indigenous American culture itself are all on the back burner, until the end of the century, until the end of the millennium, until the second coming or hell freezes over or pigs have wings ... in short, until something unimaginable occurs to make us love it again.

Or maybe that's not it all. Maybe the success of Kiss is just due to the fact that most people do love to dress up. As Munger said, "Its funny how when you put on a mask, you get a whole new personality." And Quinones, quoting Simmons, said, "You don't want to pay good money to see a guy in a T-shirt."

These things are true. But there's something else at work here as well. Sure, Kiss are fun. But Kiss are also—and I think even their biggest fans would agree with this statement—terrible. They are terrible musicians, and terrible singers, and the songs they sing have the dumbest lyrics of all time ever, and are almost tuneless to boot. Criss's drum solo—done here on "God of Thunder"—is almost mind-numbingly bad, as is Paul Stanley's weedle-o-weedle-o-wee solo on the same song. Literally any sixteen-year-old-boy could play either—which must be part of its appeal. Seriously, if Kiss weren't in costumes, any sane person would hate their guts—which is why, when they toured costumeless for ten years before this (minus Criss and Frehley), they were an incredible failure.

That's why I'm convinced that, leaving aside the costumes and explosions and the fond, fuzzy, nostalgic feelings many young men about age thirty now feel for Kiss because they listened to them when they were eight and didn't know any better, Kiss's appeal is now their actual lameness. Everyone in the audience sees through them, and their transparency makes them like Kiss even better.

In short, it's an irony epidemic in full flower, and I have proof: back when I was doing crowd interviews at Lollapalooza in New Orleans, I met a girl named Michelle, who kept telling me how awesome Kiss were instead of talking about Metallica. Of course I asked her why.

Michelle thought about it for a second. "Well you know at the end, when the band comes out to take a bow? Well, Kiss all put their arms around each other, and then one of them tripped on accident on those huge platforms and all of them came tumbling down!"

"It was," she added happily, "*so awesome,*" and I have to admit I saw just what she meant. Three months later, at the San Diego Sports Arena show, I waited breathlessly for the bow, and if Kiss didn't trip themselves up this time, it was only because four months on the road has taught them to put Peter Criss the kitty cat, the only one of them who doesn't wear platforms, on the end of the row.

The sight of him would make the pope laugh; no wonder the audience walks out of there in a good mood. After all, a joke just gets funnier the more people who get it. At this point in time, seeing Kiss in concert is almost like laughing along with the entire world. And the four people laughing hardest are Kiss themselves... all the way to the bank.

Chapter 13

Up from the Underground

History doesn't repeat itself . . . but it rhymes.

—Mark Twain

Rock 'n' roll by its very nature has always been political—the song of rebels and outcasts, the musical reflection of dissatisfaction with the status quo. In the fifties, it commented, albeit surreptitiously, on the repressive and racist nature of society; in the sixties it helped spur on the civil rights and antiwar movements; and in the seventies the punk rock movement was fueled by disappointment with economic stagnation.

But possibly the most radical and rebellious of rock—the apex of its achievements—is rap music. Since 1978 (to all intents and purposes the genre's Year One) rap has done all the things punk ought to have done, on the scale that punk ought to have done it on: had hits, altered attitudes, and changed how the world looked, felt, and thought.

Thus, a history of rap is instructive, because it shows one model of what would have happened had punk been embraced as it should have been. But it's also demoralizing—in part because rap has been co-opted and exploited, just like any other economically successful art movement; but also because rap's "punkiness," as it were, is so much deeper and more meaningful than punk's. Where punk is about frustration and alienation, rap is about racism and roots. There's no comparison in terms of significance—and yet, neither art form has been able to save itself from being sold out to the Man.

ii.

In 1978—the same year that punk was (or rather was *not*) igniting America—the Sugar Hill Gang released the song "Rapper's Delight," thus changing forever the landscape of pop music.

DIY? The trio took a turntable and a broken record (by Chic) and made it into an entire genre. Independent? Sugar Hill Records, its label, was owned by a woman, Sylvia Robinson. Groundbreaking? The record went on to sell 2 million copies, coloring a whole new universe with its infectious new beat.

"Rapper's Delight" wasn't the first rap song by any means—it was preceded not only by other rap songs, but also by music of Gil Scott Heron, the Last Poets, and other African American artists who blended rhymes with turntable technique—but it was the first one to ring out of stores, cars, and radios, like any old AM radio hit.

Rap was clearly the sound of the future—but it wasn't until 1982, when Grandmaster Flash and the Furious Five came out with the song "The Message," the song that was, is, and always will be the perfect archetype of what punk rock is all about, that rap really made its way into the psyche of rock 'n' roll. Seminal, angry, political, and yet utterly, fixedly, pop, "The Message" was a dark song, and yet because it was new and creative, it sounded downright cheerful to anyone who heard it. For the first time since the civil rights movement, black really was beautiful, and that summer, the Metro in Paris was covered with a poster advertising fares to New York City that featured a cornrowed kid with a boombox over his shoulder on roller skates. Deejays, break dancing, Eddie Murphy, Adidas, Spike Lee . . . from that point on, contemporary American black culture had a highly commercial side to it.

Rap also moved ahead a lot faster than rock, especially since acts got ahead by dissing one another, i.e., standing on one another's achievements. Not since its early years had rock 'n' roll seen an audience as educated about its subject and as eager, every month practically, for something newer, fresher, more exciting, as rap's initial followers: the whole hip-hop world was constantly upping the ante of its art form with its ever-changing array of stars.

In the following years, rap did everything punk meant to, and it did it a lot better. It succeeded on its own terms within a marketplace determined to crush it, on independent labels like Priority and Death Row, and it gave meaning and a sense of community, and a jolt of hope to an entirely disenfranchised element in society.

Moreover, if punk is punk because it's DIY, then rap was originally the punkest of all mediums, because kids who couldn't afford guitars or practice spaces were able to cull used records and low-budget recording equipment to make high-fidelity recordings of their own rapping and scratching. Much more than punk ever did, it rang a death knell for a certain type of old-fashioned music—for a sound, an emotion, an actual tempo. Funk, soul, and in particular, cheesy love ballads of the type sung by Luther Vandross and Lionel Richie and the like were banished from the kids' turntables— except in the form of samples. That shit was what parents listened to. It came in handy, but it didn't have the oomph of rap.

iii.

Post–O. J., post–Rodney King riots, I don't think you can overestimate the impact rap has had on black youth. It's one thing for white kids to say that punk liberated them from the bonds of conformity and alienation: there's no comparison between that feeling and the feeling of, say, an African American kid seeing Public Enemy perform live circa 1988. You could ask any member of any African American band, and you'd get the same answer. Here, for example, are Knowledge and Ish of the band Digable Planets, talking about seeing Public Enemy for the first time.

Knowledge: "For black kids in the black community to see a group up onstage in a major coliseum or stadium where you normally would see the Rolling Stones or something like that—to see brothers up onstage in command, brandishing guns and talkin' about black power . . . it made you feel like, 'Damn!' It gave you a sense of power for however long they were onstage."

Ish: "It was surrealistic, really! It was . . . I saw them, I was done. Definitely, it changed my life. We're in a country where we get no power, no say . . . so for us to see a group onstage showing power, and being strong, in a world where I watch the TV and my people are getting disrespected . . . for me to see people around my age onstage doing something I wished I coulda done, that was like—damn—that was power to me."

But with that power, of course, came fear—fear from the white community—and their way of dealing with fear was to assimilate not just the music, but the fashion as well. "True black neighborhoods, they didn't go out and blow N.W.A. up [to the size it became]," says Knowledge. "When you sell two to three million copies, that is not the black community: they can't really afford to buy two million copies. What happens is two or three people in the neighborhood buy the album and everyone else tapes it. Those other albums are being sold in the mall," he adds, "and then we suffer from the effects of what America spawned in the first place."

Digable Planets recognize this problem for what it is: a fundamental tenet of capitalism. "As black artists, we need to [start being] on the receiving end of the commodification of our culture," says Ish. "Like if we come up with a style that comes out of resourcefulness—like if you don't have a belt, or your parents buy you clothes that are bigger for you when you're fifteen so you can have 'em for years 'cause you don't have money to buy new pants all the time, and pants sag all the time, then why should Calvin Klein have Marky Mark on a poster and make millions of millions of dollars? ... That doesn't have anything to do with the place where it came from."

But isn't imitation the sincerest form of flattery?

Ish: "Yeah, it's a form of flattery—it flattens the community it takes from. [Because] it's not just about money, it's about your whole life, it's about feeling like you're worth something in a country that doesn't have any obligation to you.... [The white] community deals in this fantastic look at everything. Everything is aesthetic to you all, where what it comes from is a real lifestyle. So it's not about flattery really, it's about robbery. And once you commodify that, you all get all the chips, and we continue to die."

Ish's words may sound extreme, but when it comes to the marketing of rap, they're not at all off base—since rap music has essentially kept the music industry afloat for the last twenty years. Saleswise, 1996 was one of the worst since 1978; and the only million-sellers were rap. And the same was true in 1979, when rap music came along to rescue rock 'n' roll from a mire of its own making.

Consider, if you will, the world into which "The Message" was plopped. Fueled by hits like the largest-selling record of all time, *Saturday Night Fever* (762 million records shipped), 1978 had been a banner year in record sales. But in 1979, the bottom fell out of the record industry. Because of the gas crisis, the cost of petroleum—the material used to manufacture vinyl—skyrocketed; moreover, radio, once a conduit for Top 40 hits by all kinds of bands, had become increasingly polarized by the use of specific formats meant to segregate audiences into useful marketing groups, and though the polarization helped radio sell advertising, it did nothing to increase record sales.

Added to all that, during the disco era, the record industry had become caught up in a vicious cycle of expensive methods of record promoting on radio that was not conducive to breaking new rock 'n' roll acts. The result was that it became increasingly difficult for new music—for punk and new wave, the sound of which went well against the grain of current trends of laid-back easy-listening rock (like the Eagles and Linda Ronstadt) or disco (Donna Summer)—to find a niche on the airwaves. Fewer, rather than more, new rock fans were being courted, and made. And by 1980, the music industry was in serious trouble: revenues had plunged 10 percent.

Into this disaster two new factors were pitched: rap music and MTV. MTV went on the air in August of 1981, and it immediately became America's largest radio station—and the only one that reached into every region. Even at the start, when it was carried by only 300 cable outlets (as opposed to today's 2,000) it went into 2.5 million homes; thus, from the start, MTV's programming was paramount in determining the future of rock 'n' roll.

For its first few years, however, MTV remained too mainstream, too blue-collar, and too white to appeal to vast segments of youth. It concentrated on British haircut bands and American metal—pretty-boy acts who used lots of naked women in their videos. Certainly, there was no hint that rock 'n' roll had a history: "I don't think our audience is interested in the past," MTV president and cocreator Bob Pittman told *Newsweek* magazine in 1983.

But though the past didn't interest the eighteen-to-thirty-four-year-old demographic, neither, necessarily, did MTV's all-white playlist, and of the first 750 videos MTV aired, fewer than 25 were by black artists. MTV initially persisted in its early years in ignoring black music in most of its incarnations. But by 1985, rap music was easily taking the place of rock 'n' roll in the hearts and minds of America as crucial musical social commentary of youth culture. Boomboxes had replaced transistors in the streets and urban neighborhoods; hip-hop culture was everywhere.

Moreover, acts like Run DMC were reaping enormous profits from an audience that had absolutely no interest in rock 'n' roll. And in 1986, when that same band rapped a version of Aerosmith's "Walk This Way," thus irrevocably melding the predominantly white metal and the predominantly black rap audience into one multiracial mix, there was no turning back. Like rock 'n' roll, rap was going to sweep the nation with or without the help of corporate structure.

At which point, of course, the industry decided to co-opt it, beginning with the show *Yo! MTV Raps,* originally called *Rap Sunday.* Invented by Ted Demme (nephew of Jonathan), *Yo! MTV Raps* debuted in August of 1988, and it immediately proved to programmers that rap music was crucial to its audience. Even in its first weeks of existence, *Yo!* did 50 percent to 60 percent better in its time slot than the videos that used to run there. By 1990, *Yo! MTV Raps* was one of the the most popular shows on MTV. And—unlike other shows, such as *Headbangers Ball*—it consistently aired five to ten videos per show by cutting-edge rap artists, like Public Enemy, D.J. Jazzy Jeff, De La Soul, and many others, who subsequently went into regular rotation.

"MTV is adept at marketing, they can market revolution, they just dilute all the revolution out there, and make crazy, crazy money at the expense of however many people will emulate things, whether they live the lifestyle at all," sighs Ish, of Digable Planets.

MTV may have conspired to defuse rap's impact by selling it to white America—but MTV is always a little late for the train. In fact, by the time the Beastie Boys had contributed their party anthem "Fight for Your Right" to the airwaves (1986), it was becoming increasingly clear that rap music was not merely a black phenomenon: white kids loved it too. That was probably the spur that lead to the formation of the PMRC—Parents Music Resource Committee—an organization whose stated goal was to make the airwaves safe for small children by instituting "voluntary labeling" of records.

Formed in 1984 by the wives of two presidential hopefuls, Susan Baker and Tipper Gore, the PMRC was a watchdog organization whose purpose was to encourage the "self-monitoring" of record content for so-called violent, obscene, and even satanic material. The PMRC ostensibly wanted all major labels to put warning labels on the outside of records. But it also raised issues of more censorious nature. Madonna, for example, was termed "a porn queen in heat" by one PMRC lobbyist. Prince—whose record *1999* had already been subject to an attack by the PTA—was another target: apparently, artistic or musical merit wasn't one of the criteria the PMRC planned on using when labeling records. And inevitably, many of the records that fell under its evil eye were by black artists.

The PMRC's concerns reflected the growing conservatism of America under Reagan—or at least, they reflected the political expediency of catering to that conservatism. To blame society's ills—the proliferation of crack houses, unwanted pregnancies, which were occurring thanks to growing joblessness and Reagan's unending cutbacks of social services—on rock 'n' roll, instead of on the economy, was a tactic that had been tried in the fifties, and with just about as much success.

Still, during the eighties, rock was attacked by the right wing in countless legal situations, and punk and rap were of course its targets. In 1986, for example, rock artist and record-label owner Jello Biafra was tried for having included an insert of a surreal painting by award-winning Swiss artist H. R. Geiger entitled *Penis Landscape* inside the Dead Kennedys record *Frankenchrist.* He got off; a similar fate befell Luke Skywalker of 2 Live

Crew. In 1990, a Fort Lauderdale record store owner named Charles Freeman was convicted for selling a copy of 2 Live Crew's *As Nasty As They Wanna Be* album, and the band itself was also arrested for performing the material, which was deemed obscene by the Dade County police. Freeman's conviction was reversed on appeal and the band was also subsequently acquitted of all charges.

Rock 'n' roll's detractors—though it's hard to believe that it had any—must have hoped incidents like these would deter rock artists from writing controversial songs. Inevitably, however—given the nature of the beast—the opposite occurred. As joblessness increased, as social services were cut, as crack wreaked havoc on inner-city families, as AIDS became more and more prevalent, rap continued to document unerringly the emotions aroused by modern life, and not surprisingly, the emotion most often aroused, in blacks, in whites, in rock fans in general, was anger. After all, the truth inherent in a song like Public Enemy's "911 Is a Joke" makes "Anarchy in the UK" look like "Paper Roses," by Donny and Marie.

iv.

Now, rap had always been a prime target for the PMRC, but gangsta rap came under a positive artillery of fire. One song that was attacked especially was by Ice T's band Body Count. "Cop Killer" was debuted at Lollapalooza, where thousands of white teenagers cheerily sang the ironic chorus—"Wanna be a cop killer"—and watched Ice T do a duet of the Sly Stone song "Don't Call Me Nigger, Whitey" with Jane's Addiction singer Perry Farrell.

But irony on that level has always escaped the watchdogs of rock, from fifties matrons outrage at "Whole Lotta Shakin' Going On" up to the present day. A year after the release of "Cop Killer," the song became the center of controversy when the Houston Police Officers Association put pressure on Warner Brothers to remove it from Body Count's record. Then, by mutual agreement, the label dropped the artist altogether.

Still, when it comes to the topic of punk versus rap, Ice T is the guy to talk to, since he knows both communities inside out. After all, while other punk and rap artists have struggled on the one (black) hand to keep rap pure, and on the other (white) hand to assimilate its inventiveness, Ice T has moved freely between both genres throughout the eighties and nineties.

Perhaps this is because, way back in the early eighties, Ice T used to frequent the China Club and the Masque in LA—venues not known for a high number of African American attendees—where he saw the Circle Jerks, Black Flag, even Minor Threat. "I totally got off on the energy and the rage of punk," Ice recalls now. "I remember hearing those Black Flag commercials—'Daryl Gates, we're comin' for your wife! Black Flag at the Whiskey!'—and seeing those [Raymond Pettibon] posters of guns in cops' mouths."

The poster in question certainly presages Ice T's controversial song "Cop Killer" off Body Count's 1992 debut LP. But Ice T doesn't think punk was that big an influence on his music. "When I was making rap records," he says, "I was coming from a whole other background than music. When I started rapping, I was deeply involved in crime. I was out there hustling, I was pimping, I was doing everything negative. The music was just something for me to do on the weekends, something to have fun and play around with, but then my friends said, 'Why don't you rap about your life?' which was at that point negative.

"And I was like, 'No one wants to hear about drug dealing and shit like that,' but I used to make little rhymes, just for them, the kind of stuff I'd say when I was with my friends. And when we decided to put that on record, that's when they came up with the term 'gangsta rap'. But it wasn't like a preconceived notion, it was like if you were on drugs, and you just started singing about 'I'm fucked up on dope.'

"And that's kind of punkish in a way, but I think it was kinda more real, because it wasn't intentional—it wasn't like I was trying to sound crazy, it was like if an alcoholic made a record about being an alcoholic. When we sang about gang-banging we wasn't trying to make it sound fun, we just sang about it because that's what we were doing. And it just got more and more outrageous as time went on.

"But yeah," he adds, "there's a lot of parallels between [gangsta] rap and punk. Punk is an attitude, it's basically 'Fuck you and everything you believe,' and 'This is how I get down, and I'm about to break your rules for the sake of 'em, and here's my hair in spikes, fuck you.'

"Whenever I see these kids walking down Melrose all punked out with their hair in spikes," he adds, "I'm like, 'Yo, you really must need to tell people to kiss your ass!' "

Ice T pauses. "But what happens is, you get into this culture of people that do it the same way as you and you become normal, inside of your own zone. When you look at rappers, you go, 'Why you got your pants on backwards?' but among them, they're doing the right thing and everyone else is tripping. That's the whole theory of punk—and it's also like rap.

"But lately I've also been thinking that rap has a lot in common with country-and-western music," he adds. "When we'd first go to Europe, they'd call rap 'folk music.' They said, 'This is black folk music.' And if you think about it, a country-western singer sings about his neighborhood, he sings in a lingo that only he cares about, and Johnny Cash, he said he shot a man in Reno just to watch him die—that's a ghetto-boy's lyrics, right?

"Rap's really close to country music because country is music made for a particular neighborhood or climate, like our music. We sing about our neighborhood, we don't care if you don't understand it. We don't care if you can't dig it. And that's the same way a country-western singer sings. They party in their own clubs, they do their own dances, they live their own lifestyle. And when you go in their neighborhood, it's basically the same as our neighborhood, they talk a lingo, we talk a lingo, they have a dress code, we have one; and I guess to square America, it all looks outrageous, but it's culture.

"The funny thing," laughs Ice, "is then they sell all these records and everyone in the media says, 'Who bought 'em?' "

V.

Who indeed? For all its controversy, rap was always embraced by the mainstream, even without much significant radio play.

"One thing about white people," comments Ice, "is they're very, very interested in black music, versus black people being interested in white music. White people were always into the blues. . . . They were into rock when Little Richard did it, they've always been, like, very curious, about anything black culturally. They always investigate it, they find out if they like it.

"And with rap, it was like an open book to our life, by it being such a literary type of music, where it's all these words written out. [We] put the lyrics on the sleeve, and its stories and its lifestyles. . . . It's like information they get about black culture, and they started suckin' it up. It was this picture of a world, especially of Los Angeles, that no one had ever seen. When I started rapping, people were like, 'Isn't LA like David Lee Roth—all California Girls?' And I was like, 'Nah, there's a ghetto in LA.' And they're like, 'Where? How come we've never seen it?' "

One way or another, Ice T's albums, *Rhyme Pays, Power, The Iceberg,* and *O.G.,* were huge hits—and his theme song to the movie *Colors* was an international hit. But his sales slumped in the early nineties when the music became more commercial-sounding.

"When we first started making hardcore rap," explains Ice, "it was intensely nonmelodic and really, really raw. It was like, if your girl liked it, it wasn't good! So of course radio totally said, 'Fuck all you rappers.' And at that point we were totally underground, me, Ghetto Boys, Too Short... all our shit was really really underground.

"Then R & B took the beat of hip-hop and put it into R & B records, because when rap first came out it knocked all the R & B off the charts. [So producer] Teddy Riley was one of the people who started taking the hip-hop beat and putting it behind R & B singers. It was a sneak attack: R & B singers started using our beats. Then you started seeing R & B singers singing in the hook of a rapper, and now what you have is R & B singers singing rap lyrics.

"Dr. Dre, I think he was kinda a landmark crossover,'cause he had just finished producing M'Shelle, who was an R & B act, he came out with *The Chronic,* which was really an R & B album with rap lyrics on it, and that was it: boom, he went like triple platinum. Then Snoop's first album, that was R & B–based, then Biggie Smalls.

"So now what you have is so-called hardcore rap, but really what they're singing over is R & B records, and that gets you the radio play. The music is not as hard as it was; it's diluted for radio.

"It's growth, I guess," adds Ice. "But it's hard for me to make a radio record. And the cold thing is back in the old days, rappers used to get an R & B singer to sing a hook; now, we get to come in for eight bars on their songs!"

Many rappers would have taken this development as a sign to go more tuneful. Ice T took the opposite tack. In 1991, he came out with a hardcore punk band called Body Count, which was influenced, he says now, by bands like Anthrax, Slayer, and Megadeth.

"Body Count was created to allow my friends to play. Also, I'm the kinda person who, after I do something for a while, I want to do something newer, and when I can't find something new, I got to create something new. I guess I've got a lot of ideas, and I guess all my ideas don't fall under one type of music."

Of course, at the time Body Count came out, the idea of a black man doing hardcore was totally from left field.

Ice: "Yeah. But I get off on that shit, see? It's like, if I can't go against the grain, I get bored. I had the first record ever stickered, I went head up with everybody in this world as far as music, I've been on a hundred panels..."

Congress, the whole shit, done it. Rap hasn't let me down, but like Dr. Dre said, I been there, I done that."

As the "Cop Killer" controversy proves, Body Count has had its trouble with the law, but the band (now on Virgin) continues to perform, albeit on a much lower budget level than Ice T, the famous rapper, ever did. In December of 1996, for example, Body Count did a brief tour of California, punk rock style: traveling in a van, playing all the shitty nightclubs, hitting all the small towns—Sacramento, Santa Barbara, Fresno, Modesto—only in Modesto, they got shut down by the police.

In Santa Cruz, the band played a club called Palookaville, which was about half full of curious UCSC sophomores in Banana Slug T-shirts and skatepunks in ski caps and baggy pants, pumped up for a night of punk rock of old. And Body Count delivered to them exactly what they wanted: theatrical outrage, complete with scary silly costumes—a guitarist dressed like an executioner, in a ski mask; a huge and intimidating bass player; a red siren light going around and around squealing for the duration of the show. And Ice T himself, needling the crowd: "They said this town was too mellow for hardcore!" he says, and, "Fuckin' faggot-assed police tried to shut us down!"

Clearly Ice T is playing with the kind of outlaw image that rappers these days are almost required to have in order to be popular or convincing (or, at the very least, written about in the mainstream media).

"Well sure," says Ice, pragmatically. "I think that's one of the essences of rock 'n' roll. If you make it so everybody likes you, you become Pat Boone; you become something Mommy puts under the Christmas tree. And I think with youth, and people in general, there's always some edge to doing something that's a little wrong.

"Somebody got to hate you in order for it to be good rock 'n' roll. There's gotta be somebody after ya, or it's no fun. But usually if you *are* saying something, there will be somebody trying to shut you down, so it's not like you're making it up.

"But one thing that people should know is that just because people make records, it doesn't mean that their political views are correct or it just means that they're trying to yell something. Because every rapper, including myself, may not be on point. Some people think that just because you can make a record, it means you're intelligent. And that's not true. Just because someone has a guitar and enough money to get on a piece of wax, does not mean that he has the correct views. I listen to a lot of rappers who say shit that is totally outrageous to me, that's like, 'What the fuck are you talking about?' The listener has to go through it all and decide for himself. Like I always tell people, 'Don't think everything I think, 'cause then only one of us is thinking.'"

Ice now believes that some of his past music has been over-intellectualized by critics. "I think earlier, my music was crazier, because I was angrier, and unfocused. When you come out of the hood, you're just kinda angry at everything. And when I got older I learned not to be mad at everything, just be *really* mad at certain shit.... It's just that I've realized what's really the problems, and so I'm not just yelling out at dumb shit.

"But the bottom line is, first off, that rap is entertainment. Rap, everything—Slayer with their upside-down crosses, Anthrax yelling, 'I am the law!' Me, going, 'You took our parents, now we have come for your children'—it's all just entertainment. And if you get a message, or you hear something in the middle of the show, that's great, but what you want is someone to come in, pay their money, say, 'Wow that was fun.'

"If you're just out to give a message, you don't need to get people to pay. You just stand out on the corner, get a soapbox and stand on it and talk! But when you try to entertain people, you're trying to make them have fun, and that's really more important. That's why a lot of songs I make have absolutely no value: none. They mean nothing."

In 1997 Body Count released a record called *Violent Demise*, which T calls "less serious and more humorous" than his previous LPs. Meanwhile, Body Count's been on tour in Europe—with the Exploited, L7, and many other punk bands—and he says the experience has affected his writing.

"Rap and punk are so convincing," says Ice. "And it's scary to me that you can go into a country and pump up the people and then *leave*. We think we got it bad, but they got real serious shit over there. Now I've played in the Basque country, and Croatia, and Northern Ireland, and those kids, you start pumping those kids up, they got guns and they're on their way back to the war. You start seeing these kids having it bad, and it changes you. You start singing different shit.

"We played Croatia, and there were kids coming from the war, literally from the war to see the show. They're like, 'We caught a train from the *war,* and after the show we go back to the *war* and start sniping again.' I'm like, 'I can't even start telling you about South Central! I'll just shut the fuck up now!'"

vi.

In 1996, with the industry in the worst shape it's been in since 1978, rap—or what is called "urban" music in the biz—is still the most consistent-selling rock genre (though you might not suspect that merely from looking at concert revenues, television shows, or magazine covers).

But in another sense, rap is no healthier than punk, and its imminent death is literal, rather than a conceptual one. In September of 1996, for example, rapper Tupac Shakur, twenty-five, was shot and killed while riding in the passenger seat of his manager's car in Las Vegas, making him the first notable rock star since John Lennon to be shot by someone else.

Shakur, who grew up in Baltimore and Marin City and played briefly with the fun-loving Bay Area rap group Digital Underground, started his solo career in 1992, and was clearly courting the gangsta life: he was involved in many other high-profile illegal incidents—including sodomizing a fan in New York City and a puzzling shooting affair during the trial.

In fact, both his music and his public image were one long tribute to some imaginary war he was soldiering in against other East Coast rappers like the Notorious B.I.G. (who was himself mysteriously murdered in early '97). Only six days before his shooting, at the MTV Music Awards, Tupac appeared surrounded by bodyguards with a walkie talkie, saying about his enemies, "It's not like we're going to see them and rush them and jump on them. If they see us and they want drama, we're goin' to definitely bring it like only Death Row can bring it."

That Tupac actually had lethal enemies is now certain, but that Tupac also had a death wish as strong as Kurt Cobain's seems just as likely. His songs are riddled with foreknowledge of his own demise (as were the songs on Nirvana's last LP, In Utero). On the song "Only God Can Judge Me," from his second-to-last LP, All Eyez on Me—which, incidentally, sold 5 million copies—Tupac raps, "In my mind I'm a blind man doing time.... Tell me what's the use of trying, tell me what I'm living for, everybody's dropping me, and I'm knockin' on heaven's door."

And then—devastatingly—he winds up with, "The only thing that I fear is coming back to this life reincarnated." That song—like most rap songs—is a constant reminder that racism is like sexism: ingrained in almost every aspect of our lives. It's easy to ignore it . . . if you're white. But if you're black, well—that's why rap is so much more relevant than punk. The battle it is fighting is both real and righteous—and it will be until black

America stops being discriminated against and/or has evened the economic score.

That probably won't happen within our lifetime. But if one is looking for a way in which capitalism and creativity can coexist—a way in which rebelliousness and commercial success are not antithetical—then rap music is the paradigm toward which one must look. Unfortunately, as Tupac's death shows, it's a paradigm that has a pretty high price.

Chapter 14

Places in the Heart

There are places in this world where irony is inappropriate—places in the past, and places in the heart. One such place is Portland, Oregon, where the downtown has no cafés or liquor stores, just a profusion of old-man hotels and steak restaurants called things like Jake's. It looks like a scene from a depression-era photograph, all warehouses and train tracks, and evergreen-colored vistas of the Willamette River popping through the gaps between old brick buildings.

Portland is a city whose denizens will never need sunglasses: the air is so perpetually cool and dark there, it would seem like the world's biggest affectation to don them. It is, however, a place where the burning embers of punk rock are being harbored and hoarded in every corner and cornice. Slack and unpretentious, a vision in black and white, Portland bands huddle together over a little pile of coals, warming their hands and drawing strength from the fire. And nowhere is the fire so strong as in the center of Portland's queercore movement.

Greil Marcus once noted that "there is no greater aesthetic thrill than to see minority culture aggressively and triumphantly transform itself into mass culture." Thanks to Nirvana's diffusion of alternarock values throughout the very fabric of the mainstream, the past couple of years has allowed pop culture mavens to view just such a phenomenon at all-too-close range, and alas, the thrill is gone.

Sure, the economic ramifications of having an indie band like the Offspring all over MTV are inspiring, but where is the rush involved in the sight of Henry Rollins shilling for Macintosh computers, Kim Gordon hawking clothes for uber-hip anorexics, or Courtney Love on the cover of *Vanity Fair*?

If you're addicted to being a member of the underground opposition, you now have to look elsewhere for the sense of exhilaration that the sight of minority culture infiltrating the status quo can give, and at the moment, that means looking queerward.

Queercore—aka homocore, a broad term used to describe punk rock bands formed by out gays and out lesbians whose politically charged music explores aspects of being gay with a defiant mixture of humor and anger—has been cultivating itself for a quite a while, in Chicago, in New York, and bubbling around beneath the surface of the IPU (international pop underground) and riot grrrl movements.

Queercore differs radically from previous forms of gay expression in rock 'n' roll in its extreme sexual explicitness. Lyrics like "It's an orifice of elimination, it's an orifice of exploration," from Pansy Division's "Ring of Joy," for example, or Tribe 8's "Neanderthal Dyke" ("I never read Dworkin / I ride a big bike") are, by conventional standards, more than a little offensive.

To queercore acts, utter abrasiveness is part of the solution. "We've been excluded for so long that we have to balance out the imbalances," explains Tribe 8's Lynn Breedlove. "It's like affirmative action; for a while you have to go to the opposite extremes."

Homosexuality and rock 'n' roll are, of course, hardly a new combination. Bands like the Rolling Stones, T Rex, and the Kinks have all toyed with androgyny, and even effeminate actions, while Boy George, Erasure, and Morrissey have written songs that could be interpreted as queercentric. k. d. lang and Melissa Etheridge have both come out, with no discernable negative effect on their careers.

Many male rock artists have been somewhat more cautious about outing themselves, but Kurt Cobain's statement of bisexuality, followed by a slew of bands appearing, like him, in dresses, certainly did nothing to harm the new queercore zeitgeist, either.

Queercore has been around for quite some time. But it wasn't until the band Green Day took a goofball queer band called Pansy Division out on the road with them in 1995 that the subculture was allowed to peep its little head over the barricades that guard the entrance to mainstream American life—much less even think about making a dent in youth culture. "They [Pansy Division] are just spewing homosexuality and I think that's great," Green Day's Billie Joe Armstrong told MTV at the time, "I think they are the future of what's going to happen in rock 'n' roll music."

Subsequently, in its first two days of release, Pansy Division's new LP, *Pile Up*—actually a collection of B-sides and singles—shipped seventy-five hundred copies, nearly what the band's previous LP, *Deflowered,* sold in a whole year.

Pansy Division, who had been playing around San Francisco for about three years, sing punky, poppy songs about, not to mince words, buttfucking. Led by former Outnumbered guitarist Jon Ginoli, Pansy Division's whole trip is a relentless, remorseless, seemingly endless celebration of anal sex. On its debut, *Undressed,* and follow-up, *Deflowered,* each song supersedes the next in dirtiness and humor: "(Fuck Like) Bunnies" was overshadowed by "The Cocksucker Club," which was trumped by "Ring of Joy," a song that tells you to "take a good long look at a buried treasure / there between your cheeks, a hidden source of pleasure."

In some ways Pansy Division's tuneful repertoire is like one of those really bad jokes that only gets funny on its millionth utterance. Its litany of songs about men with big dicks may be queer in intention, but it is still, after all, a series of songs about men with big dicks, and therein lies its charm: by retaining one of rock 'n' roll's heterosexual constants, it really puts its message across. Kids love it because it shocks their parents even more than "Cop Killer" or "Gin and Juice." Straights love it because it's ironic and funny. And queers, of course, can consider it a call to arms.

On its 1995 LP *Pileup* (a collection of single B-sides and covers) Pansy Division invigorated an otherwise moribund punk scene via covers of songs by Spiñal Tap with the gender reversed: ("My baby fits me like a flesh tuxedo / I want to sink him with my pink torpedo"), Liz Phair ("Flower"), and a particularly seamy version of Johnny Cash's "Jackson," done as a hilarious boy-boy duet with Beat Happening's Calvin Johnson.

They even revitalize Nirvana's "Smells Like Queer [*sic*] Spirit" by injecting the already unstoppable tune with its original defiance via lyrics like "bun splitters and rug munchers too, we screw just how we want to screw" and "forget the closet, nevermind."

Lawrence Livermore, owner of Lookout! Records and the man who signed Pansy Division, says that queercore's closest analogy is to sixties activist music. "Back then there were bands who sang overtly about politics—putting politics first—while there were other bands who had similar views about being against the war and pro-pot, but didn't make it the focus of their music," he says. "Nowadays, certain [queer] bands make that a central issue of their art and music."

Queercore is not a genre, like grunge, however—it's a subculture. The bands involved may be allied with one another in their goals, but they sound entirely different from one another. Tribe 8, for example, who record for the Alternative Tentacles label, which is owned by Jello Biafra, are a loud, fast, and angry punk rock band who often pretend to castrate men onstage during performances.

In 1994, Tribe 8 were invited to perform at the prestigious Michigan Womyn's Music Festival, where they challenged mainstream lesbians' preconceptions about punk rock through their performance, and through a workshop they led to help educate those who didn't understand their message.

"They realized they missed out on asking Seven Year Bitch and L7 before they got too big to play," explains Tribe singer Lynn Breedlove. "But they know they needed to get a younger generation interested, and that PC lesbian folk music isn't going to do it anymore."

Similarly, many young homosexual men are not particularly enamored of the stereotypical gay man's delight, disco. "I've always felt," comments Pansy Division's Jon Ginoli, "that mainstream gay culture not only didn't include me, it was antagonistic to me. People were like, 'You like rock? You don't like Judy Garland?' "

According to John Gill, author of *Queer Noise: Male and Female Homosexuality in Twentieth-Century Music* (University of Minnesota Press), the recent development of queercore is an appropriate response to the current economic and political climate of America. "The cultural profile of mainstream gay culture is complacent, white, male, upper-middle-class. It has no relation to young people growing up angry and scared in the age of AIDS," explains Gill.

"In the eighties," he adds, "people were not too bothered by gay identity—they were too busy having a party. Hence the popularity of artists like Boy George or Erasure. Queercore shows that there is a new form of anger in society. Young gays are determined not to (*a*) assimilate, and (*b*) adopt the bourgeois culture they see around them."

Gill also points out that many cutting-edge purveyors of popular music have been perceived as "queer" when first seen by a puzzled mainstream. "I suspect that, early in his career, certain white people called [male] Elvis Presley fans queer."

"In the late seventies, if you were into punk rock," agrees Ginoli, "you got called a faggot anyway, whether you were or not. That's why homocore has this obvious connection to punk."

Growing up in central Illinois, Ginoli had, in fact, liked bands like the Buzzcocks, the Ramones, the Au Pairs, and the Slits. After attending college in Champaign, Illinois, he formed a band called the Outnumbered, which released two albums in the mid-eighties. He was, however, the band's only gay member. "The other guys were really cool with it, but I felt I couldn't sing openly gay lyrics because it wouldn't be fair to them."

In 1987, the band broke up. "I said, to myself, 'If I'm ever in a band again, it will be an openly gay band,' " says Ginoli. "So I figured I'd never be in a band again."

A few years later, however, having relocated to San Francisco, he saw the Austin-based rock band 2 Nice Girls. "They did this song 'The Queer Song'," he recalls. "It was really funny and gutsy and in your face, and I thought, 'Why aren't there any *guys* doing stuff like this?' "

Inspired, Ginoli went home and wrote four such songs on the spot, which resulted in the formation of Pansy Division. The group soon had a local following and an album (*Undressed*, 1993) out on the Lookout! label—the same label that released Green Day's first two albums. After Pansy D's second LP, *Deflowered*, came out in 1994, Green Day's third LP, *Dookie* (on Warner Bros.), went platinum, the band insisted on taking their former labelmates out on the road with them.

"The thing about going out with Green Day that was so great," says Ginoli, "was that we got to play to really young and diverse crowds. I always thought I'd only be playing to people like me, in their twenties and thirties who are disaffected with the gay scene, who wanted to hear something gay that wasn't techno or disco or show tunes."

Another surprise, Ginoli says, is the extreme positivity of the response they have gotten. A tour of Australia and New Zealand saw Pansy Division being greeted by ecstatic crowds.

Tribe 8 agrees. "Here in SF, there is a community of gays, lesbians, queers, and punks, all kinds of freaks from all over, and we validate each other every day," says Breedlove. "It's really important for us to get our music out by touring and going to towns where there's not a community like this, to let people know that they aren't excluded, they they are included in something, however small, however peripheral."

Ginoli: "Just being there, delivering the message, exposing the kids—it's just a way to get through to people that being gay is normal, it's something that some people are, and that they go around doing the normal things that other people do.

"Right now," he adds, "we're more popular with straight people than with gay audiences, but the gay people who do get us love us. We get thanked profusely just for existing."

What are straight people getting out of queer bands? "Don't a lot of people go to reggae shows?" asks Breedlove rhetorically. "And isn't all reggae music about the white devil?

"It's really important for white people to teach each other about racism and for straight people to teach each other about homophobia," she adds. "That's why some guys like us—because they know that their ilk has caused a lot of problems!"

There is also the possibility that Pansy Division's up-front lyrics are merely the latest way for kids to shock their parents, one step short of getting pierced. "Looking at the mail orders," says Livermore, "I can tell a lot are from heterosexual little kids who just think it's fun music. It's not just to annoy their parents, it's to annoy the jocks at their school."

Pansy Division's stance would also seem to preclude them from getting any mainstream airplay. Last year, radio station Live 105 invited the band to play on Live 105's Gay and Lesbian Parade float, but they haven't been heard on the air.

But for bands like Pansy Division and Tribe 8, the suffix "core"—a word denoting punk rock roots—is just as important as the prefix "queer." They are extremely concerned with retaining their credibility, fearing corporate co-option, the punk rock dilemma that recently skewered Green Day.

Some queercore protagonists feel that the media are already exploiting queercore by turning it into a trend that will subsequently be defused and discarded—as they have previously done with riot grrrls, angry women rockers, and a few other radical subsets of rock 'n' roll. To "go mainstream" is unpunk—and, apparently, unqueer.

But the incorporation of queer culture into the mainstream is of slightly more political importance than the vaguer ideology of opposition that indie rock represented. (After all, indie rockers, the vast majority of whom are white, upper-middle-class, college-educated males, could hardly be called an underclass.)

In light of that fact, it becomes less surprising that this burst of what Yeats would call passionate intensity would come from an all-women band. Not only is the all-guy band sound pretty much all played out, but guys who join bands have everything to gain: the respect of their peers, a girl- (or in Jon Ginoli's case, a boy-) friend, and—in this, the heyday of alternarock co-option—a shot at Sonic Youth–sized superstardom and the concomitant bucks.

Women, however, still have more to risk and almost nothing to gain from joining bands, since bourgeois culture has little to offer them that's worth thinking about. (What? Flowers? Liposuction? A date with Johnny Depp?) Thus, in punk rock, women are still margin walkers—and the band that is simultaneously marginal and potentially commercial-sounding is Portland, Oregon's Team Dresch. Less obnoxious in both its personal manner than Bikini Kill, less off-putting than Fifth Column or Tribe 8, Team Dresch stand in direct opposition to most all-girl bands in that they are completely unconflicted about their sexuality, their long-term aims, and their music.

Moreover, more than any all-female band today, Team Dresch rocks out. Its two records, *Personal Best* and *Captain My Captain,* have nothing in common with hardcore queercore, with riot grrrl, grunge, or even its members' bands' antecedents. Instead of the boring old rage of the disenfranchised female, the hoarse Medusa shouts of Donita, Kat, Kathleen, and Courtney, Team Dresch provide a precisely furious but tuneful roar—and passionate but fluttery vocals that sound like Kim Deal would if Deal sang songs by Railroad Jerk.

As if that's not enough, their songs have the energy of Biohazard crossed with melodies as hooky as Oasis's; and *Captain My Captain* opens with a kick-ass verse that could lead a generation into battle: "My mom says she loves me / but I don't think she does / 'cos she only loves me when I act just like she does." The rest of the album is equally salient, one long stretch of music that literally redefines the very boundaries of what is punk—while even questioning its very own motives on songs like "Yes I Am Too, But Who Am I Really?" and "Remember Who You Are."

Team Dresch isn't really concerned with assimilation (like L7) or challenging conventions of femininity (like Bikini Kill). Its songs are intensely personal rather than political ("Hate the Christian Right" is an exception). It is, however, in many ways modeled after Fugazi, both in band dynamics—lead vocals are shared, switched, and intertwined by Dresch, guitarist Jody Bleyle, and on the earlier record Kaia Wilson—and also in that it has a policy of playing all-ages shows and aggressively interfering with the audience if the audience gets out of hand. Like Fugazi, the band has the sheer chops to back up their moral dictates: its contextual idiosyncrasies are merely convenient adjuncts meant to facilitate the main thing, music.

Like Ginoli, Bleyle says she doesn't feel a lot in common with mainstream queer culture. "When I was at Reed, I identified way more with the rockers than I did with the women's-center people," says Bleyle. "I went to one women's-center meeting and I felt totally . . . I think what I felt was total gender dysphoria; I felt like a boy who wasn't supposed to be at the women's-center meeting; I felt like a spy who was going to say something wrong or do something wrong and get kicked out."

As for mainstream gay culture, she distrusts it as much as straight punks distrust the corporate version, like marketing by Skoal. "These days, everybody has a lifestyle marketed to them—and when it gets more specific, it gets more offensive," she comments. "I mean, we're all getting marketed to, but when you open *Out* magazine and it's that specific, and the bourbon ads are like so . . . embarrassingly homocentric . . . the more offensive is."

Like marketing punk rock to snowboarding fifteen-year-olds? "Mmm. Especially now you have punk kids with green hair in first grade. that's when it starts to seem like the hippie thing, like going to see a reggae show at the Cotati Cabaret. It's like by doing that, they've made punk ineffective. They've fuckin' . . . put the antivenom into punk."

ii.

When punk becomes ineffective, it's time to change its tune—and that's precisely what Bleyle and her friends have gone ahead and done, inventing a new-sounding voice for the disenchanted, a genre all their own. It's a stance that's somehow beyond queercore, or perhaps it's above it; soaring over the jokes and silliness that characterize it in San Francisco; soaring, also, over the murky world around it. In Portland, after all, punk must exist side by side with the burgeoning redneck world that birthed Tonya Harding, and a conservative governmental streak that sheltered Bob Packwood and doled out one of those all-purpose homophobic bills called Proposition 9.

Portland is also home to a group of people for whom the terms "gay" and "lesbian" seem totally outdated—like saying "colored person" or "Negro" rather than "black" or "African American." Dresch's Jody Bleyle is a perfect example of this type of postgay person. Charismatic, effervescent, humorous, smart, she is the embodiment of everything cool about queer. From a distance, the trousered, bespectacled Bleyle conforms to the word "dyke," but up close and personal, she confounds it utterly. The first time I met her she was lovingly toting a three-month-old baby named Isabelle, the daughter of Hazel's bassist, Brady Smith. It turned out she is Isabelle's de facto nanny, taking care of her by day while she runs her record label out of her home, in exchange for free rent in the baby's parents' basement.

An unlikely maternal streak isn't the only way that Bleyle—who runs

Candyass Records and plays drums for Hazel and guitar in Team Dresch, confounds one's expectations. Her sport of choice is golf, and she doesn't call herself a punk: in high school, she proudly admits, her favorite band was Depeche Mode.

"I listened to, like, Kiss all the time, and the *Grease* sound track and *Saturday Night Fever* sound track. I listened to Joni Mitchell for like a year straight... and Patti Smith.... Patti Smith is like my punk element, but I didn't relate her to punk, I just thought punk was..." She does a punk drum change. "All I was interested in was singing, and I didn't hear any singing, and I wanted to sing along with my records, so like I loved Patti Smith because I loved singing along with her, and I loved Olivia Newton-John because I loved singing along with her, I loved John Denver. I just loved music more than anyone else I knew, and it didn't matter what kind of music. I liked Rush. I'd learn Rush songs on the piano and learn it note for note and just sing.... I'd learn any pop song on the piano and just *sing*."

In high school, Bleyle was into music—just not punk music. "Every single day after school I recorded on a four-track with my friend John. I played music nonstop in high school.... I was in every vocal group, every jazz band ...every stage band, every marching band, I played saxophone; and every day between all my periods I played the piano down in the practice room, and every day after school I went home and John and I recorded songs on our four-track. They just weren't punk. I thought punk was tuneless.

"I was a late bloomer," explains Bleyle. "I didn't come out in high school, it was totally under my radar. I didn't define myself as a punk or a queer; I was just a musician; I was obsessed. What was it I was doing the other day that was so retarded? Oh yeah, I wanted to get my ears pierced and my friend was like, 'Jody, you're supposed to do that when you're like thirteen!'"

When Jody was seventeen, she moved from Connecticut to Portland to attend Reed College. "There was a great rock scene when I went to Reed. There were tons of bands and we'd have shows in the mailroom all the time, shows in people's dorm rooms and at houses, all the time. There were like thirty people there who were literally majoring in rock. There were people from Madison and Minneapolis, people from D.C. and from Boston...all of whom would be like, 'Here, you *have* to listen to this Rites of Spring record; here, you *have* to listen to Husker Du.' And I was just like flooded within a couple of years.

"And this was at the same time that SubPop was starting to happen and I would go down to Satyricon every night by myself and see Tad and

Nirvana and the Fluid and I just loved all that shit. It was 1987. And I worked at the radio station, I hung out there and played records, and you know, bands would come through and play at Reed and I would talk to them and take 'em to the radio station and they'd pull out records and I'd play 'em.

"The coolest thing was that people were from all over the country, and they'd say, 'Listen to this Bullet LaVolta record,' and so I'd learn about scenes from people who were really, really passionate about it because they'd grown up in those scenes. 'Cause I'm from the suburbs, and even though I grew up like three miles from the Anthrax Club in Norwalk, Connecticut, I never went to it. And people would come here and go, 'Oh, we used to play the Anthrax Club all the time,' and I'd be like, 'Duh...' I'd heard about it, I knew it existed, but it didn't interest me 'cause I didn't think they were singing there."

Then one day at Reed, Jody continues, "I said to this boy, 'Is there any hardcore music that has melodies, that people really sing?' and he goes, 'Yeah, it's called melodic hardcore,' and he brought me to his room and he played it for me and I started really getting into it, and I really loved Reagan Youth, and that's when I started listening to that and realizing that there's lots of different ways to sing beyond...Patti Smith and Joni Mitchell."

Pretty soon Jody was in Hazel, in which she played drums. But presently, she decided that Hazel wasn't fulfilling her emotional needs. "I just got sick of just being at a Hazel show and going, 'Oh, by the way, I'm queer.' I was like, 'It has to be more then this. It has to.' I started to realize how [being punk and being queer] couldn't be separated, because unless I am vocal about this part of my life all the time, it doesn't exist."

For a while, Bleyle played in an all-woman band called Love Butt, which she liked because of its noncompetitive atmosphere. But none of the other members were gay. Then she met Dresch at a Hazel gig in Olympia.

"After the show," Bleyle recalls, "I went off to her for about twenty minutes about how Tribe 8 was looking for a new drummer and I was going to try out, and I couldn't take it anymore and I wanted to play with all dykes...and blah blah blah, and I didn't even know Donna was a dyke!"

"And then I met Kaia around the same time, and she was like, 'I'm playing with this girl Donna in Olympia, you wanna play with us?' and I'm like, 'I know Donna, yes!' And ever since then it's been like...that's the way it has to be."

Now Bleyle plays in both bands, though she says Team Dresch takes up the majority of her time. "Hazel is a good foil or balance. Like, for example, if I walk into the studio with Team Dresch and I go, 'Who's got the keys to the van, you assholes!' everyone will be like, 'Uh, I'm sure,' and like, try and dialogue with me or get mad or whatever, but if I go up to Brady and say, 'Give me the key to the van you asshole,' he just takes 'em out of his pocket and throws 'em on the floor."

Bleyle's casual acceptance of the difference between male and female social relations—particularly in a band context—is where Team Dresch shows such a huge leap forward in sociosexual politics. Remember the old joke, "How many feminists does it take to change a lightbulb?" and the answer is "*That's* not a funny subject"? What separates Team Dresch from previous angry women bands—the riot gr r rls, Hole, whoever—is its humor and its courage.

But perhaps the most unique thing about Team Dresch is its nonjudgmental character. It is the first up-front gay band to successfully reduce queer issues to the dust they ought to be. In TD's hands, queer love—and hate, and lust, and betrayal—are merely love and hate and lust and betrayal: stuff that anybody can relate to. Team Dresch don't shy away from gender specifics—"Growing Up in Springfield" and "She's Crushing My Mind" and "Screwing Your Courage" are pretty damn frank—but their take on sexual orientation is all-inclusive. As Jody says, "You can't extrapolate from Pansy Division. You can't listen to their music and go, 'Well, I'm not a fag, but I understand wanting to be treated more fairly.' You listen to a Pansy Division song and you go, 'God—I didn't know you could use cock rings like that!' Whereas with our songs, the idea is just that, well, liberation is liberation."

From the straight point of view, this is crucial: it means that we—straight people—can join Team Dresch's fray with the light of battle in our eyes as well. That may sound specious—of course one can and should always support queer issues—but in fact so much of current queer culture is deliberately alienating to straight people. One can understand their impulse to shock the namby-pamby sensibilities of the despicable bourgeoisie, but there is something intrinsically defeatist about the alienating tactics of militant gay activists.

But Team Dresch are anything but defeatist. The minute you hear them, you know what's been missing from the Superchunks and Sebadohs of the world. It might be going too far to say that Team Dresch put the venom back into punk, but their goals have a lot in common with the furious passion of English punk, circa 1977. Like the British underclasses, they feel oppressed and persecuted, even in danger, just for being who they are. So before most Team

Dresch shows, the band holds a self-defense workshop onstage to teach women and queers how to defend themselves against attack.

Team Dresch also make a point of setting up shows that are friendly to queers. "Especially if it's a bar," says Jody, "we try to make sure it's advertised as a queer show, so that queers don't feel like they're going to a straight bar. Not that anyone's disinvited, but just as a step toward making it a safer space for everyone.

"Now there's lots of all-dyke bands that go on national tours that keep the connections alive." She adds: "Tribe 8 is always touring. . . . The girl network started it and it expanded it to the queer network, and then when people saw us playing people just came out of the woodwork and said, 'Hey, I'm going to do queer shows in Detroit,' or whatever. Every day people write me and say, 'You've got to come to El Paso, there's no queer music here, no punks here, no girls here . . . you've *got* to come.'"

But if there's no queer music or punks, are there people in the audience?

"Yeah, there usually is, because even if there's only forty kids that haven't made a band that's good enough to play, they usually have some band to open for us that's just getting started. Like one time we played in Minot, North Dakota, and the first girl band to be *ever* in North Dakota opened for us, and that's happened more than once. So there are people, they just usually get passed by, by every band, even Fugazi.

"We all share touring lists and secrets like, 'Oh my God, there's this awesome scene in Rapid City, South Dakota, or whatever.'"

Because she is also in Hazel, Bleyle is able to see the alternative, underground scene from every side. "A lot of the Hazel-equivalent bands in Portland can't really go on a tour by themselves; they'd have to open for a major-label band that has a song on the radio because they don't have this network. Whereas I can set up a tour in a couple of weeks that will have people at every show, because we know about these pockets."

Bleyle says the difference comes down to a band's expectations. "A lot of bands in Portland don't necessarily expect a thousand-dollar guarantee, but they're working toward that, and the way to do that is to open for big acts," she points out.

"But with a lot of queercore and girl bands, we just want to meet other people like us. If we meet twenty-five people who are packed into somebody's living room, we have a great time and we know that next time there'll be fifty people. We're willing to do that, because it feels *great* to meet twenty-five people in El Paso, Texas, who are so happy that your band came to their town!"

As Jody says, it's all about liberation—about building a community of like-minded people whom you can feel comfortable with, about forging new values and reassuring yourself that others like you exist in this, the most sterile time in our history.

"People sometimes ask me, does it feel bad or are you insecure to know that people just like you because you're in a band?" comments Bleyle. "And I say no, because if someone likes me because I'm in Team Dresch, I believe that they do know me, and that they like me, and I like them and respect them too—and that is a really great feeling.

"The word 'punk,'" Bleyle adds, "to everyone it means a bunch of different things. The kids who see me out walking around Portland who have Mohawks think that I'm a big poser, alternative rock sellout or whatever. But I know that—it's in the lyrics of our songs—that I would probably have committed suicide if Team Dresch hadn't formed.

"Because people, kids, who write me letters that say they need to meet me and that they needed to hear my music and that it's helping them get through a really hard time and they gave it to their friend who's having a really hard time...those things literally take my day from what's my point of being alive today, to going, 'Okay, there is a point.'

"People need to find each other and talk to each other and people need to know we're alive," adds Bleyle, as she scoops up a bunch of books, and her best friend's baby, and blows out the door to go to tonight's big gig. "I mean, I need to know that these people are alive one hundred per cent as much as they need to know that Team Dresch is alive."

And that, come to think of it, is really the whole point of punk. Isn't it nice to know, even if you're not queer, that sometimes—just sometimes— the system works?

Chapter 15
Time Stands Still

If you consider "punk" to be a sheerly musical term, then only a certain type of young, thin, and flashy loud-fast guitar band fits into its confines. But if you consider it as a concept, few bands are more punky than Pearl Jam, the multi-platinum-selling Seattle-based band responsible for ultra-mainstream classic rock hits like "Alive," "Jeremy," "Daughter," and "Not for You." They must be punk—else why would they be so vilified by the mainstream media?

Really, no other band attracts the kind of negative attention they do—not Hole or Guns 'N' Roses, not Marilyn Manson, not N.W.A.; not the Sex Pistols at the height of their so-called shockingness.

Pearl Jam, however, offend the more powerful members of the music business the way that punk should have done all along—not by shock tactics, but by threatening and/or ignoring the very machinery that creates record sales.

To the biz at large, Pearl Jam have done three unforgivable things: refused to make music videos, refused to give interviews, and tried—albeit somewhat unsuccessfully—to challenge the existing structure of ticket sales around the country's larger venues, first by filing a class-action suit in superior court against Ticketmaster, then by booking a tour without this agent, in alternate venues, in a failed effort to bust what they see as a ticket-pricing monopoly.

The media would have it that this last venture failed, because the suit wound up being dropped, and the tour fell apart due to weather problems and illness. But the long-term effect of Pearl Jam's efforts was to cause ticket prices to be spontaneously lowered by acts touring the country in 1995.

No wonder Pearl Jam are a pariah! They are personally responsible for vast corporate entities like Ticketmaster, MTV, and Epic Records not making as much money as they conceivably could have done, had Pearl Jam played by their rules. If punk is learning to live outside the confines of capitalism without compromising one's own aims, then Pearl Jam is indeed a punk rock band—as punk as the Pistols, at least.

The Pearl Jam organization must have lost vast amounts of money because of these efforts to challenge the status quo—but they haven't gotten any thanks for it: instead, *Rolling Stone* magazine spent a good long time over the fall of 1996 digging for dirt on the band's individual members—particularly dirt on Eddie Vedder, the band's main man and leading figure.

The magazine failed to turn up anything more damning than the fact that, seventeen years ago, Vedder was popular in high school and belonged to the drama club. The magazine used these facts to argue that Vedder is a phony: untortured, untroubled, untalented—and unworthy of the legions of fans who look to him as a lone moral being in a nasty, ugly world.

Alas for *Rolling Stone*, the only visible effect of this story was when Soundgarden played New York City, and Chris Cornell publicly used a copy of it to wipe his ass, saying, "This is all this is good for."

ii.

At the time the story ran, Pearl Jam were in central Europe, playing ten-thousand-to twelve-thousand-seat sports halls throughout Poland, Germany, Hungary, and the Czech Rupublic. In America, Pearl Jam are perceived as a band whose earnest, rather straightforward music and moralistic lyrics are embraced by well-meaning boneheads. Rich white alt-rock fans who love Sonic Youth and Jon Spencer revile them, as do ravers, hippies, and metalheads.

In Europe, however, Pearl Jam's place is less rigidly defined. And in eastern Europe—where the right to even listen to such stuff happens to coincide chronologically with the rise of Pearl Jam, grunge, punk, and alternative rock—Pearl Jam are the new messiah.

And really, why shouldn't they be? Consider the Czech Republic: one of the few countries outside England, the United States, and Germany with a punk rock tradition of its own. Contrary to the belief of Sonic Youth, Irvine Welsh, and the tenets of the musical *Rent,* the Czech Republic is still literally and figuratively the center of Bohemian life: always has been, always will be. Its most famous citizens—Milan Kundera, Jan Patocka, Martina Nav-

■ Eddie Vedder and Kim Warwick
Charles Peterson

ratilova, Franz Kafka—have always been forward-thinking, edgy individuals; this is, after all, a country whose president is both a playwright and an avowed fan of the Velvet Underground.

Heck, even Mozart, an Austrian by birth, used to premiere his operas in Prague because they weren't appreciated in stodgy old Vienna: the Czech Republic is just constitutionally art-damaged. But it is also constitutionally tragic, since the Czech Republic has a history of oppression that goes back a thousand years. From Good King Wenceslas—who was clubbed to death by his brother (Boroslav the Cruel) in A.D. 929—to politician Jan Masaryk, who was (probably) defenestrated to death by the Communists in 1948, the country has been the scene of countless political crimes, and yet its spirit has emerged indomitable and innocent, determined to shine on. Who can forget the story of Alexander Dubcek's courageous effort at fighting the Communist tanks during 1968's heartbreaking Prague Spring, or, twenty-one years later during the Velvet Revolution, the population gathering at Letna Park and shaking their keys in the face of Soviets, and whispering, "It's coming . . ."?

From the Prague Spring to the Velvet Revolution in 1989, the country then known as Czechoslovakia was held in thrall to a Soviet-built golem called the State. But in 1968, when Communist tanks rolled up Wenceslas Square, it was already too late to take back rock 'n' roll. You know the widely held theory that the Beatles are responsible for the unsuccess of Communism, the idea being that, once heard or seen, the band's irresistible and ineradicable aura was too strong for even the most committed socialist to wholly reject? In Prague, this theory does not seem unreasonable. And of course such a constitutionally arty country as the Czech Republic, once freed from the boring bondage of Communism, would embrace modern American pop culture with a vengeance.

What's more surprising is the manner in which American pop culture has embraced it back. You can't go to Prague now without noticing America's insidious influx: in between Prague's cute cobbled pavement and stately eighteenth-century buildings, the place is being overrun with the detritus of Western Civ, i.e., ski caps, baggy trousers, and vegetarian burritos.

Nowadays, on Stepanska Street across from the French School and the cyber-café, there's a snowboard equipment store called Mystique, where you can buy boards, caps, Black Flys, and Doc Martens. Near the Museum station there's a restaurant called Radost which serves pad thai and cappuccino to the tune of Portishead and the Chemical Brothers. And one cold November afternoon, while walking in the Nove Mesto, I was startled to see a branch of Catwalk, a groovy raver store in San Diego that sells used clothes, hair dye, chains, and raver tapes.

iii.

In short, since the Velvet Revolution of November 1989, the place has become overrun with Americans and Americanism and all that that implies. You can see 'em at the Globe Cafe, inhaling soy-milk cappuccinos and discussing their lactose intolerance, and the sight (or sound) of their inconsequential concerns conspires to give one pause. The joint venture—spiky castles and pad thai noodles, socialism and capitalism, MTV, and the Czech Republic's quickly-desiccating vernacular culture—is either the absolute cutting edge of post–cold war culture, or else it's depressing as hell.

The only way to come to terms with it is to look at the past. Then one feels more assured of the rightness of the present. After all, in 1977, when punk began—and incidentally, around the time that Václav Havel signed Charta 77—Czechoslovakia was at the height of its repressive years, its citizenry held in check in part by the common enforcement of Article 202 of the criminal code, i.e., "disturbing the peace."

According to Havel (in an essay in *Open Letters*), Article 202 was "one of the ways to induce in people the required 'realism,' including the surrender of one's own dignity and honor, and the acceptance of what amounts to an official moral commandment: 'Don't try to put out a fire that's not burning you.'...

"It's a law," added Havel, "that faithfully mirrors a power that is happiest when people don't socialize too much with each other...when they don't go out very often and, when they do go out, always behave quietly, inconspicuously, and with proper humility...a power that sees society as an obedient herd whose duty is to be permanently grateful that it has what it has."

The playing of punk rock is almost by definition an act of peace-disturbance, which must have made it even more attractive to those few Bohemian youths who heard it in those cold and quiet days of yore. Can you imagine its magical call to arms? Anyway, perhaps because of its proximity to Germany, or perhaps because of its Bohemianism, Czechoslavakia is one of the few Eastern Bloc nations that has a punk scene of its own. But it's not punk like you and I know it: Zappa, John Lennon, Pere Ubu, the Velvet Underground, and the Plastic People of the Universe are revered here with the same fervor as the Sex Pistols and the Damned.

This is because many Czechs heard them all at the same time, on very badly duplicated cassettes smuggled into the country circa 1979. Miroslav (Mirek) Wanek, leader of the band Uz Jsme Doma, for example, was a Czech teenager whose youth was informed by the punk zeitgeist; and in many ways his experience merely mirrors that of any old American teen. (Ben Weasel, for example. Or Tim Armstrong.) Unlike those teenagers, Mirek really had something to fight against, although Mirek was a bit young to be bitten by revolutionary fervor: he was only six when the Russians took over. But when he was seventeen years old and a resident of a town called Teplice, he saw his first punk band at a music festival in Prague called "Jazz Days," organized by a cultural organization with ties to the Western world called something like "Jazz Section."

"In those days," explains Mirek, "you could call something jazz and then it was officially okay."

Why? "I guess 'cause it's from the thirties, Russian Communists like things from the thirties. They are not afraid of old things—its everything new that is a problem."

At the festival, held in a large hall, Mirek heard two Czech punk bands, Zikkurrat and Psi Vojaci. (The latter is "Dog Soldiers" in Czech.) "I saw these bands," recalls Mirek, "and I found two things. I found punk, which I didn't know was punk, because nobody called it that. . . . And I like this kind of music, fast, few chords, and nice melodies, but a little bit in your face.

"That was one thing, but the second thing was, I found it was possible at age sixteen or seventeen to have my own band and do what I want. The people in those other bands, they were fifteen or sixteen—and I saw for the first time in my life that the same people same age like me, not something from heaven, but normal like me—that they do their own music and own songs and own style, and all these things, and I wanted to follow that. So this moment for me, it opened my mind."

At the same time—sometime within the same month, he thinks—Mirek got a copy of the Damned's first album on cassette, as well as a tape with other songs on them: songs by Fred Frith and the Art Bears, also the Residents for the first time, and "some Chrome and Pere Ubu and the Ramones and Killing Joke all on one tape. And I thought that this was all punk."

Of course, the Art Bears aren't what Americans consider punk—but Mirek's experience must have been heightened by the fact that, at that time, in Czech, the only music on the radio was Russian folk music or bad

Czech pop. "Abba, for example, was very progressive to us," recalls Mirek. "Abba was beautiful, it was like the Beatles!"

Anyway, Mirek went home to Teplice and started his own band, called Fourth Price Band or FPB, which was a way of saying the bottom rung of society. (The band sometimes used English initials and sometimes Czech on their posters, in order to confuse the police.) "The first songs I did with FPB were cover songs of all these bands. So we did the Damned, of course, we did Residents, and we did some Pere Ubu and Sex Pistols... and we tried to play them, but for all these songs I wrote Czech lyrics because I didn't understand English. Some I'd heard only the chorus, like the Damned's 'stab your back,' which I shouted over and over.

"And at the same time we started to make some of our own songs in this style.... Of course, they all sounded very similar to 'New Rose'! But from the first, I wrote Czech lyrics for that, which was not usual. At that time, a lot of people sang in English, or rather, they didn't speak English, they just followed the sound of English... what we call Swahil-English because it's not really English, just the sounds.

"Anyway," he adds, "What we did was punk, but also because of the influences of Art Bears and so on, I think it was kind of special punk."

Surprisingly, for the first few years of its existence—from about 1980 to 1983—FPB didn't have a hard time getting gigs. This was because the Communist system had a hard time regulating musical styles, and when Fourth Price Band began, the party was very taken up with suppressing hippies. These, the Party thought, could be readily identified by their *long hair.* Short hair, spiky hair—hell, even green hair—wasn't on the books as being illegal, and in Prague in those days, everything was done by the books.

"The system was really slow, and for maybe fifteen years, they had been fighting one thing: long hair!" explains Mirek. "All the time it was, 'If you have long hair, you are an enemy.' That was easily said. And now, there is somebody who has short hair... and they thought it might be the same as long hair, but what they have to use for the law is 'Long hair is bad.'"

There was one band, Extemporare, Mirek recalls whose leader signed the Charta and who had to change their name for every gig they played. "It sounds like a joke now, or whatever, but it was that slow. And a lot of these officers and people, they didn't find out about punk till much later. So for maybe one or two years it was very easy to play, everywhere, there were very many bands."

Throughout the eighties, FPB had lots of fans—not necessarily punk fans, but fans of the fight, young, old, long hair, short hair, hippies, and students alike. People came, Mirek recalls, "to be somewhere where it was dangerous to be, and symbolically to do this fight...People often ask me about the Plastic People of the Universe and about how they were all in prison for years. I respect them a lot: their fight was our fight. But they played music what we call underground, and they were really political. They had lyrics that were like 'fight communism,' things like that.

"And that wasn't punk. Punk in our country was together with new wave, and the lyrics were mostly about just some jokes, and just free thinking...just free mind....You could say whatever you want. What was dangerous at the time was that you must have a permit for each of your lyrics, you know, write them down and show them. But all these punk bands, they ignored this, and wrote whatever they wanted. And often it was nothing, just stupid things, though sometimes it was something important. And what I think was, these Plastic People, it was easier for the system fight them than it was to fight new wave and punk, because they were clear. They would sing about the fight, and there was one side, and they were the second side, it was all very clear.

"But this punk, it was about ignoring the system, not fighting it, just ignoring it. We said, 'We do what we want, we are free, we are humans, it's our life and we can use it how we want and there is no system that can stop that.' And I don't think you can imagine how these officers were really angry about it! They couldn't figure out—it was like with the hair, they couldn't say, 'Oh, it's long hair or short hair or green hair...or this lyric is wrong.' But they knew that it was."

Originally, FPB played gigs at "jazz" clubs and parties, and at weddings where, funnily enough, no one was actually getting married. But in April of 1983, there was an article in the main Communist ideological newspaper, *Tribuna*, with the headline "New Wave with an Old Coat." And this, says Mirek, was the beginning of the fight. "The article was really strange, mixing up punk and new wave up with hard rock, jazz, and Bob Dylan," he recalls. "But from this article all the officers in the whole land got directions: This is dangerous; fight."

After that, things got really difficult for Czechoslovakia's punks. "Police would check IDs and put you in prison for two days, or whatever," Mirek recalls. "They'd stop the show in midset, turn on the lights and check IDs for two hours. Oftentimes they'd just catch you and beat you, or put you in a car after, and take you and leave you out of town in the forest, with no money, no anything, and you have to walk back and it's at night and it's cold. Everytime we played we were afraid we wouldn't finish the set."

Mirek himself got caught a few times: in fact, the state authorities went to his college and had him expelled for a year. (He returned to finish up later, thanks to the kindness of some teachers there.) There were other problems too, to do with playing and existing, and finally, in 1986, Mirek left the band to join Uz Jsme Doma. (FPB's drummer formed New FPB, with two new members, but disbanded in 1987. After the revolution, they got back together to record an album of their old songs—reunited, like the Sex Pistols.) "Now we can do whatever we want," admits Mirek. "And in Europe, punk is coming back, and there are a lot of punk bands in Prague or if not punk, they follow that style. But what I see now in my country and the whole of Europe is thousands, thousands, thousands of bands that want to be like Nirvana! And I don't understand this at all because when I started punk, of course, we played covers of the Damned, but we did it our way, in a special way, maybe you wouldn't recognize these cover versions, and very soon we wrote our own."

And how did the revolution affect Czech punk?

"Basically, from the early eighties, there started to be like ten, fifteen bands, maybe five punk bands and ten new wave bands. And after the revolution, some of these bands continued to play, and everything was a lot easier . . . but some of these bands they went down because there was no quality. Before the revolution, if a band had no quality, it didn't matter so much, because there was always the fight. But after the revolution there was no enemy, so they fell down. . . .

"Punk was originally a cult of bad things," he adds. "But to me, the meaning was more, from the beginning, that negativism . . . that is like the backside of politicism. You sing about bad things because you like nice things."

Now that the nice things have come—the pad Thai, the snowboarding stores, the cappuccinos, the stereophonic equipment, he implies, punk isn't a necessity—it's merely a luxury, a status symbol even.

Last July, Mirek went to see the Sex Pistols for himself at the ice hockey sports hall at Vystaviste. "I read a lot of critics that said they are not so good, and not so dangerous right now, but you know . . . I loved it. I loved them. I think I really understand what they do and how they do it and all these things . . . I feel really near to them right now."

Mirek pauses. "You know, my idea was always that the biggest problem with the Communist system was not in the system, but in society. There are people who are snobs or like wild animals, and these people, if they have power *anywhere*—it's bad. With the Communists, these people have full mouths of talking about humanism, about freedom, about socialism and all these things, but why they [do it] is because they get good money for it, and a good job for it.

"And of course, we hated them, but my thought is, it was not something special for Communist system, it is also in America, and also in England in seventy-seven. I think there is a point where this experience, for the Sex Pistols or whatever, was very similar to ours. Of course it was a different political system, but the people are the same everywhere, we hated the same enemies. Only our enemies had a bit more power over us; they had red shirts."

iv.

In September of 1996, Michael Jackson came to Prague. He played a concert at Letna Park, the largest field in the city, and for a week prior to the concert, caused to be erected a thirty-three-foot-high statue of himself in his pseudomilitaristic garb, which was placed on a pedestal on which until recently stood a statue of Stalin. The ads for the concert in the newspaper *Mlada fronta Dnes* played on the incident of six years earlier, using the phrase "It's coming!" atop a Michael Jackson logo.

Perhaps most disturbingly, there was a moment during the concert (which sold 123,000 tickets) when Jackson baldly pantomimed scenes from Prague's recent real-life history. During "Earth Song," a tank rumbled onstage, a soldier jumped out and aimed a gun at Jackson, and was subsequently disarmed by Jackson, and then offered a flower by Jacko and a child.

Sometimes I wonder if we in America have too much freedom. And I wonder about the difference between a democracy in its infancy and a democracy in decay. To me, they look the same: full of Targets and IKEAS and Kmarts in the wings. I worry that our music is the sonic equivalent of wiping out the Jewish ghetto and replacing it with ugly high-rises.

On the other hand, maybe I'm wrong. Maybe Jackson's act of impiety suggests some glorious defiance, a proud sense that history is a meaningless joke. These countries had a culture that was nearly wiped out by the Communists (and before that, by the Germans and Prussians, and before that, by the Turks), and now they're adopting ours. Is that okay, or is it anathema? This is the question I asked myself when I was in Prague. Is the "world domination" of pop any different than the racial hegemony of Attila the Hun, who conquered Prague in the ninth century? Or is it just part of the historical process—an addition to, rather than a subtraction from culture as a whole.

I went to Prague to see my friends' band, the Fastbacks, play a gig there, but became as gloomy and downhearted as the weather itself when I received an urgent call on Tuesday from Fastback Kurt Bloch, saying the band was snowbound in the Alps and was going to have to cancel their gig opening for Pearl Jam that night.

Discouraged, I trudged off to the sport hall near Vystaviste anyway later that night; I had nothing else to do. What had happened was, the equipment truck carrying Pearl Jam's backline and sound system had gotten stuck over the increasingly snowy Brenner Pass in Austria. They could make Prague in time for the gig, but only if they bumped the starting time back till 10 P.M. and canceled the opening act (who drove straight through to Vienna instead).

To do so also meant that the forty-person crew would have to set up four trucks' worth of sound and light equipment in three, instead of the usual ten, hours, piling the amps and lights on stage instead of "flying" them from the ceiling, as is usual.

Now in America, a gig with a three-hour starting delay, horrid sound, and no opener might be resented, even by the notoriously kind Pearl Jam audiences. Not so in Prague, where by 9:30 there was an almost violently anticipatory audience. The sports hall—normally an ice hockey rink—was sold out well beyond its capacity; kids sat on the steps up and down the aisles, as well as on railings, barricades, and any ledge they could find. Kids are running around like maniacs, looking anything but bummed.

"Our dream is to see Eddie Vedder," says Alexandra, seventeen, a petite Polish girl in a tie-dyed T-shirt. Alexandra and her friend Justina have taken the train here from Warsaw. "We've been waiting four hours...and four years, so we don't mind how long we wait."

Thirteen-year-old Teresia and her boyfriend, Jirka, are from the suburbs of Prague. They heard on television that the show was delayed, but they came early anyway, just to hang out and be excited: their favorite bands are Metallica, the Exploited, and the Sex Pistols.

And all over the arena, one gets the sense that the anticipation is part of the experience, that any wait will be worth it. Pearl Jam came on at

10:30, and despite the sucky sound it was one of the better shows I ever
witnessed, a lot like those Beatles shows one sees in scratchy old footage,
which took place through one amp and were savaged by screams. Pearl
Jam was roaring, blistering, holding the huge crowd rapt in its firm grip, just
pouring it on out. Watching from the top of the arena, you could see a sea
of shining faces, singing along, surfing forward, positively praying—a vast ex-
panse of children with their lips parted and their hands in the air, emitting
hot waves of love out of their eyes and their mouths and their bodies.

And I don't know. Perhaps it is a mistake to read too much romance
into the coming of punk to Second World countries. Perhaps it is a mistake
to export these aspects of our culture anywhere at all. But say what you
will about Pearl Jam's music; heard in eastern Europe minus the ridiculously
prejudicial and contextual niceties of U.S. rock journalism, it rises above
every other band currently touring for emotional and sonic satisfaction and
depth. And what better motto for Prague could there be than "It makes
more sense to live your life in present tense"?

V.

The word "Budapest" conjures up a romantic picture of gaily dressed
ladies circa 1892, boating down the Danube River in the elegant company
of red-coated hussars. But when I arrived there with the Fastbacks in the
middle of November, I found instead a city riddled with fast-food outlets
and topless bars, as if the only aspects of capitalism that were actually
wanted when the walls came down were Pizza Hut and porn. Gone is any
aura of romance or elegance: it is dingy and foreboding, a hollow shell of its
former glory.

The city's atmosphere is like the setting of a John Le Carré novel: walking through the monolithic brown corridors of the Keleti Pu, one sees double agents at every turn.* My abiding impression of the city will always be
of the statuary-ridden horizon of the Buda side rising out of a sad gray mist
on the Danube, and a lone member of Pearl Jam, hands thrust in his pockets, wandering about the Erzsebet Bridge in the lonely manner of band
members on endless foreign tours.

Needless to say, punk rock can hardly thrive in such surroundings: although Budapest's proximity to Austria (two hours by train) has meant that

---

*Pu is short for train station in Hungarian, a word that literally translates into English as "the place
where the tracks lie side by side."

some American bands have toured here, its underground ambience is more that of sixties hippie than MTV. In the summer, Budapest hosts a weeklong music festival called Diaksziget, while underground drag clubs that play techno and house exist in abundance in the quarter.

Homemade guitar-based punk rock, however, is pretty limited, in part by the economic enormity of getting the necessary equipment—besides which, the only kind of Hungarians who could afford such stuff are not the ones who would want to play it.

This points out one of the great ironies (and failures) of punk in Eastern Bloc and Third World nations, which is that, in such places as Hungary, the rich and well-educated and well-traveled young people who have access to things like CD players and imported records are also the people who have the least use for rebellious sentiments and raucous music. In fact, they have a vested interest in disliking such a thing, maintaining instead the established order.

In Turkey, for example, a young woman told me that most of the rich kids she knows only like bad Turkish pop music, and when I thought about it, that made sense: most of the rich people I know in the States like Michael Bolton and Hootie and the Blowfish. She herself didn't come from a wealthy family, but her father was a professor at the university, and her mother was one of Turkey's first-ever female engineers. They had made a point that their children learn English and travel to western Europe when they were in their teens; now, this girl worked as a runner for Turkey's only Western music promoter—which meant she spent last week agreeably shepherding members of Pearl Jam around town, hanging out at nightclubs and giving the cabs orders in Turkish.

Unlike the Czech Republic, Hungary is quite economically depressed; and as in Turkey, only about 25 percent of its citizens have stereo equipment of any kind. Perhaps not surprisingly then, Pearl Jam's show was only about three-fourths sold—and some of that audience came from nearby Vienna. There were also about four hundred members of a nearby army base, stationed because of Hungary's proximity to Croatia (one of whom was holding up a giant banner of Jim Morrison superimposed on an American flag throughout the entire show).

Walking around the parking lot of the arena in the drizzly early evening, I also saw groups of kids who'd come from Slovakia, Slovenia, and even Bulgaria (the latter were selling stolen copies of "No Code" posters for less than fifty cents each). The metro stop near the arena also contained an outdoor market where you could buy a sausage or a fried Spam sandwich or some polyester socks; and in the drizzly November evening, I felt momentarily elated, like I'd dropped into another culture at last.

But inside the Sportscarnok was far from exotic, since all sports halls the world over look exactly the same. They are clean caverns of anonymity, ringed with gray stone corridors that lead to bland white dressing rooms and ring out with the hollow sound of sound checks—checks— checks. What takes place in these places, be it sports or rock 'n' roll, is a cattle call of sorts, but it's a call that has its appeal.

Inside the Budapest Sportscarnok, the Fastbacks took the stage at 7 P.M. and did okay with the gig, meaning they weren't outright booed, like they've been before, in Salt Lake City and in Rome. Kim in her special silver jumpsuit, Kurt frantically whipping up the crowd with his leaps and windmills, Mike in a three-piece suit, Lulu smiling giddily, did a series of quick, tuneful songs—"Fortune's Misery," "Impatience," "K Street," "Going to the Moon"—and merely looked ecstatic throughout: after five weeks on tour with Pearl Jam, they were still thanking their stars for what they consider a sudden gift of good fortune—and certain other people think a just reward for services rendered in the cause of punk.

And it's a reward they do deserve, that is for certain. The Fastbacks have long been my favorite band, but their genius became clearer as I listened, as if for the first time, to the words of "In America" near the end of their Budapest set. "Lately been thinking about what / it means to be in a country that's not all it should be / but I don't know if I'm ready to leave… do you really want to be in America? Somewhere else might be better, but I don't think that I'd be willing to get up a go."

Kurt wrote those words when he was twenty years old, when the idea of playing Prague and Budapest—hell, even playing California—was completely out of reach. But that song is as true as it ever was, and it always will be. Up until five years ago, the lines "Who says the government's on your side… think for yourself who cares what they decide?" would have gotten him jailed here, but now that they won't, it's almost even more glorious to hear them sung.

And as I listened to him sing them, I suddenly knew the answer to my original question. Is it okay that we are exporting punk rock twenty years after it was invented, sending its aged echo out into the Second World? Hell yes! These days rock 'n' roll often seems banal and clichéd and played out and over, but in Budapest and in Prague, I found that it—and I—was still entirely educable, still wide-eyed, still brimming with lust for its lessons in love.

Chapter 16
The Light's on You

My strength is that I am not alone in this world
calmly and openly I took my place in the great
struggle . . .

—Nazim Hikmet

In her essay on the movie *Nashville,* Pauline Kael once asserted that the love of country music "is about a longing for roots that don't exist." Certainly this is also what punk rock is all about: young people digging desperately for some fragile cultural roots in hard ground, in places that are pastel and suburban and hostile to things of the spirit.

If you are white and you grew up in America anywhere outside of New York City, chances are you know the kind of place I'm talking about—a beige place, with lots of fast food in it, where the aesthetic stimulus is limited to Julia Roberts movies and baseball stats. In such a place, what roots are there for a post-Boomer kid to find beneath his oblong tract home, or on the radio, or on TV? If they exist at all, they can only be grafted from the roughest of turf—from garage rock, and bad metal, and boogie, and beer—and then cultivated in the ruinous soil of the American mainstream, watered with nothing but recklessness and hope.

Given the conditions, it's a miracle that any bands were ever formed, any thoughts ever thought, any songs ever sung—and no wonder such that did didn't thrive, but were driven to perform for themselves, for nothing, for years on end, for the fun of the thing alone.

My dear friends the Fastbacks have always been just this type of punk rock gardener, unwittingly combing the hard soil of society for something to call their own, and finding it in punk rock. I wasn't there when they first got together, but I may as well have been, because life in America in 1976 was the same all over the country: a living room screening episodes of *Charlie's Angels* and the oft-watched *Brian's Song.* Even rock was limited to midnight showings of *The Rocky Horror Picture Show* and *Don Kirshner's Rock Concert*—an important thing to remember next time you're slagging MTV.

All three original Fastbacks—Lulu Garigulo, Kim Warnick, and Kurt

Bloch—were born in the early sixties and grew up in suburban Seattle. They went to junior high and high school together, although Kim didn't know Kurt, "except that he loved Queen." Lulu is a half-Japanese girl who, according to Kim, looked Puerto Rican: "She had an Afro and bright red lipstick and she always looked really badass," recalls Kim, "and she listened to Earth, Wind and Fire and the Ramones and Lou Reed."

Kim knew Lulu through her cousin Shannon; after high school, she and Kim used to hang out with Kurt and his brother Al's band, the Cheaters. The Cheaters' drummer used to leave his drums behind in Kurt's parents' basement, and one day Kurt decided he wanted to play drums in a different band. So he taught Lulu some guitar and asked Kim to play bass, and they began doing covers of songs by the Beatles and the Damned. ("We were terrible," recalls Kim, " 'cause Lulu couldn't stand and play and sing at the same time.") Presently, they drafted a fifteen-year-old neighbor boy called Duff McKagan to play drums in their band, the Fastbacks.

In 1982, the Fastbacks released their first LP, *The Fastbacks Play Five of Their Favorites*. Lulu once told me it was often compared—at least, the few times it was ever listened to—to the B-52s and the Go-Gos, the only two other bands people could think of with girls in them, but in fact, it is closer to a Ramones LP, enticingly tuneful but short and sharp, a sloppy paean to rootless existence that culminates with a song called "In America."

Because this is the thing you have to understand about the Fastbacks. They are unpretentious and shy and not very well known, three geeks plus whoever they can draft to drum, but they are also, no kidding, the best punk rock band in America. Something about them just rips up one's preconceived notions about the genre, imbuing it with a meaning that's original yet true. They're neither angry nor cool, but they are clear on the concept: to them, punk is for fun, not profit, and if it has a message at all, it is merely that they exist. As Greil Marcus wrote in the liner notes to their LP *The Question Is No,* "the Fastbacks are an unreconstructed punk band—or maybe just constructed—and full of pop. There's no attitude in their music and very nearly no style—instead a headlong, needless impulse to communicate; to come across . . . what you hear is real life, real talk, lifted, dramatized, slamming through the walls."

Duff was only in the band for about a year. In 1983, he moved to LA to join a different, less punky kind of band. When his band came to Seattle on its first tour two years later, the Fastbacks kindly allowed them to open for them, putting out a flyer with the big word FASTBACKS on top of the smaller name band, Guns N' Roses.

■ Fastbacks backstage in Budapest with Eddie Vedder

Charles Peterson

In the eighties, the Fastbacks were popular in Seattle for a while, among a tiny crowd of people: once they got to open for Iggy Pop at the Paradise, and once for P.I.L. (Where, meanly, they were all made to stand all in a row in front of the curtain, with the drummer to the side at the end.) They put out an album or two, on Kurt's friend Conrad's label Pop-Llama, and singles on many other labels. In the course of their career, they've had twenty-three different drummers. In the '80s, like most people in their twenties, all three of them had day jobs and night problems, culminating in a dark period for the Fastbacks around about 1987, when both Lulu and Kim didn't feel much like being in a band and Kurt—who did—joined the Young Fresh Fellows. The 'Bax never broke up—from 1987 to 1990, they played gigs occasionally and even released a record called *Very Very Powerful Motor*—but they were, to all intents and purposes, "on hiatus." And alas, their timing was not ideal, since it was right during the time that the Seattle music scene was slowly becoming revitalized, thanks to a new local label called Sub Pop, and a handful of bands like Mudhoney, the Fluid, Tad, and Nirvana.

In 1990, Kim went to work at Sub Pop as the office receptionist. But despite her band's long-term local reputation, they weren't signed to the label, because their sound wasn't grunge; it was too punky (not to mention girlish). After Nirvana's huge success gave Sub Pop a vast amount of cash in 1992, however, the label kindly decided to let the Fastbacks put out an album—a collection of its self-produced singles called *The Question Is No*, which cost the company exactly zero to produce and sold about two thousand copies.

In 1994, the label put out *Zucker*—again, the Fastbacks gave the label an already-made tape (recorded for free at Conrad Uno's Egg Studios) and Sub Pop helped them launch a few two-week tours. Nineteen ninety-five saw the production of *Answer the Phone Dummy,* their first non-self-funded LP, which garnered them a couple more rabid fans. Late in the year, one of those fans called up and asked them to open for three dates of his own band's six-date makeup tour of the West Coast: two nights at Salt Lake City's Delta Center (home of the Utah Jazz) and San Jose's Spartan Stadium, home of the San Jose Clash.

This fan's band was called Pearl Jam, and at some point, in anticipation of the big event, Kurt figured out that the three-day total audience of all three gigs would equal many more people than had seen their band play in its entire existence.

ii.

So Imagine being a Fastback and about to play the biggest gig of your life by a factor of twelve thousand. You would perhaps approach the Delta Center with a bit of trepidation.

First you park down in the special lot, where members of the Utah Jazz generally place their Camaros and Lexuses. Then you walk through the gaping loading dock into a maze of giant gray corridors. Presently a security guard points the way to the visiting team's dressing-room door, and you tiptoe in, feeling completely ill at ease. To make matters even more intimidating, it's all sized for your average member of the NBA, so gargantuan lockers tower over everything. The place has the feel of an expensive boardroom: there's plush carpet, pristine showers, an oversized purple couch that looks like it's made of the hide of Barney.

In short, it's not your average rock 'n' roll dressing room, which is usually distinguished by its smallness, its smelliness, and the many depictions of male genitalia that cover every available surface. I think the 'Bax might have turned and fled in sheer terror from this frighteningly white room, if it didn't have some graffiti all its own: two-foot-high letters spread across one wall, painstakingly constructed in black gaffer's tape. It reads, "Welcome Fastbacks, Love Ed Band and Crew."

Presently, Eddie himself drops by with a bottle of wine, ostensibly to say hi, but more likely to experience the pleasure that comes with true, generous gift-giving. He watches the Fastbacks shyly, from a corner, as one thing after another appears like magic—things that, even after fifteen years, have never been their share: a parking pass, a crew, a room to lock their instruments in, roadies, a catered dinner, a bottle of Tanqueray. Each little courtesy sends the band into paroxysms of excitement, until, about one half hour before going onstage, Fastbacks music starts to bleed into the dressing room, and their cup abruptly runneth over.

It seems that Pearl Jam has programmed the arena PA to play *Zucker*, the theory being that the audience will like the Fastbacks better if the music sounds familiar. "Oh, no," sighs Kim. "This is too much. Has anyone ever been so thoughtful?"

At which point Eddie, who has been curled up in a corner, suddenly disappears.

Eventually, it comes time for the band to play, and despite a warning from Pearl Jam's stage manager that they keep the set under forty minutes so as not to irritate the crowd, it goes a little better than expected. Some people even cheer for them. Out at the merch booths, the band sells four-teen T-shirts. And although afterward a few mean kids lean over the balcony railing and say to Kim, "Your band sucks! Go back to Seattle!" by this time it is way too late to hurt her feelings. Her bubble is unburstable. "I remember learning how to play 'Eight Days a Week,' " she says dreamily on the drive home. "I remember not knowing how to sing into a mike. I remember when Lulu couldn't play guitar standing up. Fifteen years but it's all been worth it, every second, just for one night. This was the payoff; this was the top."

Well, it was a fair assumption—but it turns out Kim is wrong. In January, Vedder asks the Fastbacks to play live on his private radio show, *Face Pollution,* along with Soundgarden and Mudhoney; later that month, he guest-sings along with them at a party for the movie *Hype!,* which was playing at the Sundance Film Festival, and he sings along with them on their next record, *New Mansions in Sound.*

Later that year, he asked them to open for Pearl Jam for its entire U.S. East Coast tour—and then to continue on to Europe, to play twenty-six dates in fourteen countries. At that point in time, the Fastbacks had sold a total of about ten thousand copies, all titles included—and effectively, never seen a dime. (Like most bands, whatever they earn at gigs goes into the hallowed band fund, for instruments or gasoline.) They had now been together as a unit for seventeen years.

iii.

November 1996. The previous section how the Fastbacks' equipment—bass, guitar, and drums—came to be lurching about Europe, encased in a number of anvil cases stamped "Guns 'N' Roses" (Duff having kindly lent them the necessary things in which to stow equipment when on a big tour). Up Alps and Pyrenees, through the Rhine and Loire Valleys, across various historic plains and valleys, in the company of a huge amount of Pearl Jam equipment—while following behind it, in a little red van, are the heroes of this piece, Lulu, Kurt, Kim, and Mike Musburger (who's been their drummer since 1995).

The band is being escorted around Europe by a jaded Dutch road manager named Mat, who finds their propensity to go sight-seeing in each town mildly disturbing. Mat's road-managed many an American punk band, but none that didn't need a wakeup call every morning. The 'Bax, however, have an uncanny ability to get up at seven and see the town before it's time to drive on to the next gig. "It's not rock 'n' roll," says Mat again and again, frowning.

But this is the 'Bax's ultimate rock tour, and they don't want it to degenerate into "If it's Tuesday, it must be Belgium." Ireland: Fantastic! England—not quite so great. Warsaw, Berlin, Paris, Rome . . . where the band had lire and shit thrown at them . . . all the great cities of Europe flash by, all fall.

"But every backstage looks alike, except there's no graffiti and sometimes the deli tray is better than others," comments Kim good-naturedly. "And the van is still kind of shitty and uncomfortable. Can't kick that part out. Even on tour with the world's biggest band, we've got one foot back in punk rock."

In Switzerland, the band opens for Sebadoh, and gets fabulously drunk afterward with Lou and Jason. In Groningen, the Fastbacks play their own show. It's preceded by a set by a band called the Whats, which consists of Mike, Kurt, and Eddie Vedder, who turned up at sound check, having taken the train all by himself from Pearl Jam's last stop in Germany. The Whats do Who covers and other impromptu songs, till someone in the audience yells out, "You suck! Let the Fastbacks play!"

Eddie says, "Hey—they're my favorite band too!" and cedes the stage.

And so it goes. The Fastbacks fly higher and higher—through the grimly cynical First World and into the snowy white Second, inching ever closer to the mysterious Third, the scene of all resurrections and religious experiences, to the Middle East. To a Muslim city 14 million strong, to a place that has only hosted rock concerts in stadia by acts like Michael Jackson and Tina Turner, and whose eager, plaintive kids are virgin to the joys of live rock.

iv.

Ottoman Empire writer Bahloul Dana once called it "the heaped miracle of Istanbul . . . a mountain of minarets and rainbow domes, lofting into the illimitable turquoise of the Eastern night," and to my luck-sodden eyes, Istanbul is still exactly like that: one long blue vista of blue sky, air, and water.

It is, as Orson Welles once said of Acapulco, a "bright, guilty city," but like San Francisco and Seattle, it is set in a place so beautiful that whatever shitty street you're on has a horizon overlooking it that hallows and softens all its ugliness and enpleasures its atmosphere, so that one never quite despairs of life, whatever vile smell is emanating from one's near vicinity.

In short, it is a cross between the *Iliad* and the Apocalypse, a bizarre DMZ of cultures where the past and the future meet, greet, and eat; a twisty city of sprawling, roofless tenements bordered by an ornate vista of a thousand minarets and a sky full of light made up of black smoke and pure gold.

Istanbul has a population of 14 million people, but on Tuesday, November 19, the Fastbacks became, to my knowledge, the first genuine American punk rock band to play in the country of Turkey. They were opening for Pearl Jam, of course, but even Pearl Jam's gig was a bit unusual: Turkey has hosted many big pop stars in stadia of late—Tina Turner, Michael Jackson, and Rod Stewart all played there in 1996—and the city has a jazz and blues club scene of sorts, but there is no sort of venue for a midsize rock gig. Thanks to the magic of radio, kids there know all the same rock songs that we do, but the cost of bringing even a Pearl Jam—sized band to play there is prohibitively expensive.

Metallica played Istanbul about four years ago, but other than that, the venue Pearl Jam's show was in—the World Trade Center—has hosted only two other gigs: Duran Duran and Status Quo. (Neither one drew too many people, to the puzzlement of the promoters.) The result of this dearth of pop culture is that when a band finally does make it over, the kids are ready to rock.

Ready? Okay, so that's a bit of an understatement: the Pearl Jam gig sold twelve thousand tickets, at 10 million liras each, which is a lot of money to a Turkish teenager—and a lot of tickets considering that Pearl Jam's albums have sold a total of about five hundred CDs in Turkey (though the number of cassettes is well into the thousands, as cassettes sell ten times what CDs do here).

But just because the Fastbacks are the first punk rock band to play Turkey doesn't mean that punk rock—or Pearl Jam, strangely confounded— is unknown there. This was made clear to us one night when we were taken, along with some of Pearl Jam's crew, to a nightclub called Kemanci in the Istanbul neighborhood of Kadikoy.

We got there through a wondrous maze of streets made reckless by nutsy cabs, but inside, the Kemanci Club looks uncannily like a nightclub in Manhattan or San Francisco: the walls are decorated with car parts, stuffed lizards, and American license plates, as well as a bunch of bright signs with the names of rock bands written in neon: Led Zeppelin, Rolling Stones, and...oop!—Bon Jovi.

On one wall there is a curious painting: it's an imaginative depiction of

Leonardo's *Last Supper*, with Jesus being "played" by Jimi Hendrix. To his right, he stretches out a hand toward the apostles that are dead: John Lennon, Bob Marley, Jim Morrison, and Elvis. To his left, he stretches out a hand to all his live ones: Bob Dylan, Bono, Robert Plant, and Sting.

We all stare at this painting for some time, feeling somewhat damped by its implications. Presently a band takes the stage—in English, they would be called "Cockroach." We all feel very wary: will they play originals, and suck—or horrible covers of "Stairway to Heaven"?

The lead guy—long hair, mustache, leather, and chains—clears his throat and the band begins. Their first song? "I Wanna Be Sedated." Second is Pearl Jam's "Animal," and third, fourth, and fifth are all by Green Day.

Kim turns to me, grinning, as Cockroach busts into a Bad Religion song, and says: "See, punk's not dead, it's alive and well and living in Istanbul."

I wanted to stay to interview the band, but our hosts were already pulling us out the door, and up the street to another club—Gitar Bar—where a band is playing a version of Cream's "White Room," which segues, sadly, into "Purple Haze."

"Oh my God!" exclaims Kurt, excitedly. "We've come ten thousand miles and wound up in Pioneer Square!"

And it's true: despite its dearth of McDonald's, Turkey is not quite as different as one might hope. I'm always astonished at the way every country I've ever been to is obsessed with Jimi Hendrix, partly because the subject of his songs and so on has so little to do with America—with reality, or life in general.

V.

The smallness of this world we live in is made even more evident the next afternoon, when Lulu and I take the ferry from Hayarrat to Uskudar to go to the Asian market. As usual, the Bosporus is packed with boats: big and little, old and new, ferries, yachts, tankers, ocean liners, hoopties and beaters of every description, buzzing back and forth between Europe and Asia, rounding the Golden Horn, chugging under the bridges that link up the city's islands, and looking like they could belong in any era at all, from Justinian's, through Atatürk's, to the third millennium, circa now.

The ferries have no gangways; you just leap across the water and sit on a rough bench on the side—you can lean over the water and feel its

Kurt **Bloch**
Charles Peterson

spray on your face and look out at the lovely bridge. But as Lulu and I sat down on the little bench outside the boat, the Turkish girl nearest us looked up and gasped. "You," she said to Lulu, "are you in the Fastbacks?"

Now it was Lulu's turn to gasp. "Yes...do you know us?"

"My brother worked at Sub Pop last summer," said the girl. "He sent me all your videos!"

Her name is Ipec, and she is literally the only person anyone of us even knew of in Istanbul: the tour manager had put her on the guest list earlier that day. Ipec thought our meeting was unbelievable, but to us it was by the way. After all, how many times have you seen your one friend in Hoboken on the PATH train, or run into a friend at JFK Airport? That sensation that the world is small and comfortable and with you wherever you go is just one of the byways of punk rockdom. Six degrees of separation? Try three...or even two. Once you're involved in punk, the separation factor shrinks to nearly nil.

vi.

Ipec was on her way to class at the university, so she couldn't come with us to the venue, which was out by the airport. Alas, as a venue, the World Trade Center left something to be desired. Picture, if you will, a giant square box—utterly modern except for the fact that it is spewing great puffs of black coal smoke. (Everywhere in Istanbul smells of something other than oxygen; that's kind of par for the course.)

One half of this building is being used for a trade show full of home furnishings; the other half is rapidly filling up with Turkish teens, who came in specially chartered buses from the center of town and have been waiting all day for the show to begin. (This also puzzles the promoter. "Why are they here? The show doesn't start till eight and they know it." We're like, "Oh, it's always like this at Pearl Jam shows," but he still doesn't quite seem to get it.)

Out in the parking lot, our bus met with a genuinely weird sight: a host of kids with green hair cheering on the bus as it pulls up to the loading dock, and dotted in between them a few bodies prostrate, flat on the ground. They're facing east, not Eddie: it's prayer time in Islam, and this time when I heard the muezzin, I felt remarkably like joining in.

As a matter of fact, before we arrived in Turkey, we thought the Fastbacks' set might be kinda weird: that there'd be no girls in the audience or that the band would get booed—which just shows how little we know about modern Turkey. In Turkey, women have always been allowed to retain their property; and as far back as 1909, Kemal Atatürk—one of the original "Young Turks" who overthrew the sultanate, outlawed harems and polygamy, and helped rip veils off Turkish women—said, "Is it possible that, while one-half of a community stays chained to the ground, the other half can rise to the skies?"

Turkey's had its ups and downs politically since then, from Atatürk's own scandalous massacre of the Armenians to its current human rights violations and scandals, and that's one reason that going there made me reassess some of the ways that punk rock has failed me. Punk taught me who my friends were, but it never really defined the opposition. It occurs to me now that maybe there wasn't an opposition—or not one of any moment: in Turkey, concepts like the Corporate Ogre and the PMRC seem like manufactured evils.

Thanks to freedom of speech, Americans have the privilege of being subjected to a melee of images and sounds and associations and beliefs, and none of them are serious at all; none of them have any emotional content—not Marilyn Manson, not the Smashing Pumpkins, not Danzig's devil music, nothing. Think of MTV, the ultimate egalitarian source, with its constantly flickering, utterly conflicting images: breast-implanted babes backed up against ads against breast implants; rock stars singing about the joys of drugs right up against "Don't do drugs" ads.

When that's the case, we are all thrown back on our own mental resources to sort things out, and so many of us just don't have any. America trivializes all it touches—punk, politics, whatever. Turkey doesn't have the luxury of trivializing anything. There, one's values are implanted like a racial memory, at birth. There, as in Prague, the enemy is a bit more real.

vii.

Back in Budapest, Kim and Lulu and I had discussed what Kim should wear in Istanbul: her skintight space suit, or her more usual garb, short cutoff jeans with red tights underneath. "I'll wear whatever I feel like," Kim said. "I always have; that's what I do."

"But you shouldn't show disrespect to their culture," argued Lulu.

"I'm not disrespectful of them, but they shouldn't be disrespectful of mine," said Kim. "I won't make concessions, and they can boo me if they want to."

But kids who've been waiting to hear live rock 'n' roll for four years do not boo: instead, from the word go, the electricity that powers the amplifiers shoots a bolt right through their middles and they go absolutely mad: arms in the air, chanting, waving, pushing, pulsating, jumping up and down, all to songs they've never heard in their life. To paraphrase Tolstoy, happy rock audiences are all alike. The front row of guys are all mouthing "I love you" to Lulu; the girls' faces are beaming happy, inspired, and the band is in a dream. Tomorrow they will begin flying westward again—back toward the First World, back to Seattle. Home, with its jobs and its husbands and its pets and its responsibilities, calleth: pretty soon the dream will be over.

But that doesn't mean that life's downhill from here; for if punk means anything, it means living in the moment. Minus money and ambition and "success" as America knows it—minus all the forces that have turned it into a travesty, punk is still at heart a life force. The Fastbacks know that: heck, they are one of its most important pulses.

The Fastbacks had only one other show as great as Istanbul, and that one was in Warsaw, three weeks earlier. Obviously, the more spiritually uplifting nature of those two shows has to do with economics and the emerging position of these types of nation.

I suppose you could argue that the coming of punk to places like this is a lot like the coming of McDonald's: a ruination of indigenous culture, homogeneity about to happen. But that's only if you consider rock as this static and meaningless thing, as if it were a hamburger, or an Egg McMuffin. Now, when I think of that night in Istanbul, I think also of the words of the Turkish revolutionary and poet, Nazim Hikmet: "I'm wonderfully happy I came into the world / I love its earth, light, struggle, bread."

Punk rock may not be able to liberate a nation, but it sure has liberated me. And maybe that's all a person can ask of art: for the occasional moment of noisy solace, for an instantaneous shot of hope—and a lifetime of inspiration.

End:
Habeas Corpus

It makes more sense
to live your life in present tense.
—Pearl Jam

This book was originally going to be entitled *The Death of Punk*, as if it were a murder mystery. And if it were so—third in the series, after *Murder in the Mosh Pit* and *Death Goes for a Beer Run*—then this would be the chapter where we wound up all the clues. Our detective— Inspector McLaren—would gather all the suspects together in somebody's stately home and, after a long and wandering narrative, finally announce the guilty party.

Johnny Rotten or Courtney Love? Gene Simmons or Doctor Dre? And if you really want to pinpoint the one most culpable, single-bullet party as killer, why not just finger Kurt Cobain, whose tragic suicide in April of 1994 really took the fun out of everything to do with rock?

But the question as to who killed punk is actually rather moot, because in order to have a murder, you must first produce a corpse. And how can we do that, when punk rock is happening all around us? In streets of the suburbs, on college radio, in various garages and basements and nightclubs and, most of all, inside one's imagination, the genre continues to propagate itself and prosper, all over the entire world. From the Exploited to Screeching Weasel, punk is still a font of inspiration, fertilizing the otherwise barren places in young suburbia's mind.

I know this for a fact, because every Friday for the last two years, a list has appeared automatically in my computer charting all the upcoming punk rock shows in the greater Bay Area. In vets' halls in Watsonville and Fresno, in teen clubs in Benicia and Chico, at the Phoenix Theater in Petaluma, the Epicenter in San Francisco, and of course at 924 Gilman Street, punk bands are booked from now to doomsday: Pee, Megaweapon, Ground Round, the Faggz; Janitors Against Apartheid, the Get Down Clowns, the Hi Fives, the Blockbustaz, Oppressed Logic and Natural Fonzie, the Hermaphrodaddies, Fatt Sack, Scared of Chaka, Good Riddance; Dystopia, Ringworm, the Idiots, Jack Killed Jill.

There's a jillion of 'em, each with a cleverer name than the last, appearing nightly at places like the Ptomaine Temple in San Leandro or the Sacramento American Legion Hall. Sometimes I contemplate actually going to one of these shows, but then my better judgment stops me. Like Ice T, I've been there, done that. When it comes to punk rock in grotty venues, I've seen it, I've smelled it, I know its every nuance and note. It's absolutely inconceivable to think that one of these bands could actually change my life.

But that's not to say they won't change someone else's. And besides, it comforts me to know that, whatever country I land in, be it Finland, Turkey, or Timbuktu, I could go to these little secret places and find temporary solace the way others drop in on a hatha yoga class, or a twelve-step meeting, or a church outside of your own parish.

My own parish—the one I joined at Winterland—has gotten a lot bigger of late, like a family that's added a number of new children; and with size and fecundity comes responsibility. Unfortunately, few punk rockers are willing to take up the burden that maturity brings—maturity is a bore, nor is it part of punk's initial creed. But occasionally, a punk with a bit more courage than the rest does start to shoulder the burden, and such a one is former Nirvana bassist Krist Novoselic.

Most punks who get rich use their money to start their own indie labels, but not Krist: instead, upon Nirvana's demise, he helped form JAM-PAC, the Joint Artists and Music Promotions Political Action Committee, a lobby group that is devoted to agitating Congress regarding First Amendment rights, specifically bills that aim to limit the creation, sale, and dissemination of so-called salacious rock music.

In March of 1996, Novoselic made the keynote address at the South by Southwest Music and Media Conference, and in his speech, he talked about the importance of not being intimidated by the government, even though it's understandable to be turned off by politics. Then, explaining why he got involved in lobbying, he said:

"What compels me, is the idea of civic consciousness. The true human experience is about spiritual fulfillment. We have a moral responsibility to live in a spiritually liberated society. But we cannot mandate awareness: we must take up the responsibility of contributing to the democracy, where freedom, justice, tolerance, inclusiveness, and freedom of expression come together as a constituency, and a congregation."

After his speech, Novoselic did a Q & A session, and one journalist said, "The eighties were a terrible time, but one argument says that oppression like that of the Reagan regime is what creates a backlash of great art. How do you answer the argument that censorship is self-defeating in that it fosters a climate where bands like Nirvana *must* exist?"

I forget Krist's response—something about not being able to talk about abstractions like what makes art, nor about pre-nineties anticensorship legislation, which he knows little about—but I thought, as he looked puzzledly out at the questioner, that he might well have been thinking, as I was, of all that had passed since he and Kurt Cobain formed Nirvana in 1986; of life, and of death, and of celebrity and of rock, and how none of that really matters in comparison to the greater good.

After all, a lot of what he said was directly opposed to some of Nirvana's deepest-held philosophies—"I find it hard / it's hard to find / oh well, whatever; nevermind." But it's opposed in a positive, even an avenging, way. It's as if Krist has moved past the sphere that was the birthplace of his success. Now he's attempting to give something back to the society that made him famous; to change the forces that made life so sad and bitter, which caused all the crap that Nirvana's music addressed so successfully.

You know, contact with "great art" ought to impart to its listeners and practitioners spiritual growth and self-knowledge. It seems to have done so to Krist Novoselic, but what about the rest of us? If punk rock is, by its very existence, able to edify and enlighten and liberate one's soul; if, as Brett Gurewitz posited, it has a code of ethics, then perhaps it would be as good a definition as any to say that punk is dead when living within its confines no longer elevates the mind, but on the contrary, degrades it.

Punk was meant to belittle and destroy the fatcats of rock, and for a time it did. But the fatcats are back, and more bloated than ever. And if ever there was a truism worth repeating here, it's that those whom the gods are about to destroy, they first make very rich.

Take, for example, the Smashing Pumpkins, one of the postpunk era's biggest-selling bands. In 1996, the band released a 120-minute-long double album and a five-CD set of music, earning millions upon millions in the process. That in itself is no crime—but then take a look at the Smashing Pumpkins' widely acclaimed video for their song "Bullet with Butterfly Wings," and say that they don't deserve to be destroyed by the generation coming up.

The visual text for this video comes from a photo by Sebastiao Salgado, a wide-angle picture of a Brazilian gold mine that depicts a pit full of naked miners, thousands of them, all covered in dirt and mud and sweat. They are crawling up ladders like so many ants, and the overall effect is like nothing so much as one's conception of a medieval chain gang, or perhaps a trench in the middle of a three-day battle during World War I. The photo itself is an unblinking document of the degradation of the human condition; in that video, this scene is re-created perfectly, ladder for ladder, mud splash for mud splash, at great expense—only with the sinister addition of Billy Corgan, painted blue and silver, hovering over it all and singing, "Despite all my rage / I am still just a rat in a cage."

In short, Corgan has taken a portrait of human suffering and equated it with his own, as if there is some kind of comparison between the monstrous economic conditions in Brazil and Corgan's monstrously inflated idea of his own white-boy pain. It is a gesture that seems, in its arrogance, about on par with Michael Jackson's recent erection of a giant statue of himself in various Second World countries, and the question it brings up is, does being the sad child of divorced parents create the same mental anguish as working in a coal mine for your entire life with no hope of ever getting out of it? Does selling 47 million copies of *Thriller* give one the same fascistic rights over a country as, say, conquering it and becoming its dictator does?

Most of all, it begs the question, is the world stupider than ever? I'm serious; has the world gone mad? No wonder they're calling the generation below mine—the one that likes the Smashing Pumpkins—"the D-Generation"! I mean, it's one thing to think that culture has evolved so far that it can blithely spoof and alter even the most serious of historical contexts: after all, "Nothing is sacred" is a creed that has its points. Nevertheless, it seems to me that a generation that takes for its heroes men who could even consider these actions is a society that is either decaying or as dumb as a brick.

Or take another example. Last year, images of Courtney Love—supposedly the world's most consummate punk rocker, and the only artist in well over a decade to rival the Sex Pistols in true outrage and shock value—suddenly appeared all over the place, depicting her as demure as could be. Her hair was tamed and tidy and downright ash blond, as if she'd just been called up for a role as a new roomie on *Friends*. She modeled for *Vogue*, presented an Oscar, went to fashion shows on the arm of Versace.

The sight of it all made me feel like the wife at the end of the series *Dallas,* when she woke up and found out the whole season had been a dream. Did punk even happen? Did it mean something to us…and if so, what? After all, for years punk rock was my hobby, my religion, and my one true love, and let me tell you, love dies hard. Of course, one blinds oneself to its infidelities, as one does when one wants to continue to believe: a man can betray you again and again, and you can forgive him for it easily.

But love ends on a different note altogether, when the love object can no longer be respected, when you cease to care about what it does behind your back. Courtney's new incarnation is the modern-day equivalent of Nancy Spungen having lived and gone on to become Katie Couric; as if the whole entire exercise—punk, grunge, Nirvana, Hole—had all been a great big lie; as if she too had perpetrated a rock 'n' roll swindle, and then—in the true tradition of hurricanes—moved on (in this case to the film world), leaving the alt-rock underground behind her in a shambles: disillusioned, cynical, sick of itself, corrupted.

Perhaps that is why a friend of mine from Seattle recently commented that, ever since Nirvana's demise, what she calls her "fun threshold" has been ruined. In the days before Nirvana's success, she was a struggling punker, working at an indie label by day and spending night after night watching soon-to-be-world-famous rock bands play practically in private. Now she's a highly paid business executive, flown all over the world to see bands whose music is all based on the stuff she saw in embryo, being invented.

Back then my friend was really poor, and now all her drinks are paid for and she sleeps in the best hotels. But still everything pales compared to the days when a free beer cadged from the opening band's bucket could make her whole night seem neat.

I sometimes wonder if us old punk rockers are suffering from a similar letdown syndrome. I know so many people whose lives were saved by punk rock…but I know an equal number who had their hearts broken by it as well. Perhaps we've all had too much fun—and contracted too-high expectations. Perhaps our revels are now ended, and it's time to go home to bed.

Of course, the idea that is it time to put away childish things is anathema to me, but for all that, maybe it is. Other people seem to think so, anyway: not long ago, I went into a record store to buy a copy of Fugazi's LP *Red Medicine,* and the clerk, a young, ski-cap-wearing, snowboard-loving skinhead, said pleasantly, "Oh, are you getting this for your son?"

Of course, I was enraged—angry at the clerk, at the store, at Fugazi; at punk rock itself for even nominally excluding me—and for making me feel like Fugazi was inappropriate music for me to listen to in my old age.

It didn't help to know that he was wrong—that Fugazi's members are all exactly my age; that the biggest Fugazi fan I know is a teacher who turns her car stereo off when she gets within two blocks of her school "because," she says kindly, "I don't want to ruin it for the kids if they hear me blasting out *Repeater.*

"Sometimes," she sighs, "I feel like someone who had a secret sex life in the fifties; like being an old punk is something to be ashamed of and hidden." And I know just what she means. Nowadays, I fear going to see Fugazi play live in case I overhear someone saying, "Hey, who's the grandma by the sound board?"

But, I've decided that I will not go gently into that silent night. It would be easier to give up than to grow up, but I won't be driven to listen to Mariah Carey records just to conform to some ski-capped kid's expectations. If punk's taught me anything, it has taught me to be proud of my allegiances.

And yet, this little issue—whether I'm too old for it—is just another of the conundrums that have been secreted in the fabric of the beast from the very start. Many years ago, when I first moved to San Francisco with my best friend (the Fugazi-loving schoolteacher), we used to have an ongoing in-joke about an artist called Lydia Pense. Pense was the singer for a mediocre sixties act called Cold Blood—a sort of sub–Janis Joplin type who never quite made it, and to our mean young eyes she quickly came to symbolize has-beenitis. In the mid-eighties, we used to see her gigs advertised in the paper playing various low-down clubs and bars, and caught up as we were in the punk scene, we always spared her a sneer.

Presently, the words "Lydia Pense" became a byword for music that we thought was old-fashioned and irrelevant. "He/she is a total Lydia Pense," we'd say about any band that seemed to have outlived its usefulness. This sounds very mean in retrospect, but time's caught up with the two of us, and our punishment is that we haven't been spared her fate. Nowadays, every band or band member we loved back then—Rollins, Westerberg, the Kirkwoods, Fugazi—is a "total Lydia Pense."

Worse, we ourselves are now Lydia Pensive, and we know it, and repine. After all, how much difference is there between the hippies who haunt Haight Street and listen to the Dead and punk rockers with Mohawks who have "The Exploited" written across their back?

This is the fundamental question behind the idea that punk is dead, and the concomitant question, posed earlier, as to whether, to a sixteen-year-old kid, the experience of seeing the Offspring at the Blockbuster Arena could in any way be the same experience as seeing, say, the Circle Jerks at the Masque was a decade ago.

One's first impulse is to say, "No way!" But really, I'm not so sure. Being sixteen is being sixteen, you know? "Punk rock music is rock 'n' roll music and rock 'n' roll music is rebellion," said Brett Gurewitz. "Teenagers are filled with a sense of their own mortality, and their sense of their own aloneness in the universe, and because of these things they are filled with rebellion and anger, and all the things that happen to every single teenager, and joins humanity together, because none of us are unique.

"And intense rock 'n' roll makes it better," he added. "All the better if everyone else around you is feeling it too. Then it becomes a spiritual experience."

Gurewitz may well be right. Punk's not dead, it's just resting . . . hiding its light underneath a bushel, gathering strength in foreign climes. Its flames are still burning somewhere, despite anything anyone has to say. Punk rock is Phoenician; it will rise, like the soul, on the stepping-stones of its former self. The death of punk? What a crock of shit. Punk is like youth: it will always spring eternal . . . for life everlasting, amen.

A BIBLICAL BASIS FOR MINISTRY

A BIBLICAL BASIS
FOR MINISTRY

EDITED BY
EARL E. SHELP
AND
RONALD SUNDERLAND

THE WESTMINSTER PRESS
PHILADELPHIA

Scripture quotations from the Revised Standard Version of the Bible are copyrighted 1946, 1952, ©
1971, 1973 by the Division of Christian Education of
the National Council of the Churches of Christ in the
U.S.A., and are used by permission.

BOOK DESIGN BY DOROTHY ALDEN SMITH

First edition

Published by The Westminster Press®
Philadelphia, Pennsylvania

PRINTED IN THE UNITED STATES OF AMERICA
9 8 7 6 5 4 3 2 1

Library of Congress Cataloging in Publication Data

Main entry under title:
A Biblical basis for ministry.

Includes bibliographical references.
CONTENTS: Theology and ministry in the Hebrew
scriptures / by James A. Wharton—Ministry in Judaism:
reflections on suffering and caring / by Samuel E.
Karff—Theology and ministry in the Pauline letters /
by Victor Paul Furnish—[etc.]
    1. Pastoral theology—Biblical teaching—Addresses,
essays, lectures. 2. Pastoral theology (Judaism)—
Addresses, essays, lectures. I. Shelp, Earl E., 1947–
II. Sunderland, Ronald, 1929–
BS2545.P45B5   253   81–920
ISBN 0–664–24371–1   AACR2

CONTENTS

Continued

NOTES ON CONTRIBUTORS

Paul J. Achtemeier is the Herbert Worth and Annie H. Jackson Professor of Biblical Interpretation at Union Theological Seminary in Virginia. Since 1977, he also has served as Executive Secretary of the Society of Biblical Literature. He is the author of numerous books and articles, the latest, *The Inspiration of Scripture: Problems and Proposals,* published by Westminster Press in 1980. A minister in the United Church of Christ, Dr. Achtemeier has represented his church in ecumenical dialogues, and has participated in a number of interdenominational scholarly projects.

Victor Paul Furnish is Professor of New Testament at Southern Methodist University's Perkins School of Theology. Dr. Furnish is author of several volumes published by Abingdon Press: *Theology and Ethics in Paul* (1968), *The Love Command in the New Testament* (1972), and *The Moral Teaching of Paul: Selected Issues* (1979). He was Associate Editor for New Testament of the *Interpreter's Dictionary of the Bible,* Supplementary Volume, and he is a frequent contributor to scholarly and professional journals.

Samuel E. Karff is Senior Rabbi of Congregation Beth Israel in Houston, Texas. He is also Adjunct Professor in the Department of Religious Studies at Rice University. Dr. Karff is author of *Agada: The Language of Jewish Faith*

(KTAV Publishing House, 1980) and Editor of the *Journal of Reform Judaism.*

Earl E. Shelp is Assistant Professor of Theology and Ethics at the Institute of Religion, Houston, Texas, and Assistant Professor of Medical Ethics at the Baylor College of Medicine, also in Houston. Dr. Shelp was educated at the University of Louisville (B.S.C.) and the Southern Baptist Theological Seminary (M.Div.; Ph.D.). He contributes frequently to scholarly journals in medical ethics and has edited *Justice and Health Care* (1981) and *Beneficence and Health Care* (forthcoming).

D. Moody Smith is Professor of New Testament Interpretation at The Divinity School, Duke University. He has been a Guggenheim Fellow, a Lilly Fellow, and an ATS Fellow. Professor Smith holds the B.D. from Duke University Divinity School and the Ph.D. from Yale University. Dr. Smith serves on the Editorial Advisory Council of *Interpretation* and the Editorial Board of the *Journal of Biblical Literature.* He is author of several books. His latest is *Interpreting the Gospels for Preaching* (Fortress Press, 1980).

Ronald Sunderland is Director and Professor of Pastoral Care at the Institute of Religion, Houston, Texas. His undergraduate study was completed at the University of Melbourne (B.A.) and at the Melbourne College of Divinity (B.D.). He received the S.T.M. from Perkins School of Theology and the Ed.D. from the University of Houston. He is known for his pioneering work in developing a program to equip lay persons for the congregation's pastoral ministry. He is a founding member of the Association for Clinical Pastoral Education and a certified Clinical Pastoral Education Supervisor.

James A. Wharton is Senior Pastor of Memorial Drive Presbyterian Church in Houston, Texas. He previously was Professor of Old Testament at Austin Presbyterian Theological Seminary, where he received the B.D. He

received the Th.D. from the University of Basel, Switzerland. Dr. Wharton is a popular preacher and frequent contributor to biblical journals. He serves on the Editorial Advisory Council of *Interpretation*.

INTRODUCTION

The term "ministry" is commonly used to denote a concept so basic to religious faith and practice that its meaning appears on the surface to be self-evident. Yet there is a profound lack of consensus concerning the nature of ministry. This state of affairs may be attributed to and a manifestation of divergent theologies and, especially, ecclesiologies.

Differing perceptions of ministry result in part from lack of agreement about the nature of humanity's relationship to God, the nature of religious community which ensues from that encounter, and diverse understandings of God's will for human association within and across religious, national, and cultural boundaries. In addition, differing perceptions of ministry may be attributed to the interplay of theological presuppositions with socioeconomic, cultural, geographical, and educational factors.

The apparent confusion about the foundation and expression of ministry is reflected in the relative place given the study of ministry in the theological curriculum and the priorities evidenced by the life of the local congregation. If ministry is in fact central to faith, it is paradoxical that the contribution of "practical theology" to a comprehensive understanding of ministry has only recently been affirmed. Instead of ministry being grounded in and

guided by its theological heritage, it has been influenced more in recent years by insights and practices derived from the medical and behavioral sciences. Indicative of this trend is the location of advanced training for pastoral ministry almost exclusively within general and specialized medical settings. Concurrently, opportunities for ministry were surrendered by individual members of congregations and assigned to the professional clergy. These two simultaneous but independent developments contributed to the contemporary movement away from more traditional notions of ministry validated by theological training and ordination. Certification of competency for certain specialized ministries in the form of state licensure has been one consequence of this movement.

These events point to and underscore the urgency and necessity of a renewed investigation by the classical theological disciplines into the nature and scope of ministry. The conversation between scholars and practitioners that should characterize these basic studies can result in each gaining an enriched understanding of the other's distinctive contribution to the Christian life. The Latin word behind "conversation" is *conversari,* which means "to live with." To speak of the necessity of a conversation between theology and ministry suggests the intimacy of the relationship between them and the interdependency essential to the integrity of each. An alternate approach to the conversation would be to request practitioners to reflect theologically about the resources of their experience. The former approach was adopted for this collection, namely, the initiation of this conversation by theological scholars. That is one purpose of the present volume. A second, more comprehensive purpose is to identify the heterogeneous nature of the concept of ministry, the diversity of its expression, and the richness of the resources within the Jewish and Christian traditions that contribute to an understanding of ministry. In fulfillment of these purposes the following five essays, which

examine the biblical theological foundations of ministry, are presented.

James Wharton explores how the normative traditions of Judaism contained in the Hebrew scriptures illuminate the theological ground of ministry for Judaism and Christianity. Ministry is not properly understood in this light as only referring to individual acts of compassion and comfort. More accurately, ministry is a special quality of relationship between God and people and between people and people. It is both a corporate and an individual endeavor based on the normative model of God's relationship with Israel, characterized by a divine freedom from and for Israel—and, derivatively, all humanity. Wharton explicates the implications of this root biblical notion of ministry by examining the elicited ministry of Israel to God and to human others, each distinguished by a characteristic freedom from and for the divine or human other. He concludes his study with a brief discussion of three practical implications for ministry grounded in the liberating and eliciting love of God and in the divine will-to-relationship.

Samuel Karff, a practicing rabbi, demonstrates how the Hebrew scriptures and theological traditions inform and shape contemporary ministry within the Jewish community. He uses the phenomenon of illness as an occasion to reflect on the nearly universal experience of human suffering and a caring response by the community of faith. He suggests that theologically sound ministry is guided by the principle of respect for human dignity. Ministry that is shaped by this theologically informed principle will be compassionate, sensitive, understanding, participatory, and representative of God's ministry. Karff's essay reminds the Christian of the rich rabbinic tradition as a resource for instruction. It also challenges the Christian community to appreciate anew the value of a living tradition that is responsive to the joys and tragedies of human existence.

The next three essays examine the theological convictions and ministries of the primitive Christian community as these can be discerned from the Pauline, Synoptic, and Johannine documents. Victor Paul Furnish initiates this examination with a study of the interrelationship of the apostle Paul's theology and ministry. He affirms that Paul's ministry was grounded in his theology and that his theology was shaped within the context of his ministry. Furnish suggests that service to God is the most important feature of Paul's understanding of ministry. This emphasis is consistent with the conclusions of Wharton and serves to link the Jewish and Christian traditions of ministry without diminishing their distinctive features.

Furnish portrays Paul's ministry with an explication of Paul's use and understanding of the titles "preacher," "apostle," and "teacher." He details the content of Paul's gospel and the specific pastoral priorities that issued from it. He concludes that a value of investigations of this type is the affirmation of the indissoluble integrity of gospel and mission which recommends ministry in conformity with the gospel.

Paul Achtemeier finds a similar indissoluble link between the biblical scholarship which produces theological insights and the practice of pastoral ministry. He explores selected aspects of the relationship between study of the Synoptic Gospels and the form and function of pastoral ministry. Achtemeier suggests that the nature of the Gospels of Matthew, Mark, and Luke is witness, a summons to faith. He illustrates the unique interests of each evangelist by demonstrating how the traditions were adapted in sermonic fashion and with pastoral purposes to make, clarify, or emphasize a theological point. He maintains that the Synoptic Gospels grew out of and were addressed to the communities in which they were written. They provided then, and they provide now, resources for the task of witnessing to the faith of the Christian community which grew out of the Jewish com-

munity. The Gospels address the concerns, among others, of vulnerability in ministry, persecution and perseverance, church structure, order and discipline, forgiveness, and the necessity and nature of love as the law of God. Achtemeier concludes that the distinctive presentation of Jesus, the central figure of each Gospel, by each Gospel writer reflects the theological and practical concerns of each. The Gospels were vehicles of ministry for each evangelist and resources for ministry within the primitive communities. They can perform a similar service to contemporary ministry for those willing to engage in their disciplined study.

The final contribution is a survey of the Johannine literature by Moody Smith. By contrasting John's witness to Jesus with that of the Synoptics, John's distinctive understanding of theology and ministry is discerned. Smith discusses the Synoptic problem and proceeds to identify the root and motive of Johannine preaching and, by implication, of Johannine theology. He suggests that the presentation of Jesus by John was forged in a polemical setting, and he highlights the critical significance of the claims about Jesus. Thus, Christology is the central theological issue for John. John's portrait of Jesus, like those of the Synoptic authors, asserts not only who he was but also what it means to confess faith in him.

Smith views the story of Jesus washing the disciples' feet as an exemplary and normative statement of the Johannine understanding of ministry. This account indicates that ministry is grounded in the belief that God is love and that his revelation is an expression of that love. He concludes that faith requires one to engage in self-giving service to God, Christ, and one's brothers and sisters in faith. Ministry as understood by John has a character of witness and solicitation to nonbelievers. It is expressed in concrete, specific acts and in a general disposition on behalf of another. Thus, the collection ends with an echo of a theme with which it began.

The epilogue by the editors provides a brief commentary on the substance of the essays. It identifies some of the theological and pragmatic questions that merit further investigation. It should not be surprising to note the extent of work that remains if the conversation between "theology" and "ministry" is to advance beyond its present embryonic stage.

Edited volumes are necessarily the product of collaborative efforts. The contribution of each author is gratefully acknowledged. The skillful assistance of Mrs. Audrey Laymance in the preparation of the manuscript made the tasks of the editors more bearable and enjoyable. Her dedication and talents are without equal and deeply appreciated. Finally, profound thanks are due to the Trustees of the Institute of Religion who encouraged us to pursue the task of bringing together theologians and ministers so that this creative interchange might begin.

EARL E. SHELP
RONALD SUNDERLAND

Houston, Texas

1

THEOLOGY AND MINISTRY
IN THE HEBREW SCRIPTURES

BY
JAMES A. WHARTON

The chances are excellent that we are colleagues. We are both curious about theology and what ministry is in theological perspective. In the best case we are fascinated by theology, ministry, and Judaism as they interrelate. Perhaps you are a "minister" by calling, training, and commitment. Or you may be a Jew or Christian who regards ministry as what Elton Trueblood called "your other vocation," even though you earn your living at a secular job. In either case, we share an interest in the theological realities that belong to the practice of ministry. We are interested in how the normative traditions of Judaism illuminate those theological realities.

I propose to detail some of the theological implications for ministry that I find in the Hebrew scriptures. I approach this investigation as a Christian for whom the Hebrew scriptures are of one piece with the New Testament, as a theologian in the Presbyterian tradition, and as a pastor of a local congregation. I shall not attempt to obscure these perspectives, but I hope to stimulate conversation with persons who approach the questions from quite different points of view. My hope is that common understandings between Christians and Jews on ministry may lead to a new depth of theological conversation.

The reality of ministry has been shared by Christians and Jews even though the term itself, in a more or less

technical sense, is the product of Christianized culture. "Rabbi," "priest," and "minister" are not, properly speaking, interchangeable designations for essentially identical religious offices. The religious climate of Western culture, particularly in the United States, has forced rabbi, priest, and minister into very similar roles as "religious leaders," but this has led to superficial conceptions of what "ministry" may mean for each. In the worst case, the grand conception of ministry in each tradition has been rendered trivial. "Ministry" as a distinct religiously oriented vocation may be classified legitimately among the "helping professions." It is by no means the least "helpful" among them. In a deep sense, however, ministry describes a special quality of relationship between God and people and between people and people. As such it will not submit to narrow professional or vocational definition.

The concern here is to uncover the theological roots of ministry from which all particular forms of ministry may derive. It is urgent for people who engage in "professional" ministry to do so on the basis of clear understandings rooted in the faith commitments of their respective communities. Nothing is more destructive to the practice of ministry, in my view, than the vague (or not so vague) conviction that the genuinely helpful things undertaken are actually based on disciplines that lie outside the domain of faith and theology. When that conviction is sufficiently strong, ministers think of themselves as not-quite-honest or not-quite-qualified psychologists, social workers, or sociologists. Candor, integrity, or self-esteem may make such ministers long to step out of their ministerial roles and become full practitioners of some other art or science.

Is there an understanding of self and other within the biblical faith communities that is distinctive and not merely borrowed from the behavioral sciences? If so, is it sufficiently powerful to undergird professional ministry

with a sense of its own authenticity that is not merely borrowed from other disciplines? These are critical questions. Even stout and clear convictions about what one does as a minister are difficult to maintain in the face of popular opinion that ministers are at best second-stringers in the scientifically grounded arts of helping people. Those who share the minister's faith commitments, or can at least entertain genuine sympathy for them, are apt to recognize the minister's contribution as particularly necessary or helpful. There is something sectarian, in a religiously plural society, about offering (or receiving) the professional ministrations of "clergy." It is a rare minister, priest, or rabbi who has not longed for the self-evident and generally accepted authenticity of the "regular" helping professions. It requires more than ordinary courage and confidence to bring off authentic ministry in the face of implicit and explicit questioning of one's professional "value."

From the theological standpoint it is clear that ministry is a wider and deeper affair than the trials and tribulations of "professional" ministers. Properly understood, ministry belongs to the entire community of faith and to each member of it. Yet the need for solid theological understanding of ministry comes to focus in the lives of people whose professional and personal lives are on the line. And if professionals can break through to more adequate conceptions of their own ministries, they may be in a position to help the entire faith community see the larger dimensions of ministry that engage every serious Christian or Jew. That may be the most significant reason for reflecting on "theology and ministry in Judaism."

THE MINISTRY OF GOD:
THE FREEDOM OF GOD FROM AND FOR ISRAEL

Ministry describes a special quality of relationship between self and other. The familiar word "minus" is be-

neath *"minis-*try" in whatever sense the term is used. A "lesser" person, by one definition or another, undertakes an action in the interest of a person or persons understood to be somehow "greater." Ministry may describe the service by a courtier to a king, a slave to a master, or a wage earner to an employer out of motives as diverse as loyalty, duty, compulsion, or personal gain.

The technical opposite of ministry is "magistry" (or, as the English love to misspell Latin, "mastery"): a relationship in which the will of a "greater" (magis) is imposed upon a "lesser" (minis) person as determined by relative rank or power. The modes of mastery are command, coercion, or inducement, based on a common notion of the person to whom service is due by contrast with the one whose "due" it is to serve.

In both Judaism and Christianity the quality of relationship between self and other lies near the heart of faith. How one relates to human others is the indispensable litmus by which the relationship to God as other is tested. How one relates to God as other determines the framework within which the faithful community perceives and deals with human others. This lends to Judaism and Christianity a transcendent urgency surrounding all questions of relationship between human selves and human others.

Ministry to human others is, in the ultimate sense, ministry to God. In the biblical tradition, perhaps especially in the Hebrew scriptures, there is no doubt as to who is the "magis" (the greater) and who is the "minis" (the lesser) in the relationship between God and people. The references to God's incomparable power and majesty as creator, sustainer, and ordainer of all suggests that God's mode of relationship to Israel is "mastery" and not "ministry." Only God is sovereign, worthy of unqualified praise and adoration in the universe. God alone is to be worshiped or served in the ultimate sense. "Servant of God" is the highest conceivable accolade to

which any human being may aspire.

Yet "mastery" does not describe fully the special quality of God's relationship to Israel in the Hebrew scriptures, at least not by conventional definition. The measure of mastery by a human master is the degree to which the master's will and purpose prevail among those under the master's sway. A successful tyrant may secure domination by engaging the love and loyalty of subjects, or by enticement, bribery, persuasion, threat of punishment, or raw coercion. Insofar as these fail to produce conformity to the tyrant's will, the "mastery" is incomplete and the tyrant's status and power are called into question.

By this conventional definition, the Lord of whom the Bible speaks emerges as a weak and questionable "master." The biblical story includes many apparently successful insubordinations and insurrections of individuals and nations. Nowhere, after the first two chapters of Genesis, does the Bible point to a historical state of affairs in which God's will is done on earth as it is in heaven. The sovereign rule of God is affirmed in text after text in a variety of ways, but the "kingdom of God" remains a future reality for which faithful people wait and hope. The present order reflects a vast gulf between what God wills for the world and how things actually are. In that sense God's mastery is not yet a fact.

When the Hebrew scriptures insist on God's "mastery" of the universe, as they constantly do, it is mastery by a strange definition. God's lack of mastery in the usual sense is never attributed either to unclarity of will or lack of power. Insofar as God's perfect will is not achieved on earth, the failure is not imposed upon God by any external agency, whether human, "natural," or otherwise. Somehow it is not God's weakness that surfaces in the fact of purposes and events contrary to the divine intention. The power by which God creates and sustains all things is inversely attested in the self-imposed patience and forbearance of God in the face of rejection.

It is in the context of the rebellion of people against God, and the apparent weakness of God in the face of it, that one is compelled to speak of a "ministry" of God toward Israel. The kind of service toward another ordinarily associated with a "lesser" person in relation to a "greater" begins to emerge as a mode of relationship exercised by God toward Israel. Ministry in the special biblical sense, as it is seen first of all in God's care for Israel, derives from self-contained strength, not weakness. It is above all the exercise of God's sovereign freedom *from* and freedom *for* Israel.

What is meant by God's freedom from and for Israel in the Hebrew scriptures, and how do these twin freedoms define the character of God's ministry? All forms of human ministry, in the biblical sense, derive from God's actions and attitudes toward people. My thesis is that the ministry of people to people is at its highest a reflection of the ministry of God to people as perceived by faith. At its best, our ministry is participation, no matter how fragmentary, in the ministry of God. But before we begin that exploration, it is essential to question some conventional and habitual patterns of thought about God. It is no ordinary thinking about "deity" to which the Hebrew scriptures challenge us. The breathtaking dimensions of God's freedom from and freedom for Israel, as attested in the Bible, compel us to wonder if anyone has understood to what the terse monosyllable "God" may refer. Who or what God may be, according to the Hebrew scriptures, must continually be learned afresh in the pilgrimage of faith. It is perhaps above all God's freedom that is at stake in the ancient commandment against making any graven image of God. Even the most glorious and pivotal memories of past relationship with God, which always formed the core of Israel's boldest statements about who God is, never licensed Israel to take God for granted. The God whose likeness can never be captured in wood or stone is no less free from the

Question

intellectual images in which people have been tempted
to capture and freeze the transcendent other. The attitude of wonder and the mood of awe are in order when
we presume to talk about the ministry of God.

What can be meant by the freedom of God from Israel
in the Bible? Paul van Buren[1] has made an exceptionally
keen analysis of this dimension of what the Hebrew scriptures say about God. The choosing of Israel, the creation
of the world, and the liberation of Israel from Egypt are
seen as pivotal expressions of God's freedom. This sequence is not accidental. It derives from the biblical theological insight that, in a decisive sense, Israel's perception
of God did not begin with the doctrine of creation,
though the Hebrew scriptures speak first of the making
of heaven and earth. The prior awareness that made it
possible for Israel to say its word about God as creator
was the unaccountable fact of God's will to relationship
with Israel. Western theology perhaps has not perceived
what a drastic effect this has upon the biblical story of
creation in comparison with other ancient cosmologies.

The biblical accounts of creation are hymns in praise
of the God who chose Israel to live in covenant relationship as the people of God in a special sense. Consider
what that implies about the God who creates and the why
of creation! The Hebrew scriptures offer only one "reason" for the choosing of Israel, and it is, strictly speaking,
no reason. The classic summation is Deut. 7:7–8: "It was
not because you were more in number than any other
people that the LORD set his love upon you and chose
you, for you were the fewest of all peoples; but it is
because the LORD *loves* you . . ."

This text deals with the doctrine of election worked
out in the Deuteronomistic movement of the late seventh
and early sixth centuries B.C.E. The earliest traditions of
the patriarchs point to the same unaccountable fact:
There are no compelling reasons for the choosing of
God's people apart from the sovereign freedom of God's

love and free will-to-relationship. God is decisively free
from Israel in the act of choosing. No necessity on earth
or in heaven compels or conditions the love of God. One
may theorize that God was lonely and needed company
and therefore loved. One may speculate that God is incomplete and requires responsive creatures for the fulfillment of the divine. But one finds no encouragement
from the Hebrew scriptures for such theories and speculations. Unless God is wholly free from Israel in the act
of choosing, then a cardinal dimension of what the Bible
says about God and people is stripped away.

The insight appropriated by van Buren is that this
unparalleled conception of the freedom of God from
Israel, explicit in the unaccountable fact of choosing,
stands at the heart of the biblical accounts of Creation.
Out of this same freedom, this same unaccountable and
uncoerced will-to-relationship, God created the heavens
and the earth. The antiphonal hymns to the creator God
in Genesis 1 and 2 draw conceptually from cosmogonies
that were widespread in the ancient Near Eastern world.
Yet each account has been forged, by the faith of Israel,
into hymnic testimony to a single, simple, yet wholly
unaccountable fact: In utter freedom, out of no coercion
or compulsion, God chose to create all things in the
interest of relationship. Gone are the mythic contests and
rivalries among the gods familiar from other cosmogonies. Arrow straight, all the details of each account press
toward the central mystery of a Lord who imparts existence and being in order to love. Karl Barth formulated
the point of each account unforgettably in the distinctively biblical way: Genesis 1—creation, the external
ground of covenant; Genesis 2—covenant, the internal
ground of creation. As God is free from Israel in the act
of choosing, so God is free from all existing things in the
act of creation. Both creation and election become primary witnesses to the prior and unforced love of God.

The third expression of the freedom of God adduced

by van Buren is the liberation of Israel from Egypt. We are asked to envision people in slavery, marginal people, powerless people, suffering people. The choosing of Abraham and Sarah and their descendants, if remembered at all, is a remote and apparently irrelevant memory. Again, the Hebrew scriptures do not suggest that this wretched band of people possess or have done anything that uniquely qualifies them for freedom. Deuteronomy 7:7-8 is again instructive, especially for the way in which it links the liberation of Israel from Egypt with the choosing of the fathers. Only the Lord's free oath, sworn to the fathers, moves God to set Israel free. Liberation comes solely from God's free faithfulness to God's sworn integrity, not from any compulsion derived from Israel's plight or from Israel's deserving. The freedom by which God chose, and out of which God created, is vouchsafed again in God's free act of liberation.

None of these acts of God can be seen in clear focus unless we perceive in each the prior freedom of God from the fathers, from the created order, and from the wretched slaves in Egypt. If we look for external reasons or exigencies that make these acts of relationship somehow necessary, we lose touch with the unique biblical word about the freedom of God.

Yet each of these testimonies to God's freedom from Israel is at the same time a testimony to God's freedom for Israel. God has chosen to be implicated in what happens to the fathers, implicated in what becomes of the created order, implicated in the story of slaves liberated from Egypt. The sovereign freedom by which God chooses, creates, and liberates renders God peculiarly vulnerable to the continuing story of the relationships God has brought into being.

Vulnerability is a word that Western theology has never brought easily into the conversation about God. In what sense is God "liable to being wounded," which is

what vulnerability implies? How can genuine vulnerability be brought together with thoughts about the freedom of God or God's power, majesty, and infinitude? What wounds me has power over me, and what has power over me limits my freedom.

I do not know a self-evident philosophical or metaphysical rationale that can fully account for the vulnerability of God described in the Hebrew scriptures. I am almost certain that thoughts about God's weakness, limitedness, incompleteness, or developmental character are bound to fall short of the biblical word about God's vulnerability. Even very clever philosophical or metaphysical speculations of this kind tend to make God "understandable" by placing God into categories drawn from human self-understanding. It is obvious that the Bible does this also, by describing God in "anthropomorphic" categories. How else are human beings to think or describe, except in "people-shaped" terms? Yet the Bible avoids the philosophical or metaphysical trap by multiplying and varying the anthropomorphic images and weaving them into a rich tapestry. Each image has its appropriateness and function, but no one image is adequate to provide the beginning of a "definition." On the contrary, the total testimony of the Hebrew scriptures points to a Lord so free and sovereign that no sketch of God's being and character can possibly place God at the disposal of human minds. What can be known of God is only to be experienced in a relationship offered to people by God. The unaccountable fact in the Hebrew scriptures is that God wills relationship with Israel and with all humankind. But even this "fact" is not a piece of divinely imparted information. Whether or not Israel hears, how Israel hears, and how Israel chooses to respond to what it hears are the materials of relationship with God in the context of which God's way of relating penetrates into human awareness. From the human side, at least, experience of God as the other is always open-

ended, awaiting the next turn in the story of relationship. One must somehow expect each turn in the story to disclose a new perspective upon the familiar memories of who God is. And not infrequently, in the Hebrew scriptures, a turn in the story gives occasion to wonder if Israel has ever rightly understood who God is.

To talk about God's "vulnerability" is a necessary inference from the long story of relationship between God and Israel as it is remembered in the Hebrew scriptures. Without presuming to know why or how, the Bible recalls a consistent passionate involvement of God in all the details of the individual and corporate stories there recounted. To use a blatant anthropomorphism, God cares about these people, cares about what happens to them, and cares about the ways they choose to think, feel, and express their humanity. For whatever reason, it is clear that God has not chosen to make their well-being or happiness inevitable. Nor has God chosen to make their utter degradation and despair inevitable. We can say this with confidence because either of these choices would have produced an altogether different story. The story repeatedly affirms God's unmistakable will for Israel's well-being and God's unalterable opposition to the misuse and destruction of Israel's humanity. The biblical story from the human side is as spotty and checkered on these points as any story of any people anywhere. There are hints of human wills that echo God's will for our well-being. There are instances of wanton inhumanity, by the measure God discloses to Israel in Torah, with all the painful and deadly consequences that entails. But God is no disinterested and remote observer of this checkered story. So deep and so intimate is his involvement with these people that the Bible speaks of God being "angry" or "grieved" or "pleased" when things go one way or the other. That is vulnerability, the surpassing vulnerability of one who chooses to be so intimately involved in the story of others that what happens

in their lives, for good or ill, becomes part of that one's own story. The vulnerability of God disclosed in the biblical story goes deeper than "compassion" (in the sense of "suffering with"). The peculiar vulnerability of God in the Hebrew scriptures derives from a compassion that is bound together with an exalted intention for the lives of the beloved that remains unrealized even in their best moments of fidelity and well-being. The Lord of the Bible must remain deeply "grieved," or "angry," or both at once, until the intention of God for human life is fully realized and all the children of God shout for joy as Job 38:7 says the "sons of God" did on creation day! It is the indescribable vulnerability of God to the realities of human life and to God's own wounded expectations for the beloved.

This chosen vulnerability to Israel's story, on the basis of God's freedom from Israel, describes God's freedom for Israel. The Hebrew scriptures disclose a picture of God's ministry to Israel. At its heart is God's free gift of relationship to people who are not in a position to demand it, or to expect it, except on the grounds that God has offered it, obligated himself to maintain it, and renewed the offer again and again. The familiar biblical word for that relationship is "covenant." God's covenant fidelity in relationship to Israel, expressed in so many different ways, perhaps best describes the shape of God's ministry to Israel.

One of the most enduring contributions of the biblical theology movement in the middle decades of this century was a fresh insight into the covenant-relational meaning of some of the most familiar biblical words. Words like justice, righteousness, faithfulness, truth, goodness, steadfast love, and peace are not, in the Hebrew scriptures, abstract ideals drawn from some catalog of moral values. Their biblical substance comes from the way God makes and keeps covenant with Israel. God's "justice," for example, is not documented in the Bible by the evi-

dence that God always deals identically or evenhandedly with all persons who have a claim to equal treatment. This is not to say that evenhandedness or simple fairness has no part in God's expression of justice. In fact this dimension has so great a part that God's justice can be called in question by Abraham, Moses, Jeremiah, the psalmists, or Job precisely on the grounds of "unfairness" encountered in human affairs. But Israel's confidence in the justice of God is above all confidence that God is not a covenant breaker. As long as there is trust that God is standing by the promises of covenant relationship with Israel, then God's justice can be affirmed.

It is clear that only in these terms could the tenacious affirmation of the justice of God in the Hebrew scriptures have been maintained. There is no more evidence in the story of Israel than in any aspect of human experience that the universe functions in accord with some transparent ideal of evenhandedness. Even the friends of Job, who represent the most sophisticated biblical effort to articulate a concept of divine fairness in the treatment of people, acknowledge the radical ambiguity of all human experience on this point. One must take into account a wisdom of God according to which what appears unjust may correspond to a just purpose of God beyond our ken. Or one must believe that justice delayed is not justice denied. Ultimately, so argue the friends of Job, each of us will receive precisely what we deserve. Or one must discern a larger justice in God's willingness to subject people to apparent injustice in order that the person in question may be warned, reproved, or otherwise chastised in the direction of rightness in the eyes of God.

But all of these lofty reflections are at the fringe of what the Bible says about God's justice. The root affirmations are that God has made covenant with Israel; God has kept covenant with Israel in spite of innumerable breaches of covenant on Israel's part; God renews the covenant promise again and again for no reason except

covenant fidelity. The terms of the covenant are in force from God's side; God is just. The undeniable unfairness in the human experience of life has proven incapable of unseating this trust in the justice of God in the hearts of believers. Nor have believers conceived God's justice as somehow less than or inferior to the highest ideals of human justice. They have simply anchored their confidence that God is just in the decisive memory of one who makes and keeps covenant in all the ambiguities of nature, history, and individual human experience.

But not without protest! The sense that God is just in covenant-relational terms empowers Israel to raise questions of simple fairness with the covenant Lord. Some of the most eloquent affirmations that God's justice must include simple fairness are found in the outraged cries of lament in the Bible. These are outcries to God, against God, on the grounds of God's sworn commitment to covenant justice. Israel holds God accountable for God's apparent breach of the justice that Israel has learned from God in covenant relationship. This is an "upside-down trust" on Israel's part that God nevertheless, and in spite of all evidence to the contrary, keeps covenant. The only recovery from such outrage available to Israel is recurring confidence that God is still keeping covenant. The survival of Judaism can be accounted for in no other way. The Bible continues to invite this outrage against God as a dimension of fidelity. The historical and experiential reasons for expressing it have emphatically not decreased over the millennia. But such protest draws both its edge and its tenacity from the prior and deeper conviction that God is, and that God's covenant-keeping justice is a reality.

This is not the place to explore the fresh perspective that God's covenant relationship with Israel opens up for understanding words like righteousness, faithfulness, truth, goodness, steadfast love, and peace. The discussion of God's justice has suggested how these terms derive

their distinctive biblical sense from the quality of relationship expressed by God toward Israel throughout the story. Together they begin to describe both an attitude toward Israel on God's part and a mode of dealing with Israel that constitute one side of God's ministry toward Israel. Out of God's freedom from Israel, under no compulsion or necessity, God has freely chosen to be for Israel in a highly vulnerable relationship.

There is another equally fascinating aspect of what God's ministry to Israel entails, according to the Hebrew scriptures. God seeks above all, in ministry to Israel, Israel's capacity to "minister" as God "ministers"! The style of God's self-giving in relationship to Israel, as minister, is the style of well-being God wants for Israel.

This is perhaps nowhere more apparent than in the way the great covenant-relational words describe Israel's side of the covenant. God's justice expressed toward Israel in covenant ministry elicits justice from Israel. God's righteousness elicits Israel's righteousness. God's faithfulness elicits Israel's faithfulness. God's truth elicits truth from Israel, and so with goodness, steadfast love, shalom, and "delight in the other."

When God's ministry toward Israel is complete, then Israel will have been given, accepted, and begun to express the quality of relationship that characterizes God's ministry to Israel. God ministers also in this, that the goal is not to make the helpless ones perpetually dependent upon God's ministry. Early in the biblical story, at Sinai, comes the bracing and somewhat appalling news that Israel is not only to be ministered unto, but to minister! Torah is God's gift to Israel of the possibility of reflecting in its life the ministry of God. Not "mastery" but "ministry" is the goal of God's therapy.

I am indebted to Albert Outler for the provocative image of God as therapist. In his superb little book, *Who Trusts in God,* [2] Outler implies, with typically playful seriousness, that "The Lord is my therapist" may be a more

useful contemporary image than "The Lord is my shepherd," at least for distinctly nonagrarian people. Of course, neither "shepherd" nor "therapist" is capable of describing the Lord's unparalleled caring for people which is celebrated in the Twenty-third Psalm. A cynic may associate high fees and a very spotty record of cure with the word "therapist." But the same cynic might point out that a "shepherd" is in business to fleece his sheep, not to mention such metaphor-wrecking details as lamb chops and roast mutton!

Either metaphor is useful only insofar as it suggests a style of gracious and intentional caring for those who cannot care properly for themselves without significant aid. If the metaphor "The Lord is my therapist" is to prove useful, only the style of caring that belongs to the best imaginable therapy can be appropriate. Even then, when applied to the Lord's caring, this metaphor can at best fire the imagination to wonder at the mystery of a healing grace that transcends "shepherd," "therapist," or any other human image of conspicuous caring.

I propose to take the image of God as therapist, together with many of Outler's insights, and adapt it to illustrate what has been said about God's ministry to Israel.

In the best imaginable therapeutic relationship, the therapist must be significantly free from the patient. Any urgency or necessity that forces the two into relationship is capable of destroying the therapist's objectivity and therapeutic "distance" from the patient. Without that measure of objectivity and distance the therapist's needs and agendas intrude into the foreground, diminishing the ability to focus on the needs of the other, and seducing the therapist to use the relationship for his or her gratification. Every human therapist is aware that perfect objectivity and true therapeutic distance are not possible for ordinary mortals. But every good therapist recognizes the threat, and works in the direction of achieving

greater freedom from the patient at those points where the healing process demands it. "The Lord is my therapist" suggests that the Lord is free from us in such a way that there is never a question of God having to use our relationship for some unknown internal gratification. Coercion, seduction, blackmail, or "payment" are ruled out of the Lord's therapeutic style.

In the best imaginable therapeutic relationship, the therapist is also significantly free for the patient. If the relationship is healing and caring, the therapist must be prepared to become vulnerable to the patient's story and state of mind. The painful process of hurting and healing in the patient must intrude so deeply into the therapist's awareness that the issues of healing are shared between them. Deep empathy, the capacity to sense where the patient is and how the obstacles to healing appear to the patient, is essential in order for the therapist to engage in the healing process. The threat to any mortal therapist is clear: The deeper the empathy, the greater the danger that the necessary objectivity and therapeutic distance will be compromised or destroyed. Every good therapist recognizes the danger, but takes the risk of empathy in the hope of combining compassion with objectivity to help the patient toward wholeness. "The Lord is my therapist" suggests that the Lord is free for us in such a way that there is never a question of God's lack of empathy. The endlessly varied theme of God's love for Israel in the Hebrew scriptures bears testimony to ultimate "empathy," a compassion that goes beyond *knowing* "how it is" with Israel to *sharing* "how it is" in an unimaginably profound way (two of my favorite examples are Isa. 49:15 and Hos. 11:1–4, 8–9). Yet the Hebrew scriptures forbid the inference that God's compassion so embraces Israel's experience of pain and separation that the necessary objectivity and therapeutic distance is diminished.

In the best imaginable therapeutic situation, the thera-

pist combines objectivity and empathy in such a way that therapist and patient do not remain trapped in the pathology. The therapist is able not only to empathize deeply with the patient but also to do something the patient cannot possibly do, namely, to envision a state of wholeness the patient cannot realistically envision, and to perceive the way toward it. Otherwise the two are simply doomed to wallow in the patient's helplessness. A good therapist knows that the patient cannot attain genuine wholeness by simply surrendering to the insights and "solutions" imposed by the therapist. If that happens, patient and therapist are locked into a relationship that leaves the patient totally dependent on the therapist's "wholeness." Every therapist is aware that dependencies of this kind very often, if not always, mark rather successful therapeutic relationships. Yet the good therapist always maintains the goal of a wholeness within the patient that is not dependent on the imposition of insights or solutions from without. "The Lord is my therapist" suggests that God's goal for us is that quality of interior wholeness which permits us to choose our well-being with complete freedom and joy.

God the "good therapist" thus elicits from us (rather than imposes on us) the wholeness which we, in our helplessness, cannot now perceive. God's constant invitation to Israel to walk the road of life and history in the company of the "good therapist" is the invitation to seek and experience the wholeness which God envisions for us, but which God intends us to claim as our own with all freedom and joy.

Outler sums up what I call the ministry of God as the "presence of purposive love." God's love is "purposive" in the sense that God is never content to see Israel remain in captivity to an illness that cripples and distorts the meaning and purpose of truly human being. God's love is "present" in the sense that God is always beside Israel in whatever painful turn the story may take for whatever

reason. "Loving" not only with ineffable compassion but also with unfailing commitment to keep the story going until Israel's wholeness is a joyous fact.

The "presence of purposive love" is not a bad thumbnail description of the biblical story insofar as it discloses God's side of the relationship with Israel from beginning to end! The therapeutic image also places Israel's side of the rocky relationship with God in a fascinating light. The real pain of any authentic therapeutic relationship is mirrored in Israel's story with God. The patient's hurt is real and not contrived, regardless of how the patient may have conspired to produce the illness. The patient may experience the therapist as imposing expectations for wholeness that seem quite impossible to achieve. The patient may experience the therapist as harsh and angry, and indeed any good therapist must sometimes express harshness and anger if the patient's wholeness demands it. The patient may develop an unhealthy "love" for the therapist that the therapist must shatter if what purports to be love is actually a device to avoid the pain of healing. The patient may fail to see the point or the progress of the therapy and turn away from the therapist with contempt or disgust. The patient may feel wiser than and superior to the therapist and choose the ways of illness with a vengeance. The patient may experience the therapist as distant, uncaring, and uninvolved. Yet recurring moments of insight and reassurance keep the therapeutic relationship alive and re-create a sense of common cause in the enterprise of the patient's wholeness. Following this image, much of biblical literature attests the gripping interaction of struggling people with the one whose presence is both loving and purposive, as they move together along a rocky road in the direction of wholeness!

In this light, God's ministry to Israel goes far beyond gracious interventions, acts of mercy, and provision of comfort. It includes the whole fabric of real relationships: the confrontations, the mutual disappointments, the

times of separation and reunion. Ministry on God's part is freely chosen vulnerability of relationship on the one hand and unflagging commitment to the freedom and wholeness of the beloved on the other. The point of this section has been the suggestion that this picture of God's ministry provides the root definition of ministry in biblical terms. It is now in order for us to uncover the implications of this picture for the human attitudes and actions that may be described as "ministry."

THE MINISTRY OF ISRAEL TO GOD:
THE FREEDOM OF ISRAEL FROM AND FOR GOD

The model suggested by "The Lord is my therapist" rules out the idea that Israel's ministry to God is anything like Israel doing for God the same thing God does for Israel. It may happen in a human therapeutic relationship that patient becomes therapist and therapist becomes (perhaps impatient) patient. But the Hebrew scriptures leave no room for the thought that God requires help from people in order to achieve wholeness. The yearning of God for a yet unrealized relationship with Israel and with all humankind is attested in the Hebrew scriptures (the poignant words of Isaiah 55 afford one classic example among many). Yet this yearning does not derive from what is lacking in God. It expresses God's freely chosen vulnerability to the story of people and God's free commitment to their ultimate well-being. It is for Israel and on behalf of Israel that God yearns for the fulfillment of Israel's humanity.

Yet God's ministry to Israel elicits from Israel a style of being-in-relationship that reflects in specifically human terms the style of God's being-in-relationship. There is a "service" that Israel can render to God. Indeed, God's ministry to Israel can never be finished until Israel (and with Israel, all humankind) discovers and celebrates its full humanity in the service of God. What is this "minis-

try" to God that human beings can render?

It is instructive that the Hebrew word "service" *('abodah),* when used to describe the service of Israel to God, is best rendered "worship." It is not a matter of actions designed to do for God what God cannot or prefers not to do. If that is so, all the usual references for "service" disappear. If God derives no benefit from such "service," if God is not somehow soothed, gratified, or enhanced by our attitudes and actions, what possible ministry can people have toward God? Perhaps there is none.

Israel apparently risks that its "service" ("worship") is wholly irrelevant by any pragmatic standard. What, if anything, does God want from us? We have suggested that what God wants for Israel and all humankind, according to the Hebrew scriptures, is nothing less than the full and free exercise of true humanity. As "therapist" God holds the vision of our wholeness in mind even though we are at the moment incapable of perceiving it, let alone exercising it to the full. God is the "presence of purposive love," continually eliciting every fragmentary insight or gesture that makes for our wholeness.

"Worship" in the Hebrew scriptures is a ringing "Yes!" from the human side, both to the one who heals (cf. Ex. 15:26) and, with that, to the healing process and the goal of the therapy. It is the awestruck and wondering recognition that our fullest conceivable selfhood, personhood, humanity, is the goal of the creator and liberator for us. That we should be who we were created and intended to become is the goal of God's ministry toward us. It is what God wants for us, our highest conceivable well-being. And that, as I understand it, is what God wants from us, for our sakes, not God's! Only we are diminished if this "service" is not rendered to God.

The Hebrew scriptures never suggest that Israel's service to God is "perfect." Indeed it cannot be perfect until the ultimate promise of the Hebrew scriptures is fulfilled: "You shall be my people, and I will be your God" (cf.

Jer. 30:22). That is the time when no marring circumstance separates God and people from perfect communion and fellowship. The therapy is over. Therapist and patient confront each other in sheer celebration. What was to be healed is healed, the longed-for wholeness is a fact, the long and mutually shared struggle is ended, and wholeness greets wholeness with all freedom and joy.

Yet "worship" in the Hebrew scriptures is clearly an open possibility in the far-from-perfect circumstance of Israel's journey toward wholeness. If we can press the image another step, such "interim" worship corresponds to the patient's moments of relative clarity and insight that the therapist means well and may be trusted, that the therapist's vision of the patient's future wholeness is real and realizable, and that the patient is effectively engaged in the healing process. Subjectively, from the patient's standpoint, moments of relative clarity may range from deep inner exultation and confidence to dim perceptions of tenuous possibilities. Sometimes the patient's affirmation of the therapist and self and the healing process may consist of nothing more than going through the routines of keeping appointments and engaging in the familiar patterns of conversation "as if" the whole thing held possibilities the patient is presently incapable of perceiving or explaining to anyone else.

Objectively, however, even minimum aquiescence provides the indispensable context within which all the possibilities of healing may be explored. Regardless of how the patient perceives it, perseverance in the therapy constitutes an affirmation of the therapist and of the vision of wholeness the therapist holds in mind for the patient. As long as the patient perseveres, the good therapist is in a position to turn each appointment into an occasion for eliciting from the patient those minimal and fragmentary insights that make for healing.

This is an intriguing model for perceiving what "wor-

ship" is, not only in the Hebrew scriptures but also throughout the long history of the Jewish and Christian faith communities. It has been the exception, rather than the rule, that worship explodes into triumphant and animated celebration that grips the whole community with genuine confidence and joy. The words and gestures of worship characteristically affirm grander things about God, people, and the world than the worshiping community is actually able to affirm with the full confidence of faith. The great affirmations of worship are typically not so much indicators of the superb piety of the worshiping community as they are a renewed challenge to perceive the possibilities of God, faith, and life that are the charter of the community's life.

The Hebrew scriptures demonstrate this character of worship in astonishing breadth and depth. One has only to recall that Psalm 44, which confronts God in the mode of broken hopelessness, is as much an integral part of Israel's worship as Psalm 8, which praises God for the sheer wonder of God's caring for and honoring human being in the midst of the incomprehensible vastness and beauty of the starry universe! Yet each constitutes an affirmation that God is, that our lives are in God's hands, that our relationship to God is the point of focus where the mystery of our existence is to be glimpsed.

To engage in that unlikely conversation with God, whether from the vantage point of superb confidence, deep disheartenment, or plodding routine, constitutes an indispensable aspect of Israel's worship or "service" or "ministry" to God. God demands that we become coconspirators with God in the illness-subverting plot to achieve our well-being. But Israel's story in the Hebrew scriptures is filled with instances when the forms and attitudes of "worship" do not affirm God as therapist; when worship becomes an expression of Israel's pathology; when so-called "worship" actively works against the healing process.

Again the model "God is my therapist" is instructive. Any good therapist guards against the adoring extravagance of patients who hope to purchase a cozy relationship as an escape from the pain of working out their freedom and wholeness. The therapist has to find ways of letting the patient know two things: (1) The affection or goodwill of the therapist is not for sale, and cannot be forced. (2) If the goodwill of the therapist could be bought and paid for, if the therapist allowed the patient to seduce him or her into intimacy, it would mean the end of the patient's authentic struggle for wholeness which is the point of the therapeutic relationship. In biblical terms, Israel's worship is constantly being challenged by the prophetic word that God's favor cannot be purchased (Ps. 50:8–15 and Isa. 1:11–14 are classic examples).

A good therapist also guards against the patient's desire to win the therapist's approval of attitudes and actions that are part of the pathology. The therapist takes steps to show the patient that the therapist has no intention of conspiring with the patient to intensify and aggravate the sickness which the therapy is designed to heal. In biblical terms, this mode of "worship" can be described as "idolatry": that is, the projection onto God of the urges and attitudes that constitute a rejection of God's healing intention toward Israel. The Lord of whom the Bible speaks refuses to be such a "God." Israel must borrow such deities or invent them. The Hebrew scriptures are filled with prophetic denunciations of magical or "religious" attempts to secure divine approval for pathological desires (Jer. 2:26–28 and Isa. 44:9–20 are two probing examples).

So there is a "service" or "ministry" to God that is due from Israel. Perhaps its basic form is "worship," but it is worship with a clear profile and demanding implications. Worship in Israel begins with the perception of God's covenant love, justice, righteousness, faithfulness, truth,

goodness, peace, and "delight in the other," as Israel has experienced these things from God in the story of their relationship.

Yet God also elicits from Israel these same ways of relating that God expresses toward Israel. The proper worship or service of God is a matter of perceiving God in these terms and at the same time perceiving Israel's "health and salvation" in the God-given freedom to express these same qualities of relationship in specifically human attitudes and actions. The command to worship God is well expressed in the command to "love the Lord your God with everything you've got" (Deut. 6:5, paraphrased), but this always carries with it the concomitant demand: "Therefore choose life!" (Deut. 30:19). There is no way for Israel to express its "love" for God except in the mode of the fullest possible assent to Israel's life and well-being as God has placed these things before Israel in Torah and Prophets. To pretend to have love for God without perceiving and affirming God's intention for our healing is no "service" to God. But every new perception of God's commitment to our well-being, and every fragmentary effort to affirm and express it, is the "ministry" to God that we are constantly being enabled, as Israel was enabled, by God, to render.

The basis of God's ministry to Israel is God's freedom from and freedom for Israel. Can we now say that Israel's ministry to God involves an analogous freedom from God and freedom for God? Obviously not in exact correspondence. The Hebrew scriptures affirm that life, all things that make life possible, and the whole structure of reality in which life occurs, are the gracious gifts of God's power and love. In that sense, all reality is totally dependent upon God, and every human being is dependent upon God. This "utter dependence" seems to make Israel decisively "unfree" from God (see Job 7:12–20).

Yet the same Hebrew scriptures tell the story of God and Israel in a way that it is possible for people to live

in the world *etsi deus non daretur,* to use Bonhoeffer's beloved phrase: "as if God were not there." It is not mere stupidity or bullheadedness on the part of human beings that keeps the world from being transparently and self-evidently God's world. It may be that, if God's intentions for our humanity were fully realized, all nature and history in every last detail would disclose, self-evidently, the being and purpose of God. But the Hebrew scriptures deal realistically with the fact that there is no logic in history or nature that forces human beings to acknowledge that this is God's world.

On the basis of faith, Psalm 19 affirms that "the heavens are telling the glory of God; and the firmament proclaims [God's] handiwork." There is a continual antiphonal chant in praise of God between day and night as time unfolds, and "their voice goes out through all the earth, and their words to the end of the world." Yet the riddle is that "there is no speech, nor are there words; their voice is not heard"! No human being is bound to hear the voice or understand the words. According to Psalm 19, it is the acutely understandable *Torah,* given to Israel by God in relationship, that makes it possible for human beings to perceive by faith what the silent universe is saying (Ps. 19:7–14). Without that God-given clue, Israel is in no better position than any other human community to read the reality of God from the ambiguous face of nature or history.

However one may try to account for it, Israel lives out its story with God in what must be called a context of radical freedom from God. Israel is not compelled to see, believe, or be faithful. Thereby hangs the tragic and beautiful tale of a lover's quarrel between God and Israel in the Hebrew scriptures. Apparently the Lord of whom the Bible speaks cherishes freedom at unimaginable depth: freedom *from,* so that any attitudes and actions toward any other may be freely chosen; freedom *for,* so that freedom finds its ultimate expression not in isolation

or rejection, but in love. Apparently the Lord of whom the Bible speaks is not content to exercise freedom in love without making love in freedom also the goal for the beloved.

Again, the Hebrew Bible will not submit to the idea that the relationship between God and people is or ever can be a relationship between equal partners. God is and will remain God, creator and source of everything that is. People will always be people, created, receiving, at best responding to a creator and healer who makes response possible. But the mystery remains undiminished in the Hebrew scriptures that God proposes to share with human beings a measure of God's own freedom: our responding love is not to be forced, but freely chosen, within all the real limits of distinctly human capacities to be free and choose. Our capacities are not God's capacities, but they are God-given capacities, designed into the fabric of human being. They still await full exercise in the free and joyous "Yes!" to God which is the goal of God's ministry toward us. But it is precisely in the God-given context of freedom from God that God shares the human story with us, in the direction of our healing. When the healing is complete, according to the promise of the Hebrew scriptures, our terrifying freedom from God will be the freedom out of which we express our unforced freedom for God. "You shall be *my* people, and I will be *your* God!"

As often as the people of Israel catch sight of that intended freedom and choose it by reflecting God's covenant character in their human lives, "service" is rendered to God. Israel's "ministry to God" is under way; the command is being obeyed to "love the Lord your God with everything you've got." Such ministry to God is Israel's choice for the highest imaginable freedom, the freedom to be for the beloved. This constitutes Israel's highest praise of God and, at the same time, Israel's free decision to "choose life."

Everything said thus far of Israel's ministry to God points to the quality of Israel's relationship with God. But it would be a mistaken inference from the Hebrew scriptures to suppose that Israel's ministry to God can be exhausted in the perfection of this relationship. From the beginning, the biblical story indicates that Israel is an instrument in the hands of God, a people chosen and called into the service of a larger purpose than the achievement of their highest well-being. The realities of Israel's life are completely interlocked with the realities of all human life, indeed with all the realities of the entire created order.

The external framework of Israel's special existence is the totality of creation, as the first two chapters of Genesis affirm. In the extraordinary terms of biblical faith, the natural order is not a neutral context, a lifeless stage on which the central drama of God and Israel is played out. Part of Israel's ministry to God is to articulate, in words and actions, the intention of God for everything that is. Disharmony between people and nature is not part of the intention of God disclosed in Gen. 1:1 to 2:4a. At every stage of creation, God proclaims his "Good!" upon what has been created. With the creation of the human, male and female, God places persons in the web of creation and gives them unique responsibilities. By their ordering capacities they are able to echo God's purpose for all creation, on behalf of all creation.

To return to the marvelous riddle of Psalm 19, people are in a position not only to perceive the glory of God in the created order but to give voice and concrete expression to the praise of God on behalf of the silent universe. For that reason, Israel's vision of the consummation of God's purpose constantly includes a special glory for all of nature (see Isa. 11:1–9 and Psalm 148 for conspicuous examples). It is not simply a new humanity at stake in the story of Israel but also "a new heaven and a new earth"! (See Isa. 65:17.) The ministry of Israel to

God is somehow also a ministry on behalf of all creation. The "somehow" is significant. The Hebrew scriptures do not spell out a program on the basis of which Israel has the task of perfecting creation. But Israel's proper worship of God must always include a sense of kinship with nature and the awestruck recognition that God's purpose for all creation is inseparable from the specific issues of relationship between God and Israel (perhaps most eloquently expressed in Psalm 8).

The larger dimensions of Israel's ministry to God also include the well-being of other people outside the family of Israel. The opening scenes of the biblical drama (Gen. 1–11) make unmistakably clear that God's prior concern is not with Israel, but with "all the families of the earth" (Gen. 12:3). The Adam and Eve people, the Cain and Abel people, the Lamech and Seth and Noah people, and the tower of Babel people, all humanity: these are the ones in whose story God has chosen to be implicated. The special story of God with Israel opens in the midst of God's larger story with all humankind. Again, Israel's special story with God cannot be finished until "all the nations of the earth" are united in one single chorus of praise and adoration (see Psalm 96; Isa. 2:2–4; 19:19–25; 49:6). Again, ministry to God on behalf of all people does not consist of any human program to conform the world to Israel's pattern of faith and practice. The winning of "proselytes" is not unknown or inherently forbidden to Israel. But there is no indication in the Hebrew scriptures that the health of the nations is secured by converting Gentiles into Jews. The confidence of Israel is that by seeking its well-being in the love of God and through fidelity to God's way in the world, Israel is participating in God's enterprise on behalf of all people everywhere. How the healing of the nations is accomplished through the instrumentality of a faithful Israel is not Israel's affair. But that the well-being of all humanity is at stake in Israel's love and fidelity is a constant glory

and challenge of Israel's "service" or "worship" or "ministry" to God.

Perhaps the most poignant single expression of this larger dimension of Israel's ministry to God is found in Ex. 19:3–6 (compare Deuteronomy 32). The familiar concept of "priesthood" is applied astonishingly, and perhaps recklessly, to the whole people Israel. Within Israel's own religious institutions, the concept of "priest" is based upon a "double vulnerability." The priest is vulnerable to God in specific ways that ordinary people were not understood to be. It is the priest's responsibility to live and work in peculiar contact with the "holiness" of God: to touch and handle things that belong explicitly to God, to deal with realities that would consume ordinary folk if they came in contact with them unwittingly or callously.

Yet the priesthood of Israel did not deal with the awesome realm of the "holy" for their religious perfection. One does not gain the impression from the Hebrew scriptures that the priest was either dearer to God than other people or had achieved religious "superiority" over any man, woman, or child in Israel. On the contrary, the priest is also totally vulnerable to all the people on whose behalf he ministers. To put it colloquially, the priest is always "on the spot" before God on behalf of the people, and "on the spot" before Israel on behalf of God. Not exactly a comfortable spot on which to stand! Yet it is precisely through living out this "double vulnerability" before God and people that the ministry of priesthood gets its basic biblical character.

Exodus 19 applies this priestly function to the entire people Israel! What sort of religious structure is left for Israel if the ultimate intention of God is to draw all the people into the sphere of God's "holiness" so completely that the entire community becomes a "kingdom of priests and a holy nation"? On whose behalf do priests minister if every man, woman, and child participates in priest-

hood? I see no other option than to place this extraordinary expansion of the concept of priesthood against the counterfoil of Ex. 19:4f.: Israel has been liberated and chosen as God's special "possession among all peoples." But the bottom line of God's act of liberation and choosing is: "All the earth is mine." If Israel obeys God's voice and keeps God's covenant, what God has in mind for Israel will have been accomplished—not the religious perfection of a tiny fragment of all humanity, but the equipment of a whole people to function as priests! The only conceivable priestly function for such a people is ministry on behalf of those who stand outside of God's immediate and explicit holiness.

The priesthood of Israel is the model. This cannot mean that a priestly Israel is "dearer to God" than any other people, or "religiously superior" to them. At its highest, qualification as "priests" involves the people of Israel in the special "double vulnerability": vulnerability to God on behalf of the peoples and vulnerability to the peoples on behalf of God. These are distinctly dangerous words for anyone to use, particularly a Christian, in the light of pogroms, inquisitions, and holocausts. I emphatically do not imply that Israel is the divinely ordained victim of world history, or that it is somehow right for Israel to have paid such a horrendous price in death and suffering for the "privilege" of being God's chosen people. Only a particularly vicious reading of certain "Christian" ideas has allowed people to look upon Israel as the divinely ordained scapegoat for Gentile bloodlust. Exodus 19 is emphatically not talking about victims. It speaks of priests, and that means those who carry out their God-given tasks—not for their gratification or perfection. It simply means that behind Israel's ancient and enduring search for covenant love and covenant fidelity there is the larger issue of the well-being before God of all human beings. If the entire human community should fall silent in proclaiming the

glory of God, it would still be Israel's task to affirm and celebrate on behalf of the "outsiders" that God's purpose for the well-being of "all the families of the earth" is intact and its future is sure.

There is nothing grandiose or pretentious about this priestly undertaking. The proper focus of Israel's ministry is not the shortcomings or infidelities of others. It is the modestly grand and grandly modest task of translating the covenant love of God into specific human attitudes and actions that affirm it in one's life. It is not ultimately the priest who achieves the reconciliation between God and people for whom the ministry of priesthood is intended. Nor is it the priest's place to shoulder responsibility for the piety of others. The tasks are specific, discrete, and in a certain impossible sense "manageable." The priest may honestly rest assured that the obedient discharge of the assigned functions is sufficient. The mystery of how God may use these "manageable" functions of priesthood to accomplish God's work of reconciliation is beyond the priest's wisdom and outside the priest's responsibility.

When the image of priesthood is applied to all Israel, as in Exodus 19, it seems to clarify Israel's ministry to God in this special way. It is Israel's "duty," above all, to live its life toward God with all love and faithfulness, regardless of what anyone else may do. Yet Israel remains aware that in performing this "modest" function, it has done everything possible and needful to celebrate God's healing purpose on behalf of all humankind.

If this picture is drawn adequately, then Israel's explicit ministry to God inevitably includes relationship with human others. Ministry to God, in a decisive sense, is ministry to human others. Yet it is important not to jump too quickly to this conspicuous aspect of the Hebrew scriptures. The faith of Israel must not be construed as an elaborate ideology designed to give divine sanction to ordinary acts of human decency. For one thing, "ordi-

nary acts of human decency" appear regularly in the history of the human race with and without the aid of elaborate religious ideologies. The glory of such acts is not diminished and cannot be enhanced by religious claims about them. They constitute the universal "problem of good" that is the less spectacular but equally imposing counterpart to the "problem of evil" in the world.

From the standpoint of the Hebrew scriptures the primary wonder of God, and the challenge of relationship with God, is not thinkable apart from the challenge of relationship with human others. It is precisely in the exploration of relationship with God as the Other that Israel encounters human others in a special way. Before all acts of kindness or justice toward human others, Israel is aware of a ministry to God that embraces ministry to people. The question remains as to how Israel's prior ministry to God is expressed in ministry to human others.

MINISTRY AND MINISTRIES:
THE FREEDOM OF ISRAEL FROM AND FOR
HUMAN OTHERS

Suppose it is true that God's ministry toward Israel provides the basic biblical definition of ministry: the free gift of self to others in relationship, with all the vulnerability to the story of the other which that gift involves. Suppose further that Israel's ministry is first of all ministry to God: the joyful echo or reflection, from Israel's side, of God's ministry to people. How then is Israel to conceive ministry toward human others?

One common religious answer is that service to people is a kind of virtue that is particularly pleasing to God. If believers want to show gratitude for what God has done for them, being gentle, generous, or caring toward other people is a noble means of demonstrating it. A threatening corollary of this is that while doing works of mercy

toward human others wins the favor of God, failure to do such works incurs God's anger.

Every thoughtful minister recognizes in this pattern the seeds of self-righteousness, condescension, and joyless moralism that have often crippled well-meaning efforts to "help" other people. In the worst case, other human beings become pawns on the chessboard of relationship between the believer and God. They are less significant as persons than as objects to be dealt with in order to gain favor with God and avoid God's displeasure. People being "ministered to" in this manner sense more deeply than one usually imagines, I think, that they are being "used" in the process.

Another common religious approach is that the proper goal of ministry is to secure a right relationship between the person being helped and God. It is appropriate to provide food, shelter, clothing, medical care, and emotional support for persons in need, as a way of demonstrating love and concern. But the religious need is recognized as ultimately more important than any other. Whatever else may be done on behalf of the other, the ultimate (and often hidden) agenda behind acts of caring is the person's religious well-being. In the worst case, ministry means winning the other to the believer's style of piety, belief, and practice. Ministry must be regarded as a failure, either on the minister's part or on the part of the other, to the degree that this primary goal is not achieved.

In these common religious styles, the work of ministry is necessarily a tense and anxious affair. The minister is constantly being tested on the point of his or her relationship to God. Have I done enough or done it well enough to stand approved by God? Have I succeeded in helping the other at the point of most critical need? If not, is the failure mine, the other person's, or a mixture of both? And what is to become of the others whose well-being I have proven unable to secure?

Passages can be quoted from both the Hebrew scriptures and the New Testament in support of each of these common religious stereotypes of ministry. Amos 2:6–16 leaves no doubt that Israel's uncaring oppression of the poor has provoked God's anger and precipitated the day of reckoning. Ezekiel 33:7ff. indicates that the "watchman" is held accountable to God for warning "the wicked to turn from his ways." Regardless of how wicked the others may be, God will hold the watchman guilty of their death in wickedness if the watchman does not issue the warning. However: "If you warn the wicked to turn from his way, and he does not turn from his way; he shall die in his iniquity, but you will have saved your life."

A New Testament counterpart to Amos is in James 1:27: "Religion that is pure and undefiled before God and the Father is this: to visit orphans and widows in their affliction, and to keep oneself unstained from the world." And Matt. 10:11ff. (paralleled in Mark and Luke) has been read by Christian evangelists in connection with Ezekiel 33 as a description of ministry (see also Matt. 18:6).

No doubt there is a "transcendent urgency" in biblical faith that surrounds all questions of human relationships to human others. What is the special biblical shape of this urgent concern for human others? What are the claims it places on people who undertake ministry? Does it result in perfecting one's own religious life by demonstrating the virtue of caring? Or is it a matter, ultimately, of trying to secure the religious well-being of the other? Is it inherent in ministry that the other is always in some sense an "object" in relationship to whom the minister attempts to follow the pathway of his or her own religious fidelity?

Since Martin Buber it has become a cliché in enlightened Jewish and Christian circles that "of course" one never rightly treats other people as objects, whether for religious or any other reasons. We agree that persons are

first to be treated as persons and must never be subordinated to the loftiest agenda we may have for them. The result has been a two-horned dilemma: (1) On the one hand, the merest intrusion of the dimension of God into the work of ministry raises suspicions about self-serving or religiously imperialistic motives that reduce the other to an object. In reaction against this, many ministers have tried to become increasingly "secular" in their approach to helping others. (2) On the other hand, it has become clear from "secular" researches that altruism, in the sense of genuinely unmixed positive motives toward another human being, lies outside the realm of ordinary human possibilities. We always carry our heavy agendas, needs, and expectations into every relationship with others that is not merely superficial.

If these twin problems become vivid and real for anyone who undertakes professional ministry out of biblical faith commitments, the result can be agonizing paralysis or despair. The religious motivations that define the profession are tossed into a kind of anxious limbo, not called into play in relationship to the other unless the other insists, and then only with the appropriate disclaimers of spiritual authority. Many ministers are relieved if that emergency does not arise. Yet the credentials are there, stamping the minister as one who cares "for religious reasons" by contrast with social workers, physicians, or psychologists. These secular "helpers" may also care for religious reasons, but their claim is grounded in well-understood technical competencies. There is no inherent reason for people to expect "religious" help from them.

For this reason, professional ministers often seek special secular certification to satisfy themselves and others that they really are able to help, without necessarily bringing religion into the picture. We have made great strides forward in effective caring by developing these competencies in ministers. But there is no question that one side effect has been to decrease the minister's confi-

dence that faith commitments have any consistent relevance for the practical work of ministry. Yet, in the absence of this sense, the minister often comes to think of himself or herself as either flying under false colors or engaged in an inherently second-rate profession. The temptation is intense to hang out one's shingle as a practitioner of a well-understood secular profession such as sociologist or psychologist, if only to be candid about it. Or, if the faith commitments are particularly firm, the temptation is to let religion so dominate the relationships that the charge of religious self-serving or religious imperialism is accepted and worn as a badge of honor. Without compromise or apology, such ministers want to make explicit the religious resources on which they rely and the religious motivations they bring to the work of ministry.

Perhaps least comfortable are those who drift between these poles, unwilling to lay aside their religious motivation or credentials for ministry, and equally unwilling to intrude religious commitments into the foreground for fear of treating people as objects. We need to discover an understanding of ministry that is deeply rooted in faith commitments, urgently relevant to the practical work of ministry, and yet uncompromisingly respectful of the selfhood and personhood of others.

Following the implications of God's ministry to Israel and Israel's ministry to God, what are the implications in the Hebrew scriptures for Israel's ministry to human others? Recall the way in which God elicits from Israel the quality of being in relationship that God exercises toward Israel. God's style of relating is marked by covenant love, covenant justice, covenant goodness, covenant faithfulness, covenant truth, covenant "delight in the other." When Israel responds to God in faith and trust, these same qualities emerge as Israel's style of relating, defined by God in Torah, elicited by God from Israel, but to be chosen freely by Israel as the style appropriate

to loving God with heart, soul, and might. From the standpoint of God's story with Israel, these great words are not formless abstractions describing God's attitudes. Israel remembers them expressed concretely toward Israel in the choosing of the fathers, the creation of the world, the liberation from Egypt, and in the specific dealing of God with Israel from day to day and year to year. They are not only attitudinal words but action words to be expressed concretely in real relationships.

But the roles of God and Israel are not interchangeable. There is a profound sense in which Israel can never minister to God as God ministers to Israel. Israel will never be in a position to return the favor of choosing God, creating God, or liberating God as God has chosen, created, and liberated Israel. Israel will never be able to "provide for" God as God provides for Israel with countless acts of covenant fidelity. From the beginning, Israel's acts of covenant fidelity are to find their most specific and concrete expressions in relationship to human others. The "service" of God is always inseparable from immediate and practical concern for the dignity and well-being of persons encountered in the course of Israel's story with God. Are the two services distinct and separable, one primary and the other derivative? Are they identical? Let us explore these questions in conversation with a pair of Old Testament texts, the Decalogue (Exodus 20; Deuteronomy 5) and Deut. 10:17ff.

The tradition is ancient that distinguishes "two tables of the law," one describing the duty of Israel to God and the other describing Israel's duty toward persons. But is this distinction useful? Perhaps the prior question is whether the Decalogue demands or allows this distinction. In my judgment, there is not the slightest biblical warrant for dividing the ten "words" of the Decalogue ("words" = "weighty matters," not "commandments," in the Hebrew texts) into two kinds or ranks of responsibility. Our tendency to separate duty to God from duty

to people may involve an unwillingness or an incapacity to absorb the radical word about God and people with which the Decalogue confronts us.

There are fascinating questions about the origin, antiquity, and original form of the Decalogue. Scholars argue the question as to whether this is the core statement of Mosaic Torah from which all Torah derives, or whether it is a short summary of Torah codified nearer the end than the beginning of the development of Israel's legal corpus. Or perhaps it is based on a relatively ancient original liturgical form that later was assigned the summary significance explicitly claimed for it in texts such as Deut. 5:22 and 10:1-5.

The interesting thing, regardless of how such intriguing questions are decided, is the correspondence between the Decalogue in its present form and the remarkable character of the Old Testament legal corpus as a whole. As the Decalogue embraces "religious" and "moral" or "ethical" duties, without clear demarcation between the two, the present legal corpus of the Torah confronts us with a collection of demands ranging from detailed and obscure "religious" prescriptions (cf. Lev. 19:27), to equally obscure instruction about dealing with the world of nature (cf. Lev. 19:19), to the ethics of architecture (cf. Deut. 22:8).

There is no way to press all the laws of Israel into one coherent system and demonstrate the relative importance of one law over against another. Nor was the Christian tradition on solid ground when it used the Epistle to the Hebrews and other New Testament texts as a warrant to dismiss the so-called "ceremonial law" of the Bible as "abrogated" by Jesus Christ. Christian groups who make bold claims about the whole Bible as the word of God are in a more delicate position than they realize when they use parts of Holy Scripture as God-given warrants for regarding other parts of Holy Scripture as no longer "operational"!

I am led by certain insights of Gerhard von Rad[3] to suspect that every line of Old Testament law in some way delineates an area of human experience in which the "right" of God is at stake. Thought of in these terms, the endlessly varied legal tradition of the Torah penetrates into every conceivable corner of human life with the claim: Here, too, your deciding and acting are answerable to the holy Lord.

In that light, Torah's undisciplined interweaving of what we call "religious" responsibility and what we call "moral" or "ethical" responsibility becomes more impressive. There is one sphere of Israel's covenant responsibility, not two, and it embraces duty to God and duty to people without distinction. In dealing with human neighbors we are confronted by the same transcendent Lord whom we confront in the most exalted and intentional acts of religious devotion. Nothing that happens in any detail of ordinary human interrelationships is irrelevant to God, whether individual or social, at worship or in the marketplace, within the family, clan, tribe, nation, or in international affairs.

The prior concern of God, according to the Hebrew scriptures, is for all human beings, the entire realm of history and nature (Genesis 1–11; see above, pp. 45f.). The special ministry of God to Israel is part of God's larger ministry which is universal. There is no way Israel can rightly perceive and respond to God's ministry to Israel without also perceiving this larger ministry of God and the larger dimension of Israel's service to God. Because of this, the "outsiders" appear to Israel in an extraordinary light. They are "outside" by a variety of significant ethnic, religious, and cultural definitions that Israel must take seriously if it is not to reject the special covenant claims of God. Yet within the innermost circle of the faithful, one encounters a Lord who was concerned for these "outsiders" before there ever was an Israel! The urgency to respond faithfully to the God who chose

Israel is also the urgency to perceive and greet the Lord present in the whole world of history and nature in the interest of their wholeness and well-being. What does that imply for Israel's ministry to human others?

Deuteronomy 10:17ff. is one text among many that speaks to this question. It brings the dimension of Israel's ministry to human others into focus in a startling, perhaps even shocking, way. Verse 17 is a grand hymnic affirmation of the oneness and universality of God, terrifying and invincible in power, the incorruptible judge of all things, who acts impartially toward all human beings (cf. Isa. 11:3f.: "With righteousness he shall judge the poor, and decide with equity for the meek of the earth"; and cf. Psalms 94; 96; 98).

In Deut. 10:18, God is praised as the one who defends the cause and stands beside those who are disadvantaged and without recourse in the familiar human structure for securing justice and well-being. The familiar biblical words "fatherless," "widow," and "sojourner" represent, *pars pro toto,* all such disadvantaged and powerless people, without remainder. But it is here that the common religious idea is exploded that the virtue of "charity" is primarily a mode for the righteous to achieve or demonstrate their religious perfection. Here Israel must confront the unqualified affirmation that God loves the "sojourner"! In dealing with the "outsider," Israel is dealing with the Lord's beloved!

Distinctively in Deuteronomy, God's love is the foundation of Israel's election (Deut. 7:6ff.). It is this same quality of love that God elicits from Israel toward God (Deut. 6:5). Shockingly, God declares the same love for the outsider (Deut. 10:18). In the next breath comes the commandment, "Love the sojourner therefore!" As God loves Israel, as Israel is commanded to love God, now Israel is to perceive God's love for the sojourner and respond by participating in God's love.

But it doesn't stop there. Every shred of condescension

toward the sojourner, whether ethnic, moral, religious, or social, is stripped away from Israel in the next phrase: "For *you* were sojourners in the land of Egypt!" The same love by which you were liberated, constituted as God's people, and called to love God without reservation—that same love rests upon these outsiders. Meet yourself in these people. Recognize your need in their need. Recognize the justice, freedom, and mercy God wants for you in the justice, freedom, and mercy God wants for them. Recognize your well-being in their well-being. Recognize God's love for you in God's love for the alien. Above all, respond to God's love for you by participating in God's love for the alien.

This is the distinctive logic of ministry to human others in the Hebrew scriptures. It is a direct echo of Israel's election, an answering ministry of Israel to God, expressed toward other human beings because that is the way God expresses love to Israel. For this reason the relationship of faith for Israel can never become a tight lover's circle excluding those who do not, for whatever reason, share its intimate delights. There is only one love, not four, that flows from God to Israel, from Israel to God, from God to the alien, and from Israel to the alien. The source of this distinctive love described in the Bible is God. Israel's love toward God and neighbor is at its highest and best a joyous echo of, a free participation in, the love God has granted.

In Deut. 10:17ff. the question remains unanswered: Will love also flow from the alien to Israel, from the alien to God? In any case, Israel's command to love the alien is not conditioned by such expectations. There is no limitation that says ". . . provided the alien loves you in return." And there is no codicil saying that love for the alien is designed to seduce or coerce the alien into Israel's style of faith or response. It is enough to express God's love for the alien without imposing terms or asking anxious questions about the ultimate outcome.

It is in this sense that Israel is decisively free from all human others in the work of ministry. It is never a question of conveying God's love to the other. Before any act of loving or caring there is the startled recognition that God's love is already there for the other, as surely (and exactly on the same basis) as the love of God is there for Israel. The love that empowers God's ministry or Israel's ministry is not based on external necessity. If God's love is reflected in ministry toward the other, it is freely chosen love, celebrating love, answering love. All pragmatic questions about the how, the how long, and the ultimate "effectiveness" of ministry, important as they are, ultimately belong in God's hands. Israel does not depend on human others in order to reflect God's love, nor do the human others depend on Israel for the love of God.

But Israel and human others are given to each other in the love of God, in order that the single love of God for Israel and for the alien may be celebrated between them. When Israel chooses, out of God-given freedom from the other, to exercise its God-given freedom to be for the other, then God's love is celebrated in human affairs.

Deuteronomy 10:17ff. illustrates these dimensions of ministry because of its demand that Israel recognize itself in the alien. This implies that Israel must also perceive, in its acts of ministry, that the alien also is to be free from Israel, and even free from God in the same sense that Israel is free from God. Only the alien can choose whether to be free for God, and perhaps also free for Israel. If that is so, then Israel is called upon to do two apparently difficult and contradictory things in the work of ministry: (1) Israel is called not to surrender its integrity as a covenant people of God. (2) Israel is called not to surrender its love for the alien, or drop its ministry, even when the alien refuses to respond in love. To surrender either would be a failure to perceive and reflect the love of God. The biblical story insists that God's

"integrity," God's "holiness," is never surrendered in the infinitely vulnerable work of sharing Israel's life and history. Yet the story insists equally that no rejection of God on Israel's part, nor any failure, is capable of diminishing or altering God's "everlasting love" (Jer. 31:3). This kind of love, without surrender of self or other, describes the frontiers of ministry to human others to which Israel is called. Ministry toward human others, in that measure of freedom from and freedom for the other, and in the mode of granting the other the same kind of freedom from and freedom to be for, is Israel's ministry and service and love toward God.

Jesus may have been most Jewish when he linked Deut. 6:5 and Lev. 19:18 in response to the question about the "great commandment." I heard a chance acquaintance, a young New Testament scholar, talk about his researches into possible Aramaic originals underlying the Greek text of Matthew. He had provisionally concluded that Matt. 22:37ff. might have sounded something like this in Aramaic: " 'You shall love the Lord with all your heart . . .' This is the great and first commandment. And the second is a parable of it, 'You shall love your neighbor as yourself.' " I am not competent to judge the linguistic merits of the case, nor do I know how far my young friend has been able to convince his New Testament colleagues. I am persuaded that this way of putting the matter comes close to expressing the dynamic interchange between love of God and love of neighbor I encounter in the extraordinary phenomena of Torah. It is not so much a question of which is "primary" and which is "secondary." It is rather the astonishing biblical insistence that the love of God is to be expressed in specific attitudes and actions toward the neighbor, and the love of neighbor that participates in and reflects God's love of one's neighbor *is* the love of God. Even in Matt. 25:40 and 45, where Jesus puts the matter most radically, I am not convinced that he goes beyond Deut.

10:17ff., for in dealing with the "least" of one's human brothers and sisters, one is dealing with God's beloved, and therefore with almighty God.

If that is so, then in the broadest sense every human interaction is the occasion for "ministry." In every human contact the ministry of God to Israel and Israel to God will either be expressed or fail to be expressed to some degree. This does not have the consequence of leveling out all ministries or reducing the love of God and people to a vague abstraction. The incredibly varied and vivid details of the covenant claims made upon us in Torah make clear that none of us is ever in exactly the same situation as anyone else. The gifts, talents, opportunities, and circumstances of no two persons are identical. In the biblical story, prophet, priest, king, shepherd, matriarch, grain merchant, judge, bondmaid, farmer, queen, prophetess, soldier, are not interchangeable! "Ministry," the calling to reflect and celebrate the love of God in relation to neighbor, is not the same for each one. Yet the invitation and the claims of Torah rest upon each one. That means that "ministry" is the God-given possibility for each one according to who they are, what they have, where they are, under whatever circumstances they may live.

In the biblical story, God is singularly unimpressed by the differences between us on the points of competence, fitness, equipment, credentials, or status. On one occasion a rather harried and somewhat frantic prostitute was minister to all Israel (Josh. 2). On another, a shepherd boy was minister to a king (I Sam. 16:14ff.). A famous prophet endured the indignity of receiving ministry from black birds (or was it "Arabs"? cf. I Kings 17:4ff.)! This should perhaps give an appropriate sense of humor to those of us who bring to the task formidable resources of training, experience, wisdom, skills, perhaps very specialized ones. The possibility of ministry is as near for any of God's people as the next human being. If the miracle

happens between them that God's ministry is perceived, celebrated, and shared, then "ministry" has happened at the greatest imaginable depth. Yet if one brings specialized resources to the task, one may be certain that every part of those resources will be called upon. The claims of covenant love never require less of us than we actually possess.

The liberating consequence of this for professionally trained ministers is that we can take ministry absolutely seriously, as engaging the absolute best we have for the task, without having to take ourselves with absolute seriousness. In the biblical sense there is only one ministry. It is the ministry of God to Israel and to the entire world of history and nature. But there are as many ministries as there are people and groups who have been gripped by the ministry of God and choose to reflect it by claiming the God-given freedom to be for people.

If this is where our notions of ministry begin, then there are a variety of implications, some of them very practical, for what contemporary Jews and Christians may conceive as ministry. I cluster them under three headings: (1) Freedom from and for the other; (2) Celebration of the freedom of the other toward us; (3) A liberating sense of humor.

1. *Freedom from and for the other.* Ministry toward human others involves a special kind of detachment and a special kind of involvement. On the face of it, detachment sounds like the opposite of ministry. Yet if the freedom of God from as well as for Israel is our basic model, we are bound to explore what it may mean to be detached from those we seek to serve in God's name. Two basic kinds of attachment are immediately exposed as counterproductive for ministry. Ministry in the biblical sense cannot be based on my personal need to be a helper or to be recognized by the other as a helper. Such needs are present in all of us, but biblical faith demands that we recognize them for what they are, marks of spiritual ado-

lescence that the Lord intends us to grow beyond. The more we internalize the line "My help comes from the LORD, who made heaven and earth" (Ps. 121:2), the more ridiculous it appears to think of ourselves as "helping" anyone. We are the needy ones, and the "need" of the other is in that sense a mirror of our condition. Such "help" as may result from the work of ministry always happens between us and the other, for the strengthening of each of us, and it comes ultimately from God, not from either one of us. In ministry we may not count ourselves attached to the other in the sense that without the other our own basic needs cannot be met. If we are so attached to the other, then the other becomes for us an "it," and "ministry" becomes simply another form of self-gratification or self-aggrandizement. It is a strange postulate of faith that we do not need the other in order to minister to him or to her.

It is an equally strange postulate of faith that the other does not "need" us. If that is true, it would seem to destroy the whole logic of ministry. Yet the more we internalize the line "My help comes from the LORD, who made heaven and earth," the more clearly we recognize that we preside over no resources that are indispensable for ourselves or any other human being. To approach ministry with the idea that the other "needs" us in any fundamental sense sets up a relationship of necessary dependence that compromises both the freedom and the dignity of the other.

For caring people who preside over resources other people desperately lack, it may be impossible to avoid altogether this sense of being bound to other people by the intensity of their need. And the other may inevitably develop feelings of dependence on the one who ministers, regardless of the minister's own attitudes. But biblical faith forbids us to surrender to such feelings on either side. For the sake of our own God-willed freedom, as well as the freedom of the other, it is the work of faith

to claim again and again a holy sense of detachment. If we can perceive at some depth that we do not ultimately need the other, and the other does not ultimately need us, in order for God's ministry to happen between us, then we are beginning to explore the kind of freedom from compulsion and necessity that marks God's freedom from us.

Yet it is precisely out of such essential freedom from the human other that the possibility of genuine involvement on behalf of people emerges. There is no ministry in the biblical sense that is not freely chosen as a grateful response to God's free involvement with us. Caring seriously for other people necessarily involves varying degrees of drudgery, frustration, and pain. Yet there is a remarkable difference between freely choosing these liabilities for the sake of love, out of the motive of gratitude to God, and having them imposed from without.

For "professional" ministers, the very structure and pattern of professional life constitute an enormous temptation to lose sight of this indispensable inner key to ministry. We are expected, institutionally, to be caring persons whether or not we happen to feel like it on a given day. The sheer predictability of the next day's demands, and the taken-for-granted expectation by all sorts of people that we will be available and effective, constantly threatens to rob us of any serious sense of freedom we may have had in "choosing" to minister. The case is compounded for professional ministers by the economic reality that we are expected to "earn our keep" by demonstrating our capacity to care. Who can sustain a sense of freedom to be involved on behalf of other people when they and their needs are simply thrust upon us every day?

From the perspective we have described, there are two appropriate responses to this terribly unfree fatigue that often overtakes professional ministers. The first is to recognize that in the absence of any sense of freedom from

and freedom for the other, ministry by biblical definition is simply not our possibility. To face that fact squarely is no surrender. It is only the frank recognition that we who set out to minister in God's name to human others are ourselves constantly in need of the ministry of God: we are like the unformed chaos, waiting for God's creative word; like Israel in Egypt, waiting for God's liberation. It is the deep awareness that nothing separates us from the profound need of all those "others" that we feel are being "thrust" upon us in the routines of a pastoral day.

But this recognition, this awareness, is not the end of the possibility of ministry. On the contrary, it is only from this depth of our need that God breaks open ministry as our human possibility. We have simply been brought back to painful awareness that we never did possess resources and strength of our own which we could then generously "dispense" to other people. The sense of unfree fatigue that overtakes us is simply a measure of our naive and wrongheaded assumption that we are "strong" and the others "weak," that it is our strength that is being "drained" in our attempt to minister to others, that these others are somehow thrust upon us as our burden to carry.

So the first appropriate response to fatigue in ministry is a theological one: It is to recognize our own need, not as an indication of our ultimate failure, but as a necessary return to the starting point from which alone ministry in the biblical sense always begins. It may be that we need physical rest, emotional support, psychological therapy. Needy people often do, and faithful people need have no reluctance to admit the fact and to ask for the ministry of others. But it is essential not to suppose that by doing these practical things we are replenishing the basic resources out of which we may again attempt to minister to others. If the foregoing description of ministry in the biblical sense is accurate, it is precisely in acute awareness

of our own weakness, not our own strength, that ministry becomes our possibility.

That brings us to the second appropriate response to fatigue in ministry, which is to accept again the liberating ministry of God. It is for such tired and unfree people that the liberating love of God is given, in sovereign freedom from us and freedom for us. Every fresh perception of this grace discloses the fact that we and those we presume to "help" are identical in our need for the ministry of God. The help we presume to offer is not our own, and its "expenditure" is not a drain on our human resources. On the contrary, to receive and share the love of God is the only means we have ever had to experience the liberation God intends for us and all people.

This awareness will not prevent us from becoming fatigued in ministry, whether physically, emotionally, or psychologically. But it should disclose the fatigue as a sign of the ordinary human limitations we share with all people, and not as an indication of some radical failure in ministry. The wonder of faith is that it is precisely through the fragile and limited character of ordinary human lives that God chooses to disclose and mediate the infinite resources of God's grace. It is this same wonder that creates the special freedom from the other that keeps us from taking either ourselves or the other with absolute seriousness and that enables us to confront our own utterly real human limitations without losing heart. But it also creates the special freedom to be for the other, even in our brokenness and fatigue. Rightly understood, this freedom to minister to others—even if it is only a weary silent prayer when our human resources are at their lowest ebb—is the avenue to renewed freedom, renewed strength, and renewed joy.

2. *Celebration of the freedom of the other toward us.* Ministry toward human others also involves celebration of the freedom of the other toward us. Everything we have said about our freedom from and for others also describes the

kind of freedom that genuine ministry intends for the other. We are in a position to understand and experience in our lives, at considerable depth, the unfreedom and fatigue of those to whom we minister. The symptoms may be radically different. It is vital to perceive that no two of us ever have the identical experience of life. It is always our part to cherish and learn from the uniqueness of every human being with whom we come in contact. No one is ever merely another statistical example of some general rule of human experience and human response to it. So great is the freedom for which God intends us!

Yet ministry in the biblical sense does involve awareness of the kind of freedom which is the ultimate goal of every fragmentary act of ministry. It is the same kind of freedom which, when perceived and accepted by faith, constitutes both the warrant and the energy for ministry on our part. Not that our aim is to transform the other into a carbon copy of ourselves. That would be the rankest unfreedom both for us and for the other. Rather, it is precisely the aim of ministry to celebrate with the other the freedom from others (including us!) and the freedom to be for others which is the goal of God's ministry to us both.

If that is true, then both the minister and those to whom ministry is offered are equally "beggars in search of bread," to borrow a figure from D. T. Niles. The privilege of making the search together with another human being is the highest privilege of ministry.

This places all notions of the "practical results" of ministry in a liberating perspective. Each of us is in search of the "presence of purposive love" (see above, pp. 34ff.). Yet that is a quest none of us can make for anyone else. We can only point to God's purposive love by the quality of freedom we bring to the work of ministry. If our own freedom from and freedom for the other is genuine, then the other will sense a constant invitation

to be free from us as an important goal of our work together. We may not succeed in breaking through the unfree feelings of dependency the other may form toward us, but it is our place not to acquiesce in or foster such feelings. In the extreme case, it may be part of "purposive love" to terminate a relationship in ministry in which the other offers no mode of relating except a fixed pattern of increasing dependency upon what the other conceives as our "superior resources." The chances are excellent that these extreme dependencies have been created, wittingly or unwittingly, as much by our own complicity as by the stubborn insistence of the other. Frank acknowledgment to the other of the mutual failure may at least open the possibility that a different ministering person may be able to point, more effectively than we have managed, to the freedom *from* the ministering person that is a significant goal of ministry.

In one sense, this sounds like a practical "failure" in ministry on our part, and we may need to count it as such. But if we are clear enough about our own deep need for God's ministry, it need not continue as a crippling failure either for us or for the other person. In the best instance it may disclose better than any other course just how little and how much any minister (in the biblical sense) may presume to offer a human other. If the other expects more from us than the concerned company of another "beggar in search of bread," then the other expects more than we have to give, at the fundamental point. If the other expects less than the superb gift of freedom from others in order to be free for them, then the other expects less than God offers to give through the fragmentary efforts of very human "ministers." In that light, pragmatic concern about "success" or "failure" in acts of ministry is replaced by a tireless impulse to perceive, second, and celebrate every fragmentary sign of genuine freedom in the other.

It cannot be the expectation of ministry that the free-

dom of the other from us will issue in the decision to be free for us, to love us in return, to appreciate us, or perhaps least of all to "see things our way." In that regard, the most "practical" of all the results of ministry rest securely in other hands than ours, in the hands of God whose liberating love for unfree people like us far exceeds our best intentions, let alone our performance. Human ministry, in the biblical sense, is never "finished" —if that means achieving some envisionable goal of human wholeness or well-being. The only serious indication that someone has been "helped" through our ministry are the signs, not always perceptible to us, that the other has discovered his or her weakness as a perfectly adequate basis upon which to undertake ministry to others. We are not in the business of "saving" people. That is God's business. But the biblical word about ministry does invite us to celebrate, in very practical ways, the love of God that liberates us from, and therefore for, the people for whom God gives us to care. It is our freedom we celebrate, as well as theirs, when the relationship of ministry discloses signs in the other that God's gift of freedom has been accepted and is being shared.

3. *A liberating sense of humor.* Ministry toward human others involves doing very serious work of a kind that forbids us to take ourselves or the other with absolute seriousness. What could be more serious than the deliberate effort to express God's own love toward people about whom we already know that God loves them to the uttermost? Yet the Hebrew scriptures forbid us to believe that we are capable of generating such love out of our own emotional, spiritual, or intellectual resources. If we detect the impulses of such love for others moving in us, we can only greet the fact that God's love, upon which we depend for life, is apparently having its intended impact upon us. We are at best stewards, never proprietors, of even the initial motivations that stir us to think of dealing positively and constructively with

human others. Interior resources to care for others are things to pray for, and to celebrate when they are received. We know from the outset that we cannot manufacture them.

What a liberating thought that is. I not only do not have the burden of manufacturing my own goodwill toward the other, it is inherently quite impossible for me to do so! Ministry grounded in the love of God is, above all, sheer celebration of the God-given capacity to receive, share, and express the love of God for me and the other.

I may indeed face a given task of ministry toward another as a heavy chore for which I must generate the appropriate moral, emotional, spiritual, and intellectual heroism in order to begin. If so, I may be impressed most by the drudgery, frustration, and pain, and—perhaps above all—by the sheer unpleasant impossibility of really accomplishing anything significant on behalf of the other. Or I may sail into the task with the exalted notion that it is my job to intervene in the lives of others, and to secure for them a kind of well-being that only I can provide.

But it is at just such points that the biblical word says to us: "Don't take yourself so seriously!" Neither our own well-being nor the well-being of the other rests ultimately in our own hands. Even the capacity to care is a liberating gift of God, and God's caring for us and for the others goes far beyond any benevolent feelings we can generate on our own. Even our failures in caring— and we will fail!—are embraced in the exquisite care of God, whose forgiving love greets us even in our failure. If that is true, as the biblical word insists, there is nothing for it but to find specific ways to celebrate God's love for us and for the others by risking our own acts of caring.

As often as this somewhat hilarious state of affairs strikes us in the approach to ministry, then our attempts at caring are buoyed up by a certain laughter of the spirit.

We are free to risk failure, because our failures are not God's last word about us or about those we serve. But, more importantly, we are free to succeed in expressing God's caring, without the oppressive weight of supposing that we have done anything heroic or spectacular. Where God's ministry succeeds through us, we have done nothing more than celebrate with a human other the one love by which each of us lives and sustains hope. Perhaps it is true that only on the basis of such spiritual lightheartedness are we free to minister seriously, in God's name, to any human being. The appropriate prayer, then, on undertaking any task of ministry, goes something like this: "You know me, Lord, what my gifts and skills are, what I can and cannot do. Show me myself in this other. Each of us is beyond help unless you minister to each of us equally. Let your love happen between us, through our fragmentary means of relating. Forgive us and keep us both in your care. Amen." Having said that, expect miracles, remembering that the greatest miracle of which the Bible speaks is God's will to be faithful to us through and beyond our failures or even our tragedies. And every penultimate indication of human healing in response to ministry is a God-given sign of the wholeness for which God intends us. To undertake ministry on these grounds is an exercise not only in faith and love but also in hope—hope for oneself, for the other, and for the entire human experiment. It is designed to be the most liberating, authentically serious, and joyous calling on earth.

2

MINISTRY IN JUDAISM:
REFLECTIONS ON SUFFERING AND CARING

BY
SAMUEL E. KARFF

Two Jews were engaged in a theological argument. One was a doubter; call him doubting David. He questioned passionately the reality of God, and, with even more vehemence, the concept of a God of justice and love. The second gentleman, call him Jonathan, was extremely distressed by David's remarks. In opposition to David, Jonathan affirmed the existence of God, the reality of the divine covenant with the people Israel, and God's providential care of the world. David rebutted Jonathan's defense of God. They debated until David suddenly said: "I am sorry, I must leave. It is time to recite the afternoon prayers."

Astonished and unnerved, Jonathan blurted: "Are you serious? You have spent all this time questioning the faith of our fathers and now you are ready for prayer?" David replied: "I am not sure always that God cares for his world, but I am sure that it is a *mitzvah* (a commandment) for a Jew to recite his afternoon prayers."

This story illustrates that considerable flexibility in matters of theological affirmation is a fundamental characteristic of Judaism. Judaism tends to be less concerned than Christianity to require assent to formal creeds. Rather, Judaism seeks more to guide behavior, to define clearly the *mitzvot,* the commandments that a Jew is expected to observe. Judaism assumes the reality of a cove-

nant between God and Israel and proceeds to define how a Jew ought to respond to that covenant.

This does not mean that Judaism is not concerned with theological reflection; rather, theological questions are very much a part of the biblical and rabbinic world. Prophets, sages, and simple folks had moments when God's caring love or his fidelity to the covenant was doubted. The *aggadot* (stories in the Bible and Talmud) reflect such crises of faith and the yearning to reaffirm trust in God's power and goodness in the presence of sickness, suffering, and death.

By whatever means an ancient rabbi described adversity, his intent was to strengthen the believer's trust in the God of the covenant. Yet he was not devoted primarily to *agada* (interpretation in the form of stories to strengthen faith). Rather, he was devoted to *halacha*, which instructed the conduct of a faithful Jew. Whether or not traditional *agada* has successfully "resolved" the problem of suffering, the *halacha*, the system of Jewish law, defines and mandates the way in which a Jew can best express love for God in God's world.

The theological and pragmatic questions posed in the imaginary debate between David and Jonathan are not ancient artifacts of religious lore that are irrelevant to contemporary life. People of faith still address these fundamental concerns. What is God's will for humanity? What meaning can be given to human adversity? What is God's role in tragedy? What does God command of the faithful in response to human pain and suffering? What resources, both scriptural and traditional, are available to inform attempts to express and offer divine and human concern and comfort?

These questions highlight some of the problems which from time immemorial have tested the faith of believers and challenged justifications for ministry. All suggested answers are necessarily limited by human finitude and prejudiced by historical circumstances. Nevertheless, the

issues remain and merit fresh initiatives at resolution by each generation of believers. This essay addresses these issues by providing some reflections on how the ministry of caring can be grounded in and derived from the theological tradition of Judaism.

My discussion of ministry in Judaism will focus on the phenomenon of illness as an example of how theological reflection shapes and gives substance to ministry. I encourage the reader to apply the findings of this study to other areas of ministry in a faithful and creative manner. In order to fulfill the limited purpose of this essay, I shall consider first several Jewish responses to the problem of innocent suffering. Second, I shall offer a perspective on the ministry of caring that emerges from the biblical and rabbinic sources.

SUFFERING: A CHALLENGE TO FAITH

Elisha ben Abuya was one of the most colorful personalities in all rabbinic literature. He was a revered scholar, a teacher of teachers, a rabbi of rabbis. He lived during the second century of our era. He is remembered most as a man who underwent a crisis of faith and became a rabbinic dropout. According to a talmudic account, Elisha lost his confidence in divine justice when he observed two contrasting scenes. One Sabbath he paused from studying the Torah to watch a man ascend a tree, remove a mother bird and her little ones from the nest, and climb down safely. Elisha knew that two commandments of the Torah had been violated. The man had climbed a tree on the Sabbath in violation of the prohibition of work and he violated the commandment in Deuteronomy which prescribes that if one chances upon a mother bird in her nest and takes the young, the mother bird shall remain free. The man who violated these injunctions of the Torah left the scene with no ill effects.

The following day Elisha noticed another man climb a

tree. It was no longer the Sabbath. Observing the commandment, the second man released the mother bird before taking the offspring. Yet he who obeyed the biblical injunction was bitten by a poisonous snake and died. Contrasting these two episodes in his mind, Elisha was overcome by despair and declared: "There is no justice, there is no judge."

If God is infinite power and love; if he cares for his creation, then why should a righteous person be bitten by a poisonous snake and die? If God is just, then why is fidelity to the covenant repaid on occasion with suffering and death? Why do the innocent suffer? These questions of practical theodicy are often addressed to those who minister. Many who suffer ask consciously or unconsciously in one form or another, "Why, why me?"

In most instances like these, neither a formal attempt to explain the ways of God nor a recitation of responses excerpted from Theology 101 is expected, desired, or perhaps needed by the questioner. The minister or rabbi may be of most help by offering a verbal or nonverbal gesture of empathy, solidarity, and love. If this perception is accurate, then why should an essay on ministry permit a digression into theodicy? One answer is that there are occasions when an afflicted person needs simple reassurance that life is not absurd in spite of all appearances. The pastor in these circumstances ought to help the sufferer reaffirm faith in God's purposes.

Students of Hillel and Shammai once posed the issue in this way: Given the conditions of human life and the reality of evil, would it have been better for humans not to have been created? The school of Shammai argued that it would have been better. The school of Hillel agreed but added that since mankind has been created, let people live as responsibly as possible. More typical than these two conclusions is the rabbinic dictum: It is incumbent upon mankind to praise God for the good *and* for the evil encountered in life, i.e., if evil is the price of

God's creation, then life is worth its price (Berachot 33b).

There is another principal reason why a discussion of theodicy is by no means a gratuitous digression. The struggle to reaffirm the goodness of creation and a meaning for life may be experienced not only by those who suffer but by those who minister. The success by which the struggle is met will affect the morale of the former and the effectiveness of the latter. Pastors also have spiritual needs. They cannot be exposed relentlessly to innocent suffering without experiencing periodic crises of faith. The one who ministers also needs assurance that God's covenant with mankind abides, and that life is more than a dirty trick. A rabbi or pastor who comes to terms with the conditions of life and is able to praise the Lord is far better equipped for the task of ministry than one who pretends that the issue does not exist, or who has refused to personally wrestle with it. In this sense a Jewish perspective on theodicy is not a frivolous digression but an essential part of any discussion of pastoral ministry in Judaism.

A Jewish theodicy cannot be derived from a study of Scripture alone. The diligent student must examine how biblical themes were elaborated by the rabbinic spirit. Rabbinic thought is dependent upon the Bible but is not reducible to biblical texts. One cannot understand classical Judaism, that configuration of thought and norm which has shaped Jewish life for the last fifteen hundred years, without studying early rabbinic texts which began with the teaching of the Pharisees in the first century B.C.E. and end with the canonization of the Talmud in the sixth century C.E.

Jewish responses to the question of innocent suffering are rooted in Scripture and fleshed out in rabbinic texts. They may be classified under the following headings: (1) Inauthentic righteousness—the innocent may only appear so; (2) The suffering servant—we may suffer for

God; (3) Chastisement of love—discipline by God; (4) Reliance on future salvation—the hedge of time; (5) Divine self-limitation—the price of human freedom; and (6) A covenant with hidden clauses—the limitations of human understanding.

Before we survey these responses, it is helpful to note that biblical covenant theology affirms one God who created and rules over nature, calls persons into being, and enters into a covenant with them. Mankind is free to obey or disobey God's commandments, but not without consequences. Deuteronomy proclaims, "I have set before thee life and death, the blessing and the curse; therefore choose life, that thou mayest live, thou and thy seed" (Deut. 30:19).

Elisha ben Abuya's discovery that a person who follows God's laws may be wounded mortally by a snakebite affronted his faith in a meaningful covenant. He asked: "Why do good people suffer?" He replied: "Because God is not trustworthy; the covenant is a deceit." Meaningful alternatives to Elisha's conclusion are found in biblical and rabbinic thought wherein efforts are made to reconcile the power and love of God with the reality of unmerited suffering.

Inauthentic Righteousness

One of the most striking responses was the suggestion, made by one of Job's comforters (Bildad), that there is a causal connection between sin and suffering, illness and death. Many biblical texts support this idea. Miriam was stricken with leprosy because she unjustly lashed out at her brother (Num. 12:9f.). Aaron's sons died because they offered "strange fire unto the Lord" (Lev. 10:1f.). On the other hand, King Hezekiah presumed that his illness and impending death were undeserved. When he pleaded that he had been faithful, God accepted his plea and healed him (II Kings 20:1–11; cf. Isaiah 38).

Some rabbinic sages asserted that God's moral provi-

dence was all-encompassing: "No man bruises his finger on earth unless it is decreed in heaven" (Hullin 7b). It followed: "If a man sees suffering, let him examine his conduct" (Berachot 5a). The implication of this Deuteronomic view is that if a righteous person or family member suffers, it may be that one is not as unblemished as one seems (Ps. 37:25).

The Suffering Servant

An alternative response is also found in talmudic thought: One may suffer in the very course of serving God. Second Isaiah declared that Israel's anguish was more than a measure of the nation's sin. Israel suffered also for the sake of others and for God. This is a common Jewish interpretation of the "servant" poems. In Isa. 50: 4–9, Israel is likened to a prophet commissioned by God for a mission. Sheldon Blank, in his translation of Isaiah 53, commented that by being God's prophet people, Israel suffered more than it deserved because God chose Israel as a lesson, an example to other nations, and because bearing God's message to an unredeemed world necessarily brought suffering to the messenger.[1]

This concept of suffering for God is amply elaborated in rabbinic Judaism. In the midst of Emperor Hadrian's persecution of the Judean community, Rabbi Akiba, a contemporary of Elisha, imagined the nations of the world asking Israel tauntingly why it did not abandon God and forsake its mission. Akiba implied in his response that Israel suffered and died not because of the depth of its sin but to sanctify God's name in a world that did not yet acknowledge God's sovereignty (Mekilta Shirata, Beshallah). Akiba himself was destined to die a martyr's death and, according to the Talmud, exclaimed in the midst of his agony: "Now I know what it means to love the Lord with all my soul" (Berachot 61b).

There is some suggestion in the servant poems of Isaiah that Israel suffered vicariously, but this theme did

not attain the centrality in biblical Judaism or in rabbinic Judaism that it has held in Christianity. Nevertheless, the Hebrew Bible and rabbinic literature incorporated some sense of the atoning power of suffering (Isa. 53:12). This theme, relatively minor in classic Jewish thought, was destined to become a pivotal affirmation of Christianity.

Chastisement of Love

The biblical concept of suffering as a chastisement of love, elaborated in rabbinic thought, is rooted in Deuteronomy: "As a man chastens his son, so the Lord thy God chastens thee" (Deut. 8:5). Second Isaiah and Jeremiah developed the theme of loving parental discipline and instruction. It is partly embodied in Second Isaiah's understanding of Israel's suffering as a servant of God. Second Isaiah declared that God loves Israel and has not abandoned her. Her suffering is intended to discipline her and is in part a lesson to the nations (Isa. 40–55). Jeremiah bemoaned the fact that the people did not respond to God's intention: "They set their faces harder than stone, they refused to come back" (Jer. 5:3). He projected the response that God wanted to hear from his people: "You disciplined me, and I accepted discipline. . . . Now take me and let me come back, for you are the Lord my God" (Jer. 31:18).

In rabbinic literature suffering may possess an atoning power. Suffering disproportionate to one's sins may be a "chastisement of love," a way of reconciling the sinner to God in this world in order that the fullness of divine grace may be received in the world to come. The story is told that when Rabbi Eliezer fell sick his disciples entered his house to visit. In great pain Eliezer greeted them with the words, "There is a fierce wrath in the world." Hearing this, the disciples broke into tears of empathy, but Akiba laughed. When the disciples demanded an explanation, Akiba replied that until now things were going so well for his friend that he feared

Rabbi Eliezer may have received all of his reward in this life. Having been cleansed of the debt of sin, Eliezer would now be fully rewarded in the next world. Hearing Akiba's words, Eliezer asked challengingly: "Have I neglected anything of the whole Torah?" (i.e., Did I need atonement through suffering?). Akiba replied: "You, O master, have taught us that there is no totally just man who does not sin" (Sanhedrin 101a).

This talmudic story and its sequels asserts that suffering may be a chastisement of divine love. It should be noted, however, that the rabbis were not unanimous in embracing the notion of suffering as a chastisement of love. One rabbi prays: "In your abundant compassion forgive my sins, but not by bringing suffering and evil diseases" (Berachot 17a).

Reliance on Future Salvation

The concept of suffering as a chastisement of love is linked in rabbinic texts to one's ultimate reward in a world to come. There is some intimation in the Hebrew Bible that the problem of suffering may be resolved only in a future realm. But while intimations of an "afterlife" are found in Daniel, Isaiah, and Ezekiel, the primary burden of Hebrew scripture was to seek a resolution of the conflict between God's goodness and human suffering within the perimeters of earthly existence. The psalmist who saw no just reason for his affliction questioned God's providence but concluded with the hope— even more, the expectation—that God's faithfulness would in time be vindicated (see for example Psalm 22; cf. Psalms 6 and 92).

The concept of time as God's vindicator means that in the future the apparent contradiction between God's power-love and unmerited suffering will be resolved. This hedge of time blossomed into the biblical messianic hope. Jews were encouraged to believe that "in the end of time" or "in latter days" the contradictions of life

would be resolved. At present those without goodness hold power, while those who are good are powerless. But someday a righteous ruler will be enthroned. There will come a day when goodness and power will be united on earth as they are in heaven. On that day political and cosmic disharmonies will be resolved (Isa. 11:1–9).

The Pharisees offered the fullest eschatological response to the reality of suffering in God's world. These forerunners of the rabbis went beyond the notion of future vindication in this world. They moved the boundaries of hope to "the world to come" by developing a theme found in the later biblical period, i.e., the belief that God's dominion and presence extended beyond the realm of the living (see Ps. 139:7–8).

The notion of reward and punishment in a postmortal realm stems from the Maccabean period (second century B.C.E.). Louis Jacobs noted that at this time three interrelated eschatological ideas coexisted: (1) the immortality of the soul, (2) the doctrine of the Messiah, and (3) the resurrection of the dead. Jacobs explained that immortality of the soul was initially a concept of personal fulfillment, while resurrection focused on the community of Israel. He suggested that the two were combined so that an individual was presumed not to have lost his soul at death. Thus, the soul lived on in heaven, and sometime after the coming of the Messiah the body would be resurrected and the soul restored to the body on this earth.[2]

Rabbinic Judaism's attitude toward the "afterlife" vis-à-vis this earthly existence was one of coaffirmation. The rabbis appear to have affirmed both the unique and unrecoverable glory of our mortal span and the crown of fulfillment available to God's children in the world to come. A belief in an eschatological redemption from the brokenness of this earthly existence served as a comfort, consolation, and means of bridging the gap between God's power-love and the innocent suffering of this life.

Divine Self-Limitation

If the vindication of God's power-love is deferred to the future either in this life or in the world to come, then the question arises: Why should there be a time lapse before the fullness of God's glory is manifest? This delay implies that God the Creator and Ruler of nature and history is subject to some restriction. One suggestion is that the gift of human freedom is a self-imposed restriction on God's power.

In the Bible, Adam (representing mankind) was called to covenant. He was given the power/freedom to obey or disobey the senior partner in the covenant. Adam's freedom and power were tempered ultimately by the ineluctable encounter with death. Nevertheless, within the boundaries of his mortality, Adam's freedom implied some divine self-limitation at the very dawn of sacred history. Adam was free to act independently of God. The fact of human freedom implies that not everything that occurs is necessarily the purposive will of God. Thus, there is a basis for a distinction between the suffering and evil that God *wills* and the evil that God *permits.*

The concept of divine self-limitation is implied rather than explicitly formulated in Scripture. If God had his way, Israel always would have observed his will. The prophets suggested again and again that the drama of history included a divine pathos or disappointment (Jer. 2:5). God seems to say, "I gave them freedom, and look how they abused it."

The implications of man's power were substantially extended in rabbinic thought by the notion of *yetzer* (primal energy), which is God's creation. The rabbis suggested that *yetzer,* properly directed, enabled one to be God's constructive partner. A rabbi noted: "The greater the man, the greater his *yetzer,*" i.e., the person of great promise is a person with greater energy for good or evil. The intention of God is that one hallow or consecrate

one's *yetzer* to the service of the Creator.

In addition to the energies God gave mankind for consecration, even more crucially, God has given Israel the Torah as instruction. Those who adhere to its precepts are believed to diminish the power that evil has over them in the world at large. While a dualistic solution to the problem of suffering won the hearts of some Jews, the classical rabbinic tradition resisted it. It is not a personified Satan's mischievous antics but mankind's abuse of freedom that remains the most pervasive sign of divine self-limitation. God alone speaks the final word in the drama of history. For all their God-given powers, human beings remain junior partners in the covenant of life. Only penultimately does God appear to be self-limited by his creatures.

A Covenant with Hidden Clauses

The ultimate biblical response attributes the problem of innocent suffering not to intimations of divine self-limitation, but to human finite understanding. Isaiah sounded the keynote. "As the heavens are higher than the earth, so are my ways higher than your ways and my thoughts than your thoughts" (Isa. 55:9). The author of the Book of Job sounded an even more powerful note on this theme. Job insisted that his suffering was without moral cause. He refused to accept his suffering as just punishment for sin. Although his comforters suggested otherwise, Job was vindicated. The Lord who spoke to him out of the whirlwind did not deny Job's innocence, nor did God deny that good people may suffer.

Job discovered that he and the comforters he scorned had shared a desire to unveil the mystery of the infinite and to reduce the covenant to an irresistible proposition. In his struggle for faith, Job realized that his finitude made it impossible for him to penetrate fully the mystery of divine providence. He was summoned to trust God, though the covenant had hidden clauses. Job struggled,

rebelled, and doubted, but finally accepted his finitude. His life became bearable and meaningful because he chose to serve and trust a God who is both hidden and revealed. Job learned to trust in the presence of mystery and to affirm that beyond the mystery there is meaning.

The rabbis also acknowledged that not all suffering was deserved, nor was the purpose of such suffering always perceived. Mankind must ultimately trust in a God whose covenant has hidden clauses. One of the sages put it succinctly: "It is not in our power to understand the suffering of the righteous, or the prosperity of the wicked" (Avot 4:19). Faith is a struggle. One must trust at times in spite of an apparent contradiction between the power and goodness of God and the pervasiveness of innocent suffering.

The Theodicy of Maimonides

The theodicy of Moses Maimonides, one of the giants of Jewish thought, provides an additional dimension to the view of God limited by his purposes. This medieval rabbi, physician, and philosopher who lived during the late twelfth and early thirteenth centuries was deeply influenced by neo-Aristotelian thought. He struggled to formulate a compelling rational ground for the painful experiences of human life. As an outstanding physician he beheld daily evidence of human affliction. He also knew from personal experience the anguish of emotional suffering.

At age thirteen, Maimonides and his family witnessed the persecution of Jews at the hands of the Almohades. His entire family was forced to go into exile. Some years later Maimonides' brother David, the mainstay of family support, died in a shipwreck. The death of his brother was traumatic to Maimonides. About eight years later he wrote: "On the day I received the terrible news I fell ill and remained in bed for a year, suffering from a sore boil, fever and depression and was about given up.

. . . He (David) has passed away and left me disturbed in my mind in a foreign country."[3] Maimonides ended his report by quoting Gen. 37:35, words that Jacob recited when he heard of the death of Joseph: "I shall go down to the nether world to my son in mourning." Maimonides recovered from his depression and subsequently became one of the most prodigious figures in human history.

Maimonides recognized that pain and suffering was in part the price of our bodily nature and that a proper rational understanding of God and the world was a principal ally in reducing the power of pain over human life. Maimonides' reflections on theodicy drew upon and amplified certain themes found in biblical-rabbinic Judaism. His consideration of innocent suffering led him to three conclusions: (1) God's goodness and love are not compromised by encounters with the reality of evil. God does not directly will suffering. Rather, God "permits" or accepts suffering as the necessary price of the creative process. (2) Human partnership with God imposes a human responsibility for the preservation of life and the alleviation of pain. Much of what is considered evil is not only the price of creation. It also can be the price of an abuse of human freedom or a failure to understand the conditions of life and to fulfill the intended purpose of creation. (3) The quality of one's relationship to God may enable one to attain significant victory over suffering partly in this world and totally in the world to come.

The biblical and rabbinic responses to suffering form the classical theodicy of Judaism, forged during countless generations of rabbinic debate and study of the Scriptures. Maimonides' quest for understanding, the search for a reconciling vision, has engaged every generation of thoughtful believers. Those who minister to suffering individuals draw on the insights of our heritage and test them in the crucible of contemporary experience. Depending on temperament and circumstance the believer

could affirm that suffering is deserved, that suffering is part of being God's servant, that there will come a time when our faithfulness will be vindicated, that suffering may be the price of God's creative plan, or that the ultimate recourse is to trust God and be faithful to a covenant with hidden clauses.

Search for a Practical Theodicy

Gershom Scholem has stated that the task of theology is to speak of God in ways that "preserve the purity of the concept of God without loss of His living reality."[4] It is not easy to speak of God without overpersonalizing him, which risks creating God in human images. It is difficult in the depths of human anguish to commune with a nonpersonal energy, power, or force. I have opted for the classical rabbinic approach to religious language: Use reasonably bold anthropomorphic imagery and remind yourself from time to time that God transcends all our images. I think of, address, and, in moments of grief, feel the presence of one who is conscious of prayer, active to love, to heal, and to redeem the promise of his creation. The key to my personal theodicy is the notion of a God of infinite goodness and power who is self-limited by his freely chosen purposes for mankind in the world. This concept is implicit in the biblical-rabbinic tradition and in the philosophy of Maimonides.

As a creature of the twentieth century, I have experienced both the creative power and the silence of God. His power is manifested in his creative gift of structures and the life processes of the world and the human organism. This structure makes human thought, planning, and knowledge possible. But the gift of a structured world is also an act of divine self-limitation.

God's good gifts impose a price from which not even the Lord may be able to spare us. The complex human organism which renders us capable of special sensitivity, creativity, and love also renders us more vulnerable to a

wider range of suffering than the lower animals. An ancient rabbi intuited this when he pointed out that lower organisms do not suffer from nervous stomachs. The gift of life itself exacts a price; a living organism is by its very nature a dying organism. All that lives must die.

What is true in the realm of nature is also true in the realm of history. God's redemptive power was present to our ancestors in Egypt and is present in our own experience. But the God who is active in history is also at times silent. He who liberated a people from Egyptian bondage hid his face at Auschwitz. The gift of history, a dialogue between God and man, exacts a heavy price. Man is a creature who may say a destructive *no* to his creator. Hitler was a demonic fruit of freedom, a bitter symbol in our time of divine self-limitation.

In nature and history we experience both God's power and God's silence. We experience the wondrous gift of life and the tragic curse of untimely death. We experience the unyielding demand to "let my people go" and the ashes of the oppressed who were not freed by God or man. Where does God's power in this earthly realm end and his self-limitation commence? The drawing of that line is the mystery of divine providence. Our prayers of petition are grounded in the hope that the line will be drawn in our favor. The ancient rabbis pictured God struggling between his attribute of justice and his attribute of mercy. This insight may be extended to embrace the image of a God who struggles between his desire to sustain human freedom and his desire to spare one from the consequences of abusing that freedom. God grieves over the suffering of his creatures. He grieves over the painful price that he and his creatures must pay for the drama of life and history.

God's loving presence is our ultimate ally in weathering the storms of life. We can resist God's help. We can permit our suffering and anguish to embitter and destroy us, or with his help we can wrest victory from adversity.

Whether or not we formally acknowledge God, he is present in every human effort to wrest some meaningful, life-affirming blessing out of the depths of suffering and anguish. Many creative achievers like Beethoven, Freud, Keller, and Didion have struggled against barriers and boundaries that served only to renew and refocus their energies. I cannot believe that God wills disabilities, but I believe that God is redemptively present in helping people to cope with them.

God's redemptive power is not manifested only in celebrated lives. I think of persons with whom I have ministered over the years. A couple who lost a young son in a tragic rifle accident wove a life of compassion and tenderness for underprivileged children in their community out of the fabric of their broken hearts. I think also of a young woman who became a paraplegic through a ski accident at age twenty-two. After a successful battle against despair, she found meaning in a militant campaign to provide a physical environment in public buildings that will render these structures accessible to persons in wheelchairs. These cases reveal that God's providence may not spare us from suffering and sorrow, but God's redemptive power may enable us to experience blessing even in the depths of pain.

When all has been said and all our theological stories have been proclaimed, the mystery of God's ways abides. The line where God's power and self-limitation meet is hidden from our eyes. The full meaning of suffering is not revealed to us. We grope in a land of shadows. We are called to trust that beyond the mystery there is meaning. We are summoned to accept God's universe on his terms and to proclaim that despite the reality of innocent suffering there is a loving, caring, redemptive presence at the heart of life.

That struggle was revealed to me in some handwritten notes that the mother of an eleven-year-old girl gave me.

One note was written in the hospital room where her only daughter lay dying from the ravages of leukemia.

> I am sitting by the bedside of a dying child—my child. I ask myself, O Lord why, is there any justice in the world that the life of an innocent child should be taken at age eleven? She never did anything to bother anyone, but has been through the tortures of hell with a fatal blood disease complicated by a series of infections. . . . Susan never did anything in her life except bring joy to her parents. Sometimes she was willful, demanding as an only child of middle-aged parents. I don't doubt that we spoiled her. She was pretty, willful, good-natured, and mature far beyond her years, compassionate toward people, keenly aware of current social problems. . . .

The letter concludes:

> After a simple funeral service our lives will have to go on, but there will be no more light. She was our light and our hope. Blessed is the will of the Lord who has given us life and who has taken it away.

Between the death of Susan and the funeral service, the mother wrote another letter in which she elaborated upon the loveliness of Susie. This letter concludes:

> And so, at eleven she is gone, but is life easily measured in days or months or years? Susie touched many lives and will live beyond in my heart through the privilege of having known her. Her parents, in the eleven years she spent with them, enjoyed the closest thing to heaven that is granted to man on earth. May God bless her always.

At such times all explanations, all attempts to understand God's ways are inadequate. What is needed most is a renewed love for each other and a renewal of power to trust the God of love who has summoned us into covenant with him.

In situations like this, people of faith are called to

minister to those who suffer the hurts of life. Whatever
the occasion of ministry (sickness, death, separation, vocational loss), believers are called by God to share the
burden of adversity and to affirm the eternal presence
and love of God who has chosen us for fellowship with
him. A response of compassion to the adversity of another is elicited from the believer by God's gracious
action in incorporating the believer into the covenant
community. God's initiative toward the believer should
be reflected in the believer's initiative toward others.

We turn therefore to examine the nature of a ministry
of caring that acknowledges concerns of theodicy and is
built upon Jewish theological premises. I will focus on
illness as one instance of adversity, drawing from both
talmudic and biblical sources in order to describe the
shape and content such ministry takes.

THE MINISTRY OF CARING: A JEWISH PERSPECTIVE

Serious illness by its nature is demeaning. It is an as-
sault on bodily powers. It dramatizes one's dependence
on others. The governing principle of ministry to the sick
is embraced in a word appropriated so generously in our
time. The word is *dignity*. The Talmud says that one who
is in the presence of a sick person is confronting the
shechina, the indwelling spirit of God, who hovers over
the bed of the sick one. Respect for the dignity of the sick
is linked to respect for the *shechina*. Hence it is taught
that when visiting a person confined to bed, one must not
stand over the patient but sit on a chair or stool so as not
to be on a higher level or to flaunt one's well-being and
mobility. If the patient is stretched on the ground, then
one must act reverently and sit on the ground (Nedarim
40a). Respect for the dignity of a sick person is an act of
deference to the sick person and to God who hovers
above the patient's bed.

The *halacha,* the tradition of Jewish law, contains additional stipulations governing the visitation of the sick that are designed to confirm and clarify the meaning of human dignity. The sick person is accorded special privileges (or exemptions) with regard to the fulfillment of covenant obligations. For example, Yom Kippur is a fast day and the holiest day in the Jewish year. The tradition stipulates that if a *patient* wants to observe the fast and the *physician* objects because the patient is too weak, the patient is obligated by Jewish law to eat. On the other hand, if the *physician* says the patient is strong enough to fast, but the *patient* doesn't feel able, the latter's testimony is decisive and the fast should not be observed.

The Talmud prohibits the visitation of those suffering with bowel troubles, eye troubles, and headaches (Nedarim 41a). Why? Because one whose bowels move frequently may be embarrassed by the presence of visitors. Speech, it was believed, could be also injurious to people suffering from eye trouble and chronic headache. It is necessary to question the early rabbis' medical. knowledge, but the underlying principle is valid. Under some circumstances a patient's dignity and health may be served best by not visiting. The prospective visitor, however, may not salve his conscience at the expense of the patient's comfort.

A concern for the morale of a sick person is illustrated in the following talmudic statement: "Formerly they placed a perfuming pan under (the bed) of those who were dying of intestinal disorders. Those who suffered from intestinal disorders were embarrassed (shamed) at being so singled out, whereupon it was determined that the perfuming pan should be placed under all patients' beds" (Moed Katan 27b).

The impact of contemporary health care has affected the ministry to the sick in a number of significant ways. For one thing, the hospital has eclipsed the home as a center for ministry to the sick. The reasons for this are

numerous and have been amply discussed elsewhere. The preference for care of the sick in the hospital has served to shield the modern family from the reality of death and dying. The assembling of families at the bed to receive a parting word is much less common today because the dying process is often extended through respirators and intravenous feedings beyond the level of personal consciousness, and because of a desire to deny death. Consequently we have deprived ourselves of experiences at home or in the hospital that would enhance life's meaning for the dying and their kin.

Surely there is much to be said for the dignity of being permitted to die in familiar surroundings rather than in the sterility of a hospital. But I have known families and patients who felt more comfortable in a hospital setting. Effective ministry may be offered in either setting. When hospitals become, for a variety of reasons, the setting for care of the sick, a primary goal for patient care is to infuse that alien place with the nurturing symbols of hearth, home, and synagogue.

Ministry to those commonly called "terminally ill" requires special sensitivity if the dignity of the person is to be honored. While Judaism generally has encouraged medical intervention to extend life, there has always been a subtle distinction between extending life and merely prolonging the process of dying. There are occasions when death comes not as a conqueror but as a friend. A concern for the dignity of the sick may require a diligent intervention to extend life. On the other hand, under some circumstances it may require sharing a person's yearning for release from an unbearable limbo of a "life" that is not life.

In this regard the Talmud contains a strange story. When Rabbi Judah lay dying, a group of his rabbinic colleagues gathered outside his home in a continuous prayer vigil. They hoped that their prayers would result in an extension of Rabbi Judah's life. But the Rabbi's

housekeeper, who knew the hopelessness of his situation and loved him deeply, could not stand to watch him suffer. She not only refused to join his rabbinic colleagues in their prayers, she threw a huge earthen jar down from the roof in order to interrupt their prayers. The Talmud cites the housekeeper's action with approval (Ketubot 104a). Rabbi Nissim Gerondi, who lived in the fourteenth century, developed the implications of this rabbinic story. He discussed the duty of visiting the sick and praying for their recovery. He concluded that there are times when one may ask God in his mercy that a sick person be permitted to die.[5]

Our situation is more complex than the one confronting Rabbi Judah and his rabbinic colleagues. Once they had finished praying there was relatively little by way of medical intervention that could affect the timetable of life and death. We live in an age of sophisticated medical technology, which cannot conquer death but can prolong the process of dying. Rabbi Judah's housekeeper could interrupt prayers. We can unplug respirators. Is it ever right to do so? These issues address all who offer a ministry of care, and cannot be avoided.

Fortunately much of our pastoral ministry enables us to witness the balm of healing, the renewal of energy, and a return to the mainstream of life. The rabbi is both a minister to the dying and a partner in the healing of the sick. This, at least, is the claim of our tradition. The healing power of visitation is by no means confined to the rabbi.

Rabbi Abba, the son of Rabbi Hanina, said: "He who visits the sick takes away one sixtieth of his pain (illness)." "If so," quipped another rabbi, "let sixty visit him and restore him to full health." Whereupon Rabbi Abba qualified his statement to suggest that there are limits to the healing power of visitation, but that what power there is remains exceedingly great (Nedarim 39b).

One formulation of this healing power is rather pragmatic. We are told that a pupil of Rabbi Akiba took ill. The sages did not visit him. Rabbi Akiba did, and because the attendants swept and sprinkled the ground before him (which kept the room more sanitary) the patient recovered. When Akiba returned later the pupil said: "My Master, you have revived me." Whereupon Rabbi Akiba left and lectured to his disciples: "He who does not visit the sick is like a shedder of blood" (Nedarim 40a). The contemporary resonance of this talmudic principle is palpable. By attention alone a visitor may contribute to the maintenance of optimal conditions for a patient's recovery. Of course, when the rabbis spoke of the healing power of visitation, they generally had something else in mind.

Rabbi Yohanan once fell ill and Rabbi Hanina went to visit him. "Are your sufferings welcome to you?" he asked. The patient, Rabbi Yohanan, replied: "Neither they nor their reward." In other words: "I would gladly trade the rewards of accepting chastisements of love if I could be spared those chastisements."

Rabbi Hanina flashed a knowing glance at the sick Yohanan and said: "Give me your hand." Rabbi Yohanan gave Rabbi Hanina his hand and he was healed. The question was asked: "Why could not Rabbi Yohanan raise (heal) himself?" The reply: "Even as the prisoner cannot free himself from jail, so the sick person cannot liberate himself from illness. He needs the caring attention of others" (Berachot 5b).

There is a sequel to this talmudic story that illustrates the place of empathy in visitation to the sick person. Rabbi Eliezer fell ill. He must have been a man of great physical beauty who took pride in his body. Rabbi Yohanan went to visit Rabbi Eliezer. Rabbi Yohanan noticed that Rabbi Eliezer was lying in a dark room. But when Rabbi Eliezer exposed his arm, light radiated from it. Despite his illness and its effect on his body, Eliezer's arm

was still so beautiful that it seemed radiant. When Yohanan saw that his friend wept he asked, "Why do you weep?" Eliezer replied: "I am weeping on account of this beauty that is going to rot in the earth." Rabbi Yohanan replied: "On that account you surely have reason to weep." And they both wept (Berachot 5b).

There may be another mood and need in time of illness and suffering: the need to express uncensored feelings, including self-pity and anger. Psalm 88 reflects this possibility. The poet was suffering and he was angry. Feeling betrayed by God, he proclaimed in effect: "What are you doing to me? You want me to serve you and praise you and bear witness to you? Well, I can't do it from the grave!" It is part of the dynamics of comfort and healing to express feelings, even if these feelings include anger against God. These emotions and actions are understandable and permitted within Judaism.

The tradition of affirming one's integrity even in the presence of God is strongly rooted in biblical Judaism. Sheldon Blank[6] called this the "promethean element" in biblical prayer. Words of anger, protest, and bold confrontation are spoken by the faithful. Abraham challenged God's justice at Sodom and Gomorrah: "Will the judge of all the earth not act justly?" (Gen. 18:25). Jeremiah accused God of deceiving him (Jer. 15:18). Job held to his integrity: "Yea though he slay me, still will I argue my case before him" (Job 13:15).

This readiness to challenge God is accentuated in rabbinic exegesis of biblical texts. After the incident of the golden calf, God says to Moses, "Now therefore let me alone, that my wrath may wax hot against them and that I may consume them . . ." (Ex. 32:10). Rabbi Abahu expounds: "If it were not written in scripture we could not say it. [Scripture] teaches that Moses took hold of the Holy One, blessed be he, as a man takes hold of his friend, by his garment, and said to him, 'Sovereign of the Universe, I shall not let you go until you forgive and

pardon them' " (Berachot 32a).

This promethean mood is amply represented in tal-mudic Judaism but it does not stop there. The eighteenth-century Hasidic rabbi, Levi Yitzhak of Berditchev, once uttered a Yiddish prayer which has become a classic. He stood on the pulpit of his synagogue and proclaimed:

> Good morning to you, Lord of the World. I, Levi Yitz-hak, son of Isaac of Berditchev, am come to you on a legal matter concerning Your people Israel. What do you want of Israel? It is always "command the children of Israel." I, Levi Yitzhak, son of Isaac of Berditchev, say, I shall not go home or budge from my place until there be a finish, until there be an end of exile.[7]

It is hardly accidental that in the aftermath of the Nazi Holocaust the most compelling response has been given by the novelist Elie Wiesel. Wiesel personally endured the Holocaust. He was a teenager when his family was transplanted to the death camps. Wiesel alone survived. He emerged bruised, haunted, and imprisoned by a nightmare which shattered his world. He has written a series of autobiographical novels blazing with anger and bitterness. One of his characters said: "Never shall I forget those moments which murdered my God and my soul and turned my dreams to dust."[8] What is common to all promethean words is that an anguished challenge has become part of the dynamics of comfort and reaffir-mation. Blank wrote of these spokesmen: "They hold fast to God even when they question His decree. Though they defy, they do not deny Him."[9]

One Christian colleague asked: "What is there that might make Jews more prone to challenge God without fear of blasphemy?" The answer may lie in the biblical and rabbinic images of the covenant. Biblical man's re-sponse to God's presence may be characterized by the words "creaturely and creative." Man's feeling of depen-dence is countered by a feeling of genuine power for

decision. Finite humanity freely and spontaneously participates in a dialogue with unlimited Being, and that dialogue defines the structure of human life.

Rabbinic literature preserved this concept of an irreducible dialogue in its understanding of the covenant between God and Israel. Man's boldness stems from two dimensions of that covenant. The conditional dimension dares to define contractual expectations of God as well as the human partner. In this context the rabbis picture Israel saying to the Holy One, blessed be he: "Master of the Universe, I do not know who dealt wrongly with whom and who failed to keep his promise, whether Israel dealt wrongly with God or whether God dealt wrongly with them" (Sifre 130b). The conditional dimension of the covenant casts Israel as a dignified partner in fulfilling the promise of creation. The sense of real power and responsibility emboldens one to challenge the senior partner. Paradoxically, the unconditional dimension of the covenant that casts Israel as a child of the loving father also encourages honest dialogue. One does not fear that a misspoken word will break the bond. "The congregation of Israel spoke before the Holy One, blessed be he: Sovereign of the Universe, though I am poor in deed, yet I am thine and it is fitting that I should be saved" (Pesachim 118b). Thus both the conditional and unconditional dimensions of the covenant encourage a pattern of bold honesty and dignity in the presence of God.

The God of the covenant who commands the faithful to attend the sick is also involved as healer. It is therefore a commandment for one who visits the sick to pray for them and with them. God's redemptive power may be enhanced through the communion of prayer. It is a blessing to be loved by God and to be conscious of his love in the active communion of prayer.

Some persons were believed to be especially gifted in "opening the gates of heaven." Once, we are told, the

son of Rabbi Gamaliel fell ill. He sent two scholars to Rabbi Hanina ben Dosa to ask him to pray for him. The rabbi went to an upper chamber and prayed for the sick child. When he came down he said, "The fever has left him." They said to Rabbi Hanina, "Are you a prophet?"

He replied: "I am neither a prophet nor the son of a prophet, but I learned this from experience. If my prayer is fluent in my mouth, I know that it is accepted." Gamaliel attested that the fever had subsided (Berachot 34b).

The tradition holds that prayer may unleash the healing grace of God. No person, especially one in the throes of illness, should feel obligated to censor his or her petitions to God. Even if the divine struggle between power and restraint is resolved against the petition, the sharing itself, the baring of the soul to God, may bring its own reward by drawing the person closer to the Eternal One in a communion based on the very deepest of needs.

More positively, the communion of prayer may itself engender healing power. The person in conscious relationship with the Eternal Thou may be renewed in his "will to live," armed against bitterness and despair, and able to draw on the divine presence and power to meet the demands of an uncertain future. Communion with God through prayer may bestow that trust and confidence which is part of the anatomy of healing.

One of the implications of covenant theology is that God's power to enter lives redemptively is affected by the human freedom to turn toward or resist his presence. Thus a Hasidic rabbi asked rhetorically: "Where is God?" And he replied: "Wherever we let him in." Here we come close to the heart of the power of petitionary prayer. Surely the God in whom I believe does not withhold his healing love from his children even in moments when they do not turn to him in prayer. "The Guardian of Israel neither slumbers nor sleeps" (Ps. 121:4). God is always active to maximize his redemptive activity in the

world that he has created. We are God's partners in redeeming the promise of creation. We share in this ministry of redemption when we, physicians, clergy, or lay persons, minister to the sick. We enhance God's redemptive power when we take care of our bodies and when we use knowledge to advance healing.

Intercessory prayer in Judaism is rooted in a strong sense of the community standing before God. If such care is a religious obligation for the whole fellowship of Israel, then the person receiving the ministration is affirmed as a member of that sacred community. The petitions appeal for healing in order that the stricken one may serve God again by assuming the full privileges and responsibilities of one bound by the covenant. The petitioner also calls God to remember his commitment under the covenant with his people Israel. One of the great fears of illness is isolation. Prayer reaffirms the love of God and his care of individuals as well as the sick person's abiding participation in a covenant community which has known God's redemptive love.

CONCLUSION

The difficult question of theodicy seemingly defies rational solution. Mankind has been taunted not so much by the reality of pain but by the experience of suffering that seems undeserved. The attempts to resolve this paradox that have proved most satisfying are those which confront the issue in the context of the promise of divine grace. In the face of questions that remain unanswered, God is believed to abide even in the midst of human suffering, and is continually present to his people. It is because of the assurance that God is present with his people that the believer may confront the crisis of illness with poise and confidence. God will cause his name to be present with his people. He will be seen and known for what he is in the situation of illness as we become aware

of his presence and act accordingly. It is enough to hear the promise and act in faith. When Moses asked to be shown the ways of God, demanding evidence of God's presence, he was told, "My presence will go with you." The rabbis reminded Israel that the name "I am the Lord," "I am he who is present" (Leviticus 19) included the saying: "You shall love your neighbor as yourself: I am the Lord." Therefore, "I am the Lord" means "I am he who is present beside thy neighbor." The all-pervading reality is the presence of God which enables each person to achieve his fullest life as a creature of the covenant.

When a sick person and the one who ministers are brought together through the crisis of illness, they are together in the promise that God is present to those who call upon him. This ministry offers a tangible opportunity to express compassionate concern for another. It opens one to the pain of the world. It compels the visitor to confront human vulnerability and finitude. It encourages one to count blessings and place trivialities in perspective. And, it offers each the possibility of encountering the *shechina,* as one who dwells with his people.

3

THEOLOGY AND MINISTRY IN THE PAULINE LETTERS

BY

VICTOR PAUL FURNISH

There can be no question about the decisive influence Paul's theology and ministry have had on the Christian church. The apostle's friends and adversaries alike, both ancient and modern, are agreed on that. What his friends and adversaries do not agree on is whether Paul's influence has been for the better or for the worse. There is not even clear agreement on what one should identify as the chief sphere of his influence.

Is one to think of Paul first of all as a *theologian,* an interpreter of the meaning of God as revealed in Christ and as proclaimed in the gospel? It is clear that Pauline theology has played a major and sometimes decisive role in the development of Christian doctrine across the centuries. Paul was undoubtedly one of the seminal thinkers in the earliest church, and while he was certainly not a "systematic theologian," the theological issues which he helped to define and with which he struggled have remained fundamental down to our own times.

On the other hand, there are those who argue that Paul's chief impact on the development of Christianity was rather more "practical," that his enduring importance is due to the evangelical zeal with which he proclaimed Christ far and wide. One can argue that apart from his bold and tireless mission to the Gentiles, Christianity would have remained a Jewish sect and, at length,

would have lost its own identity completely.

There is a large measure of truth in each of these ways of describing Paul's importance for Christianity. He is rightly honored, both as one of the church's most profound interpreters of the gospel and as one of its most zealous preachers, a stunningly effective missionary to the Gentiles. But neither of these descriptions of Paul's importance, taken by itself, is adequate. Nor does it really help simply to affirm them both, although this moves us in the right direction. The greatest contribution Paul made to the church was undoubtedly his impressive demonstration of how these two—the Christian gospel and the Christian ministry—are fundamentally and absolutely inseparable. He saw this more clearly and articulated it more forcefully, both in his letters and in his life, than anyone else in the early church. He saw that "the truth of the gospel" (Gal. 2:14) must manifest itself concretely in the life of the Christian community and in the individual lives of Christian believers wherever they are in the world. Thus, one may say that Paul's theological reflection and his missionary zeal were but two sides of the same coin, two equally necessary and necessarily equal modes of his Christian obedience. His commitment to the Gentile mission was profoundly rooted in his understanding of the gospel—that is, in his "theology." His "theology," in turn, took shape within the context of his ministry.

This vital nexus of theology and ministry is clearly present in the Pauline letters, most of them written to congregations Paul himself had founded.[1] Here one sees both the profoundly "situational" character of his theology and the thoroughly theological character of his ministry. Paul's understanding of the gospel not only motivated his preaching and defined its content; it also influenced the order of objectives for his ministry and his actual ministerial practice. It is this interrelationship between theology and ministry, between Paul's gospel and

his mission, that is explored in the following pages.

Because our primary sources for this study are letters written to specific congregations (or, in the case of Galatians, to several congregations) for specific purposes, we are inevitably brought into touch with a further dimension of Paul's career, his *pastoral* activity. The pastoral side of Paul's ministry has received only scant attention, at least in the scholarly literature.[2] This is unfortunate, particularly because Paul's letters are themselves the products of his pastoral activities and offer us direct and immediate access to them. Moreover, we have Paul's own testimony that his pastoral concerns loomed large in his apostolic work. After presenting a lengthy recital of his apostolic hardships he adds, "And, apart from other things, there is the daily pressure upon me of my anxiety for all the churches" (II Cor. 11:28). This is not mere rhetoric; the truth of this comment is validated on every page of the apostle's letters. There, one sees him dealing with the needs of those for whose nurture in Christ he obviously cares very deeply.

It is worth pausing here to emphasize the significance of this pastoral concern for which Paul's letters provide so much evidence. This is not exactly what one would expect of Paul. He himself emphasized that his call was to preach the gospel to those who had not yet heard it (Gal. 1:16; Rom. 15:18–21; cf. Rom. 10:14–15). His sense of apostolic vocation could prompt him to cry out, "Woe to me if I do not preach the gospel!" (I Cor. 9:16), and to make every effort to preach Christ where Christ had not yet been named (Rom. 15:20–21). How was it that this same person could feel such ties of responsibility binding him to the churches of his founding that he could also say of them: "Who is weak, and I am not weak? Who is made to fall, and I am not indignant?" (II Cor. 11:29). The answer is that Paul's pastoral ministry, no less than his missionary activity, was rooted in the character and meaning of the gospel to which he was committed. The

obedience to Christ he sought to win from the Gentiles (Rom. 15:18) involved their becoming one in Christ (Gal. 3:27–28), members of Christ's body (I Cor. 12: 12–27; Rom. 12:4–5), bound to one another as members of God's family (cf. Gal. 6:10). Thus, Paul's rhetorical questions, "Who is weak, and I am not weak? Who is made to fall, and I am not indignant?" are but specific pastoral applications of his more general statement, made in another letter to Corinth, about the oneness of Christ's body: "If one member suffers, all suffer together; if one member is honored, all rejoice together" (I Cor. 12:26).

One must grant that the word "pastor" is notably absent from Paul's own letters. In fact, it occurs only once in any letter even ascribed to him, viz., Eph. 4:11–12: "And his gifts were that some should be apostles, some prophets, some evangelists, some pastors and teachers, to equip the saints for the work of ministry, for building up the body of Christ." The word *pastor* is Latin for "shepherd," and it is indeed the Greek word for shepherd *(poimen)* which is used in Eph. 4:11. The same image is applied elsewhere in the New Testament to Christ himself as the Shepherd of God's flock, the Pastor of God's people (John 10:1–18; Heb. 13:20; perhaps also in I Peter 2:25; cf. Matt. 26:31). However, the only place in the New Testament where Christian ministers are called "shepherds" is in the list of ministerial functions given in Ephesians 4. The same usage is found not much later (early in the second century) in the letters of Ignatius (To the Philadelphians 2:1; cf. To the Romans 9:1), and then subsequently right on down to our own day. The fact remains, however, that Paul himself does not appear to have applied this shepherd metaphor to the practice of ministry. He was inclined, rather, to employ images derived from family relationships, so that he could present himself to his congregations as their brother, as their father, or even as their mother.[3]

In any case, the Pauline terminology for ministry is less

important than the apostle's constant effort to conform his practice of ministry to his understanding of the gospel, and it is this interrelationship of theology and ministry which deserves our careful examination. It will be useful, first, to gain some overall understanding of three major facets of Paul's ministry: his proclamation of the gospel, his establishing of congregations, and his nurture of them. This will be followed by a more detailed look at the content of Paul's gospel, and at the specific pastoral priorities which followed from that. Finally, these points will be substantiated with reference to Paul's dealings with one particular congregation.

It would be naive to suppose that Paul's ministry as such should or could provide a model for ministry in our day. "New occasions teach new duties," as the poet says, and as Paul himself had more than one opportunity to learn, even over the relatively brief span of his own ministry. The church's obligation to reexamine the meaning and the practice of Christian ministry is ongoing, and its constant and difficult task is to accommodate its ministry to changing realities without abandoning the unchanging Reality of the gospel. The social, political, economic, and even the environmental, realities of our day differ fundamentally from those of Paul's day. The apostle's missionary tactics and pastoral strategies are not automatically applicable twenty centuries later.[4] The importance of Paul's ministry for the practice of ministry in our day is of a different order. It demonstrates the indissoluble integrity of gospel and mission, and it shows us how each defines and supports the other. Moreover, it offers us an example of what it means for one's ministry to be conformed to the gospel, even in the face of adversity and apparent failure.

PAUL AS "PREACHER, APOSTLE, TEACHER"

One of Paul's earliest interpreters, the anonymous author of the so-called "pastoral epistles,"[5] has left us a formulation of Paul's ministerial activities which accords so closely with the data from Paul's own letters that we may use it as a guide in our initial probe of theology and ministry. In II Tim. 1:11, Paul is represented as having written: "For this gospel I was appointed a preacher and apostle and teacher." The same formula appears in I Tim. 2:7: "For this I was appointed a preacher and apostle . . . , a teacher of the Gentiles in faith and truth." Paul himself never schematized his ministerial work so neatly. Yet each of these titles—preacher, apostle, teacher—points to an important aspect of Paul's self-understanding as a minister. If we are careful to fill in this outline with materials from his own letters, we shall gain a good general understanding of how significantly Paul's ministry was related to his theology.

Paul as "Preacher"

The apostle leaves us in no doubt about the central theme of his preaching. He tells the Corinthians that his gospel is "the word of the cross" (I Cor. 1:18), and he reminds them that when he came preaching to them at first he knew nothing among them "except Jesus Christ and him crucified" (I Cor. 2:1–2). This theme will be explored in some detail below when we consider Paul's gospel as such. For the present it will be sufficient to make just two observations about Paul's conception of preaching and of himself as a preacher.

1. *As a preacher of Christ, Paul is bearing a message which has been assigned to him by another, viz., by God.* This point is absolutely fundamental if we are to understand the Pauline conception of ministry. He regarded his work as a *ministerium* in the strictest sense of that word: as the

service of a greater by a lesser. His ministry was the service of God; it was a *ministerium Dei.* When Paul writes about his own ministry, he does not think of this in the first instance as "serving his congregations." He thinks of it, first of all, as serving God. He uses at least half a dozen different terms to emphasize this: not only the word "steward" (I Cor. 4:1–2), but three different words that can be translated "servant" (I Cor. 3:5; 4:1; II Cor. 4:5), and two different terms that portray his preaching to the Gentiles metaphorically as the priestly service of God (Rom. 1:9; 15:16). His being bound by the word of God, and in and to the service of that word, freed him from the awful tyranny of trying to "please" his congregations. To the Galatians, who are being lured by what must seem to them a safer gospel than Paul's, he writes: "Am I now seeking the favor of men, or of God? Or am I trying to please men? If I were still pleasing men, I should not be a servant of Christ" (Gal. 1:10).

This should serve to alert us to the fact that Paul's preaching was something much more than a "personal testimony" about what God had done for him. He was certainly conscious of the radical transformation that had been wrought in his life: but his own "religious experience" was not the content of his preaching. Such details as one can glean about his own spiritual biography come almost entirely from polemical passages in his letters (e.g., Gal. 1:11–24; Phil. 3:2–11), not from passages where he is recapitulating the cardinal points of his preaching. Only when we recognize that Paul's preaching was a *ministerium Dei,* and not just personal religious testimony, are we able to understand how he could rejoice even when Christ was proclaimed for the wrong reasons, by those who acted from unworthy motives and out of pretense (Phil. 1:15–18). The word Paul preached was not about what God had done for him; it was a word from God that spoke of what God had done in Christ for all those who believe. This brings us to the second point

we must bear in mind as we consider Paul the preacher.

2. *Paul conceived of preaching, both in its origin and in its effect, as an event.* The distinction commonly made between an "occurrence" and an "occasion" might be applied here. An "occurrence" can be anything that happens, no matter how accidental, incidental, or unimportant. An "occasion" is a specific event, not some random or chance occurrence. An "occasion," we may say, fulfills and enhances the time it occupies; an "occurrence" merely uses up time. Now in the Pauline understanding of ministry, preaching is an *occasion,* not just an occurrence. It is a special event, both because it is the delivery of a word from God and because that word is given for the fulfillment and the enhancement, for the "redemption," of the time it occupies. Paul identifies the preaching of the gospel, not primarily with the speaking, but with the "demonstration of the Spirit and of power," that is, with the reality and meaning of God's presence which is disclosed when the word is preached (see I Cor. 2:1–4). An occurrence of the spoken word thus becomes an occasion, as the time filled with the speaking is revealed as God's time, time given and claimed by him.

When we think of preaching, we are usually thinking of the spoken word, of the sermon, of public address. That was most often in Paul's mind, too—but not exclusively. He was able to conceive of his whole ministry as a proclamation of the gospel, as when he wrote to the Philippians: "What you have learned and received and heard and seen in me, do; and the God of peace will be with you" (Phil. 4:9). In such a comment the event character of "preaching" is emphasized. It is also emphasized when, writing of the Corinthians' assembling for the eucharistic meal, he reminds them: "As often as you eat this bread and drink the cup, you *proclaim* the Lord's death until he comes" (I Cor. 11:26). The underlying presupposition here is significant. The word from God that Paul preached was also an *event* in the sense that it was re-

ceived by and constantly "repeated" in the life of a believing community. In Rom. 10:5–21, Paul describes the
gospel as "the word of faith" which comes "near" in
preaching. One of the points in this eloquent passage is
that there can be no righteousness without faith, no faith
without preaching, no preaching without a preacher, and
no preacher without God who sends the preacher forth
with a message. But the most important point of this
passage and of the context within which it occurs is that
the gospel is not truly preached until it has been heard
and obeyed. The *reception* of the gospel is as much a part
of the event as its *delivery*. The community of faith that
is called into being through the preaching of Christ not
only lives from the gospel; it also lives for the gospel. In
its life and ministry, and in the lives and ministries of
those who are individually members of it, the preached
word must be heard and obeyed, and spoken over and
over again. For Paul, the preached word is not some
timeless truth flung to the winds; it is a word of address
that summons to faith and seeks an "eventuating" in the
concrete life of the human community. We are thus
brought to a consideration of a second word by which
Paul was described in the pastoral epistles.

Paul as "Apostle"

"Apostle" was Paul's own favorite description of himself, and when he names those whom God has appointed
for special service within the body of Christ, "apostles"
heads the list (I Cor. 12:28). Above all, Paul relates
apostleship to the *establishment of the gospel,* and this is the
distinction of the "apostle" within the body of Christ.

I have used this phrase, "establishment of the gospel"
(it is not Paul's own phrase), in order to emphasize and
elaborate a point I have already made about Paul's view
of preaching. As an *occasion,* as a real event, the preaching
of the gospel is far more than public discourse about
God, Christ, faith, and salvation. Christian preaching is

not just *de*clamation, it is *pro*clamation. It calls for a response from those addressed and seeks to "eventuate" within their experience that which is proclaimed. For example, when a government "proclaims" a state of martial law, it seeks at the same time to win assent from the citizens and thus to establish what is proclaimed. Similarly, when Paul proclaimed the gospel, he sought to win obedience to it, and thus to establish it in the experience of his hearers. I use the term "apostle" as a reminder of this crucial aspect of Paul's ministry. As an apostle he was concerned for what may be called the "eventuating" of the gospel; he was concerned that the *eventuality* of his preaching of the gospel should be a new life, concretely manifested among those to whom he preached.

At the beginning of Romans, then once more near the close, Paul has provided us important formulations of this objective. In Rom. 1:5 he writes, "We have received grace and apostleship to bring about the obedience of faith for the sake of his name among all the nations." And in Rom. 15:16–21, reflecting on his "priestly service of the gospel of God," he writes of himself as "a minister of Christ Jesus to the Gentiles," and of his ministry as designed "to win obedience from the Gentiles, by word and deed" (vs. 16, 18). Here, characteristically, Paul is talking about the establishment of the gospel, not about the founding of religious societies. Paul the apostle carried no ecclesiastical blueprints with him. The challenge of his preaching was not to "come to church" but to "obey the gospel." The formation of Christian community was a vital part of the "eventuality" of Paul's preaching, but it was regarded as the consequence of obedience to the gospel, not as the first or fundamental act of obedience itself. When Paul describes himself as "a skilled master builder" who "laid a foundation" in Corinth (I Cor. 3:10), he is not thinking of the organization of a church there, but of the preaching of Christ: "For no other foundation can any one lay than that which is laid,

which is Jesus Christ" (3:11). As an apostle he was—to use his own metaphor—a planter. He sowed the seed of the gospel, others could help to tend it, but only God could give the growth (I Cor. 3:6–9). Paul understood the "eventuality" of faith's obedience, no less than the gospel itself, to be a gift from God. His apostolic ministry was rooted in and empowered by this firm conviction.

The apostolic role I have been describing is often thought of by Paul as a *parental role.* He not infrequently refers to his readers as his "children" (e.g., I Cor. 4:14; II Cor. 6:13; Gal. 4:19), and he thereby represents himself to them as their "father" (e.g., I Cor. 4:15) or even as their mother (see, e.g., Gal. 4:19). In a number of these instances the metaphor is used to remind Paul's congregations how the gospel had come to be established among them through his apostolic ministry. Paul thinks of himself in one place as the father by whom his readers have been begotten (I Cor. 4:15), and in another place as the father of the bride, who has betrothed them to Christ (II Cor. 11:2). Once he portrays himself as a mother in labor through whom his readers have been born in faith (Gal. 4:19), and once more he likens his apostolic activity to the task of a nursing mother (I Thess. 2:7–8).

Paul's letters are replete with evidence like this of his sense of closeness to and pastoral responsibility for his churches (e.g., II Cor. 2:4; Phil. 4:1; I Thess. 2:19–20). Perhaps most eloquent of all, there is the apostle's remark at the conclusion of a long list of hardships endured for the sake of the gospel. "And, apart from other things," he writes, "there is the daily pressure upon me of my anxiety for all the churches. Who is weak, and I am not weak? Who is made to fall, and I am not indignant?" (II Cor. 11:28–29). Paul's apostolic ministry of establishing the gospel involved him not only in planting the seed of faith but also in its cultivation and nurture. Thus we are brought to our third term.

Paul as "Teacher"

The apostle recognized teaching as one of the gifts of the Spirit (Rom. 12:7; I Cor. 12:28–29; cf. I Cor. 2:13), and he clearly valued it above speaking in tongues when it came to public worship (I Cor. 14:6). He never specifically refers to himself as a "teacher," however, and apostles and teachers are presented as two distinguishable categories in his list of those whom God has appointed to service in Christ's body (I Cor. 12:28). Nevertheless, he is conscious of being a teacher, and of course in his letters we have tangible evidence of the fact, the scope, and the character of his teaching ministry. The letters themselves are essentially teaching instruments. His own consciousness of this role comes to the surface when he writes of sending Timothy to remind the Corinthians of "my ways in Christ, as I teach them everywhere in every church" (I Cor. 4:17).

The parental imagery to which I have referred also involves Paul's sense of being a teacher and a disciplinarian. This application of the metaphor is particularly striking in the Corinthian letters. It is also present, however, when Paul likens his anxiety about the Galatians to the pain of a woman in labor, and to the frustration of a concerned parent (Gal. 4:19–20). And it is present when he writes to the Thessalonians, reminding them of his earliest ministry in their city: "You know how, like a father with his children, we exhorted each one of you and encouraged you and charged you to lead a life worthy of God, who calls you into his own kingdom and glory" (I Thess. 2:11–12).

This last text helps to document the first of two general points I would like to make about Paul as teacher: *Paul's preaching and teaching were inseparably interrelated aspects of his apostolic ministry.* The distinction so often made between "kerygma" and "didache," for example, can be very misleading.[6] No neat distinction is possible between

Paul's preaching and teaching, or between his evangelizing and his exhorting. Precisely these two together constituted Paul's mission to Thessalonica, as he reminds his converts there in I Thess. 2:11-12. They had been "exhorted," "encouraged," and "charged" to "lead a life worthy of God," who through the gospel had called them into his own kingdom. Paul's teaching ministry, his concern for Christian nurture, is inseparable from his fundamental apostolic concern to proclaim and establish the gospel of Christ.

In the second place: *Insofar as we may identify a distinguishing objective for Paul's teaching, it was to build up the body of Christ.* The teachings in Paul's letters may be variously classified and analyzed: some are general, some are quite specific; some are more abstract, some are decidedly concrete; some pertain to doctrine, some pertain to conduct; some are more and some are less specifically Christian; some are supported with the authority of Scripture or of the Lord, some are offered as Paul's apostolic opinion; some are supported by an appeal to common sense and reason, some are supported by appealing to what all good Christians do; etc. However, basic to all of the different kinds of teaching in the Pauline letters, there is the apostle's concern for "building up" (Greek: *oikodomein*). That is Paul's own favorite expression for what we would call "Christian nurture."

"God's building" (I Cor. 3:9) is one of the images Paul uses for the community of faith called into being by the gospel. Although he thinks of himself as first of all the one who lays foundations on which others build (I Cor. 3:10-15; Rom. 15:20), he is also very much aware of his own ministry of "building up." Twice in chs. 10-13 of II Corinthians he emphasizes that the Lord has given him authority for "building up," not for "tearing down" (II Cor. 10:8; 13:10; cf. 12:19), and in these places he has reference to "pastoral care" in its broadest and deepest sense. He was thinking not only of the moral and

spiritual edification of individual Christians. He was also thinking of the upbuilding of the congregation in Corinth, of its chastened and strengthened witness, worship, and work in the Lord. He sought to correct the Corinthian slogan, "All things are lawful," by reminding them that not everything is "helpful" or "upbuilding" (I Cor. 10:23–24). It is love, *agape,* which builds up, he wrote (I Cor. 8:1), and thus it was to a life lived in love to which the Christians under Paul's care were constantly admonished (e.g., Rom. 13:8–10; 15:2; I Cor. 16:14; Gal. 5:13–14; 6:2; I Thess. 5:11).

Paul and the Renewal of Christian Ministry

To what extent and in what ways is Paul's understanding of himself as "preacher, apostle, and teacher" pertinent to the church's concern for the constant revitalization of its ministry? It must be acknowledged that the apostle's conception of Christian ministry was in certain respects conditioned by his belief that Christ's return was imminent, and with it the close of the age. Thus, for Paul himself (in contrast to later writers, e.g., the author of the pastoral epistles), the church was regarded as an eschatological community in the strictest sense, and its various ministries in the world were presumed to be wholly provisional and temporary. Nevertheless, the most decisive component of the Pauline conception of Christian ministry remains unaffected by the church's changing eschatological expectations and worldly circumstances. Of absolutely primary importance is the understanding of ministry, in all of its aspects and particular tasks—not as the service of "the world," or of "the church," or of "individuals," or of "society" in some vague sense—but as *the service of God.* When it understands its ministry in this way, the church recognizes that its ultimate accountability is to no human agent or agency, that it is liberated from the bondage of every lesser claim, and that it is freed for the true service of God in the world. The

implications of this for several related aspects of Christian ministry today may be briefly indicated.

First, this Pauline conception of ministry liberates *preaching* to become the genuine proclamation of a word from God, even as it places the preacher under a judgment that transcends all worldly judgments. The proper challenge of Christian preaching is not to say something new, to say it better, or even to say it more persuasively; neither is it to say simply what is on one's mind or what is on one's heart, as if preaching were only a matter of personal testimony. It is certainly not to say what the people want to hear, or to say what will most readily advance the prestige of the church or the preacher personally in the eyes of the world. Rather, the first and fundamental challenge confronting the Christian preacher is to be faithful to the gospel of which he or she is a minister. That this requires both understanding it and being able to communicate it effectively is clear. But it is equally clear that this liberates the preacher and preaching from the terrible tyranny of the temptation to be "innovative" or "original," either in one's ideas or in one's presentation of them. In short, the preacher is the bearer of a tradition, and Christian preaching is first of all a witness to the gospel which is defined, interpreted, and handed on in that tradition.

When preaching is conceived in this way, I believe, it will perforce become at once more scriptural and more relevant. It will become more scriptural because scripture is the fountainhead of all Christian tradition. And preaching will become more relevant, because it will no longer be subject to the whims, moods, prejudices, or "personal charisma" of the preacher. This need not mean, and indeed it must not mean, that preaching will become more authoritarian or doctrinaire. The tradition itself, as it is present in Scripture and as it has been received in the church, is rich and diverse in its witness to the gospel. The church's custodial obligations to the

tradition have included from the beginning the obligation to interpret, adapt, and apply the gospel. The preacher, then, is also and necessarily an *interpreter* of the tradition, to and for the world, but always from within, and subject to the correction of the tradition itself, and of the whole believing community to which it is entrusted.

In this connection we must also remember that Christian preaching in the Pauline sense is always an *event.* It is an "occasion," the meaning of which transcends the particularity of what is said and of the person who says it. It is important that Christian preaching originated in the setting of synagogue worship, in the context of prayer and praise, where scripture was read, hymns were sung, and blessings were given and received. This liturgical heritage, never lost though often endangered in the church, has been a concrete and dramatic demonstration of the fact that Christian preaching is part of a larger event, to which it surely contributes, but from which it also receives. The renewal of preaching and the renewal of worship must go together. Preaching is liturgy and the liturgy is itself proclamation. The larger and more profound Event to which they both belong is what Paul called "the Holy Spirit," come with cleansing and healing power to redeem and to claim God's people (see, e.g., I Cor. 2:4–5; I Thess. 1:4–5).[7]

Not only preaching, but also the various tasks of *church organization and administration* properly derive their meaning from a conception of ministry as the service of God. As we have seen, Paul's sense of apostolic vocation involved him in the founding and care of churches, of specific Christian congregations. It is significant, however, that he understood this as the planting and cultivation of the gospel, as its "eventuation" in the lives, both individual and corporate, of men and women where they were in the world. As a church organizer and administra-

tor Paul was serving the gospel, he was functioning as a minister of God.

Unfortunately, however, as the church came increasingly to the realization that it needed an institutional structure appropriate to its indefinitely prolonged ministry in the world, the danger increased that its energies would be turned more to its own preservation and stabilization and less to its primary task of serving the gospel. A recovery of the Pauline understanding of ministry will alert us to the continuing presence of this danger, and it will challenge us to avoid it.

One must acknowledge that the church, particularly in a "Christian society," is tempted to make the enhancement of its own institutional life and the advancement of its own institutional goals major concerns. Church officials naturally tend to define the responsibilities of church organization and administration with reference to the standards and criteria of secular associations and businesses. For instance, organizational goals and priorities are often determined with primary regard for what is "financially realistic," for what will further the social position of the organization itself, or even—though this is hardly ever stated explicitly—with regard for what will make a given congregation or denomination most "competitive" in relation to others. In these and many other, subtler ways, however, the church is betraying its proper ministry, which is not to serve itself or its own institutional aims, but to be a faithful servant of the gospel, an agent for its eventuation in society.

This is not to say that the church is released from the responsibility to organize and administer its institutional life wisely and carefully. On the contrary, exactly because the church exists to obey and serve the gospel, the highest claims are placed upon its organizational behavior and upon the quality of its institutional structures and management. But the issue is one of priority, and it is clear that the church, understood to exist for the purpose of

serving God, must ask first of all what is necessary for its faithful witness to the gospel, not what is expedient or efficient for its own institutional security. This means, further, that the pastor when occupied as church administrator is no less a servant of the Word than when she or he is standing in the pulpit or conducting the liturgy. When the administrative offices and the various boards, agencies, councils, and committees of the denominations and of local congregations define their goals and priorities with primary reference to the requirements of the gospel, then their work is itself Christian ministry of the highest order. The promise of the gospel is that one gains one's life as it is lost, that one finds life as it is given for others. This applies no less to the church as an institution than to its individual members, and it has direct and sometimes inconvenient implications for the church's programs and policies.

The church, conceived as the body of Christ, lives only by and only for the gospel. Admittedly, the task of organizing and supervising those various bodily functions of which Paul wrote in I Corinthians 12 has become significantly more complex since then, and so has the matter of the church's life within and mission to the world at large. But this only accentuates the importance of the Pauline insight that the church fulfills its mission only to the extent that it is a servant church, devoted not to its own security, but to the planting and cultivation of the gospel.

It is appropriate, finally, that we consider the implications of this for the various kinds of pastoral activities that may be grouped together under the heading of *Christian nurture.* The description of Paul as "teacher" has served to introduce us to this topic, but Christian nurture is inclusive of much more than the church's educational ministry. It involves, as well, such things as facilitating growth in the Christian life, strengthening the fabric of the Christian community, giving guidance and support to its members as they confront perplexing moral choices,

providing leadership as the church itself formulates its response to pressing social issues, comforting the sick and the bereaved, and giving counsel and aid to those in any kind of need. If the church is to be responsive to its call to establish the gospel, then the cultivation of the gospel in the lives of people and in the life of the Christian community becomes no less important than its planting. Paul understood and even emphasized this, although he wished that he could devote his own chief efforts to the planting, not the cultivation. Despite his own wishes, however, it became evident in his actual practice of ministry that one cannot effectively plant the gospel without at the same time providing for its cultivation and maturation. In Pauline terms, this task of Christian nurture is nothing else than the work of "building up" the body of Christ.

How does the dynamic of gospel and mission, or theology and ministry, function with respect to the responsibility for Christian nurture? Perhaps the matter can be expressed as follows: Where ministry is understood and practiced as the service of God, there is a concern that the promises and claims of the gospel be brought to ever-deeper effect and wider scope in the lives of believers. That is Christian nurture. Christian nurture distinguishes itself from all other kinds of edifying activity by reason of its constant reference to that gospel from which it derives its meaning and objectives. It does not ignore or despise the world's wisdom as such, but neither does it confuse that wisdom with the truth of the gospel, which stands in judgment over all human values and standards. When nurture is authentically Christian, it does not aim merely at the "self-realization" of individuals, as if their salvation were coequal with the development of their "human potential." Christian nurture must give due regard to the realities of human personality and of social relationships as these are perceived by the various behavioral and related sciences. But it must not give undue

regard to these; it must not—if it is to remain *Christian* nurture—forfeit its basic commitment to the gospel, that is, to the conviction that life is a gift from Another and not the "development" or "realization" of one's own personal potential. Perhaps, then, one may describe the task of Christian nurture, at least formally, in this way: It seeks to enable believers to receive the gift presented in the gospel, and to facilitate the concrete enactment of that gift, including its inherent claims, in their lives.

To conceive of the church's nurturing ministries in this way might well prompt some reconsideration of both the goals and the techniques of Christian education, pastoral counseling, and other related tasks. It might also open the way to a renewal of interest in *church discipline* as not only a legitimate, but indeed an essential aspect of Christian ministry. The image here must not be of the pastor as an authoritarian judge, calling church members to account and assessing appropriate penalties. Rather, and in keeping with the New Testament—and specifically the Pauline—view of church discipline, the image will be of a disciplined community of believers, that is, a community of believers committed to the gospel and thus "discipled" to the Lord it proclaims. The image will be of a community which stands under the Word of that gospel, and in this *understanding* of that Word knows itself to be held accountable to it. Church discipline will occur as that community of disciples subjects its beliefs and its witness, its life and its actions, to the judgment and renewing power of the gospel from which it lives. Conceived in this way, church discipline is not a now-and-then procedure invoked in special cases, but a constituent and ongoing aspect of the church's life, an essential part of that Christian nurture by which the believing community renews itself in the gospel and builds itself up into Christ.

PAUL'S GOSPEL AND FAITH'S VITAL SIGNS

The relation of theology and ministry in Paul's letters and in his own practice will be clarified still further if we inquire more carefully into the nature and meaning of that gospel from which he understood his mission to derive. This will allow us, in turn, to identify with greater precision the priority objectives toward which his ministry was directed and by which his ministry was particularly characterized.

Paul's Gospel

Romans 1:16–17 is the passage from which any discussion of Paul's gospel must proceed. "For I am not ashamed of the gospel: it is the power of God for salvation to every one who has faith, to the Jew first and also to the Greek. For in it the righteousness of God is revealed through faith for faith; as it is written, 'He who through faith is righteous shall live.' "

The first thing to notice here is the identification of the gospel with God's saving power. Thus, the point is made again that "gospel" in the Pauline sense is best understood as an *event,* not as a message. It is God's own powerful coming and working for salvation (see also I Thess. 1:5; I Cor. 2:3–5); and it is certainly not a message contrived, however cleverly, by human beings (I Thess. 2:13). It is God's own word *at work* among believers with a power that transcends the fragile earthen vessels in which it comes (II Cor. 4:7).

Paul frequently associated this transcendent power with God's power to raise the dead (e.g., I Cor. 6:14; 15:42–43; Phil. 3:10, 21). Most of all, however, Paul understood God's saving power to have been manifested in the cross, in Christ's death. In Pauline theology, the theme of Christ's resurrection is in fact secondary to the emphasis on Christ's saving death.

Willi Marxsen's penetrating analysis of the development of the resurrection narratives helps us to appreciate this fact and its significance.[8] Christian faith was not born when Jesus' followers saw him risen from the tomb and then deduced from that evidence that he was their Lord and Savior. Rather, their preaching of Christ as their risen Lord grew out of the meaning they found in his death, a meaning which was inherent in their experience of him and his teachings during his lifetime, and which was crystallized and confirmed for them by what they found in Scripture. Thus, Paul's affirmation of Jesus' resurrection is of one piece with his affirmation of the redemptive significance of Jesus' death. To speak of Christ's resurrection is to affirm the life-giving power of his death.

Paul's "theology of the cross" is nowhere clearer than in the first two chapters of I Corinthians. There he emphasizes that his preaching of the gospel is "not with eloquent wisdom, lest the cross of Christ be emptied of its power. For the word of the cross is folly to those who are perishing, but to us who are being saved it is the power of God" (I Cor. 1:17–18). It is clear from the parallelism of this statement and Rom. 1:16 that Paul's gospel is "the word of the cross." The saving event made present in the gospel is Christ's death.

Let me try to be more exact. What is that "power" of the cross which is made present in the gospel for the salvation of those who believe? Romans 5:6–11 can be of help to us in answering this question. Here the apostle wants to emphasize Christ's death as the definitive instance and the decisive confirmation of God's reconciling love: "God shows his love for us in that while we were yet sinners Christ died for us" (v. 8). This is a love that justifies (v. 9) and reconciles (v. 10) and that enables Paul to write of that "peace with God" experienced by those who believe (v. 1). This passage makes clear that for Paul the power of the cross is the power of love,

God's love operative in the cross. The "word of the cross" is that God loves us, and in that word we are at once freed from death and claimed for life. Later in Romans, Paul writes: "If God is for us, who is against us? He who did not spare his own Son but gave him up for us all, will he not also give us all things with him?" And the question, "Who shall separate us from the love of Christ?" is answered with the moving affirmation that nothing "in all creation will be able to separate us from the love of God in Christ Jesus our Lord" (8:31b–32, 39).

"God is for us" (Rom. 8:31b). That is Paul's own simple and yet profound summary of "the word of the cross." The saving power of the cross he understands to reside in the love of God which is instantiated in Christ's death. This theme finds expression also in II Cor. 5:14, where Paul alludes to the familiar creedal affirmation that "one has died for all." Taken by itself that formula would mean that Christ died in our place, bearing the penalty for sin which was rightfully ours to pay; or else, using the closely related metaphor, that his death was paid as a ransom for our life. The conclusion would seem to be: "Therefore, all the rest may live." But Paul surprises us, and thereby he discloses something else important about his conception of the power of the cross. "One has died for all; therefore," writes Paul, *"all have died."* When by faith one receives God's love, one participates in Christ's death. What this means, more concretely, is explained a few sentences later: "If any one is in Christ, he is a new creation; the old has passed away, behold, the new has come" (II Cor. 5:17).

We may recall that Paul interprets Christian baptism in just this way (Rom. 6:3ff.). Such texts are so familiar to us, and the terms within them have become so highly charged over the course of twenty centuries of theologizing that we need constantly to find fresh ways of expressing their meaning. What, for example, is the meaning of

the bold Pauline metaphor that speaks of our "old self" being "crucified with [Christ]"? In Philippians 3, Paul has provided us with a rather more concrete description of what this had meant in his own case. It had meant giving up the "righteousness" he had gained on his own as defined by "the law." He did not give this up because he had failed to achieve what he had sought. On the contrary, he testifies that he had been "blameless" as regards righteousness defined by the law (Phil. 3:6). There is nothing remarkable about abandoning one's *failures*. But Paul abandoned his *accomplishments*, because as he suggests, they could not lead him beyond himself. The life he sought to fashion and furnish for himself, on his own terms, proved illusory. But in "the foolishness of the cross" Paul was confronted with an entirely different kind of possibility. There he was confronted with the reality of God's love, that "God is for us" and that life is a gift of his love. He had come to understand that where that gift is received by faith there is new life, a new creation. There one finds a righteousness that does not depend on one's own persistence and energy, but on the persistent working of God "for us." "What do you have that you have not received? And if you have received it, why do you boast as if it were not a gift?" Those are questions Paul put once to the Corinthians (I Cor. 4:7), and they are fundamental. In his view, all that we have and are is a gift. It is the saving power of the cross to confront us with this gospel and, where it is received by faith, to eventuate that gospel in our experience. The power of the cross inheres in the love that meets us there, that gives us our life and claims us for God (Gal. 2:20).

Before we conclude this attempt to summarize Paul's "theology of the cross," it will be useful to return to the text at Rom. 1:16–17, with which we started. The second sentence of the text refers specifically to "the righteousness of God" which in the gospel "is revealed through faith for faith" (v. 17a). "Righteousness" is not meant to

describe an "attribute" of God as he exists in and of himself, but as he exists in relation to his people. It refers to his faithfulness to the covenant which he has established with them, and to the love and the justice of which that covenant is the sign and the seal. Paul also associates God's righteousness with the attainment of life. This is why he quotes from Habakkuk: " 'He who through faith is righteous shall live' " (Rom. 2:17b; cf. Hab. 2:4). God's righteousness is his life, and it becomes the life of his people when they acknowledge themselves to be God's covenant people. "Righteousness," then, is first and foremost a relational term. When Paul writes of the righteousness which faith receives, he is not thinking of the imputation of some moral quality, but of being drawn into a "right relationship" to God.

How, then, are we to understand that "faith" which justifies and brings us alive to God in Christ? It will help us to answer this if we note that, for Paul, the opposite of faith is not "doubt" but "sin." "Faith" for Paul is not a certain disposition of mind or attitude, e.g., "believing where we cannot prove" (Tennyson). Faith is a disposition of one's whole life, an act of the will. The apostle understands sin to be the refusal to accept one's life as a gift, the attempt to live life as if it were at one's own disposal. For him, sin consists in that effort, ultimately futile, to invest life with meaning and purpose through one's own acquiring and achieving. As Paul himself phrases it, more theologically, in Rom. 1:21, sin is the refusal to "honor [God] as God or give thanks to him." Faith is the exact opposite. Faith means to accept life as a gift and to give thanks for it. Faith means to accept the good news that "God is for us," that life is a gift of love. And faith means to be committed to the "eventuation" of that gospel in the world, through the obedience of love.

Faith's Vital Signs

Physiologists have long since identified certain bodily organs and functions as those upon which life is directly dependent. In a modern hospital, therefore, the physicians and nurses are constantly attentive to a patient's "vital signs," such as pulse, respiration, and digestion. These they seek not only to monitor and maintain, but to strengthen when they falter and to restore when they fail. In a healthy body they must all be present and strong. Since Paul himself finds the body metaphor appropriate for describing the believing community, it may not be inappropriate for us to expand that metaphor enough to inquire into faith's "vital signs." Granting that the body of Christ lives from and for the gospel, that its mission is to embody that gospel; and granting, too, that Christ's body must like any organism be appropriately nurtured—granting all this, what may be identified as the vital signs of the faith by which this body lives? Put another way, what does that congregation look like which is being "built up" into Christ? Or put still another way, what pastoral priorities did Paul understand to be incumbent upon him in his own practice of ministry? What concrete manifestations of their obedience to the gospel did Paul seek to monitor, maintain, and strengthen in the congregations under his pastoral care?

As soon as such questions are asked, and before the vital signs of faith can be specified, we must remind ourselves once more that Paul and his fellow Christians lived with the fervent hope and expectation of the Lord's imminent return and, with that, the close of history and the transformation of the world. There are complex and important historical, theological, and also sociological reasons for this early Christian apocalypticism, but a discussion of them here would lead us too far from our central

topic. There are two important ways, however, in which that eschatological expectation influenced Paul's practice of ministry.

1. *Paul's eschatological expectation precluded his setting any long-range social objectives.* The word I wish to stress here is "long-range." Paul's ministry provides us no unambiguous models for the church as an agency of social change or for the pastor as an agent of social reform. There are some practical reasons for this (e.g., Christianity in Paul's world had a radically different status in society than Christianity has in most of the modern Western world), but the chief reason is theological. Paul believed that "the appointed time has grown very short" (I Cor. 7:29a) and that "the form of this world is passing away" (I Cor. 7:31b). This belief conditioned significantly the priorities of his ministry. For example, he placed no priority on the formation or perfection of long-range ecclesiastical structures; the church as an institution was part of this transitory world. Again, he placed no priority on defining the characteristics of the "Christian home and family"; these, too, were part of the transitory social order. Similarly, one finds in Paul's ministry no concern for the abolition, or even the reformation, of the institution of slavery; that was simply a "given" of the economic system of his day which, again, was destined to pass away. And, to cite one final example, there is no reflection on "the best" or "most Christian" form of government, no "political philosophy" in the Pauline letters, no sense of priority about establishing principles for the Christian's relationship to the civil authorities; for at "the end," says Paul, Christ "delivers the kingdom to God the Father after destroying every rule and every authority and power" (I Cor. 15:24). Pauline eschatology precludes these kinds of priorities. When we have acknowledged this, however, there is yet a second point which must be made about the apocalyptic component in Pauline theology.

2. *Paul's eschatological expectation did not preclude, but rather intensified his concern for the Christian's life in this present world.* We must make a distinction between long-term goals and objectives for life in the world, which Pauline eschatology precludes, and a concern for life in the world while this age endures, which Pauline eschatology by no means precludes. A careful examination of Paul's letters will show that he had virtually nothing to say about the time, the manner, or even the consequences of the Lord's return. He had a great deal to say, though, about the Christian's conduct in this present world in prospect of that return. Significantly, insofar as our sources permit us a judgment in the matter, the same reluctance to be caught up in detailed apocalyptic speculations was characteristic of Jesus' preaching, although his call to repentance and obedience was issued on the presumption that the Final Day was at hand.[9] For Paul, as for Jesus, the reality of one's ultimate accountability to God is a fundamental sanction for obedience in the present, but neither for Paul nor for Jesus is the reality of that ultimate accountability dependent upon any particular, detailed eschatological scenario.

When we have recognized that, even though long-range social objectives are not among the priorities of Paul's ministry, the apostle is earnestly and urgently concerned for the life and conduct of believers in this present world, then we have been brought back again to the question about faith's vital signs. What vital functions did he seek to maintain and strengthen in the congregations to which he ministered? The letters disclose his prioritizing of three essential functions in the body of Christ.

First, the body is to manifest in its own life as a community the life and death of Christ in which each of its members shares. This vital sign of faith can be described with Paul's own term, *koinonia,* variously translated as "fellowship," "partnership," "participation," "communion," "community," etc. As Paul uses the word it has

both a "vertical" and a "horizontal" dimension, and in each of these respects *koinonia* is emphasized as one of the vital signs of faith. The vertical dimension bespeaks Paul's conception of the Christian life as sharing Christ's sufferings and death, and thus the hope of his resurrection (see Phil. 3:10). But this vertical dimension of *koinonia*, which may perhaps be designated by the word "communion," always involves the horizontal, for which one may use the word "community." Paul clearly understands that one's communion with Christ is inseparable from one's membership in the believing community. He writes sometimes of the partnership of believers "in Christ" (e.g., I Cor. 1:9); and at other times of their partnership in the Holy Spirit (e.g., II Cor. 13:14), in the gospel (Phil. 1:5), in faith (Philemon 6), in grace (Phil. 1:7), in adversity (e.g., Phil. 4:14), and in comfort (II Cor. 1:7).

Paul's prioritizing of *koinonia* is directly related to his understanding of Christian existence as "life in the Spirit." One has but to note his affirmation (Rom. 5:5) that "God's love has been poured into our hearts through the Holy Spirit" to see how he comes to describe the new life, redeemed by and into love, as life "according to the Spirit" (e.g., Rom. 8:4ff.; Gal. 5:16ff.). Believers are bound together, not by a common ethnic origin (there are both Jews and Gentiles in Christ), nor by their common social status (there are slaves and free and males and females in Christ), nor even by their common "religious experiences" or spiritual gifts (for those are diverse). They are bound together as members of Christ's body and shareholders in the Spirit. They belong to a reality and live out of a reality which is more than the sum of all its parts. That is Christian *koinonia*, and wherever faith expresses itself in love, as Paul says it must (Gal. 5:6), *koinonia* is present. It is the circulation of Christ's love within the body which forms it into a genuine *koinonia* and which constitutes its essential life force.

Another of faith's vital signs, if we are to be guided by Paul's priorities in ministry, is *eucharistia,* "thanksgiving." In Paul's view, the body of Christ exists for the praise of God and to "give him glory." The two vital signs of *koinonia* and *eucharistia* are meaningfully conjoined in the benediction of Rom. 15:5–6. In the first half we meet in turn the "horizontal" and "vertical" dimensions of *koinonia:* "May the God of steadfastness and encouragement grant you to live in such harmony with one another, in accord with Christ Jesus . . ." And then, in the concluding phrase, there is Paul's characteristic concern for *eucharistia:* "that together you may with one voice glorify the God and Father of our Lord Jesus Christ." This benedictory formulation also suggests that, just as it is Christ who defines the meaning of the believers' lives together in community, so it is Christ who is the norm of the community's praise of God.

It is important to realize that when Paul writes of thanksgiving he is thinking about more than a particular form or attitude of prayer, although thanksgiving includes that, to be sure (e.g., Phil. 4:6). He is also thinking of something more than the corporate praise rendered by the whole congregation gathered for worship —although he is thinking of that too, and often emphasizes it (e.g., I Cor. 14:16–17; II Cor. 1:11; 4:15). For Paul, *eucharistia* in its most fundamental sense is that which inheres in a life committed to God and given over to doing his will. The praise of God which finds expression in prayer and other formal acts of worship, public or private, is authentic thanksgiving only insofar as it is a genuine outgrowth of that faith commitment by which the believer's every action is shaped and guided. Thus, in Rom. 12:1–2 Paul urges his readers to present themselves to God, their lives, their routines, their decisions, their time, their energies, their resources. He calls this a "living sacrifice," and he identifies one's commitment to seeking and doing God's will as one's "spiritual wor-

ship." This is *eucharistia* as Paul understands it, and the many concrete moral teachings that follow in Romans 12 and 13 illustrate and specify how this praise of God is to be enacted in the Christian's everyday life.[10]

Once this Pauline understanding of true thanksgiving is grasped, it becomes clear why *diakonia* must be listed as a third and closely related sign of vital faith. "Ministry" is often the best English translation for this Greek word, and so it might seem redundant to identify *diakonia* as one of Paul's priority objectives in his ministerial work. But the root meaning of the word is "service/serving," and it is quite clear that Paul's pastoral activities were in no small part directed to establishing and renewing his congregations in the service of God. Another word for service, the verb *douleuein,* appears in his letters, and this, too, must be taken into account. It is related etymologically to the noun *doulos,* "slave," which the apostle uses several times in describing himself in relation to Christ, his "Lord" (Rom. 1:1; Gal. 1:10; Phil. 1:1). But Paul does not apply these terms for a servant ministry only to himself and to other *individuals* appointed for ministerial service with him (for example Timothy, I Thess. 3:2) or in his churches (for instance Phoebe, Rom. 16:1). The church as such is called to ministry; each congregation is understood by Paul to be commissioned for service. Several different kinds of evidence from his letters confirm this and provide us an idea of why he sought to monitor, maintain, and strengthen *diakonia* as one of the vital signs of faith.

For one thing, there is the term "saints," which Paul frequently applied to his congregations. It means literally, "holy ones," and in the terminology of the Old Testament from which this concept derives, to "be sanctified" or "made holy" means essentially to be set apart or "dedicated" to the service of God. Therefore, one need not be surprised that Paul can address even such an unruly congregation as the one in Corinth as "sanctified

in Christ Jesus, called to be saints" (I Cor. 1:2). Some biblical traditions and writers, it is true, tend to include the idea of "purity" within that of "holiness," but Paul does not. Christians can be addressed as "saints," not because their lives are blameless, but because their calling as Christians is to serve God.

There is further and more explicit evidence of this Pauline view. Many scholars are agreed that we hear in I Thess. 1:9–10 an echo of the apostle's earliest and most basic missionary appeal. There he reminds the Thessalonians that at their conversion they had "turned to God from idols, to serve a living and true God, and to wait for his Son from heaven, whom he raised from the dead, Jesus who delivers us from the wrath to come." Paul develops the meaning of this service of God to which the gospel summons when he speaks of "serving Christ" and shows what that means. Every believer, he insists, even those who were "freeborn" as regards the slave system of his day, must view him- or herself as "a slave of Christ" (I Cor. 7:22), that is, bound over in service to the Lord. That one's service to Christ involves serving others is brought out clearly in the discussion of Romans 14 about the "strong" and the "weak" in the congregation. Each member of the community should "walk in love" toward every other member, and should cause no one any injury (Rom. 14:15). When one *"thus serves Christ,"* Paul concludes, one "is acceptable to God and approved by men" (v. 18). *Diakonia,* then, is one of the signs of life in the body of Christ, and when it ceases to be a vital force, both Christian community and the praise of God likewise fail.

Paul's concern that the Christian serve Christ by "walking in love" is also present when he speaks of the believer's obligation to "walk according to [or: by] the Spirit" (Rom. 8:4; Gal. 5:16; an equivalent idiom in Gal. 5:25). These are readily interchangeable expressions because Paul understands God's love to have been "poured

out" precisely in the coming of the Spirit (Rom. 5:5). Thus, the quickening power of the Spirit is nothing else than the enlivening power of God's love to which faith is the response and by which faith finds concrete expression in the believer's life (Gal. 5:6). The interrelationship of these fundamental Pauline ideas explains why in Rom. 12:7 *diakonia* is itself mentioned as one of the gifts of the Spirit and one of the manifestations of the Spirit's presence in Christ's body. If there is any doubt about the importance Paul places on *diakonia* as one of faith's vital signs, that must finally be dispelled by his words in Gal. 5:13–14, where love's service is presented as the essence of God's law.

Paul acknowledges that there are various ways of serving within the body of Christ, just as there are various gifts of the Spirit (I Cor. 12:4–6); but he is quite clear on the point that all of these are to be devoted to "the common good" (I Cor. 12:7). *Diakonia,* then, is another way of describing the "upbuilding" of Christ's body which we have previously associated with the concept of Christian nurture. In this regard, it must be acknowledged that Paul had little to say, apparently, about the church's servant role in society at large beyond the believing community itself. Some modern Christians criticize him, therefore, for what they take to be a much too limited understanding of the scope of Christian love and service. At the same time, other Christians have found in Paul a biblical warrant for their own view that the church should look upon the world only as a field for "conversion" and not as a field for service. Both of these positions need to be corrected.

On the one hand, it is not remarkable that Paul had so little to say about the church's service in the world as such. As noted above, his social vision was limited by his eschatological expectations. Moreover, the opportunities Paul's congregations would have had, as congregations, for concerted community action would have been ex-

tremely limited, if they existed at all. The resources of those in the church for responding to whatever opportunities may have opened up would have been very meager indeed. What resources Paul's congregations could muster were properly used, first of all, for those within the church itself who, not least *because* of their conversion to the gospel, were cut off from most of the usual sources of public welfare.

On the other hand, what is remarkable is the extent to which, despite the limitations imposed by social conditions and his own eschatological expectation, Paul *did* have a vision of service to the world beyond the church itself. This is not developed, but it is certainly present in at least two passages in which believers are urged to express their faith in love. "As we have opportunity, let us do good *to all,*" he writes to the Galatians (Gal. 6:10). When he adds, "especially to those who are of the household of faith," it confirms that by "all" he had intended no restrictions on the Christian's responsibilities to other persons. The additional phrase should not be interpreted as compromising the initial admonition, which stands in any case. The point is, rather, that if service is not a priority concern within Christ's body, it surely cannot find expression outside it. The other text is I Thess. 5:15, a summary admonition all the more emphatic because of its brevity: "See that none of you repays evil for evil, but always seek to do good *to one another and to all.*" Paul could hardly have been more explicit about the unlimited scope of the *diakonia* to which the believer is called. It seems clear that, just as faith is only faith when it is enacted in love (Gal. 5:6), so the church is only the church when by that love it is animated to service, both within its own community and beyond it.

Toward an Understanding of "Pastoral Care"

We have seen that Paul's most fundamental convictions about the meaning of the gospel—that God's power

for salvation is love instantiated in the cross, and that that love is at once a gift and a claim to be received by faith and enacted in the believer's life—determined the priorities by which he operated in his ministerial practice. Guided by Paul's image of the church as Christ's body and by his own ministerial practice in which these priorities were operative, one is led to an understanding of pastoral care which may now be formulated as follows: *Pastoral care is the work of monitoring, maintaining, and strengthening the vital functions by which the community of faith is quickened and built up into the body of Christ, as those vital functions are represented in its* koinonia, *its* eucharistia, *and its* diakonia.

There is no minimizing the awesome responsibilities assumed by those who are charged with pastoral care in the church. Paul himself was conscious of the burden he bore as a pastor (II Cor. 11:28), although one must not forget that he could also describe his pastoral work as "fruitful labor" (see Phil. 1:19–26), and that precisely when he had to acknowledge his own inadequacies as a person ("Who is sufficient for these things?" II Cor. 2:16b), he was renewed in his awareness of God's enabling power (II Cor. 2:17 to 3:6). The complexities of the modern world, the vast expansion of the church, and the radically altered position the church occupies in much of today's world have confronted it with enormous new challenges, as well as with impressive new resources for responding to them. The danger is not so much that the church will fail to appreciate the complexity of the new problems and opportunities with which it is confronted, but that, alternately intimidated by and enamored of them, it will be distracted from giving attention to those vital functions which are its very life.

It is not legitimate to try to derive from Paul's teaching or practice any one specific model for Christian community, thanksgiving, and service. The forms in which those

three vital functions of Christ's body come to expression must change with changing times and circumstances. Ministerial leadership that seeks to impose prefabricated forms of *koinonia, eucharistia,* or *diakonia* on a congregation cannot be called pastoral care in any genuine sense. Whether such forms be "traditional" or "innovative" is really immaterial. If they are *imposed,* their fate will be like that of transplanted organs which prove to be incompatible with the host body and are soon rejected. Rather, the forms of Christian community, thanksgiving, and service must take shape from within the congregation. The pastoral task is not to dictate what those shall be, but to facilitate their formation.

I have previously described pastoral care as "the work of monitoring, maintaining, and strengthening the vital functions by which the community of faith is quickened and built up into the body of Christ . . . ," and it is with some hesitation that I now introduce the concept of *facilitating* to describe the pastor's role in doing that. The pastor's role as facilitator must not be misunderstood as it is whenever it is reduced to that of "convenor," "discussion starter," "resource person," or "business manager." The pastor's fundamental job is to "facilitate" the congregation's obedience to the gospel, and this means, concretely, to guide it into forms of *koinonia, eucharistia,* and *diakonia* which are appropriate both to the gospel and to the world in which that congregation is called to obey. Thus, a ministry is not truly "pastoral" unless it is also effectively "priestly" and "prophetic." One may not unfairly associate the pastoral role with the vital sign of *koinonia,* the priestly role with *eucharistia,* and the prophetic role with *diakonia.* Thereby the point is made all the clearer that just as these vital signs of faith are inseparable, so are the pastoral, priestly, and prophetic roles within the body of Christ.

PAUL AND THE CORINTHIANS:
A CASE STUDY

The thesis that Paul's theological convictions directly and significantly influenced his practice of ministry can be verified in the particular instance of his dealings with the Corinthian church. We know enough about the political, commercial, and cultural life of Corinth in Paul's day to be able to appreciate the fact that his ministry there faced complexities and had to be conducted under pressures similar in many ways to those experienced by Christian ministers in our own day. We also know many things about the church there: its sociological makeup, its theological outlook, its competing factions, its moral standards and questions, its fear of authoritarian leaders, and yet its need to have apostolic heroes, its particular suspicions of Paul, etc.[11] Moreover, in the apostle's letters to Corinth we have firsthand evidence of how he responded to the needs and opportunities he faced in that city over a period of several years. At least four characteristics of his Corinthian ministry may be noted, and taken together they enable us to confirm our earlier observations about the relationship between Paul's theological convictions on the one hand and his pastoral commitments on the other.

1. *Paul's persisting pastoral commitment to the Corinthian congregation.* How often, given the religious pretentiousness, the spiritual arrogance, the incessant infighting, the moral confusion, and the personal slanders hurled at him, the apostle must have been tempted to put the woes at Corinth behind him and devote himself to other, more promising and less frustrating fields of service! A modern "cost-effectiveness" analysis that measured the time and energy expended in relation to quantifiable results would likely have pointed him to that decision. But Paul's Corinthian ministry is noteworthy, first of all, because he *persisted* with it where others would have given up. He

wrote to the Corinthians repeatedly; he sent Timothy to them (I Cor. 4:17; 16:10–11). After Timothy's mission failed, Paul himself made a hurried trip to Corinth, interrupting his work in Asia (the "painful visit" referred to in II Cor. 2:1); and when that, too, failed, he dispatched to Corinth yet another associate, Titus, whose delay in returning increased Paul's anxiety and caused him to break off a mission in Troas (II Cor. 2:12–13). Titus finally did return with an encouraging report (II Cor. 7:6–7, 13b–16), and Paul was moved to send him back again to Corinth, along with others, to continue the work of ministry there (II Cor. 8:6, 16–24). Subsequently, Paul planned yet a third visit to Corinth for himself (II Cor. 12:14; 13:1–4, 10) and apparently managed to accomplish that on his way to Jerusalem with an offering (Rom. 15:24–29).

The apostle's pastoral commitment to the Corinthian congregation is also apparent in the fraternal and parental images which are especially frequent in I and II Corinthians. The Corinthians are addressed as "brothers [and sisters]" (e.g., I Cor. 1:10, 11, 26; 10:1; 14:6, 20, 26, 39; 16:15; II Cor. 1:8; 8:1; 13:11), even as "beloved brothers [and sisters]" (I Cor. 15:58). Both the depth and the character of Paul's pastoral concern for them are especially visible, however, in those places where he conceives of the Corinthians as his "children" to be nurtured, guided, guarded, and disciplined in the ways of Christ (I Cor. 3:1–2; 4:15–20; II Cor. 6:13; 11:2; 12: 20–21; 13:2). It must be emphasized, however, that Paul tried not to be an overly "possessive" presence in his pastoral role. He is deeply troubled, not just embarrassed, by those in Corinth who boast that they somehow "belong to Paul" as his personal converts and followers (I Cor. 1:12–15; 3:4–9); they show that they have not fully grasped the meaning of "the cross of Christ" on which his preaching is centered (I Cor. 1:17).

2. *Paul's perceptive theological analysis of problems in Cor-*

inth. Most of us, faced with the formidable array of "practical" issues and problems Paul faced in Corinth, would be apt to preoccupy ourselves with alleviating the symptoms only. But Paul, ever alert to the vital signs themselves, does not allow himself to be diverted from what is most fundamental.

One example of Paul's theological perceptivity is present at the very beginning of I Corinthians. It is significant that he does not blame the factiousness in the congregation on the other Christian leaders, Apollos or Cephas. Rather, he perceives that it has arisen from the Corinthians' failure to grasp the meaning of his own preaching of the cross, and from their confusing of the gospel with the sort of special religious wisdom they had been predisposed to seek and possess. Paul must now remind them that the gospel does not involve cultic heroes but a cross, and that the wisdom it presents is the "foolishness" that Christ was crucified for their redemption (I Corinthians, chs. 1, 2). This gospel, he insists, neither offers nor requires unique ecstatic experiences or particular spiritual gifts; indeed, the Corinthians' own pretensions in this regard are decidedly *pre*mature (see I Cor. 2:6 to 3:4). Paul saw clearly that in Corinth faith had been misunderstood as conveying new religious *privileges* and a new spiritual *status,* and that neither the radical nature of the gift nor the radical scope of the claim of the gospel had been grasped. What the Corinthians needed most to learn was that the gospel undercuts and makes relative all human pretensions and religious claims with its proclamation that the believer belongs to Christ, even as Christ belongs to God (I Cor. 3:23). This fundamental theological point is stressed over and over again, in many different ways, as Paul threads his way through the intricate and sensitive "practical" issues on which he gives counsel in the remainder of I Corinthians.

3. *Paul's determined reiteration of the "theology of the cross."* Not only at the opening but also at the close of I

Corinthians Paul emphasizes the terms in which he had preached the gospel to them: as the "cross of Christ" (I Cor. 1:17), "the word of the cross" (1:18), "Christ crucified" (1:23; 2:2), and that "Christ died for our sins" (15:3). This same kind of summary of his gospel is interjected into the discussion of apostleship in II Corinthians (5:14–15), and time and again as he addresses the practical matters of Christian life and conduct he reemphasizes his theology of the cross (see, e.g., I Cor. 8:11–12).

Because Paul regarded the eucharist as a powerful liturgical sign of the believers' common participation in Christ's body through his death (I Cor. 10:16–17), he considered the Corinthian abuses of that rite to be a peculiarly revealing symptom of the root theological problem. Their "profaning the body and blood of the Lord" (11:27) should not be identified with their specific mishandling of the consecrated elements of bread and wine. Rather, it was the fact that the more prosperous members who were able to arrive earlier for the preceding congregational meal went ahead and ate heartily without thought for the poorer members who, arriving later, would also have less to bring with them to eat (11:17–22). What should have been a proclamation of the Lord's death (11:26) had been turned into a virtual denial of its meaning. Instead of a community of brothers and sisters bound together in the common praise of God and the service of his people, the Corinthian congregation was becoming simply another religious association, its central cultic rite little more than a perfunctory appendage to a "church supper" benefiting primarily those who needed it least. Paul could thus claim that there was no real "eucharist" in Corinth, because there was no true *koinonia* and no true *diakonia* of one another.

We have good evidence that the Corinthian Christians found it difficult to understand that faith offers the believer no immunity from hardship and distress (see I Cor. 4:8–13; cf. 2:6–16). But for Paul faith means to acknowl-

edge one's dependence on God and to give him thanks, and he is able to accept the suffering that comes to himself and to other Christians, not as an obstacle to faith but as a help to it—"to make us rely not on ourselves but on God who raises the dead" (II Cor. 1:9). Here again Paul's "theology of the cross" finds expression: Christian faith is directed toward the God of Jesus Christ, in whose death-resurrection God has acted redemptively for all. Paul's description of his own apostolic existence is applicable to every believer: "always carrying in the body the death of Jesus, so that the life of Jesus may also be manifested in our bodies. For while we live we are always being given up to death for Jesus' sake, so that the life of Jesus may be manifested in our mortal flesh" (II Cor. 4:10–11).

4. *Paul's keen sense of having been called into the service of God.* In the Corinthian letters, Paul's sense of his work being the service of God is especially apparent (see, e.g., I Cor. 4:1; 9:16–17; II Cor. 6:4). First, he emphasizes that of himself he is insufficient for the work of ministry; his competence comes from God alone (II Cor. 2:16b; 3:5–6). If there is anything that "commends" his ministry as such, it is not his achievement, but his sufferings (see II Cor. 6:4–10). These disclose his own mortal weakness, and thereby enable the "transcendent power" of God to be the more effectively revealed (II Cor. 4: 7–12; cf. 11:16–30; 12:1–10; I Cor. 4:8–13).

Second, Paul's sense of ministerial vocation leads him to emphasize, particularly in his letters to Corinth, that finally he is accountable to God alone. The most important passage to consider here is I Cor. 3:1 to 4:7, where he insists that those who lay the foundation of Jesus Christ and build upon it must stand the test of God's judgment (I Cor. 3:10–13). "So let no one boast of men," he writes (3:21a), because we all belong to God and our ultimate accountability is only to him (3:21b–23). Thus is the true ministry of God liberated from the

tyranny of constant concern about the world's judgment as well as from the tyranny of self-doubt (4:3). "It is the Lord who judges me" (I Cor. 4:4b; cf. 4:5; II Cor. 10: 17–18). That was a genuinely liberating word for Paul, and it can be for us, too. In his Corinthian ministry, then, we see Paul resolute against almost constant pressure to establish himself and his ministry by human credentials. "What we are is known to God," he writes them (II Cor. 5:11–12). That is enough.

CONCLUSION

It is a temptation to idealize great men and women of the past, to make their accomplishments appear not only "larger than life" but also less flawed and finite than they were. Paul's ministry is not easily idealized, however. We do not have to rely exclusively on secondhand accounts of his work (like Acts, where there is undoubtedly some measured idealization of Paul), but have a group of letters from his own hand. This means that we are never far from the sober reality that Paul faltered and failed like any mortal. We have evidence that Paul specifically refused to adopt a style of ministry that could in any sense be termed "heroic." His refusal to conform to such a model, even in Corinth where for many people apostolic legitimacy seemed to depend on religious heroics, shows how deeply committed he was to another understanding of ministry.

Paul's own understanding of ministry grew out of his commitment to the gospel as "the word of the cross," and out of his perception that "the power of the cross" is the power of self-giving, serving love. For this reason he could accept his own weaknesses, hardships, and failures as themselves an integral part of his apostolic witness. He cataloged these frequently for the Corinthians (I Cor. 4:8–13; II Cor. 4:8–12; 6:4–10; 11:23–33; 12: 1–10), not by way of an excuse for ineptitude, nor to

elicit their sympathy and aid. Rather, he presented these as confirmation that what he had been able to accomplish for the gospel was not really his accomplishment at all, but God's. He must have experienced the temptation to become a mere "peddler of God's word," tinkering with it to make it more attractive and to enhance his own prestige as its spokesman, but he rejected this way (II Cor. 2:17; 4:2). He refused to compete for profit with the popular religious propagandists of his day, although he probably could have achieved greater "statistical success" in Corinth had he done so (see II Cor. 11:7–21a). As it was, his strange ways made him suspect there, and earned him the unflattering epithet "crafty" (II Cor. 12:16).

Even more striking, Paul dared to ask his congregations, indeed even his congregation in Corinth, to join him in this kind of ministry: "Be imitators of me, as I am of Christ" (I Cor. 11:1). He reminds them that they share with their apostle the sufferings of Christ, and thus also the comfort with which God comforts his people (II Cor. 1:3–7). The ministry of the church as a whole, no less than his own, must be conformed to the gospel, the word of the cross. It is to be a ministry through which God's power, made present in the cross as suffering, serving love, is constantly represented in the disciplined work and worship of a believing community.

Here, then, is Paul's greatest legacy to the church of our day, and to its ministry. It is not that he was the first great Christian theologian, because he was not a systematic theologian, and he himself was heir to a rich theological tradition. And it would be both inappropriate and ironic to honor him as a "successful missionary," through whose tireless efforts forces were set in motion which would one day "win the world for Christ." That would be an inappropriate claim because it is a much too simplistic conception of the origin of the Christian mission. It would be, moreover, highly ironic, because Paul him-

self consistently declined to measure his own "success" in the usual external ways. Indeed, his most important contribution was to show that a Christian ministry can only be validated as such when it is devoted to the service of God and to the "eventuation" of the gospel of God, understood as "the word of the cross," in the world. Such a ministry is not to be judged by how much it "achieves," but by how well it serves to monitor and maintain faith's vital signs in the body of Christ.

4

RESOURCES FOR PASTORAL MINISTRY IN THE SYNOPTIC GOSPELS

BY
PAUL J. ACHTEMEIER

It is not always apparent that biblical scholars have pastoral concerns in view when they conduct research and publish its results. Nor is it always apparent that practitioners of pastoral ministry have such research and its results in mind as they carry out their duties. Nevertheless, the two are indissolubly linked. Given the nature of the biblical materials, faithful study of them will lead to results applicable to the pastoral task. Given the nature of the pastoral ministry of the church, responsible practice must remain faithful to the witness of the Gospels, or it will lose its true reason for being.

This essay explores selected aspects of this relationship between Synoptic Gospel studies and the form and function of pastoral ministry. (1) I shall discuss not only the content but also the shape and nature of these Gospels (i.e., Matthew, Mark, and Luke), to see whether the kind of literature they are sheds some light on the guidance pastors may find in them for their responsibilities. That task is undertaken in the first section. (2) Because our Scripture has grown out of the life of the community of believers as they sought to be faithful to the God who had called that community into being, and because the pastoral task concerns itself primarily, if not exclusively, with contemporary communities of faith, I shall examine the relationship of Synoptic Gospel and community in

the second section. I shall attempt to discern some linea-
ments of the interrelationship of each Gospel and the
community out of which it grew and for which it was
written, to see what light may be shed on the way that
interrelationship can be configured in contemporary
times. (3) Finally, because the Gospels point away from
themselves to their central figure, Jesus of Nazareth, crucified and risen, I shall, in the third section, look at the
content of the Synoptic Gospels, to see in what way their
story of Jesus is to affect the ministry of pastors to the
people of God. What is learned of the nature of the
Synoptic Gospels and their relationship to their originating community will inform the discussion in the final
section.

GOSPELS AS WITNESS:
THE NATURE OF THE SYNOPTIC GOSPELS

Scholars have concluded over the past several decades
that the Synoptic Gospels do not represent an attempt to
record the history of Jesus of Nazareth. Attempts to write
the life of Jesus using the Synoptic Gospels as sources
proved conclusively that the evidence necessary to produce such a history is simply not present in the Gospels.

It is obvious that much of the information one would
want to know about an important person is missing from
the Gospel accounts of Jesus. We don't know the date of
his birth. There are two accounts of circumstances con-
nected with his birth which differ so widely that one is
forced to choose either one version or the other. Any
attempt to "harmonize" them into one account runs
afoul of material unique either to Matthew or to Luke.

Further information needed for a history of Jesus is not
given in any form. His childhood years, education, formative influences, vocational decision, his call to ministry,
are absent from the canonical records. Even the material
that tells of his ministry does not contain the kind of

information needed to develop a history of Jesus. Too often, intervals are designated by such phrases as "after some time," or "after that," or "not many days later," making it impossible to determine accurately the time span involved. Jesus' itinerary is different in each of the Synoptic Gospels, apart from the fact that each Gospel includes unique material, and each omits important material contained in the other two.

Above all, modern biography needs some indication of the mental and psychological development of the person. What events in the person's life were significant for later perceptions? Why did the person act in the way he or she did? What formed the character and world view that influenced, if not dictated, later activity? It would be interesting to know, for example, at what point Jesus felt called to be Messiah. Did his family life influence him? Was his propensity to call God by the familiar "Abba" (our equivalent would be "Daddy") influenced by the father image he knew in Joseph? Was his religious understanding influenced by his relative John the Baptist? When did Jesus learn the law of God in the Pentateuch? What did he learn in his synagogue? What were his teachers like? The list of questions goes on and on, and all are important for any biography of Jesus.

This means that any history, or life, of Jesus must be based as much upon guesswork as upon available evidence. An interesting thing about such guesswork is that the biographer tends to fill in the gaps in such a way that the Jesus who emerges is suspiciously like the author or at least his religious ideal. That was the burden of Albert Schweitzer's massive *The Quest of the Historical Jesus,* [1] in which he showed, among other things, how the religious ideals of any given period shaped the picture of Jesus that emerged from such attempts. After fruitless years of many attempts, the historical Jesus remains, at least from the perspective of modern historical writing, the man who remains unavailable, and in that sense, unknown.

Whatever else the Synoptic Gospels may or may not be, therefore, they do not contain the materials necessary to construct a satisfactory biography of Jesus' life. This has implications for the way the Synoptic Gospels ought to be approached. Attempts to deduce from a Gospel account the psychological motivations, or the personal reasons, for a given sequence of events will require generous amounts of imagination. The raw material is not there. Sermons based on pious imagination have a way of being benign, and sometimes malignant, reflections of the cultural and religious ideals of the preachers. This comes perilously close to reversing Paul's dictum that he preached Christ as Lord, and not himself. If a task of preachers of the Word is to preach the Word of God, and not their own religious and cultural ideals, then sermons must be shaped in terms of the intentions of the text. The modern understanding of history is not one of those intentions.

Study of the Synoptic Gospels has indicated that the differences between the Gospels of Matthew, Mark, and Luke are due not to different or superior historical information or traditions, but rather to the theological points each author wanted to make. Redaction criticism has informed this conclusion. Redaction criticism seeks to determine how much material in a Gospel came to its author in the form of tradition, and how much of the Gospel's shape and content resulted from the writer alone. One way to do this is to compare the text of a Gospel with the source the author used in producing that text. A careful examination of the differences between the text and the source will help to determine the motivation for the changes that are discoverable. As more passages are examined, a pattern of editorial changes and additions may emerge which provides clues to the theological intention underlying those alterations. If, for example, as most scholars agree, Mark is one of the sources used by both Matthew and Luke, but independently of

each another, one can, by carefully comparing the way Matthew and Luke used Mark, determine some of the theological motivations for the shape and arrangement of that material. A few examples will illustrate this.

In the beginning of Mark's Gospel, it is evident that John the Baptist plays an important role in the story of Jesus. The opening verses may be paraphrased: "The beginning of the gospel of Jesus Christ was John the Baptist, appearing in the wilderness, preaching a baptism of repentance for the forgiveness of sins." A further clue to the importance of John is the description of him in words that bear linguistic echoes of the description of Elijah in the Greek translation of the Old Testament (LXX, IV Kings 1:8). Clearly, John is to remind the reader of Elijah, who was expected to return and announce the advent of the Messiah.

The death of John the Baptist is told in horrifying detail (Mark 6:17–29), with the clear impression given that the martyr death of John means that he was Jesus' forerunner in his preaching and in his manner of death. Like Jesus, he is wrongfully put to death by political authorities, but for essentially religious reasons. So similar are John and Jesus that after putting John to death, Herod, on hearing what Jesus was doing, concluded that Jesus must be John come back to life (Mark 6:14–16). In answer to the question about the return of Elijah to herald the coming of the Messiah, Jesus made clear that John the Baptist filled that role. This meant that John was the final prophetic voice before the appearance of the awaited deliverer, namely, Jesus himself (Mark 9:11–13). Clearly John/Elijah played a key role in the career of Jesus of Nazareth, God's Christ, as Mark portrays it.

If Luke's use of the traditions about John the Baptist is compared to Mark's, some indication of how the author of the Third Gospel understood the Baptist's importance can be discerned. We receive a hint in the way Luke begins his Gospel. Although Luke contains stories about

the annunciation and birth of both John and Jesus, from the outset Jesus is the more important figure. This is indicated in Luke 1:39–56, where the unborn John reacts to the voice of Jesus' mother, and Elizabeth who bears John acknowledges that the child of Mary is superior (esp. vs. 41–43). It is further indicated in Luke 2:41–52, where Jesus appears in the Temple and astonishes with his wisdom the teachers of the law. While Luke has parallel accounts for Jesus and John of the annunciation (John —Luke 1:5–25; Jesus—Luke 1:26–38), birth (John—1: 57–66; Jesus—2:1–21), and praise of the infant (John— 1:67–80; Jesus—2:22–40), there is no parallel to Jesus' appearance in the Temple. Clearly, Jesus is the superior one.

Furthermore, although Luke knows that John began his ministry before Jesus, Luke omits Mark's description of John the Baptist in terms of the prophet Elijah (Mark 1:5–6). Luke's unwillingness to see in John the figure of Elijah returned is further evidenced by Luke's use of the traditions about the death of John. Instead of telling the story of John's martyr death, Luke simply records that Herod had John imprisoned, and we indirectly learn that he also had him beheaded. This indirect manner is most revealing. Mark records Herod's words, when he hears about Jesus: "This John, whom I beheaded, has risen." Thus he identified Jesus with John. Luke changed the verse to read: "John I beheaded; who is this about whom I hear these things?" (Luke 9:9), thus eliminating the identification by Herod of John and Jesus.

The climax of Mark's identification of John with Elijah the forerunner, and thus a key element in the ministry of Jesus, occurred when Jesus made that identification (Mark 9:11–13). Apparently there was no way Luke could reshape this material and still have it conform to his understanding of John the Baptist, and so he simply omitted it.

As this exercise has made plain, Luke is as unwilling to

identify John the Baptist with Elijah as Mark was insistent upon it. For Luke, it was not John but Jesus who is to restore all things through his inauguration of God's kingdom and therefore, since two could not play that role, and since the tradition of Elijah turned on the idea of Elijah as restorer, Luke eliminated an identification of John with the ancient prophet. Apparently for Luke anything that detracted from that importance of Jesus must be eliminated. Luke gives no comfort to anyone thinking that John could be the true restorer, and hence worthy of veneration. The theology of the Gospel writer, in this case the author of Luke, is therefore very much a part of the Gospel itself and helped to shape the presentation of the traditions about Jesus of Nazareth.

There are other motives apparent in the differences between the Gospels. In some cases the form a story took was confusing, or open to misunderstanding, so the tradition was reshaped to eliminate the problem. One example, from Matthew's use of Marcan material, is all that space will allow to show this. In Mark, where Jesus points to the significance of John the Baptist, we read: "And they asked him, 'Why do the scribes say that first Elijah must come?' And he said to them, 'Elijah does come first to restore all things; and how is it written of the Son of man, that he should suffer many things and be treated with contempt? But I tell you that Elijah has come, and they did to him whatever they pleased, as it is written of him'" (Mark 9:11–13). Surely it is right to infer that Jesus has referred to John the Baptist as the returned Elijah, even though he did not explicitly say it. Matthew, perhaps aware that some had missed the point of this tradition, added this sentence to the account: "Then the disciples understood that he was speaking to them of John the Baptist" (Matt. 17:13). In this way, possible ambiguity was replaced by absolute clarity: John is Elijah.

There are, in addition, places where the alterations are made simply to prevent routine misunderstanding that

would deflect attention from the point under consideration. For example, in the account of the call of Levi, and
in the subsequent debate about Jesus' association with
sinners (Mark 2:13–17), it is not clear in whose house the
debate takes place. Mark 2:15 reads, literally, "And it
happened that he was reclining in his house, and many
tax collectors and sinners were gathered around Jesus
and his disciples . . ." It looks as though the debate took
place in Jesus' house, yet the antecedent of "he" in v. 15
seems to be Levi, about whom v. 14 says, "And he got
up and followed him." Or is the antecedent the "him,"
i.e., Jesus? Obviously these concerns could deflect attention from the point being made: Jesus does not follow the
Pharisaic rules of exclusion when it comes to people who,
in their eyes, are impure. If this point is deflected by
confusion about whose house is being talked about,
something ought to be done. Luke does it. The comparable verses in Luke are: "And abandoning all he got up
and followed him. And Levi held a great feast for him,
and a great crowd of tax collectors and others were there
with him" (Luke 5:28–29). The confusion about the
house has been eliminated (it was Levi's house) and the
point of the tradition is made clear.

Examples like these can be multiplied many times
over. The differences between the Gospels are not due
to superior historical information. Rather, they are intended to make another theological point, to clarify a
theological point, or to assure that the theological point
is not obscured. The intention of each Gospel is to witness to the theological significance of Jesus of Nazareth,
risen and regnant, who walked among fellow human
beings, taught them, and helped them.

The point of the Gospel is the point of a sermon, not
a historical biography. The sermon must adapt the tradition to new circumstances among its listeners. It must
clarify areas of potential uncertainty about the meaning
of the text. And it must make the theological point neces-

sitated by the situation to which the preacher is called to minister. The point of the Gospels is pastoral, not historical. Therefore, to assume that changes were made to correct history rather than to aid in pastoral understanding is to miss the point of the Gospels. To raise the question of the resources for pastoral ministry in the Synoptic Gospels is in fact to identify the kind of literature the Gospels are. They grew out of, and are intended for, the pastoral use of the reader and the preacher. The nature of the Gospels is not history. Their nature is specific witness to the meaning of Jesus of Nazareth. It is precisely the sermon that performs the act of witness in the context of the church.

The point is Jesus, not what he did or what he said, although these are important. The gospel witness includes what he said because of who he was, not the other way around. Jesus is not important because of what he said; rather, what he said is important because of who Jesus was. Let me illustrate this with a consideration of the opening verses of the Sermon on the Mount in Matthew 5–7, namely, the Beatitudes (Matt. 5:3–12).

The form of the beatitude—an announcement of blessing upon a certain person or class of persons—is not the creation of Matthew or of Jesus. Beatitudes are common in the Old Testament, and they frequently occur in the Psalms, especially in the opening verses (e.g., Ps. 1:1; 32:1; 41:1). Furthermore, beatitudes are characteristic of the Wisdom Literature of Israel and can be used to announce the blessed state in nonreligious terms (e.g., Wisdom of Sirach 14:1, 20; 25:8). Nor are the beatitudes in Matthew the only ones remembered of Jesus. Others are scattered throughout the Gospels (e.g., Matt. 11:6/Luke 7:23; Matt. 13:16/Luke 10:23; Luke 12:37; and John 13:17). People other than Jesus also use the form in the Gospels (e.g., Luke 11:27 and 14:15). They appear in other places in the New Testament, for example in Paul (Rom. 14:22) and in the Revelation to John (1:3).

The beatitudes do not represent ethical exhortation to some virtue as much as they simply declare a blessing on some person or act. If some of the causes for blessing happen to be virtues (e.g., Sirach 14:1, 20), others simply state a fact (Luke 11:27; 14:14; Sirach 25:8), or a more particular contingency (e.g., Rev. 1:3; John 13:17; Matt. 13:16).

Against this general background the series of beatitudes in Matthew 5 may be examined. They are the longest series of such sayings in biblical and apocryphal literature. They here begin a discourse of Jesus. They are unique in that they do not simply acknowledge a state or recognize a virtue. They also bless a person in the present for something that will occur only in the future. Furthermore, these beatitudes do not represent a catalog of virtues that the Christian is to produce in order to be regarded favorably by God. If this were true, the first half of the beatitude would name the virtue to be achieved, and the second half would identify the reward. Yet the form of the beatitude is never used this way in Jewish literature. Nor does this seem to be the function of the other New Testament beatitudes. Rather than exhort to virtue, beatitudes identify certain realities as good or blessed.

Additional clues to the significance of these beatitudes in Matthew are derived from the structure of the language. The rewards promised in vs. 4, 6, 7, and 9 are expressed in the passive voice (e.g., "they shall be comforted; they shall be satisfied"). This is an example of the reverential passive, by means of which one avoids mention of God. This form was an expression of Jewish piety which felt it would be sacrilegious to pronounce the name of God, the sacred tetragrammaton, Yahweh. Thus, instead of "May God bless you," one could say "May you be blessed." Anyone who knew the religious customs would immediately know, from the passive

form, that it was a prayer that God might bless the hearer of the words.

This is the linguistic structure of the Beatitudes in Matthew 5. The point is that God will comfort those who mourn, will fill those hungry for righteousness. The other Beatitudes fall into this pattern as well. Taking this insight into account, the Beatitudes may be rendered in the following way:

> Blessed are the spiritually poor, for God will give them his kingdom.
>
> Blessed are those who mourn, for God will comfort them.
>
> Blessed are the meek, for God will give them the earth for their inheritance.
>
> Blessed are those who are hungry and thirsty for righteousness, for God will satisfy them.
>
> Blessed are those who are merciful, for God will be merciful to them.
>
> Blessed are the pure in heart, for they shall see God.
>
> Blessed are the peacemakers, for God will call them "my sons."
>
> Blessed are those who are persecuted because of righteousness, for God will give them his kingdom.

Expressed in this way, Jesus speaks for God in the Beatitudes. He announces what God will do in the future. The structure points to two realities with which the reader must come to terms: (1) Jesus can speak with authority of the future, and (2) Jesus can speak for God, because he knows what God will do. This places the hearer of the Beatitudes at a point of decision. One must decide whether Jesus can speak bindingly for God, and hence one must believe that what the Beatitudes say is true—or one must decide that the content of the Beatitudes cannot be true, in which case Jesus may be ignored.

The choice is not an easy one. What the Beatitudes bless is counter to the system of rewards under which we

live. It is not the meek who inherit the world, but the violent and the aggressive. We do not erect statues to the people who plead for the avoidance of war, but to the generals who win them. Those who do deeds of mercy in large cities are more likely to be mugged than to be shown mercy in return. Either Jesus can promise in God's name, or he is propounding a cruel hoax on those most vulnerable to such cruelty. Can we accept Jesus as the one who speaks for God? If not, what choice is there but to oppose him? On this choice, on the significance of his person, the meaning of the Beatitudes depend.

If he is accepted as one who can speak for God, we find in the Beatitudes some of the contours of God's eschatological rule. It means sheer grace. Those who lack and suffer in the world will benefit in the kingdom. Mourners will find divine comfort. Why do they mourn? They live in an age in which mourning is appropriate, an age dominated by conquest, intolerance, suppression, extortion, and the violation of the rights of many. Who could rejoice in such a world? Only those who profit from such activity. Those who mourn a sin-infested age will find comfort in God's benevolent and just rule.

The same is true of the spiritually impoverished who, finding no way to achieve righteousness in a religious legal system tilted against them, can hunger only for that righteousness which brings fellowship with God. They will find satisfaction when God in his rule welcomes them into fellowship with him because he was their only hope. For those who have relied on their own goodness to establish a relationship with God, that kingdom must mean the same disappointment as the laborers in the parable received, seeing others labor less but receive the same reward. Those who show mercy will receive a divine mercy denied to those who deny mercy to others, like the man in the parable who, though forgiven the millions he owed, nevertheless was unwilling to forgive the ten owed him.

In sum, for those whose only hope is God, the kingdom is joy, peace, comfort, mercy, and fellowship with the God who does not disappoint those who hope in him. For those who are satisfied and joyful in the present order, the kingdom of God must mean a reversal of values that will be painful. This is the reality presented to those who hear the Beatitudes. Whether or not we accept them will depend on our judgment about Jesus and his relationship to God. If he can speak for God, and make promises about reality that God will keep, the Beatitudes present a vision of God's coming rule. If Jesus cannot speak for God, he must be rejected as one who gives false hope to the bereaved. What decision we make about Jesus will determine what we think of his words, the significance of his works, and what happened to him on the cross and, three days later, in the grave.

The Gospels are witnesses to who Jesus was, and what he said and did. They are not dispassionate history. Rather, they are a summons to faith. They are a witness to the significance of Jesus by whom, they affirm, God visited humankind and gave new shape to the future that he would eventually come to rule in visible majesty. It is not the pastor's task to wring from a distant history some insight useful to the proclamation of the Christian faith. Rather, it is the pastor's task to hear the summons to faith expressed in the Gospels, to respond to it, and, with faithful responsibility, to pass along that summons to others in the context of worship.

The evangelists shaped the traditions that they received in order that a central point might be heard. If a detail or the shape of the inherited tradition deflected attention from the point or gave rise to an inappropriate reflection, the detail or shape was changed to suit the audience for which the evangelist wrote. The point of the Gospel is to witness to faith in Christ, around whom a decision of faith must turn. The materials in the Gospels are shaped to elicit this decision in more and less obvious

ways. The intent of the Gospels is pastoral. They provide resources for the task of witnessing to the faith. This thrust points to the close relationship between Gospel and community, which will be examined next.

GOSPEL AND COMMUNITY

Modern scholars have concluded that the Gospels are addressed to the communities of faith out of which they were written. If some knowledge can be gained of how the Gospels related to their communities, and what they sought to achieve in that relationship, some clues may be found for the way we ought to be related pastorally to the communities of faith that we have been called to serve.

There is only indirect evidence about the relationship between Gospel and church in the Synoptics. This situation is different from that in the Pauline letters. Paul's letters are addressed to churches; what Paul liked and disliked is clear for all to see.

Direct evidence about the state of the churches to which the Gospels were addressed is absent in them. Direct statements that indicate what the Gospel authors sought to encourage, and what they found discouraging, are similarly lacking. Compounding the problem is the fact that the Gospels are cast in a literary form in which points must be made by shaping and arranging the traditions that were already in existence. The student must be careful in what is assigned to the community and what to the traditions. It cannot be assumed that every saying of Jesus in the Synoptic Gospels represents some situation in the author's community that he wished to address. One cannot assume, for example, that the saying about wealth in Luke 18:25 ("It is easier for a camel to go through the eye of a needle than for a rich man to enter the kingdom of God") reflects the condemnatory attitude of poor Christians in Luke's community toward the wealthy, despite Luke's bias in favor of the have-nots (cf.

Luke 1:51–53 and 6:20, where "in spirit" does not appear). One cannot make this assumption for two reasons. First, this saying appears in all three Gospels. It is possible that Luke included it simply because it was contained in the traditions about the sayings of Jesus. Indeed, in this instance, Mark appears to be Luke's source, as Mark is for the same saying in Matthew (Matt. 19:24; cf. Mark 10:25). What is inferred about the state of the community from this saying in Luke therefore would have to be inferred also about the communities of Mark and Matthew. Second, one cannot assume that it is a condemnatory statement. It would apply equally to wealthy Christians as an admonition to give up their dependence on wealth, since in the Christian community, wealth does not confer the status that it does in the secular world. Other sayings about wealth could have the same intention. The account of the "widow's mite" in Mark 12:41–44, for example, could serve not so much as a condemnation of the wealthy, but as an admonition to the wealthy in the Marcan congregation to share the financial burden in proportion to their wealth.

Care is required to deduce the shape of the community to which each Synoptic Gospel was addressed. One may not simply assume that every saying of Jesus reflects some belief or attitude of the community, which everyone in the community shared. If Paul's letters are an indication, everything was not always well with every church. It is reasonable to expect that the Gospels would intend to correct as well as reinforce views of the community of faith to which they were addressed.

The task is complex but nevertheless important, as much recent work on the Gospels has shown. The attempt to locate and describe the kind of impact the Gospels had on the world into which they were projected, as well as the influence that world had on the shape of the gospel message, has occupied and continues to occupy many New Testament scholars. If hints about the rela-

tionship between Gospel and community are indirect, they are nevertheless present and can be uncovered. One way to uncover them is to examine the shape of each Gospel in comparison with the others, to find where emphases are placed and where differences exist. Such a comparison will reveal the large amount of space Mark devoted to the account of Jesus' last days in Jerusalem. Clearly, Mark thought those days were of enormous importance for an understanding of the significance of Jesus of Nazareth. Couple this insight with the total inability of anyone, even his closest disciples, to understand the meaning of Jesus of Nazareth during his earthly career, and add the direct command of Jesus to his three disciples not to speak of what they had seen on the Mount of Transfiguration until after the resurrection (Mark 9:9), and the pattern emerges that Mark thought the passion of Jesus was the key to understanding him. Indeed, so important was the passion for a true understanding of who Jesus was, and what he was about, that Mark thought it was as impossible to understand Jesus prior to those events as it was easy after them; immediately after his death, even a centurion who helped kill him recognized who Jesus was (Mark 15:39).

Normally one does not spend a great deal of time on things that are going well, but tends to concentrate on things that need correction. This assumption is amply borne out by the Pauline correspondence. It seems fair to conclude that the author of the Gospel of Mark felt that the meaning of Jesus' death and resurrection were in danger of being diminished. Part of the purpose of that Gospel, therefore, is to call attention to the key role of the passion of Christ to a clear understanding of the meaning of his whole career.

Mark did not think the suffering of Jesus was an unfortunate accident, or a minor setback which was soon overcome and all but obliterated by the resurrection. Those who expect of the Christian faith a deliverance from all

future sufferings and pain are warned by Mark's Gospel
that suffering was an integral part of the fate of the one
they revere. Following Christ can hardly be understood
as a guarantee that life will be nothing but painless and
uninterrupted joy. For Mark, the path to glory for Jesus
lay through the valley of the cross, and Jesus' followers
are therefore armed, not for the avoidance of suffering,
but with the confidence that suffering, real and bitter
though it be, is not the final word. Those who take
Mark's Gospel seriously are thus prepared to face the
inevitable struggles and pain life brings, and to survive
them victoriously.

To follow Christ means to be open to the pain and
suffering, the confusions and despair, of those who come
seeking help. In these situations the one who follows
Christ must know that pain and suffering are not the final
reality, yet in this world they cannot be avoided. If
Christ's path to glory led through his own vulnerability
to the world's pain, a vulnerability demonstrated when
he hung dying on the cross, then our path, too, will lead
through our own vulnerability to the hurt of our fellow
human beings, as we seek to minister in Christ's name.
All vulnerability, all laying open of our lives to the needs
of others, belongs to those who follow the crucified Lord.
Yet the crucified Lord arose, and in that sure knowledge,
vulnerability becomes not a burden but a joy, as we
minister to others in the name of our crucified and risen
Lord.

In addition to what can be learned from the total structure of the Gospel about the point each evangelist intended to make, there are additional indications that can
be gleaned from an examination of smaller portions of
the larger narratives. For example, material in one Gospel that is not in another Gospel may provide a clue to
the intention of the author with respect to his community. An example can be taken from Matthew.

To understand Matthew, some observations are neces-

sary about one of his sources, i.e., Mark. In Mark 13, there is a prophecy of Jesus about what the future will be like. Interspersed among the cosmic signs that are to come prior to Jesus' return, there are references to the difficulties into which the community of Christians will fall. There will be false Christs appearing (vs. 6, 22), Christians will be put on trial in synagogue and civil court (v. 9), and betrayals will reach into the immediate family of believers (v. 12). The point is to urge Christians to remain steadfast and faithful through coming persecutions (vs. 13b, 33). Because of the prominence given to this material in Mark, one may infer that such tribulations had come upon his community. Mark was attempting to assure his community that these events presaged the coming of Jesus, that they were due to worsen, and so the Christians had to hold firmly to the faith. The impression is that the community was being hounded by enemies from without and was in danger of abandoning the faith.

Matthew's additions to this material are illuminating. There is, for example, material added after Mark's references to being hated "for my name's sake" (Mark 13:13a). Matthew adds: "And then many will fall away, and betray one another, and hate one another. And many false prophets will arise and lead many astray. And because wickedness is multiplied, the love of the majority will grow cold" (Matt. 24:10–12). Here the disintegration has penetrated the Christian community. No longer is the chief threat of dissolution posed by outside forces. The pressure has caved in the walls of resistance, and the community is divided against itself. Many are "offended" at Jesus (literally, "scandalized"), which clearly means that they have renounced their faith. Having done so, they betray their former fellow Christians, exposing them to persecution and sowing hate where once Christ's love had reigned. Schisms have opened with sectarian preaching; the community is fragmenting; indeed, it is threatened with complete dissolution as Christian love

cools and hardens into hate and divisiveness. What Matthew had to say to his church may have relevance for how such conflicts are met in our churches.

That Matthew was speaking to such problems is evident from some of the material he has assembled. This is especially clear in ch. 18. The only Gospel that uses the word "church" is Matthew, and one of those uses is in ch. 18. Matthew included a parable about a shepherd who left ninety-nine sheep to look for one that was lost. Luke also used this parable, but the way each writer presented the parable gives insight into his respective interest. Luke thought the story referred to the need for unceasing missionary activity designed to bring lost sinners into the Christian fellowship. The pursued sheep is identified as "lost" (Luke 15:4, 6), and the parable concludes with the observation that such pursuit is valid because of the great joy God has when a sinner repents. Clearly, Luke saw this parable as speaking to the mandate of the church to reach out to sinners who need the good news of salvation in Christ.

Matthew, on the other hand, because of the problems faced by the church for which he was writing, saw another point. For Matthew, this parable pointed to the need to pursue an erring fellow Christian, lest he be lost from the Christian community. In Matthew, the sheep is not "lost," it has been "led astray" (Matt. 18:12, 13), and the language Matthew used to describe the search allows, as Luke's did not, the possibility of failure to find that straying sheep (compare Luke 15:5: "And when he finds it," with Matt. 18:13: "And if it happens that he find it"). Apparently Matthew knew that such attempts did not always succeed. The conclusion of the parable is shaped accordingly: It is counter to God's will that one of these "little ones" should perish in such a manner. Even the phrase "little one," reveals Matthew's point, since it was used by Jesus in Matt. 18:6, a few verses earlier, to identify "one who believes in me." The para-

ble is introduced by Matthew with the same thought in mind: One is not to despise a "little one" by failing to pursue him or her with the full intention of restoring that one to the Christian fold.

To this parable, Matthew appends some straightforward advice on dealing with those who stray (Matt. 18: 15). This Christian church business is serious, Matthew seems to say, and careful steps must be taken to preserve in wholeness and health the community of faith. But there are limits. The church is not a collection of likeminded people free to alter the rules of fellowship as the situation may seem to demand. They march under higher orders, and those who fail to keep step are not to be accommodated, they are to be purged. The straying sheep is to be pursued, but the possibility of failure in the pursuit exists.

The question here is forgiveness. To the story about Peter's query of how many times forgiveness is to be exercised ("seventy times seven" according to Matt. 18: 22, whereas a somewhat similar story in Luke 17:2–4 speaks only of seven times), Matthew adds the parable, unique to his Gospel, about the servant who refused to forgive a small debt owed to him, despite his having been forgiven one much larger (Matt. 18:21–35). The point is transparent: Should not those who have received Christ's mercy be under obligation to show a similar mercy to fellow sinners (v. 33)? Indeed, that is what God demands (v. 34). The structure of the community is to be forgiving love. As though to give the final word on how the community is to organize itself, Matthew concluded this portion of his Gospel with these two stories which make clear the obligation of Christians to exercise the incredible mercy God has shown to them. The structure of the community is the structure of grace. For Matthew, both words are significant: structure and grace. The church is not an amorphous, if loving, blob. It is the community of faith, and its structural integrity is to be

upheld. Erring brothers and sisters are to be admonished, and, if the good of the community as a whole makes it necessary, ejected. But the structure is to have as its motivation the act that constituted the community: God's forgiving, merciful love toward sinners, placarded in his Son. Structured grace is the reality of the Christian community.

Matthew makes the point unavoidable in another way, when he speaks of love as the structure and meaning of the law. The purpose of the law is to provide a structure within which people may function as a community by limiting certain acts that are harmful and, in the case of religious law, by encouraging those activities which enable a community to function in accord with the will of God. Thus, the purpose of the law given to Moses on Mt. Sinai was to enable a ragtag band of slaves who had lived under Egyptian law to function as a "chosen people." Since the Hebrews had no notion of what a "chosen people" was, or how it ought to function, the law was an act of grace, conferring on them the opportunity to conduct their common life in a way acceptable to the God who had chosen them.

That is the law of which Jesus speaks in Matt. 5:17–20. Matthew intends for us to understand that Jesus thought keeping the law was the most important thing a person could do. Matthew records Jesus as saying: "Do not think that I have come to destroy the law or the prophets; I have not come to destroy but to fulfill" (v. 17). After commenting on the value of the smallest letter or even the smallest part of a letter of the law, Jesus concluded: "For I tell you that unless your righteousness is considerably greater than that of the lawyers and Pharisees, you will not enter the kingdom of heaven" (v. 20). Jesus advised others to obey the law (e.g., Matt. 19:17–19; 23:2–3a), and he could himself act in perfect accord with those words, even to the point of having tassels on his

garment, in accord with the command in Num. 15:38 (Matt. 9:20).

On the other hand, Matthew recalls that Jesus acted in opposition to the apparent force of these positive words about the law. Jesus did not fast (Matt. 9:14); he broke the Sabbath (12:1–14), contradicted the Mosaic law on marriage (19:3–9), counseled others that the Levitic law regarding dietary practices was insignificant for true righteousness (15:16–20), and gave the impression that he had a low estimate of the Temple (21:12–13; 26:61). This presents a certain dilemma: Was Jesus honest when he spoke highly of the law and obeyed it, or was he honest when he disparaged the law and broke it? Either there is a contradiction, or Jesus understood "fulfilling the law" in a way not readily apparent to his opponents, who were the official custodians and interpreters of the law.

That the latter is the meaning Matthew intended is clear by another passage. In response to a question by Pharisees about the greatest command in the law, Jesus answered that the greatest command has two parts: love of God and love of neighbor. He concluded: "On these two commands hang the entire law and the prophets" (Matt. 22:40). Clearly, the command to love God and every fellow human being is the substance of the law. Apart from this twofold command, the law and the prophets would lose their significance.

This means that the Jesus of Matthew's Gospel intends by his actions not to destroy the law, but to fulfill it. Everything is done to fulfill the true law, whether it is understood this way or not by his Israelite contemporaries. Jesus, by word and deed, reinterprets the law in terms of its true intent: love of God and neighbor. Apart from such love, whatever is done will not fulfill the law. Where love is present, the law is fulfilled, no matter what other interpretation has been given to the law. The absolute validity of the law of love leads to a breaking of some

of the commands of the law, as Jesus' words and acts make evident. Unless the last jot and tittle of the law of love for God and neighbor are fulfilled, the law is abrogated. Where love is found, there is righteousness greater than that of lawyers and Pharisees who followed a different interpretation of the law.

This understanding is emphasized in the illustrations that Matthew placed after the original statement about righteousness and law. One thing needs to be clear. "Love" refers to compassion, and to the acts that grow from it. That God "loves" us means that out of his compassion for us he sacrificed his Son to redeem us from sin. As Paul writes, God loved us while we were his enemies (Rom. 5:10). For this reason we are commanded to love our enemies. Christian love, or compassion, is the opposite of emotional reactions. We "love" our enemies by doing good to them, even if emotionally repelled by them. The command to love our enemies is not a command to turn our emotions about. It is a command to act counter to our emotions if necessary and to do good to those whom we hate. Because "love" has been perverted in contemporary usage, I will use the more neutral word "compassion" in what follows.

In the reinterpretation of the law as a law of compassion, Matthew uses a number of illustrations. The demand for compassion is as broken by attitudes that are counter to compassion as when the proscribed act is performed (Matt. 5:21–26). To look with lust on a fellow human being ruptures the relationship of compassion as much as an adulterous deed (5:27–30). To divorce a wife for the trivial reasons permitted by some rabbis (burning the dinner, putting too much salt in the soup, etc.) is to neglect compassion by being primarily interested in oneself and not the good of another (5:31–32).

Even the strange statement about oaths has a proper place (Matt. 5:33–37). Elaborate rules had been developed on what kind of oaths were and were not binding.

To use such oaths could deceive another into thinking that one was giving a binding word when one was not. This practice ruptures compassion by seeking one's own good at the expense of another. It puts one's desires above the good of a neighbor.

This is also the point of the saying about retaliation (Matt. 5:38–42). When one is insulted—the meaning in Jesus' world of a slap in the face—retaliation in kind means that one is preoccupied with self at the expense of neighbor. We are to seek the good of, to be compassionate toward, even those who insult our person. Similarly, if a person needs material aid or personal help, one is to assure that the needs are met, and thereby act compassionately. One is to give to those who need, and lend to those who desire it, all with the good of the petitioner in mind.

Two observations are helpful here. First, this is not a prescription for nonviolent behavior in all circumstances. A slap in the face is not a violent deed; it is an insult, and it is understood as such in this text. A program of pacifism must be based on passages other than Matt. 5:39. Secondly, this is not a prescription to respond to all requests, however harmful these requests may be to the one who asks. This is not compassion; it is permissiveness. To give something to a person in the full knowledge that the gift will harm the receiver would rupture the duty of compassion. To be compassionate does not require one to be stupid.

The final example is the climax: even those who act toward you in total disregard of compassion are to be treated compassionately (Matt. 5:43–48). As God is perfect in his compassion toward us (5:48), so we must strive to be compassionate in the same way toward our neighbors. Compassion is not to be limited to those from whom we expect it in return. We are also to show compassion to those from whom we cannot expect it in return. To do this is to fulfill the law and the prophets in

their primal intent, and thus to exhibit a righteousness which is greater than that shown by lawyers and Pharisees.

For Matthew, this should be the structure of the community of faith. Compassion is the solution to the fracturing and bickering community to which Matthew wrote. The community of faith has as its cornerstone compassion because Christ, the chief cornerstone, is God's act of compassion toward mankind. This is why compassion is the structuring element of a community that owes its existence to God's act in Christ. Those communities in which compassion rules will heal their divisions and caustic bickerings, both in Matthew's time and today. The structure of the community of faith is love of God and neighbor, a love that looks to the interest of others over self-centered preoccupations.

This means that the Gospels offer resources for the way churches as communities of faith are to be structured and operated. The grace of God makes possible radical compassion within the community of faith. Grace remains the ground from which compassion springs. The reality of divine grace *is* compassion, shown supremely in God's lifting his Son upon the cross, and three days later lifting him from the grave. That reality will be at work in the community of faith that allows it full course. Matthew's advice to his divided community can provide pastors with resources for aiding parishioners in structuring their individual lives and their lives together within the community of faith.[2]

Matthew, as well as the other Gospels, obviously had more to say to the respective communities, and to individuals within them, than these words about compassion, although these words are fundamental to all else. It would be helpful to distinguish what was intended as advice to their contemporaries from what was reported because of its intrinsic value for the information of the community of faith. I do not suggest that this latter mate-

rial can be omitted by anyone pursuing pastoral resources in the Synoptic Gospels. I am suggesting that pastoral resources in the Gospels may be more visible when we find them in a form originally intended for specifically pastoral purposes.

One key to detecting material addressed to the evangelist's own community is the identification of the recipients of Jesus' words. Matthew's advice to his troubled community took the form of Jesus' words to his disciples. That form provides an indication of what material was intended specifically as instruction to the community. What better way to address members of the community of faith than to do so in the form of instructions for disciples?

There are other formal criteria to justify this conclusion. A glance at any of the Synoptic Gospels shows that while some of the material addressed to crowds is of more general interest, the material addressed to the disciples in almost every instance is by its content applicable to, and intended for, the community of faith. A clear example of this is in Mark, where Jesus tells about the sower (Mark 4:1–20).

The parable of the sower (Mark 4:3–9) is addressed to the crowds that flocked to Jesus. So pressing is the crowd that Jesus retreats to a boat which, located a bit offshore, enables him to address the multitudes that otherwise apparently would have crowded him into the sea. The parable points to unexpected results from ordinary beginnings (the point also of the other parables in this chapter, Mark 4:26–29; 30–32). This may be a parable on the ministry of Jesus: his unspectacular announcement of God's impending kingdom will nevertheless finally be seen to have been the dawn of its visible coming. At least Mark presented it as the key to all other parables, and thus it must in some way have been linked to Jesus' total career (Mark 4:13).

The explanation given privately to the disciples no longer remains a parable. The meaning is clear. It is

almost an allegorical exposition of the way in which the proclaimed gospel is received by different types of listeners. Only those elements are explained which bear on the missionary task of the disciples. The point is that discouragements come in the course of preaching. But the people who truly accept the word bring forth amazing fruit as the result. Whatever the parable meant originally, the explanation is clearly aimed at the missionary task. It arms against premature discouragement when the inevitable rejection occurs. When the explanation is given to the *disciples,* as against the crowds to whom the parable was addressed, the content bears directly on the community of faith, in this case on its missionary task. In this way the disciples become a window on the community as they are instructed by Jesus.

This is true in the other two Synoptic Gospels. One example will suffice. Later in Mark's Gospel, the formal announcement is made that Jesus' fate involves suffering. Peter's confession, the first prediction of the passion, and Jesus' rejection of Peter's unwillingness to contemplate such a fate for Jesus make the point (Mark 8:27–33). To that Mark appends advice directed to both crowds and disciples. This advice bears on the fate of those who follow a crucified Lord. Future recognition by the lordly Son of Man returned in divine power will turn on one's willingness to embrace the fate of the suffering Son of Man as he moves to the cross. The epitome of this advice to the community is formulated in terms of the cross: "If anyone wants to come after me, let that one deny himself and take up his cross, and follow me." To follow Jesus is clearly to take on a new master. The center of existence is no longer self; it is Christ.

Willingness to follow Jesus to the point of martyrdom is surely the highest form of devotion. Quickly the disciples expressed their willingness to take it upon themselves! Led by Peter, they pledged their intention to die with Jesus (Mark 14:29, 31). Their failure to live up to

these pledges is openly placarded by Mark as well (v. 50). It is easy to imagine one's own courage sufficient to martyrdom when that possibility is remote to the point of invisibility. Yet this is the danger. Mark's readers, comforting themselves that should martyrdom be unavoidable they could summon the courage to follow Jesus, could shelve the advice on giving up self-centeredness until such time as martyrdom might be required.

Yet daily living requires of the community the spirit of self-giving which reaches its final expression in martyrdom. Advice to the church along this line needs also to be given. Luke seeks to solve this problem by reformulating Jesus' command: "If anyone wishes to come after me, let him deny himself, and take up his cross daily, and follow me" (Luke 9:23). With this one word, all daydreaming of future fulfillment of self-denial is punctured, and the hard reality of ordinary life lived for others takes its place. Luke, continuing the practice of speaking to the community through the disciples (the "all" in 9:23 draws its referent form from v. 18, where it is Jesus and the disciples), has made the command easier and harder. If a cross is not required, self-sacrificial life is needed even short of its ultimate expression.

A reading of the Synoptic Gospels while remembering this point (that when Jesus instructs the disciples he regularly has the community in mind) will provide resources for preaching, instruction, admonition, and counsel. Drawing on the material to use as it was meant to be used, one will find the contours of the Christian life portrayed in memorable form. The power that sustained the community of faith over the centuries becomes the power needed for it to survive today in troubled times.

THE GOSPELS AND JESUS OF NAZARETH

There is little doubt that Jesus of Nazareth is the focus of the Gospels. Who he was and his significance are

themes that dominate the Gospels. This final section will examine examples of these themes for resources in pastoral ministry. We shall examine first an element of who he was, then some of what he said and did, and finally, what happened to him.

The fundamental question in Christian faith is Christological: Who is Jesus? A variety of titles are given to him in the New Testament: Christ, Son of Man, Son of David, Son of God, Lord, and many more. Many of his deeds and sayings turn on who he is. One fundamental aspect underlies all of Jesus' titles, words, and deeds. That aspect concerns Jesus' relationship to the people of Israel and their sacred literature, the Old Testament. All three Gospels make evident that Jesus cannot be understood apart from the history of the Hebrew people with their God, and the promises God made to them.

Although the relationship of Jesus to the Old Testament witness may not be as evident in the Gospel of Mark as it is in the other two Synoptic Gospels, it is nevertheless there. The beginning of Mark's Gospel, both in the form in which Mark wrote it and in Mark's understanding of its beginning (cf. Mark 1:1–3), is presented in terms of the fulfillment of an Old Testament promise which is quoted with the appearance of John the Baptist. John, the forerunner of Jesus, even in the form of his death (see Mark 6:17–29), is to be understood as Elijah, whose return was promised to the Hebrew people (see esp. Mark 9:10–13). Therefore, Mark makes clear, one cannot understand the opening act of the career of Jesus without recognizing that it takes place as fulfillment of Old Testament prophecies and expectations.

Again, the parable of Mark 12:1–10, with its account of the wicked tenants of the vineyard, is patterned after the song of the vineyard in Isa. 5:1–7. The parable is meant to show the fate of Israel in its rejection of Jesus. Even when Jesus is turned away, it is in terms of the Old Testament! Finally, the passion of Jesus, the theological

key to the Gospel of Mark, is interpreted in terms of Psalm 22, both in terms of what happened (e.g., the soldiers cast lots for his garments, Mark 15:24, cf. Ps. 22:18; the high priests and passersby mocked him, Mark 15:29–31, cf. Ps. 22:7–8) and in terms of what Jesus said (Jesus' only words from the cross in Mark are the opening words of Psalm 22). In these and other ways, Jesus must be understood in relation to God's promises to Israel or he can only be misunderstood.

The Gospel of Luke also makes clear, in slightly different but no less convincing ways, that Jesus is the fulfillment of the promises of God contained in the Old Testament. The language with which Luke composed his Gospel and Acts, with its distinctive flavor of Septuagint Greek, points unavoidably to the roots from which Jesus emerged. Luke makes the point more obvious. The Magnificat, for example, which Mary delivers on the occasion of Elizabeth's visit, is clearly modeled in theme and language after the prayer of Hannah in I Sam. 2:1–10. This hymn, modeled after the piety of the Old Testament people, shows that Jesus is the fulfillment of the mercy God spoke to Abraham and his descendants (Luke 1:54–55). The place where Jesus was born, the city of David, namely, Bethlehem, indicates that Jesus should be understood as the fulfillment of the promise God made to the Israelite king (II Sam. 7:12–13). Jesus' birth in a city far from the home of his parents emphasizes the significance of the place. Remember that Luke was unwilling to cast John the Baptist in the role of Elijah because he wanted nothing to distract from the fact that Jesus, and no one else, was the fulfillment of Old Testament faith. Further, in the first public utterance of Jesus, his sermon in Nazareth, Luke's Jesus seeks out the passage from Isaiah (61:1–2) which speaks of the spirit-filled servant of God, and tells his listeners: "Today this scripture is fulfilled in your hearing" (Luke 4:21). Luke means that all Jesus subsequently did and said was as the

spirit-endowed servant of the God of the Hebrews, fulfilling by those words and deeds the promises of God.

This fulfillment is continued, after Jesus' ascension, in the church, when God's spirit descends upon it at Pentecost (Acts 2). Thus the church that calls Jesus its Lord is also understood as the continuing fulfillment of God's promises to his chosen people. To give one more example, the risen Christ, appearing to his disciples, opens their minds to understand the Scriptures (Luke 24:25). It is clear that Christ is not only the fulfillment but also the key to the comprehension of the Old Testament writings. In these and other ways, both in his Gospel and in his account of the early church in Acts, Luke makes clear that Jesus is understood only in terms of his roots in the Hebrew people from whom he descended. To miss this point is simply not to understand the importance of Jesus for Luke.

It is Matthew who makes the relationship between Jesus and the promises in the Old Testament most obvious and unavoidable. The characteristic formula, "This happened to fulfill what was spoken by the prophet," and its variations, occurs and recurs in Matthew. All aspects of Jesus' career—his conception (Matt. 1:22), events that swirled around him (2:17), his travels (4:14), his acts (12:17), his words (13:14, 35), even his final fate (21:4; 27:9)—are surrounded by the evidence that what happened to Jesus was as fulfillment of God's commerce with his chosen people. So convinced is Matthew that Jesus is the fulfillment of Israel that he can find links where, to our understanding, no explicit prophecy occurred. A prime example is the flight into Egypt of the young Jesus and his family. This happened, says Matthew, to fulfill what God had spoken through Hosea: "Out of Egypt have I called my son" (Hosea 11:1). But Hosea did not speak this as prophecy. He spoke it as historic fact referring to the exodus from slavery in Egypt. How can Jesus "fulfill" what was already an accomplished fact by the

time the prophet spoke it? The answer is that for Matthew the final fate of Israel remained unfulfilled until the advent of Jesus. The career of Jesus was so much a part of the total drama of God's dealing with his chosen people that until it occurred all events in the history of Israel remained provisional and unfulfilled. So intimately is Jesus tied to the people of Israel that their history remains less than history until it is capped and completed, and then begun anew, in Jesus of Nazareth. For that reason Hosea spoke unknowingly of the coming one in whom Israel's task and fate, its promise and its goal, would be fulfilled.

There is other evidence of this view in Matthew. The genealogy that ties Jesus to the two recipients of divine promises in the Old Testament, Abraham and David, is one example; Matthew's preference for "kingdom of Heaven" over "kingdom of God," thus identifying Jesus' central message with Old Testament piety is another. Matthew's conviction is that the Christological problem could be solved if one began with the relationship between Jesus and the story of the chosen people in the Old Testament.

In all three Gospels the fulfillment goes beyond the promise. God is not trapped by history. He freely changes the meaning of the past by his acts in the present as he moves his creation into the future where he will assume visible rule. Thus, one cannot view God's relation to the past with complacency. Rather, one must be open to the new things he will bring forth.

This has a number of implications for the way ministry is conducted. Let us mention two. First, the history of Jesus Christ, the Lord of the church, whose roots lie in the chosen people of Israel, means that there is a special relationship between those who confess Jesus as Lord and the descendants of Abraham according to the flesh. Anti-Semitism among Christians is the surest evidence that even the most rudimentary understanding of the mean-

ing and significance of Jesus has been missed.

Secondly, the creativity of the divine fulfillment of the divine promise ought to warn against any thought that God is somehow trapped in the pages of the New Testament, or the Bible as a whole, and that one can predict how he will fulfill his final promises in Christ. *That* he will fulfill them is a matter of the certainty of faith and the trustworthiness of God. *How* he will fulfill them is a matter of the open future and the sovereignty of God. Like those who saw Jesus, but held fast to *their* interpretation of God's Old Testament promises, those who similarly hold fast to *their* New Testament interpretations will find that when God has fulfilled his promises events will simply have passed them by.

In addition to Jesus' links to the chosen people of the old covenant, there are resources for pastoral ministry in what Jesus said. Here I concentrate on selected parables and relate them to the problem of the self-understanding of the Christian in general and the pastor in particular.

A problem in evaluating some of the parables is that too much is expected from them. Meaning is sought for each and every detail. One mistake is to press from the parables as much theological juice as we can. A second mistake is to read them from a resolutely religious perspective. Surely, we reason, Jesus must have wanted to communicate religious truth by means of them, so the lessons are sought.

Both of these approaches are wrong. Jesus communicated detailed theological truth in the form of straightforward sayings. He used the parables for another purpose. Interpretation of the parables as moral or theological tales is belied by the evidence. For example, the wise young women are anything but moral when they refuse to share the oil they have brought with those who did not bring enough (Matt. 25:8-9). Their actions run directly counter to a command of Jesus (Matt. 5:42: "Give to the one who begs from you, and do not refuse

the one who wants to borrow from you"). Other examples could be cited (Luke 15:11–12; 16:1, 5–7; 18:4–5; Matt. 13:44).

Similarly, and closely related, the practice of suppressing normal reactions to the events recited in order to find pious motives for all the acts perpetrated in parables should be forsaken. The parables are stories of the world as it is, not as it ought to be. The reactions to them must be the kind of reactions such activity would normally provoke. To hide disgust at the dishonest steward, or dismay at the owner of the vineyard who pays everyone the same wages, however long and hard they have worked, and then to substitute for those reactions some theological piety, is simply to prevent the parable from functioning as it ought.

For many of the parables, the point is not so much in what they tell us, theological or otherwise, as in the reaction they elicit from us. By causing these reactions to surface, dimensions of ourselves are revealed that we try to ignore or suppress. They reveal something about the kind of persons we are, and why we need the redemption Christ brings. Let me illustrate this.

Consider the parable of the Pharisee and the tax collector who pray in the Temple (Luke 18:9–14). The self-righteous Pharisee thanks God that he is good and righteous, does what is good and righteous, and is surely superior to the poor, miserable tax collector. The humble prayer of the truly honest tax collector admits that as a sinner he can only plead for mercy. Our reaction is predictable. We identify with the tax collector and feel gratitude that we are decent and humble, rather than self-righteous like the shameful Pharisee. The parable has performed its function. It has laid open our own self-righteousness, allowing us to see ourselves for what we are. The parable can lead to a discovery that no amount of pious rhetoric could bring about. Our reaction to the parable as a whole, rather than any theological meaning

found in its detail, leads to a new insight into ourselves, and into the insidiousness of sin as it seeks to use pious thoughts in the corrupting service of self-interest.

It is this function that makes the parables invaluable as aids in the minister's self-understanding. It will do the same for the congregation. But before the light is focused on others, it must shine in the dark corners of our own lives. And it is the purpose of these and other parables to probe those dark corners, break open our last defenses, and expose us to the cleansing light of the grace of God. This function is one of the great resources for pastoral ministry in the parables of the Gospels.

In addition to the parables, there are records in the Gospels of some of the things Jesus did. Perhaps the most striking and puzzling are his acts of power, commonly called "miracles." The New Testament word is really more descriptive and more accurate: *dynameis,* from the same root as our word "dynamite." In the Gospels, they show the incredible power at Jesus' command.

To understand what the Gospels report with this kind of story, it is helpful to know the way such stories were treated, told, and regarded in the New Testament world. People who could do such extraordinary things populated the imagination of the Greco-Roman world of the first century of our era. Such activity aroused wonder and amazement, not to say incredulity in some quarters. To say that miracles were "common" in the Hellenistic world is something of an overstatement. Such acts are never common. Common occurrences are not, in ordinary parlance, "miracles." Yet such stories were part of the folklore of the age. They were told of many people doing many things. In several instances these events were quite similar to the acts attributed to Jesus, especially casting out demons and walking on the sea.

When this kind of story achieves wide popularity, it develops a recognizable pattern as it and others like it are told and retold. A form develops that best conveys the

point intended. The material is then told in this form.

This happened with miracle stories in the Hellenistic world. The pattern had basically three elements, each one capable of expansion of detail and complexity. First, the problem was stated. A person was sick, or possessed by a demon, or blind, or dumb, or deaf, or endangered, or the like. Accompanying the statement of the problem, there was frequently an appeal for help either by the subject or by someone else on the subject's behalf. Secondly, the miraculous solution was recounted. Through a gesture, or a phrase from an exotic language, or manipulation, or power from plant or animal, or any combination of these, the problem was resolved. The third element was a demonstration that the problem had been resolved and that it was not an illusion or a trick of some kind. A dead person brought back to life ate a meal to prove that he or she really had been restored fully to life; a lame person walked, and even carried a burden, to prove the cure was a true one; a blind person did something only a sighted person could, like leaving the normal, well-known paths or surroundings to which he or she had previously been limited. An expression of amazement on the part of the onlookers is often an element in this proof that the miracle happened. The witness of a group of bystanders added objectivity to the claim that the resolution actually happened.

Problem, solution, and proof are thus the three elements, in that order, which characterize the normal Hellenistic miracle story. There is nothing mysterious about the formula. These are the three necessary elements for such a story. Fewer than these three, and there is no story. More than three are not necessary if the sole intent is to recount a miracle.

The Gospel miracle accounts conform to this pattern. The story of the healing of Peter's mother-in-law takes two verses in Mark (1:30–31), but the whole framework is there. Peter's mother-in-law had a fever about which

the disciples told Jesus. Jesus took her by the hand and raised her up, the fever left her, and (the proof) she made a meal for them. The story may be longer. In the story of the healing of the blind man in Mark 8:22–26, the actual working of the mighty act is described in much more detail: Jesus has to apply spittle and lay his hands on the blind eyes twice before sight is fully restored. But then the man is capable of taking a route home that he formerly could not take. The framework of the miracle story, however, is not of primary interest for this study. Rather, details that are included in the story but not necessary to it are important. Obviously, if there are elements that go beyond the basic components, some point is being made other than the recitation of an act of power. There are very few miracle stories recounted of Jesus without some material included that is extraneous to the telling of a miracle. These make a point other than that Jesus could do such things.

Miracle stories are subject to widely varying interpretations. They give ambiguous information about the one who does them. It is not clear that the power to perform such deeds must come from God or be used for benevolent purposes. Demons exercise similar power and are malevolent in intent. The sheer act of power tells nothing about the source or intention of that power. Opponents of Jesus could use his miracles to discredit him (saying that he casts out demons by demonic power—Mark 3: 22), just as others could see in those acts the power of God (Mark 2:12). If a miracle story is to convey anything more than the impression that the person performing it is out of the ordinary, the impression must be built into the story. This is the case with most of the Gospel accounts of Jesus' mighty acts.

There is more in these stories than simply material to aid in interpreting Jesus' character. The miracles frequently include elements that make them highly useful for ministry in the modern world. I cite two examples

from the Gospel of Mark to show what I mean.

The first example is the familiar story of the healing of the paralytic let down through the roof by four companions (Mark 2:1–12). The framework of the miracle story is clear; after the introduction sets the scene (vs. 1–2), the problem is stated (vs. 3–4). The problem is compounded by the crowds that prevent easy access to Jesus. Letting the paralytic down through the roof is understood as an enacted request for help. The solution is divided between vs. 5a and 11, and the proof, including the bystanders' reaction of amazement, is found in v. 12. There is, however, more to the miracle story than that. Verses 5b–10 concern a dispute about whether or not Jesus has the right to pronounce sins forgiven. Some lawyers take exception to Jesus' doing this, and Jesus responds. This exchange is not necessary for the miracle story. It appears to have been inserted into the middle of an otherwise regular miracle story. Attention is called to the place where the miracle story is suspended, and then continued, by the repeated phrase "he says to the paralytic" in vs. 5 and 10. It is as if the reader is told not to miss the fact that what is contained between these identical phrases is more than might have been expected.

This discussion (vs. 5b–10) is meant to aid in understanding what the miracle (vs. 3–5a, 11–12) is all about. The discussion turns on whether it is proper for anyone to pronounce sins forgiven, since that is something only God can do (v. 7). The implication is that when Jesus says that, he is not only blasphemous but fraudulent. Jesus never denies the premise that forgiveness is the divine prerogative. Rather, he sets a test. After equating the phrases "rise, take up your bed and walk" and "your sins are forgiven" (v. 9), Jesus tells the paralytic to walk, and he does. As v. 10 makes clear, that the paralytic walks is proof that Jesus can forgive sins, because the two phrases are the same, and Jesus speaks both to the paralytic (vs. 5, 11). The reality and power that flow from the com-

mand to walk, visibly demonstrated, must then be assumed to flow from Jesus' words that remit sins. The same power is at work in both instances, and, as the lawyers have already said, it is God's power. What the story intends to say is that Jesus' announcement of forgiveness of sin has the same power and is as effective as his command to the paralytic to walk. The visible walking of the paralytic is proof of the invisible efficacy of the announcement of forgiveness.

This story means that sins forgiven in Jesus' name are in fact forgiven! Matthew preserves a saying in which that power is conveyed to the church (Matt. 18:18–19). He concludes with the declaration of Jesus that where people are gathered in his name, he is there. In Jesus' name sins are forgiven. I wonder if ministers are aware of the miraculous power inherent in the words they use.

Similar insights are gained from a study of the first act of power that Mark records: casting out the demon in the synagogue of Capernaum (Mark 1:21–27). What is unusual here is the framework Mark has put around the story. The point of this material is the power, not of demonic expulsion, but of Jesus' teaching (vs. 22, 27). Again, this is a deliberate attempt to make the point that the same power that allows Jesus to overcome the demon is also present in his teaching! To have his words, therefore, is to be in contact with his incredible, divine power. If this interpretation is correct, then the resources in the teaching of Jesus, contained in our Gospels, are simply breathtaking. To preach the words of Jesus is to handle not only the word of truth, but the word of incredible power. It is a pity when that power is ignored or misused in sermons for lack of adequate preparation or seriousness.

We have now considered briefly some examples of the significance of who Jesus was and of what he said and did. Yet the nerve of the Gospels' understanding of the significance of Jesus of Nazareth has not yet been touched.

This central element is the passion, and above all, the resurrection of Jesus. All that he did and said is significant finally because in him God made visible his plan for humankind, a plan dependent on God's grace and benevolence toward his creation. In the passion week, culminating with the open and empty grave, the meaning of Jesus of Nazareth finally became clear. Long before the Gospel narratives were put in their present form, the passion and resurrection of Jesus intoxicated the preaching of his early followers. It is no accident that cross and resurrection are the key to Jesus for Paul, for whom absence of the resurrection would make faith and preaching vacuous (I Cor. 15:14, 17). It is no accident that the first attempt to tell the whole story of Jesus, the Gospel of Mark, is dominated by the passion week. It is no accident that one of the key additions later Gospel authors made to Mark's account was appearances of the risen Christ.

The resurrection proved the true significance of Jesus for the Gospel narratives because that event changed the way humanity is to look at itself and its future. Humanity did not in the moment of the resurrection lose its sinfulness or self-centeredness. But the inevitable determination of the future by these characteristics was removed. Sin and self-centeredness were stripped of their final potency. That is the power of the resurrection: It has the power to alter the past. What Adam did, Christ has undone. We are no longer prisoners of the past. We are freed of its burden. We can face with happy confidence a future under God's benevolent control.

Some of the followers of Jesus, crushed by the defeat of the cross, sought to console themselves by some last small acts of faithfulness to his cold and bloodied corpse. They found instead an empty tomb, and that awe-filled word: "He is not here, he is risen." In the moment thus announced, reality was totally transformed. The course of the future was revealed: It is in God's hands; the

outcome is victory over death. In that moment the past was transformed. It became once more the repository of promise, rather than of condemnation. Those who follow the risen Christ know that the future is assured. However dark the present may appear, God is strong enough to redeem and transform it in his love into his own rule of grace.

It is the resurrection that distinguishes Christians from others. Those who follow the risen Christ know that, despite our best efforts at evil, we cannot thwart the final rule of a benevolent God. Those who follow the risen Christ know that whatever their fate and the fate of the world may seem to be, in the end it must be transformed into the kingdom of a merciful God. Those who follow the risen Christ know that finally life is not a tragedy but, in the classic sense, a comedy in which the final resolution is not pain, despair, and defeat but joy, victory, and laughter. That is why the Christian can confidently stride into a future known to be in the hands of a merciful God.

This is the resource for pastoral ministries, whatever form they take. In the confidence that God cannot finally be defeated, we do what we can, in word and deed, to spread the good news among people so that they, realizing the redemption that awaits them, may share the joyful anticipation of God's final, glorious rule.

5

THEOLOGY AND MINISTRY IN JOHN

BY
D. MOODY SMITH

My personal history, first as a Christian, then as New Testament student, has revolved about a fascination with the Fourth Gospel. It is the greatest riddle of the New Testament and of Christian origins generally. When was this Gospel written? Who wrote it? Under what religious and cultural influences was it composed? What is its relationship to the other Gospels? Indeed, what is its relationship to Jesus? Is the Jesus of John in any sense the Jesus of history? Or is that figure a construct arising out of the piety and theology of primitive Christian faith? I have not always been able to parse the riddle of the Fourth Gospel into so many subriddles. Yet for many years I have been aware of the problematic character of the Fourth Gospel as it stands alongside the other three.

THE RIDDLE OF THE FOURTH GOSPEL: WHY IS IT SO DIFFERENT FROM THE OTHERS?

From childhood I can remember the oft-repeated claim of some preachers that Jesus was either what he claimed to be (Messiah, Son of God) or the most colossal egomaniac and fraud the world has ever known. The posing of that alternative was a kind of evangelical tactic to eliminate the moderate middle, or all liberal or quasi-liberal, critical or quasi-critical, views of Jesus. They are

excluded by virtue of Jesus' own claims. There was no gentle Jesus meek and mild, nor even a young and fearless prophet of ancient Galilee. There was and is only the strong Son of God, walking across the face of the earth performing astounding miracles and proclaiming, "I am the way, and the truth, and the life; no one comes to the Father, but by me."

Even before my mind was illuminated by theological training, I had become aware that this latter view of Jesus was largely the product of the Gospel according to John. Even the possibility of the more modest or restrained view of him could arise only on the basis of the Synoptic Gospels. I was later to learn, if I did not already realize it, that the Jesus of the Synoptics was already the Christ of Christian confession in the hearts and minds of the Gospel writers and the early congregations for whom they wrote. They are anything but value-free, objective, historical accounts. Yet the Synoptics—or at least the Synoptic tradition—breathe the air of first-century Palestine; that is, those Gospels evoke the religious and cultural atmosphere in which Jesus worked in a way that the Fourth Gospel does not. It may be that it too breathes the air of first-century Palestine, but in a different sense. For in the Fourth Gospel, Jesus continually speaks of himself in the language of Christian confession, while in the Synoptics he is much more restrained, and in Mark he appears reluctant even to accept the title of Messiah or Christ when it is proffered him by his followers.

I find it difficult to avoid the conclusion of two centuries of critical scholarship that a historical, or a historian's, view of Jesus must begin with the Synoptic Gospels (Matthew, Mark, and Luke) or their content, i.e., the Synoptic tradition.[1] By this I do not imply that everything in the Synoptics is historically authentic, while nothing in John is. On the contrary, much in the Synoptic Gospels, including their outline or structure, is the creation of the Christian communities and writers which pro-

duced them. By the same token, it is most probable that there is authentic, historical data to be mined from the Fourth Gospel. (For example, John rather than the Synoptics may be correct in having Jesus crucified the afternoon before, rather than the day of, the beginning of the Passover celebration.) But when all is said and done, I find it difficult to believe that the picture of Jesus which emerges from the Synoptics and their several strands of sources or traditions does not take priority over the Johannine, or that the Synoptic Gospels or traditions could have arisen *after* the one found in John had been widely disseminated among the early Christian churches. If the Johannine portrayal of Jesus had been the original, it would be hard to understand how and why the Synoptic one ever developed—and not in one isolated Gospel, but in three Gospels, each of which represents multiple strands of compatible tradition. One may always revive the venerable view that John represents an arcane, secret tradition, equally authentic historically, as the well-known scholar Oscar Cullmann has recently once again proposed.[2] Yet this resolution of the matter is less than satisfactory. If Jesus talked in two different ways, why does one way appear in the Synoptics and the other almost exclusively in the Fourth Gospel? Moreover, the literary style and vocabulary of the Fourth Gospel, even of the Johannine Jesus, finds its closest analogy not in the other Gospels, but in the Johannine epistles.

If we are to consider the important matters comprehended by the title "Theology and Ministry in John," it is necessary to tackle the problem of John and the Synoptics. The question is not which represents the point of view of Jesus. In every Gospel, Jesus' point of view is to be found only as it is refracted or reflected through each evangelist's prism. To be completely realistic, there is no possibility of going behind the Gospels to recover a picture of Jesus and his message that is "objective" in the sense that it avoids their tendencies or perspectives.

In fact, there is no distinctively Christian reason for deeming that desirable. Rather, we assume that John, although not a historically superior (in the sense of factually more accurate) account, is a faithful and authoritative witness. The intention and result of his writing is to speak to such questions as are here raised in the name and on the authority of Jesus. Our purpose, which will accord with the evangelist's purpose, is to inquire how and to what extent John's portrayal of Jesus expresses his understanding of theology and ministry. This inquiry is based upon the conviction that what John has to say needs to be heard with and alongside what other New Testament witnesses say. If put in a proper and sufficiently broad perspective, they complement and even correct, but do not contradict or cancel out one another.

Our immediate and primary purpose, however, is to understand John's distinctive insight and contribution. In order to do so, one needs to know whether or to what extent the Fourth Evangelist knew, assumed, and approved of the other Gospels as he wrote his own. Thus appears the question of John and the Synoptics. It is the theologically most important aspect of the question of John's relationship to the rest of early Christianity. There is a sense in which the Gospel of John seems to build upon the witness of the others. Was it originally intended to do that? In what relation to one another do they stand?

At this point we should enter a qualification about the overall purpose of this presentation. In addressing "theology and ministry," we do not presume to cover the whole of Johannine theology, or even the Johannine concept of ministry, in the scope of this essay. That is obviously too big an order. After dealing with the question of John and the Synoptics and its implications, we shall next attempt to identify the root and impetus of the distinctly Johannine Christian preaching and, by implication, of Johannine theology. Only then will it be possible to treat the matter of church and ministry.

At this juncture, I want to do three things. First, I will say something about the ingredients of the problem of John and the Synoptics, that is: What are their similarities and differences and what do they mean? Second, I will indicate briefly how the church fathers and modern interpreters have viewed this problem. Third, I will point out salient facts and considerations that must be involved in any solution of it, particularly as they bear upon the task of interpretation.

The Ingredients of the Problem: Similarities and Differences Between John and the Synoptics

John, like the Synoptics, tells the story of Jesus from his encounter with the Baptist through his crucifixion and the discovery of the empty tomb. In both there is a scene with Peter near the center point in which the questions of Jesus' role and identity and the disciples' relation to him emerge as central issues. In each Gospel Jesus gathers disciples, teaches, debates with opponents, performs signs or miracles, goes up to Jerusalem at a Passover, there encounters severe opposition, and—after a final meal with his disciples—is arrested, tried, crucified, and buried. On the third day women find the tomb empty. In addition, there are some instances in which the wording of the Fourth Gospel is exactly the same as in one or more of the Synoptics, usually Mark. These are not nearly so numerous or extensive as the agreements among the Synoptics, but they nevertheless exist. The character of Jesus' teaching in the Fourth Gospel, while different, is not necessarily incompatible with what is found in the Synoptics. The famous love command of John (John 13:34; 15:12) has with good reason been regarded as an apt summation of Jesus' teaching. If Jesus talks much more about his messiahship and divine sonship in John than in the others, these theological convictions are not, after all, unlike those of the Synoptic evangelists. What is latent in the Synoptics is patent in John.

Moreover, the general purpose of John's Gospel, as stated in 20:30f., is not fundamentally different from that of the Synoptics.

Yet alongside such significant affinities and similarities must be ranged a variety of substantial divergencies or differences. The ministry of Jesus in the Synoptics takes place in Galilee and might well have occurred within a period of one year. In John, the ministry encompasses about three years; there are three Passovers (John 2:13, 23; 6:4; 12:1), perhaps four (5:1). Jesus goes up to Jerusalem at least three times (2:13; 5:1; 7:10). After 7:10 he is no longer in Galilee at all, although there are subsequent periods when Jesus withdraws from public view (10:40–42; 11:54). In John, Jesus is portrayed in Jerusalem or Judea far more than in Galilee (2:13 to 4:3; 5:1–47; 7:10 to 20:31), so that one gains the distinct impression that he spent most of his time there during the period of his public activity. Thus the itinerary of Jesus, the structure of the Gospel, and the geographical location of Jesus' ministry in John differ from what we find in the Synoptic Gospels. But the divergencies do not end there. The substantial content of John (i.e., the specific stories, sayings, and controversies) is different. While much of the content of each of the Synoptics is paralleled in the other two, most of what is found in John has no parallel in the Synoptics and vice versa.

The parallelism or similarity of content between John and the Synoptics lies mostly in the passion narrative. According to H. F. D. Sparks's Gospel parallels,[3] there are 93 pericopes or sections in the Fourth Gospel. Of these, only 25 have Synoptic parallels, while 68 do not. But in the passion-resurrection narratives (John, chs. 18–21), 14 of the pericopes have Synoptic parallels, while only 11 do not. This discrepancy is really even broader than these figures reveal, for within the passion narratives the extent of verbatim agreement with the Synoptics, especially Mark, is greater than elsewhere. More-

over, the order of events in the passion is very much the same, whereas in the pre-passion parts of the Gospel there is only the most remote or general similarity between John and the Synoptics.

If one looks at the evidence from the standpoint of Mark, for example, the picture is similar. Of the 106 Marcan pericopes (again according to Sparks), only 21 have Johannine parallels, while 85 do not. But of the 24 Marcan pericopes in the passion-resurrection narrative (Mark, chs. 14–16) 15 have Johannine parallels, and only 9 do not. The comparison of John with either Matthew or Luke would reveal even more striking discrepancies. Because John and the Synoptics end on the same note, with the same general episodes of crucifixion and resurrection, and with many of the same individual narratives, one gets the impression that the Gospels are more similar than they actually are. Of the pre-passion narratives of Mark, which comprise most of that Gospel, only a few (Jesus' encounter with the Baptist, the miracle of the feeding of the five thousand, the walking on the water, and the confession of Peter) have reasonably close Johannine parallels. It is true that John, like Mark, contains an account of Jesus calling his disciples, but the actual call narratives are quite different in the two Gospels. Moreover, the Johannine and Marcan narratives of the so-called confession of Peter (in Mark at Caesarea Philippi, in John not) are so different as to call in question our identification of them.

It is a striking fact that no Marcan healing miracles or exorcisms are found in John. The obverse is also the case, none of the Johannine healing miracles is found in Mark. Since, by and large, the Marcan healing narratives represent the bulk of the Synoptic miracle tradition, it is fair to say that John and the Synoptics contain different miracle traditions, which scarcely overlap.

Not only the miracle narratives or traditions differ, however. The style and tone of the Fourth Gospel, as

well as the presentation of Jesus' message, are different. Nothing typifies this difference more than John's handling of the miracles. In the Synoptics, especially Mark, Jesus admonishes his disciples to keep silence about his miracles, as if he is reticent about them, or about their significance. But in the Fourth Gospel, Jesus demands faith in himself precisely on the basis of such miracles. They have become signs revealing who he is. Jesus' teaching and controversy are of a piece with his signs. With good reason it has been said that in the Synoptics Jesus proclaims the coming kingdom of God, while in the Fourth Gospel he proclaims himself as king. In John, Jesus' teaching centers upon that subject which mostly is only suggested, or hovers in the background, in the tradition of the other Gospels, namely, Christology. Both to his opponents and to his disciples the Johannine Jesus expounds his messiahship and divine sonship openly. That is the principal content of his teaching. If in the Synoptics awesome powers of human and supernatural evil seem to overtake Jesus, in John he goes to his death of his own volition and remains clearly in control, not only of himself, but of those who seek his demise.

Past Efforts to Explain or Solve the Problem

How can one account for John's extensive and significant differences from the other Gospels without at the same time ignoring the similarities? That in a word is the problem of John and the Synoptics. The orthodox fathers of the early church resolved it on the premise that John wrote in full cognizance of the other Gospels and in one way or another intended to supplement them or even at points to correct them. It was therefore commonly assumed that John wrote after the other Gospels had been composed and were circulating among the early churches. Clement of Alexandria at the beginning of the third century wrote that John, realizing the other evangelists had recorded the physical facts, undertook to set

down a spiritual Gospel. His assessment has seemed to accord so well with the character of the Fourth Gospel, as well as its differences from the others, that one sees it cited frequently.[4] Eusebius of Caesarea thought that the differences between John and the others could be accounted for by the realization that John related what Jesus did before the arrest of the Baptist (cf. John 3:24), while the other evangelists reported only what happened afterward (Mark 1:14f.).[5] As a way of explaining the whole of the Fourth Gospel in its differences from the Synoptics this obviously will not work. But as modern critics have seen, there may well be some truth in it. John appears to be in touch with a period of Jesus' ministry when he was a contemporary or possibly a rival of John the Baptist rather than his successor, as in the Synoptic Gospels.

Modern critical opinion has agreed more often than not with the tradition that John took cognizance of the other Gospels in a positive way as he wrote. But the two most significant works on the problem of John and the Synoptics in this century have in different ways challenged that assumption of tradition and the earlier critical orthodoxy.

The first was a 1926 monograph by the German scholar Hans Windisch, *Johannes und die Synoptiker* (John and the Synoptics).[6] Windisch expressed dissatisfaction with the traditional view, at that time shared by most critical scholars, that the Fourth Evangelist, writing after and in full cognizance of the Synoptic Gospels, intended to supplement them. He pointed out that John contains not only a great deal of material not found in the Synoptics, which could be regarded as supplementary, but also much, especially in the passion narrative, which clearly parallels and in effect duplicates them. Moreover, one looks in vain in the Fourth Gospel for any explicit indication of such an intention on the part of the author. That is, there are no clear indications at appropriate places that

the evangelist wishes the reader to supplement his own account from one or more of the Synoptics or, conversely, that he wishes the material he supplies to be used to supplement them. The Fourth Gospel rarely (perhaps at 3:24) evinces the intention of correcting the Synoptics. More often than not, in the case of a discrepancy, John simply differs from or contradicts the Synoptics. All in all, the Fourth Gospel does not look like a document in which the author intended to weave one narrative alongside another or to play an obligato in accompaniment of another. It is an independent Gospel designed to stand on its own two feet. Following this line of reasoning to a logical but extreme conclusion, Windisch maintained that, far from aiming to supplement the other Gospels, the Fourth Evangelist actually intended to displace them with a superior Gospel of his own creation. In other words, he found them inadequate vehicles of the Christian message and undertook to compose a really satisfactory Gospel to stand in their stead.

A dozen years after Windisch's book, and strangely without any reference to it, the Cambridge don Percival Gardner-Smith published a slim volume in which he argued that the belief that John was dependent upon the Synoptics was based on far less extensive and convincing evidence than its adherents generally supposed.[7] Thus, in effect, Gardner-Smith undercut Windisch's position, for John could not have intended to displace what he did not know!

Going expeditiously through the Fourth Gospel from beginning to end, Gardner-Smith pointed out John's many and striking divergencies from the Synoptics, and suggested that these divergencies were difficult to understand as deliberate alterations by the Fourth Evangelist designed to advance his own distinctive theological purposes. Rather, they look more like alternative and independent renditions of the same or similar narratives. Granted there are instances in which John seems to fol-

low the Synoptics, especially Mark, verbatim, these are never very long (i.e., they generally consist of fewer than a dozen words), nor are they numerous. As a rule, they are comprised of just such phrases as might be preserved in oral tradition. A good example is Jesus' word to the paralytic in Mark 2:9 and to the crippled man in John 5:8: "Rise, take up your pallet, and walk." The command, identical in wording, appears in two clearly different narratives in Mark and John. The narratives are miracle stories of a similar type, but it is hard to imagine John's having constructed his on the basis of Mark. More likely, thinks Gardner-Smith, the entirely independent stories contain a catch phrase that Jesus was widely known to have used, and which became current in the oral tradition.

Many scholars, particularly in the English-speaking world, but also elsewhere, found Gardner-Smith's case against John's dependence upon the Synoptics persuasive. By the mid-1960's there was developing a consensus that John did not know, or at least did not use, the Synoptic Gospels in the composition of his work. One need only mention such names as Dodd, Bultmann, E. R. Goodenough, and Raymond E. Brown. The Belgian scholar Frans Neirynck quotes with approval an earlier statement of mine on the existence of such a consensus.[8]

Yet, significantly, Neirynck does not agree with that consensus. He rather belongs to a growing number of scholars who once again espouse the view that John knew the Synoptics. Indeed, Neirynck and scholars associated with him think that John was using the Synoptics as he wrote, and they ask themselves how and why he altered (or preserved) elements of their account. This resurgence of the opinion that John knew the Synoptics is based upon the redaction-critical method of Gospel study. Basic to this method is the identification and separation of tradition and redaction in the Gospels. One attempts to determine what material the author had at his

disposal (tradition) and how he arranged it and wove it together (redaction). How the author uses his material and what he himself composes (as distinguished from what he receives) then become crucial factors in the interpretation of the Gospel.

Scholars who once again espouse the view of John's dependence on the Synoptics have become convinced, for example, that elements of identifiable Marcan redaction have been taken up by the Fourth Evangelist. Thus, not only do Mark and John share a common or overlapping tradition, but John must have known and used Mark. To cite a concrete instance, it is argued that the arrangement of Peter's denial in conjunction with the trial before the Sanhedrin is a Marcan construction, i.e., a Marcan redaction, with no earlier, traditional, basis. Because this arrangement is found also in John, one can infer that John knew not only a tradition common to Mark, but the Gospel of Mark itself.[9] (It is, of course, presupposed that John is later than Mark and not the other way around.) Moreover, a German Catholic scholar, Anton Dauer, believes he has discovered that the *source* upon which John's passion narrative is based was influenced by the Gospels of Matthew and Luke.[10]

Such arguments as these do not go uncontested.[11] Nevertheless, it is fair to say that the question of the relationship of John and the Synoptics, which only a few years ago seemed on the verge of being settled in favor of John's independence of the Synoptics, has been reopened seriously with a vigorous counterattack from several quarters on what had become the predominant viewpoint.

The Significance of the Problem for Interpretation

The problem of John and the Synoptics probably never will be "solved" in the sense that an overwhelming majority of scholars will agree one way or the other. It would be presumptuous even to suggest a solution on the

basis of our brief survey. One may, however, note several points that emerge from an assessment of the evidence and the scholarly discussion of it which are important for the interpretation of John's Gospel.

First, the classical traditional and critical view that John, whether or not dependent upon the Synoptics, is nevertheless not prior to them remains highly probable. If the Johannine portrayal of Jesus had emerged first, the Synoptic one would have seemed problematic. Even Bishop John A. T. Robinson, who dates John earlier than A.D. 70, takes it to be a shade later than the Synoptics.

Second, even if he did not know the Synoptics, John clearly knew a gospel tradition similar at many points, on the basis of which he offered his own theological elaboration. He at least knew, and presumably expected his readers to know, certain gospel facts and traditions (that Jesus was baptized by John, who Pilate was, etc.) in a form not unlike the Synoptic. John could be read with understanding only by someone already imbued with the Christian tradition. Someone unacquainted with it, or outside it, would be as perplexed as Nicodemus or as offended as the chief priests and Pharisees by this strangely fascinating book. This determination, if true, has the following corollary. John might have been the only Gospel of an early Christian community; but, if it was, it apparently did not incorporate all of the Gospel tradition known to that community (John 20:30f.).

Third, although the fact that the content of John is so different from the Synoptics, and vice versa, does not prove that John did not know the Synoptics, the independence theory comports well with precisely this state of affairs. It is difficult to understand John as an attempt to supplement the Synoptics or even to interpret them, if one means by interpret to explain the specific content of our Synoptic Gospels. Windisch's view, that John intended to supplant the Synoptics, is not impossible, but like the supplementation theory it founders on the lack

of any explicit evidence in the text itself. Yet Windisch may be right about John, at least in this respect: If the Fourth Evangelist knew the Synoptic Gospels, they were not for him standards of orthodoxy in the sense of bearers of the only orthodox tradition, even to the extent that Mark seems to have represented standard tradition for Luke and Matthew. John goes his own way.

Finally, we need to ask how our own theological and hermeneutical perspective may be informed by this assessment of the problem. How should it inform our overall grasp of the text as a source for theology and preaching? To say, "Not at all, for this is a strictly literary or historical problem," will not do. After all, Christian traditions arose out of history and have been transmitted largely through literature. Our views on such questions will and should inform us theologically. Of course, we cannot allow our preferences to dictate our conclusions in such matters. It is a good critical rule to suspect and test rigorously views that we have assumed or like! I would actually prefer to think that the Fourth Evangelist, whoever he was, wanted his readers to know the Jesus of the Synoptic tradition as the necessary background for reading and understanding his Gospel. But despite recent moves back in the direction of that traditional view by scholars of different persuasions and church backgrounds, for the reasons just indicated I remain somewhat skeptical. Moreover, the strange, extraordinary character of the Gospel of John must not be leveled off for the sake of a quick and easy compatibility with the others. If that presents a difficulty for Christian theology, it is somewhat relieved by this fact: The fathers of the church in their wisdom allow both the Synoptics and John to stand side by side in the Christian Bible. We have the obligation to take both seriously. When we are merely attracted and challenged by the still-human figure that emerges from the traditions embodied in Matthew, Mark, or Luke—especially Luke—we are brought up

short by the Johannine Jesus, who demands that we decide who he is and whether or not we belong to him. But lest we become complacent about that lordly, divine figure and satisfied to repeat, "He is the way, the truth, and the life, no one comes to the Father but by him," those other Gospels remind us of another and indispensable dimension of Christology and faith. There was a Jesus who lived a human life under the same conditions that oppress us, defeat us, but also offer us the possibility of meaningful, authentic life. To live as followers of Jesus is not just to say, "Lord, Lord," but to participate in that life and in those struggles as he did. Whatever may have been the case in antiquity, the riddle of the Fourth Gospel can finally be answered adequately only by those who know the other three.

Yet for the purpose of this discussion I want, so far as possible, to set aside the other three or to refer to them only in order to address such questions as these: What are the distinctive aspects of Johannine theology? How do they determine or contribute to his view of church and ministry? Whatever may be said about John's relationship to the Synoptics, it is clear that he intends to set forth an original, distinctive, and largely independent presentation of Jesus. We are on exegetically and theologically good grounds if we first ask about John's view of theology and church, theology and ministry. We shall then be in a position to see how it relates to the positions of the other Gospels and New Testament witnesses.

JOHN AS CHRISTIAN PREACHING

In looking at the peculiar problem of the relationship of the Fourth Gospel to the Synoptics, we noticed that there are similarities in form and content, as well in as their portrayals of Jesus, which justify the assumption that they are different representatives of a common genre. With reason they are all called Gospels. Yet there are

also very great differences, which are often minimized or overlooked. Anyone brought up in the Christian tradition tends from an early age to assimilate the different Gospels and to blur their differences. Therefore, it has become necessary and important to emphasize those differences.

Both the similarities and the differences come to light in a remarkable way in John 5. In this chapter the characteristic themes of Johannine theology find expression. By examining it we shall be able to see why the Gospel of John qualifies as distinctly Christian preaching, in a way that even the Synoptic Gospels do not.

The chapter begins rather abruptly. For good reason John has been called a seamless robe. The narrative moves with such clear unintentionality, and often so smoothly, that the characterization seems apt. Yet at some points there are lacunae, breaks, abrupt stops and starts; and this is one of them. Jesus was last seen in Cana of Galilee, and while there he had caused the official's son, who lay at death's door in Capernaum, to become well. All of that, and whatever else may have been in the author's mind, seems to be summed up in the laconic "after this" of John 5:1. As the RSV renders it, "After this there was a feast of the Jews, and Jesus went up to Jerusalem." John then briefly recounts a miracle story in which Jesus heals a man whose illness is not clearly specified.

> Now there is in Jerusalem by the Sheep Gate a pool, in Hebrew called Bethzatha, which has five porticoes. In these lay a multitude of invalids, blind, lame, paralyzed. One man was there, who had been ill for thirty-eight years. When Jesus saw him and knew that he had been lying there a long time, he said to him, "Do you want to be healed?" The sick man answered him, "Sir, I have no man to put me into the pool when the water is troubled, and while I am going another steps down before me."

> Jesus said to him, "Rise, take up your pallet, and walk."
> And at once the man was healed, and he took up his pallet
> and walked. (John 5:2–9)

The story has some curious features. The name and location of the pool have long been matters of dispute. The names Bethzatha, Bethesda, and Bethsaida appear in different manuscripts. (The pool with its five porches may have been discovered recently by archaeologists. If so, the discovery illumines the historical background of the account more than John's purpose in recounting the story.) Even before Jesus speaks to the man, he knows that he has been ill for a long time. When Jesus asks the man whether he wishes to be well, he does not answer directly, but describes his problem in getting into the pool "when the water is troubled." Jesus pays as little attention to that response as the man apparently paid to Jesus' question. "Rise, take up your pallet, and walk," says Jesus. The word of Jesus exactly parallels Mark 2:9, where it occurs in quite a different healing narrative. As we have already noted, Jesus may have said such a thing more than once, and it would be easily remembered. The man's remark about not being able to get down into the pool when the water was stirred up sounded so strange that some ancient copyist provided an explanation after John 5:3: "An angel of the Lord went down at certain seasons into the pool, and troubled the water: whoever stepped in first after the troubling of the water was healed of whatever disease he had." (That is v. 4, absent from modern translations.) This explanation may provide the legendary belief that underlies the story and makes sense of it historically, but it is not part of the original text.

The difficulties of the story do not obstruct John's using it to portray Jesus and to say what in his view is crucially important about him. Probably the story was traditional, a story about Jesus' healing a person, very much like many such stories that circulated in the early

church and are found now in the Gospels. Possibly its traditional character accounts in large part for the peculiarities. Maybe the evangelist himself did not know where the pool was, exactly what illness affected the man, or why the movement of the waters was thought to effect a cure. Nevertheless, the story also has a Johannine character, whether imposed by the evangelist or found already in the tradition. Jesus knows, supernaturally and without asking, that the man has been lying ill for a long time. He does not wait to be approached (contrast John 4:47; Mark 2:2–4; 5:25–28; 7:25, 32; 8:22; 10:47), but initiates the healing. When the man responds to his question, Jesus seemingly takes no notice of what he has said, but gives a command that effects the healing suddenly and with no preparation. Such behavior is not uncharacteristic of the Jesus of the Fourth Gospel, who knows Nathanael before they meet, knows all about the Samaritan woman, who has never met him, and tells her about herself. He typically initiates the conversation or action. He often seems not to notice what has been said to him, but speaks at another level. (This is a characteristic of the Johannine technique of misunderstanding. Jesus' interlocutors do not have the theological knowledge to comprehend what he means. By the same token, he utters statements that seem to make little or no contact with what preceded.) None of these features may be entirely unique to the Fourth Gospel (cf. Mark 2:8 and 5:30; 1:29–31 and perhaps 5:7–9, respectively). Yet they are certainly more frequent in John than elsewhere.

What we see so far is a miracle story that is not unlike a number of other miracle stories of the Gospel, except that it has certain Johannine features. It is likely that John draws upon tradition, and we shall find reason to infer that he builds upon that tradition in order to portray Jesus in a distinctive way. Indeed, he uses it to make clear what to him is most important about Jesus. There is, however, as yet only a hint of the course the narrative

will take. First, the man manifests his healing; he takes up his bed at Jesus' command and walks. In a typical Synoptic miracle story this would be the end of the account or nearly so. (There one sometimes finds a brief indication of the amazement of onlookers, but even that is absent.) In John, however, we are still near the beginning. The reader is next told that the healing had occurred on the Sabbath (John 5:9). This is a motif familiar to the reader of the Synoptics. Jesus becomes involved in controversy because he violates, or to many seems to violate, the Sabbath. But in contrast to what is often found in the Synoptics (e.g., Mark 3:1–6; cf. 2:23–28), the Sabbath motif has not figured prominently, or at all, in the story itself. Only now is it introduced. Probably it was no part of the traditional healing narrative, but it is traditional at least in the sense that John gets it from tradition. He knows that Jesus was often accused of breaking the Sabbath.

But it is the healed man, not Jesus, who now is accused of breaking the Sabbath by carrying his pallet (John 5: 10). (Similarly, in Mark 2:23f., Jesus' disciples are attacked for plucking grain on the Sabbath.) The healed man responds by saying that Jesus has commanded him to do it (John 5:11). The Jews then ask the healed man to identify the one who has commanded him. Nothing like this is found in the Synoptic Gospels. There it is no secret who works miracles and heals people, although Jesus may command people to remain silent about his miracles. We also observe yet another striking feature in the way this narrative is developing. The people who challenge the healed man are described as Jews. They doubtless were Jews; but in this setting everyone, including Jesus, presumably would have been a Jew. There is something odd about this.

Who is called a Jew, or when is a member of Israel called a Jew and by whom?[12] In the Synoptic tradition it can be assumed that everyone is a Jew unless otherwise

designated, so no one is ordinarily called that. Only when non-Jews appear is the term used. Thus the wise men from the East inquire about one born "king of the Jews" (Matt. 2:2) or Pilate designates Jesus "the King of the Jews" (Matt. 27:37 and pars.) after his Roman soldiers have mocked him, using the same title (Matt. 27:29 and pars.). When he hangs upon the cross, the Jewish chief priests, scribes, and elders, however, cry out, even in derision, "He is the King of Israel," not, "He is the King of the Jews" (Matt. 27:42). All this corresponds closely to first-century Palestinian Jewish usage. Jews do not ordinarily refer to themselves in that way, except when assuming an outsider's perspective. John's usage, on the other hand, does not conform to what we would expect from Jewish circles in first-century Palestine. The narrator somehow stands outside the orbit of Judaism in that he seems no longer to consider himself, or even Jesus and his disciples, to be Jewish. Of course, John can have Jesus addressed as a Jew by the Samaritan woman (John 4:9), and Jesus can even claim to be a Jew himself (4:22). The evangelist knows that Jesus is from Nazareth (1:45f.) of Galilee (7:41). Yet when Jesus or his retinue confronts hostile people, the latter are characteristically and routinely referred to as "the Jews." Moreover, these Jews can distinguish between disciples of Jesus and disciples of Moses (John 9:28) as if one had to choose between the two.

What we find in John is then clearly a departure from Synoptic usage. Even there Jesus may set himself off from Moses in an unprecedented way. He calls the Mosaic divorce law a concession because of "your hardness of heart" (Mark 10:5). In the Sermon on the Mount he counterposes to Mosaic law his own, authoritative, "but I say to you," which characteristically radicalizes the Mosaic command. Yet all this occurs in a context of Jew talking to Jew, and on the assumption that the Jewish

scriptures contain the Word of God, which the Jews as such could understand.

Jesus' original disciples did not regard themselves as having abandoned Moses any more than he himself rejected him, and the Synoptic tradition reflects this state of affairs. When in a Q saying (Matt. 12:41–42; Luke 11:31–32) Jesus implies he is greater than Jonah or Solomon, it is perhaps noteworthy that he does not say he is greater than Moses. In John, however, Jesus says or implies that he is greater than Jacob (John 4:12–14), Abraham (John 8:56–58), and Moses (John 6:32–33, 49–51; cf. 5:45–47).

Both John and the Synoptics were in all probability written in and for Christian communities which understood themselves to be such. That is, they were written in and for Christian churches as distinguished from the synagogue. Yet in the Synoptics the tradition still embodies, to a recognizable degree, a time and a perspective different from the authors' own—whether it be the perspective of Jesus or that of the postresurrection Palestinian church, which lived in a Jewish environment where Aramaic was still spoken and people still looked for the coming redemption of Israel. (Cf. Luke 24:21 and Acts 1:6, which, although quite possibly compositions of Luke, are intended to convey the perspective of an earlier time.) On the other hand, John reflects thoroughly an entirely Christian point of view, one in which it cannot be taken for granted that everyone is a Jew. Not only is this the evangelist's perspective, but it permeates the material of which the Gospel is composed. And it is in this respect that John differs significantly from the Synoptics.

By commonly referring to Jesus' interlocutors as "the Jews," John creates the impression that Jesus does not belong, or no longer belongs, to the Jewish community or world. By the same token, neither do the disciples (John 9:28), nor, indeed, does the evangelist himself.

Not only John, but Jesus also, speaks from the perspective of a community separate and distinct from Judaism. Jesus, as well as the evangelist, talks like a Christian.

But we are getting ahead of our text. There follows upon the Jews' question to the healed man about the identity of his benefactor a rather strange interlude:

> Now the man who had been healed did not know who it was, for Jesus had withdrawn, as there was a crowd in the place. Afterward, Jesus found him in the temple, and said to him, "See, you are well! Sin no more, that nothing worse befall you." The man went away and told the Jews that it was Jesus who had healed him. And this was why the Jews persecuted Jesus, because he did this on the Sabbath. (John 5:13–16)

Jesus is at first absent, but then he encounters the healed man in the Temple and warns him. The warning goes unheeded, for apparently the evangelist would have us understand that the man betrayed Jesus to the Jews—that is, betrayed his identity—with the result that the Jews persecuted Jesus. The man had not known at first who Jesus was. Curiously, after the second encounter he knows, but the text never says Jesus told him! There may well be an intentional contrast between this man, who instead of affirming or confessing Jesus betrays him, and the man born blind, of ch. 9. The latter doggedly insists upon the reality of what Jesus has done for him in the face of severe questioning, and even harassment, and finally confesses his faith in him (John 9:38). In any event, the fact of tension or opposition between Jesus and those who have been identified as the Jews is now established. They persecute him because of what he has done on the Sabbath, namely, heal a man, and Jesus at length speaks in response.

Interestingly enough, Jesus speaks in answer to no direct question but to the presumed situation as a whole. "My Father is working still, and I am working," he says

(John 5:17). Jesus never justifies his breaking of the Sabbath with such an imperious statement in the Synoptics, even though he may imply that he is "Lord of the sabbath" (Mark 2:28). There he appeals to the precedent of David (Mark 2:24–26), to common sense (Mark 3:4), or to commonly accepted practice (Luke 13:15; 14:5). Here he compares his working on the Sabbath with God's working. I think it unlikely that Jesus actually said this about himself. More probably, here the confessing community speaks. If the Johannine church believed that Jesus was in the beginning with God (John 1:1–2; 17:24) and was at present with God in glory (17:24; 20:17, 26–29), it could believe that as the Father always worked Jesus continued to work, whether during the week or on the Sabbath. (Of course, according to Gen. 2:3, God rested on the seventh—the Sabbath—day. Yet contemporary Jewish exegesis of this passage did not unanimously take it to mean that God continued to rest every Sabbath.[13])

Jesus' response actually goes far beyond what is called for by the situation. In fact, it injects an entirely new and disturbing element into it. A view of Jesus that does not arise directly out of the situation as previously described, out of the healing narrative, suddenly presents itself. It is a view well calculated to arouse the ire of any Jew who does not share the Christological views of the Johannine community: "This was why the Jews sought all the more to kill him, because he not only broke the sabbath but also called God his own Father, making himself equal to God" (John 5:18).

It is probably significant that the Jews' persecution of Jesus is suddenly presented as already in progress, already attaining its full intensity (they were seeking to kill Jesus), without its development having been described fully in narrative form. Intense opposition between Jesus and the Jews dominates the Fourth Gospel from this point onward. Heretofore, the reaction of the Jews (John

2:13–22), and of their representative Nicodemus (John 3:1–21), has been more perplexity than hostility. The same is true of the Samaritan woman's reaction. Hereafter, although there may be moments of uncertainty or ambiguity, the Jews of the Fourth Gospel, including those who have believed in Jesus (John 8:31), are not only estranged from Jesus but hostile to him.

From this point onward, John not only preaches Jesus as the Christ of Christian confession but presents him in a decidedly polemical way. This Jesus is the Christ of Christians, but not necessarily the Messiah of Jewish expectation. The Christological preaching or teaching of John is from here on the occasion for offense on the part of the Jews. It is not just Jesus' claim to be the Messiah, a claim they reject. What Jesus claims for himself strikes the Jews as an intolerable offense against their religious beliefs, especially monotheism. Thus Jesus' claim to be working still with the Father (John 5:17) is construed by the Jews as a claim to be equal to God. In all probability this construction of Jesus' claim is in at least some sense correct, and is acknowledged by Christians to be so. Despite the fact that the claim that Jesus is making himself equal to God is a cause of profound offense, it is not denied or disclaimed outright. Indeed, it cannot be, for, rightly understood, it represents the distinctive Christological claim that has arisen in the Johannine church.

Nevertheless, the claim is explained. Jesus does nothing that he has not seen the Father doing and claims nothing more than the Father has granted him:

> Jesus said to them, "Truly, truly, I say to you, the Son can do nothing of his own accord, but only what he sees the Father doing; for whatever he does, that the Son does likewise. For the Father loves the Son, and shows him all that he himself is doing; and greater works than these will he show him, that you may marvel." (John 5:19–20)

Yet the net result is that Jesus presents himself as the revelation of God, the eschatological salvation-bringer:

> Truly, truly, I say to you, he who hears my word and believes him who sent me, has eternal life; he does not come into judgment, but has passed from death to life.

> For as the Father has life in himself, so he has granted the Son also to have life in himself. (John 5:24, 26)

The offense is qualified, explained, and later justified by appeal to witnesses: John the Baptist (John 5:33), Jesus' works (5:36), the Father himself (5:37), the scriptures (5:39), and, therefore, Moses (5:45–46). Yet offense it remains, for precisely what is the meaning of the Baptist? What do Jesus' signs or works portend? Where is the Father's witness to be sought? How are the Scriptures, and therefore Moses, to be interpreted? All of these questions are at issue in the interchange between the Johannine Christians and those with whom they debate. Because there is agreement on none of them, there can be no agreement on the validity of the claims made by, or for, Jesus.

It is a matter of considerable historical import and interest whether, or to what extent, the claims made for Jesus in the first instance led to the polemical situation we find in the Fourth Gospel. Did the Christology expressed in the Johannine Gospel precede and give rise to the polemic? Or has that Christology evolved over a period of decades as questions and challenges to claims made in the name of Jesus resulted, not in the moderation of those claims, but in their accentuation or perhaps their qualification in ways that heightened rather than reduced the offense? I think the latter is the case and that such a process is what we find reflected in John 5.

Christology did not begin with Jesus' proclaiming himself, as he does in the Fourth Gospel. It did, however, begin with Jesus' announcing God's salvation, the advent

of his kingdom or rule. However else Jesus may have conceived of himself, he was certainly conscious of his role as the herald of that kingdom. The earliest church, composed of his disciples and others, proclaimed him the Messiah at his resurrection. (If Jesus thought of himself in such terms, he did not announce it publicly during his career.) Paul argues that in Jesus Christ, God acts to pronounce the ungodly righteous while at the same moment revealing his wrath against human sin. The Synoptic authors rework and arrange traditions originating in Jesus' historic ministry to present him as the fulfillment of emerging Christian conceptions of messianic expectation. These conceptions originated in Judaism and were mined out of the Old Testament, the early Christians' Bible. Yet by and large they represented a reformulation of those expectations in the light of Christian perceptions of the significance of Jesus' career. As we see these formulations, in the New Testament at least, they are fundamentally conditioned or shaped by belief in Jesus' resurrection and in the saving effect of his death.

There may have been forms of early Christian belief in which death and resurrection were not so prominent. For example, some early Christians may have lived out of eschatological hope for the establishment of that rule of God which Jesus proclaimed (Mark 13, Revelation, forms of Q?). It is an oversimplification, but not entirely misleading, to say that as such fervent eschatological orientation and expectation of an imminent consummation waned, the thought and preaching of Christians centered increasingly on Jesus himself as the eschatological salvation-bringer. More and more, salvation is found and proclaimed in him. There is a sense in which John represents the culmination of this tendency. Thus the Johannine Jesus is portrayed as performing those acts of judgment and salvation, i.e., the giving of life, which had been the prerogative of God. They had been the primary object of expectation and hope for the eschatological future:

> Truly, truly, I say to you, the hour is coming, and now is, when the dead will hear the voice of the Son of God, and those who hear will live. For as the Father has life in himself, so he has granted the Son also to have life in himself, and has given him authority to execute judgment, because he is the Son of man. (John 5:25–27)

Not surprisingly, Jews, and quite possibly also Jewish Christians, found such talk dangerous and blasphemous. Jesus makes himself equal to God. Therefore, Jesus responds at length in John 5:30–47 to possible objections to the claims made for him, and his words sound like a rejoinder to objections already raised against him:

> You search the scriptures, because you think that in them you have eternal life; and it is they that bear witness to me; yet you refuse to come to me that you may have life. I do not receive glory from men. But I know that you have not the love of God within you. I have come in my Father's name, and you do not receive me; if another comes in his own name, him you will receive. How can you believe, who receive glory from one another and do not seek the glory that comes from the only God? Do not think that I shall accuse you to the Father; it is Moses who accuses you, on whom you set your hope. If you believed Moses, you would believe me, for he wrote of me. But if you do not believe his writings, how will you believe my words? (John 5:39–47)

Curiously, the Jewish objections to which Jesus speaks or the situation of opposition he describes here have not yet appeared in the narrative, but in the following chapters (esp. chs. 6–10) they will be heard increasingly. The fundamental objection boils down to this: The Jesus of Christian confession and proclamation (not the historical Jesus) is an impostor for whom blasphemous claims are made (John 7:47; 8:48, 52; 10:20). "You, being a man, make yourself God" (10:33). The Johannine Christian answer to this objection is virtually to fly in the teeth of it:

Jesus answered them, "Is it not written in your law, 'I said, you are gods'? If he called them gods to whom the word of God came (and scripture cannot be broken), do you say of him whom the Father consecrated and sent into the world, 'You are blaspheming,' because I said, 'I am the Son of God'? If I am not doing the works of my Father, then do not believe me; but if I do them, even though you do not believe me, believe the works, that you may know and understand that the Father is in me and I am in the Father." (John 10:34–38)

Yet the bold accusation that Jesus makes himself equal to God, or makes himself God, is not allowed to go unchallenged. At one point that is crucial for the Johannine Christians it is qualified. "I can do nothing on my own authority," says Jesus (John 5:30); "as I hear, I judge; and my judgment is just, because I seek not my own will but the will of him who sent me."

This qualification will not, of course, satisfy the objectors, whether Jewish, pagan, or Christian. It is very interesting, and I think significant, that in the history of Christian doctrine the Jewish objections to the boldness, or the baldness, of Johannine Christology reappear, if in less overtly hostile form. The Ebionites, the Antiochene Christology, the Arians, and others shrink back from the identification of Jesus with God that is the dominant, if not unqualified, thrust of Johannine Christology. Modern liberal Christianity shares in this reservation. Even the ancient church did not ignore it. By embracing the Chalcedonian "truly God and truly man" the church seemingly endorsed an interpretation of Johannine Christianity that accentuates this most distinctive, or offensive, aspect. Yet it nevertheless allowed for a larger chorus containing some mellower and less shrill tones. It affirmed Jesus to be "truly man" as well. Moreover, in its canon of Scripture the church preserved voices and traditions that balance the Johannine proclamation. John's Gospel may be said to be Christianity or at least Chris-

tology taken to a logical or illogical extreme, an extreme case of being Christian. It needs balancing out.

Two things, however, need to be remembered about the Johannine Christology. First, it arose in a polemical setting. In all probability the denial of more modest or traditional claims led, not to their withdrawal, but to the advancing of more sweeping and offensive claims. Second, the Johannine Christology lays bare what is involved in distinctively Christian confession and preaching. So as an extreme case of being Christian, it is also a valuable exploration of the depth and character of Christian conviction, hammered out under pressure, probably under threat. At the same time it represents a very narrow view, theologically and existentially. If, as seems likely, the Johannine community felt "hemmed in" by a hostile world, that narrowness is reflected in its doctrine and ethos. John's is a Christianity for tough times. It may, and I think does, contain its moment of eternal truth (if one wishes to speak in that way), but it does not provide a complete or adequate perspective for all seasons.

Having looked at the Johannine preaching, let us now explore more closely the Johannine ethos, and therefore the Johannine conception of church and ministry.

CHURCH AND MINISTRY
IN JOHANNINE PERSPECTIVE

The theology of John did not arise in a vacuum. Probably the development of that theology was related to a polemical situation that had led to the separation of Johannine Christians, or the embryonic Johannine church, from the synagogue. Such an understanding of the setting of John's Gospel owes a great deal to the seminal book of J. Louis Martyn, *Theology and History in the Fourth Gospel.* [14] He construes the debate over whether Jesus was the Christ, first within the synagogue and then between the sundered communities, as the motive force that gives

the Fourth Gospel its distinctive character.

It may be hazardous to infer too much about specifics of the setting of the Fourth Gospel from its portrayal of the conflict between Jesus and the Jews or Pharisees. Nevertheless, the thrice-repeated reference to expulsion of those who confess Christ from synagogues (John 9:22, 12:42, 16:2), if it reflects a historical situation at all, points to a period well after the historical ministry of Jesus. The question of confession of Jesus as the Christ was scarcely the issue constantly confronting and troubling his contemporaries. That this question became acute at the time of the Roman War and thereafter is probable, although its roots go back earlier. It is interesting to observe that Jewish authorities are portrayed as already hostile to the proclamation of Jesus as Christ in Acts 1–5, i.e., at the earliest period. But this may be anachronistic. At the time of the arrest of Paul in Jerusalem (Acts 21) the issue between Paul and the Jewish authorities in Jerusalem seems to be observance of the law (Acts 21:24–25). That Paul had been persecuted by synagogue authorities is clear (II Cor. 11:24–25). Before that, Paul himself persecuted the church, as both he (Gal. 1:13; I Cor. 15:9; cf. I Thess. 2:14–15) and Acts (ch. 9) attest. But also in Acts (5:33–42) the Pharisee Gamaliel urges the Council to take a wait-and-see attitude to the claims made for Jesus. Not until John's Gospel is the question of whether Jesus is the Christ presented so unequivocally as the single issue dividing Christian believers, whether Jewish or Gentile, from "the Jews." Certainly such a situation did not obtain in Jesus' own day, nor is it reflected in the Synoptics.

A polemical setting of Johannine Christianity would account for the vigor, and even vehemence, of the Fourth Gospel's Christological affirmation. John is, so to speak, "hemmed in," and the result is a narrow focus on what the community thinks is essential, the confession of Jesus as Son of God which constitutes its *raison d'être*. This

confession is deepened beyond what is otherwise known in early Christianity, or certainly in the gospel tradition. The cosmic significance of Christ, already suggested in Paul (Phil. 2:5–11; Col. 1:15–20) and Hebrews (Heb. 1:2–3), is now expressed in a Gospel, a narrative of Jesus' career (John 1:1–2), and by the Lord himself (John 17: 24). That God has acted in a decisive way in Jesus (cf. Rom. 1:1–4, 16–17; 3:21–22), a cardinal theological tenet of early Christianity, is now taken to mean that Jesus is, at least functionally, equivalent to God. The equation of Jesus and God in revelation is complete:

> Jesus said to him, "Have I been with you so long, and yet you do not know me, Philip? He who has seen me has seen the Father; how can you say, 'Show us the Father'? Do you not believe that I am in the Father and the Father in me? The words that I say to you I do not speak on my own authority; but the Father who dwells in me does his works. Believe me that I am in the Father and the Father in me; or else believe me for the sake of the works themselves." (John 14:9–11)

How or why does this happen? What basic theological instinct or perspective finds expression in such Christological claims? Exegetical answers range from the view that the Johannine Jesus is docetically conceived, that he authenticates himself as revelation through the *doxa* (glory) of supernatural signs, knowledge, and word (Käsemann) to the position of Bultmann that "the revelation is present in a peculiar *hiddenness.*" Bultmann writes: "This is the paradox which runs through the whole gospel: the *doxa* [glory] is not to be seen *alongside* the *sarx* [flesh], nor *through* the *sarx* as through a window; it is to be seen in the *sarx* and nowhere else."[15] Bultmann comprehends and expresses the nature of this paradox perhaps better than John does. But it is not a sheer imposition upon the text. The same Jesus who tells the Samaritan woman all she has done also grew weary from

a journey and sat down at the well to rest. It is not the intention of the Fourth Evangelist to present the revelation of God in Jesus in such a way as to negate his humanity or to make his experience foreign, and therefore irrelevant, to his followers. "As the Father has sent me," says the risen Jesus (John 20:21), "even so I send you." "If they persecuted me, they will persecute you; if they kept my word, they will keep yours also" (15:20). "I do not pray that thou shouldst take them out of the world, but that thou shouldst keep them from the evil one" (17:15). The author of the closely related First Epistle of John writes (I John 2:5b–6): "By this we may be sure we are in him: he who says he abides in him ought to walk in the same way in which he walked." And again (I John 3:16): "By this we know love, that he laid down his life for us; and we ought to lay down our lives for the brethren." In Johannine thought, the believer's life in the world recapitulates certain crucial aspects of Jesus' own ministry.

Now, at length, we can consider the question of the nature of ministry in John. At the outset we should be aware of the sheer lexical data. The word "ministry" or "to minister" *(diakonia/diakonein)* is rare in John, and the word "church" *(ecclesia)* does not appear at all. But it would be wrong to infer from this that there is nothing in John answering to the concepts of church and ministry. We have already seen that in John the disciples of Jesus constitute a distinct and separate group over against the disciples of Moses. This situation does not correspond to the time of Jesus itself, when Jesus and his disciples stood within the Jewish community. Rather, it more likely reflects a tension between the synagogue and the emerging Johannine Christian church, probably in the latter part of the first century. There is then at least an implicit Johannine ecclesiology. What about a conception of ministry?

One way to pursue this question would be to ask about the understanding of church order in John, or about the

actual church order in the Johannine community. It cannot be shown that either the Gospel of John or the Johannine epistles evince a highly developed church organization. Because of the narrative, quasi-historical, or biographical nature of the Gospels, it is difficult to infer from them the kind of church order they espouse or represent.[16] This is, if anything, especially true of John. But because the Twelve are seldom mentioned and never named, because Peter seems to be put down in favor of the Beloved Disciple, because the importance of direct access of the believer to Jesus is emphasized, because the risen Christ seems to preside over his church through the Spirit-Paraclete; for all these reasons it is widely held that John represents a "low" ecclesiology or a view of church order in which ministerial office has not developed, or has not been allowed to develop. Rather, every believer is related to Christ in the same way. There is no ministerial hierarchy, perhaps not even the distinction of ministry and laity. The downplaying of the Twelve would be commensurate with an ecclesiology in which the concept of apostolic authority was not espoused or emphasized as the touchstone of churchly ministry. Also, in the Johannine epistles, probably later than the Gospel, no clear conception of ministry or church order appears. II and III John are the work of someone who styles himself "the Elder," and the First Epistle of John is presumed to be by the same person, but this is not certain. (Obviously all the letters as well as the Gospel are from the same or related early Christian circles or schools.) Whether "elder" is even a title comparable to that found in Acts, Paul, and the pastoral epistles, is not completely certain. Probably it is. From III John 9, and the mention of "Diotrephes, who likes to put himself first," one may infer that church organization and order has become a problem in the Johannine community. Beyond that it is impossible to say much with certainty. Who represents the nascent episcopal office and authority? Diotrephes? Or perhaps

the Elder? There is scarcely sufficient evidence to decide. I should like, however, to prescind from this and related questions in order to approach the subject of ministry in the Fourth Gospel from a different angle.

It is true that Jesus does not speak of himself as performing a ministry or ministering in the Fourth Gospel. By contrast, the term *diakonein* (to minister, or serve) occurs in a crucial context in the Gospel of Mark. At Mark 10:45 (RSV) Jesus says, "The Son of man also came not to be served [ministered to] but to serve [minister], and to give his life as a ransom for many." Moreover, the concept of Jesus' ministering or serving, which is at home in the Synoptics, seems at first glance to be foreign to John. The absence of the term would appear to suit John's high Christology.

Yet this is not quite the case. There is in John, and only there, a narrative that portrays Jesus performing the most humble ministry or service, although the words *diakonein/diakonia* are not used. It is, of course, the story of Jesus' washing the disciples' feet (John 13:1–20). This story stands in John's account of the Last Supper at about the point at which the Synoptics would lead us to expect the institution of the Lord's Supper, which, of course, is not found in John. There is, however, in Luke an interesting "missing link" connecting the Marcan concept of ministry *(diakonia)*, the Johannine foot-washing story, and the institution of the Lord's Supper. In the Lucan narrative (Luke 22:25–27) there follows after the institution a kind of brief farewell discourse of Jesus in which he speaks of ministering or serving *(diakonein)* in terms similar to Mark 10:45:

> And he said to them, "The kings of the Gentiles exercise lordship over them; and those in authority over them are called benefactors. But not so with you; rather let the greatest among you become as the youngest, and the leader as one who serves. For which is the greater, one

who sits at table, or one who serves? Is it not the one who
sits at table? But I am among you as one who serves."
(Luke 22:25–27)

Probably Luke draws on Q material (cf. Matt. 23:11) as
well as on Mark 10:45. Moreover, Luke 12:37 records
another saying of Jesus about service *(diakonein):*
"Blessed are those servants whom the master finds awake
when he comes; truly, I say to you, he will gird himself
and have them sit at table, and he will come and serve
them." Certainly this suggests the Johannine foot-washing scene.

On the assumption that John knew Luke, Barrett
thinks that John has probably developed the Lucan sayings into the story which we find in the Fourth Gospel.
This is not impossible. But as real as are the affinities
between Luke and John, there is much to be said for
Bultmann's proposal that John here employs a traditional
apothegm, related to Lucan tradition, which he has an-
notated and edited to express his own point of view.[17] It
is after all, quite a jump from the sayings of Luke to the
Johannine story.

John certainly used tradition related to the Synoptic.
Possibly he knew, or at least knew of, one or more of the
Synoptic Gospels. But this story is found only in John,
nowhere else. Yet its earthy character implies an origin
not far removed from the Synoptic tradition, if not the
historical Jesus. The very obvious twofold interpretation
also suggests that the evangelist is here working with
tradition. According to John 13:6–11, the washing of the
feet symbolizes Jesus' saving work, especially his death:

He came to Simon Peter; and Peter said to him, "Lord,
do you wash my feet?" Jesus answered him, "What I am
doing you do not know now, but afterward you will
understand." Peter said to him, "You shall never wash
my feet." Jesus answered him, "If I do not wash you, you
have no part in me." Simon Peter said to him, "Lord, not

my feet only but also my hands and my head!" Jesus said
to him, "He who has bathed does not need to wash,
except for his feet, but he is clean all over; and you are
clean, but not all of you." For he knew who was to betray
him; that was why he said, "You are not all clean." (John
13:6-11)

Here the foot washing is clearly a ministry or service that
Jesus performs for his disciples, his church. In vs. 12-17,
however, there is another interpretation of the washing
of the feet.

When he had washed their feet, and taken his garments,
and resumed his place, he said to them, "Do you know
what I have done to you? You call me Teacher and Lord;
and you are right, for so I am. If I then, your Lord and
Teacher, have washed your feet, you also ought to wash
one another's feet. For I have given you an example, that
you also should do as I have done to you. Truly, truly, I
say to you, a servant is not greater than his master; nor
is he who is sent greater than he who sent him. If you
know these things, blessed are you if you do them. (John
13:12-17)

Bultmann quite reasonably takes this second interpretation to be traditional, a part of the apothegm the evangelist used. It highlights the moral demand implicit in Jesus'
act.

The first interpretation (John 13:6-11), which centers
around Peter's misunderstanding of the event, seems to
be the distinctly Johannine one. Certainly it accords more
closely with Johannine theology and style. Peter evinces
the kind of misguided loyalty and impetuousness attributed to him elsewhere in the Gospels. He at first
refuses to allow Jesus to wash his feet. When Jesus tells
him he does not know now what he (Jesus) is doing, but
he will know "afterward" (the *meta tauta* surely refers to
the crucifixion and resurrection), a typical Johannine
motif emerges. The disciples do not understand now, but
they will understand in retrospect (cf. John 2:17, 22;

12:16). Then Peter declares even more strongly that Jesus will never wash his feet (13:8a), and Jesus says to Peter that if he does not wash him, Peter will have no part in him. This elicits from Peter what the reader perceives as a typically Petrine expostulation: "Lord, not my feet only but also my hands and my head!" (v. 9). This is also a typical example of Johannine misunderstanding. Peter thinks Jesus speaks of a physical washing, when something more profound is at stake. Jesus then makes a rather enigmatic rejoinder: "He who has bathed does not need to wash, but he is clean all over; and you are clean, but not all of you (v. 10). (I follow Bultmann, who accepts the reading of Codex Sinaiticus, in which "except his feet" is omitted.) The bathing is the washing of the feet, which symbolizes Jesus' service for the disciple, the saving work which he accomplishes. Bultmann equates this service with Jesus' word, but it can scarcely be separated from his death (John 3:16; 6:51; 10:11; 15:13f.).

John the evangelist has laid these two interpretations back to back in such a way that they make sense together. The service that Jesus performs for the disciples in washing their feet is his salvific work, culminating in his death. This work must be accepted by the disciples. Accept it is all they can do in the first instance. They dare not refuse it. Christ acts decisively for the salvation of his disciples. Yet the disciples' acceptance of this work of Jesus comes to fruition only as they recapitulate it on behalf of one another. This is the significance of the second interpretation (John 13:12–17). What Jesus says here accords rather well with the Marcan teaching about Jesus' service or ministry *(diakonia/diakonein)*. According to Mark, what Jesus does for his followers they must recapitulate among themselves. (The Johannine sayings actually have Synoptic and other parallels: John 13:15 (I Peter 2:21); John 13:16 (Matt. 10:24; Luke 6:40); John 13:17 (Luke 10:37).

We have thus arrived at a cardinal tenet of Johannine

theology. Jesus' love for his disciples is recapitulated in their love for one another. At the beginning of the Last Supper we learn that Jesus loved his disciples, who were in the world, to the end (John 13:1). At the conclusion of the meal he gives them a new commandment, to love one another as he has loved them (13:34). This, not incidentally, is in John's view the most persuasive form of evangelism (13:35; cf. 17:21, 23). Jesus lays down his life for his friends (15:13), after having first enjoined his disciples to love one another as he has loved them. In I John this dual motif, the disciples' boundless love for one another recapitulating Jesus' love for them, is strongly reiterated: "By this we know love, that he laid down his life for us; and we ought to lay down our lives for the brethren" (I John 3:16).

John understands faith in Jesus as belief in him that finds specific and concrete manifestation in the disciples' mode of life. This realizing of faith in life belongs to the essence of faith. The author of I John never tires of making this point. In fact, he makes it quite clearly and eloquently:

> Beloved, let us love one another; for love is of God and he who loves is born of God and knows God. He who does not love does not know God; for God is love. In this the love of God was made manifest among us, that God sent his only Son into the world, so that we might live through him. In this is love, not that we loved God but that he loved us and sent his Son to be the expiation for our sins. Beloved, if God so loved us, we also ought to love one another. No man has ever seen God; if we love one another, God abides in us and his love is perfected in us. (I John 4:7–12)

The indissoluble connection between what we call theology and ethics is stated simply and beautifully, but also forcefully:

> If any one says, "I love God," and hates his brother, he
> is a liar; for he who does not love his brother whom he
> has seen, cannot love God whom he has not seen. And
> this commandment we have from him, that he who loves
> God should love his brother also. (I John 4:20–21)

John's seemingly dogmatic, and somewhat strident, Christology has as its other side a vital, ethically pregnant conviction that in Jesus, God expresses his love for the world, especially for believers. If there is a Johannine conception of ministry—and I think there is—it is grounded in the belief that God is love and his revelation is the expression of that love. To believe, to live in and by the light of God's revelation in Jesus, is to participate in that love, to love God, Christ, and one's brothers and sisters in faith. This broadly based conception of ministry or service is incumbent upon the disciple of Jesus. If there are specialized ministries, they must be grounded in this fundamental ministry.

Nevertheless, there is a narrowness about this grand conception that is perhaps more apparent in the epistle than in the Gospel, but it is present in both. God loves the world and intends to save it (John 3:16). Yet the world is by and large rejecting the definitive expression of that love, Jesus Christ the Son of God. The result is judgment. The hostility and tension between the disciples and the Jews is only an archetypal instance of the polarity between Jesus and his disciples, i.e., the church on the one hand and the world on the other. There is a relationship of proportionality, if not polar duality, between Jesus, the disciples, and the church on the one side, and Satan, the Jews, and the world on the other. The well-known dualism of the Johannine literature is the linguistic, conceptual product of a profound sense of estrangement and hostility.

This sense of estrangement makes it difficult for the Elder to affirm, with the evangelist, that God loves the world. In fact, it is interesting to compare the forthright

statement of John 3:16 with I John 4:9: "In this the love of God was made manifest among us, that God sent his only Son into the world, so that we might live through him." God's Son comes into the world, but the love of God is made manifest "among *us . . .* so that *we* might live through him." God's love seems only to benefit the Christian community.

I do not know that the author of I John, much less the evangelist, would want to be held to so narrow a construction of the effect of the saving work of God, if we were able to question him. Quite possibly the exigencies of expulsion from the synagogue (John 9:22; 12:42; 16:2) have given the Johannine church a dim view of the world, as well as of Judaism. However that may be, the tendency to reject the world in favor of the beleaguered community, and thus to see God as rejecting the world in favor of that community, is strongly at work in the Johannine literature.

This is particularly evident in what seems to be the sharp limitation, whether intentional or not, of the realm in which the ethical imperative, the love imperative, is taken to apply. Whom are believers to love? The answer seems to be that we are to love other believers: "Love one another. . . . By this all men will know that you are my disciples, if you have love for one another" (John 13:34–35); "This commandment we have from him, that he who loves God should love his brother also" (I John 4:21). Many interpreters (e.g., Bultmann, Furnish) are loath to concede that in the Johannine view Jesus' command to love is limited to the circle of his disciples, i.e., the church. Strictly speaking, this may not be the case. The Synoptic Jesus' command to love your neighbor as yourself (Mark 12:31; Matt. 22:39; Luke 10:27) is not rejected in John, it is true. There is no injunction to love your neighbor and hate your enemy (Matt. 5:43). One may argue that the command to love the brethren really raises the question of who your brother is. If all men and

women are brothers and sisters before God, the command to love one's brother is equivalent to the command to love all people. However true in principle that may be, it does not seem to be what the author of the Gospel (and the epistle) had in mind. His concern was with relationships within the church. Love among the members of the community establishes its unity. This unity, the realization and manifestation of love, is the basis of the community's witness to the truth of Jesus as well as of its very existence:

> By this all men will know that you are my disciples, if you have love for one another.

> I do not pray for these only, but also for those who believe in me through their word, that they may all be one; even as thou, Father, art in me, and I in thee, that they also may be in us, so that the world may believe that thou hast sent me. (John 13:35; 17:20–21)

Ministry in John is self-giving service. It is conceived, at least in the first instance, as an intramural relationship. As Jesus lays down his life for his friends, so they are willing to lay down their lives for each other. Through this ministry, however, a positive relation to the world may be established, i.e., people may be converted. As to the concrete and specific form this ministry may take, it is usually less dramatic than laying down one's life. Washing one another's feet, of which a modern equivalent is difficult to produce, is neither sacramental nor sentimental. It is the symbol of that practical ministry which defines the very life of the Johannine community. The community lives in and for such mutual service. Apart from it there is, effectually, no revelation, no faith, and particularly no ministry and no church:

> Beloved, let us love one another; for love is of God, and he who loves is born of God and knows God. He who does not love does not know God; for God is love.

No man has ever seen God; if we love one another, God abides in us and his love is perfected in us.

If any one says, "I love God," and hates his brother, he is a liar; for he who does not love his brother whom he has seen, cannot love God whom he has not seen. (I John 4:7–8, 12, 20)

In conclusion, we return briefly to the problem of John and the Synoptics, not as an interesting literary and historical conundrum, but as a matter germane to theology and preaching in the church. The origins of the distinctly Johannine theology, particularly Christology, lie not in the Synoptic tradition, or in a direct line of development from Paul, but rather in the peculiar polemical situation of the Johannine community. The claim that Jesus was the Messiah was confronted by rejection within the Jewish community. The resulting controversy, now reflected in the Fourth Gospel's accounts of Jesus' conversations and debates with his contemporaries, led to schism and alienation. Out of it the Johannine Christian community emerged. In some measure the high Johannine Christology with its dogmatic overtones, as well as the Johannine church, is a product of polemic. Yet at the same time that Christology does not contradict the other Gospels or the theological developments evident there. Certainly John knew a gospel tradition similar to what is found in the Synoptics, if not the Synoptic Gospels themselves. His Gospel, although not deliberately written to supplement them, nevertheless makes sense, and takes on an added dimension of depth, when read alongside them. The Fourth Gospel by itself might well have led to a heretical form of Christology and Christianity that the author himself did not intend. For theological, specifically Christological, purposes John needs to be read with the Synoptics. It is not wrongly construed as making explicit what is mostly latent or implicit in them.

Moreover, the Johannine interpretation of Jesus'

teaching as fundamentally the command to love one another is also not foreign to the Synoptic tradition. Interpreters have not erred in perceiving in John's "new commandment" the epitome of Jesus' teaching. In all likelihood, the inwardness of this command ("love one another" as contrasted with "love your neighbor") to which we have pointed has something to do with the polemical circumstances of the Gospel's origin and history. (There are some good reasons why Johannine Christianity has been referred to in recent scholarship as sectarian.) Interpreters are obligated to understand and appreciate this history as best they can. When we begin to speak of the concept of ministry in John, however, we have not only the right but the obligation to think of a somewhat broader context or picture. In and of themselves the Johannine writings warrant the depiction of Christian ministry as the expression of love, not only in a general disposition but in concrete and specific acts on behalf of one's brother or sister in Christ. Mission then comes about as, so to speak, an overflow from the world's observation of such expressions of love. When put alongside the other Gospels and the New Testament writings generally, once again John is found to bring to very pointed expression the teaching of early Christianity, of the New Testament, and indeed, of Jesus himself. This last judgment may belong to the realm of faith as much as to that of historical criticism, but it is not a judgment devoid of historical integrity.

EPILOGUE

This study was motivated by the desire to bridge the chasm between classical theological studies and the daily practice of ministry. Certain broad, general questions prompted us to seek answers concerning the interdependence of these two pursuits: theology and ministry. The vitality of each is handicapped without the benefit of the insights of the other. The essays included in this volume provide an introduction to the resources to be found in biblical literature that may inform and animate the conversation now begun. In addition to the achievement of the primary purpose, the essays serve also to provoke questions that require further study.

The contributors are to be commended for providing essays that not only inform but also generate a desire to pursue these concerns. They have been careful not to delineate explicitly the implications of their foundational studies for the practice of ministry in the modern world. Nor have they addressed the broader questions concerning the constitution and function of the institutional church. The reluctance to address these matters is an indication of the difficulty of applying biblical norms to a pluralistic environment radically dissimilar from that of the biblical era. However, the admitted difficulty of applying biblical norms does not excuse us from taking up the implicit challenge posed by this task.

The issues identified below are suggestive of the sorts of practical and theological concerns that demand further explication. It is unreasonable to expect five essays of limited scope and purpose to provide a definitive systematic theology of ministry. Yet each contributor has demonstrated how the issue can be approached profitably. It is incumbent upon pastor-practitioners to join the conversation. Those who are engaged in ministry should no longer need to be chided for a failure to invest the time necessary to reflect theologically on pastoral contacts and conversation. It was noted in the Introduction that the practicing pastor should bring this unique perspective to the study of the interrelationship of theology with ministry.

One of the distinctive contributions that pastor-practitioners may make is the translation of the root notions explicated in this volume into contemporary ministry. For example, they can examine the implications of these biblical insights for the following questions and areas of interest:

—To what extent is ministry constitutive of, or an appendage to, the life of faith?
—To what extent can one adapt the gospel to changing circumstances without compromising its integrity?
—What is the relationship of lay to ordained ministries? Are specific ministries intrinsic to the clergy office and to lay persons? In particular, is pastoral care a function of the clergy, or of the congregation *qua* congregation?
—What are the distinctive contributions to ministry that women provide?
—Are pastoral practitioners sufficiently alert to the benefits and liabilities of a close association with the behavioral and medical sciences?
—Does the scope of ministry encompass sociopolitical

action intended to establish a more just social order?

—Is ministry being corrupted or usurped by advocacy of a theocratic state?

—How can one minister in a pluralistic religious world without being paternalistic?

These questions are merely suggestive of the issues that merit careful consideration. The essays in this volume constitute a substantive and helpful orientation to the nature of the relationship between "theology" and "ministry" implicit in biblical literature. The insights of others interested in a "theology of ministry" will be welcome additions to the conversation and inquiry that is vitally important to the life of the people of God.

EARL E. SHELP

RONALD SUNDERLAND

NOTES

1. Theology and Ministry in the Hebrew Scriptures

1. Cf. Paul van Buren, *The Burden of Freedom: Americans and the God of Israel* (Seabury Press, 1976), pp. 9–34, esp. pp. 14–17.

2. Albert C. Outler, *Who Trusts in God: Musings on the Meaning of Providence* (Oxford University Press, 1968).

3. Cf. Gerhard von Rad, *Old Testament Theology,* tr. by D. M. G. Stalker, Vol. I, *The Theology of Israel's Historical Traditions* (Harper & Row, 1962), pp. 241f. and 263f.

2. Ministry in Judaism: Reflections on Suffering and Caring

1. Sheldon Blank, *Prophetic Faith in Isaiah* (Harper & Row, 1967), p. 84.

2. Louis Jacobs, *A Jewish Theology* (Behrman House, 1973), p. 307.

3. Solomon D. Goitein (ed. and tr.), *Letters of Medieval Jewish Traders* (Princeton University Press, 1974), p. 207.

4. Gershom Scholem, *On the Kabbalah and Its Symbolism,* tr. by Ralph Manheim (Schocken Books, 1965), p. 89.

5. Cited in Solomon Freehof, *Modern Reform Responsa* (Hebrew Union College Press, 1971), p. 200.

6. Sheldon H. Blank, *Prophetic Thought: Essays and Lectures* (Hebrew Union College Press, 1977), p. 91.

7. Quoted in Nahum N. Glatzer (ed.), *In Time and Eternity: A Jewish Reader,* tr. by Olga Marx et al. (Schocken Books, 1946), p. 946.

8. Elie Wiesel, *Night,* tr. by Stella Rodway (Hill & Wang, 1960), pp. 43f.

9. Blank, *Prophetic Thought,* p. 92.

3. THEOLOGY AND MINISTRY IN THE PAULINE LETTERS

1. The New Testament contains thirteen letters ascribed to Paul, but most scholars have difficulty in accepting all of them as authentic. The standard introductions and commentaries discuss the reasons why Paul's authorship of the Pastoral Epistles, Ephesians, Colossians, and II Thessalonians is often questioned. The seven certainly-Pauline letters are Romans, I, II Corinthians, Galatians, Philippians, I Thessalonians, and Philemon, and these alone will be employed in the present discussion. The six remaining letters, and also the Book of Acts, provide evidence for how Paul's theology and ministry were received and perceived in the decades following his death, but they are less than dependable guides as one attempts to understand the theology and ministry of Paul himself.

2. Studies by W. E. Chadwick, *The Pastoral Teaching of St. Paul: His Ministerial Ideals* (Edinburgh: T. & T. Clark, 1907), and C. F. Heinrici, *Paulus als Seelsorger,* Biblische Zeit- und Streitfragen VI/i (Berlin: E. Runge, 1910), are now seriously dated, and were not really adequate to begin with. John T. McNeill devotes only a few pages to Paul in *A History of the Cure of Souls*

(Harper & Bros., 1951), while William A. Clebsch and Charles R. Jaekle deal only generally with the earliest church in their *Pastoral Care in Historical Perspective,* 2d ed. (Prentice-Hall, 1978); cf. Don S. Browning, *The Moral Context of Pastoral Care* (Westminster Press, 1976), pp. 52–55. John Knox's essay on "The Ministry in the Primitive Church," in *The Ministry in Historical Perspectives,* ed. by H. Richard Niebuhr and Daniel Day Williams (Harper & Brothers, 1956), pp. 1–26, contains some helpful insights about Paul's ministerial practice, as does the short article by S. Maclean Gilmour, "Pastoral Care in the New Testament Church," *New Testament Studies,* Vol. 10 (1964), pp. 393–398. The excellent study by Walter Brueggemann, "Covenanting as Human Vocation: A Discussion of the Relation of Bible and Pastoral Care," *Interpretation,* Vol. 33 (1979), pp. 115–129, occasionally cites Pauline texts, but only within the context of a quite general discussion of biblical theology.

3. Paul frequently addresses his readers as "brothers [and sisters]," even those in Rome who belong to a church he had never visited (e.g., Rom. 10:1; 12:1). Paul's use of parental images for himself is discussed below.

4. I have made a similar point about Paul's concrete moral instructions in *The Moral Teaching of Paul: Selected Issues* (Abingdon Press, 1979), especially Chapter 1.

5. See note 1, above.

6. I have discussed this issue at greater length in *Theology and Ethics in Paul* (Abingdon Press, 1968), pp. 99–111.

7. See William N. Willimon's excellent discussion of *Worship as Pastoral Care* (Abingdon Press, 1979), in which the priestly and pastoral roles are presented as having a reciprocal and necessary relationship.

8. Willi Marxsen, *The Resurrection of Jesus of Nazareth,* tr. by Margaret Kohl (Fortress Press, 1970).

9. See Rudolf Bultmann's still classic exposition of the eschatological basis of Jesus' call to repentance, and of the meaning of this eschatological element, in his *Jesus and the Word,* tr. by Louise Pettibone Smith and Erminie Huntress Lantero (Charles Scribner's Sons, 1934).

10. On this passage see Ernst Käsemann's essay, "Worship and Everyday Life: A Note on Romans 12," in his *New Testament Questions of Today,* tr. by W. J. Montague (Fortress Press, 1969), pp. 188–195.

11. For details the standard commentaries on I and II Corinthians may be consulted.

4. RESOURCES FOR PASTORAL MINISTRY IN THE SYNOPTIC GOSPELS

1. Albert Schweitzer, *The Quest of the Historical Jesus* (1906; E.T., 1910; Macmillan Co., 1968).

2. Cf. William G. Thompson, *Matthew's Advice to a Divided Community, Matthew 17:22–18:35* (Rome: Biblical Institute Press, 1970).

5. THEOLOGY AND MINISTRY IN JOHN

1. Recently C. K. Barrett has sharply rejected any too sanguine estimate of the historical value of the Fourth Gospel. Cf. *The Gospel According to St. John,* 2d ed. (Westminster Press, 1978), p. viii: "I do not believe that John intended to supply us with historically verifiable information regarding the life and teaching of Jesus, and that historical traditions of great worth can be disentangled from his interpretative comments."

2. See Oscar Cullmann, *The Johannine Circle,* tr. by John Bowden (Westminster Press, 1976), p. 94.

3. H. F. D. Sparks, *A Synopsis of the Gospels: The Synoptic Gospels with the Johannine Parallels* (Fortress

Press, 1964) and his *The Johannine Synopsis of the Gospels* (Harper & Row, 1974) were used in this analysis.

4. Cf. Barrett (*The Gospel According to St. John,* p. 115), who quotes the saying according to Eusebius of Caesarea, *Ecclesiastical History* VI. xiv. 7.

5. Eusebius, *Ecclesiastical History* III. xxiv. 7–13.

6. Hans Windisch, *Johannes und die Synoptiker;* subtitled *Wollte der vierte Evangelist die älteren Evangelien ergänzen oder ersetzen?* (Leipzig, 1926).

7. Percival Gardner-Smith, *Saint John and the Synoptic Gospels* (Cambridge University Press, 1938).

8. Frans Neirynck, "John and the Synoptics," in M. de Jong (ed.), *L'Évangile de Jean: Sources, rédaction, théologie* (BETL, Leuven [Louvain]: Leuven University Press, 1977), p. 73.

9. Norman Perrin, *The New Testament: An Introduction* (Harcourt Brace Jovanovich, 1974), pp. 228f.

10. Anton Dauer, *Die Passionsgeschichte im Johannesevangelium* (SANT, Munich: Kösel, 1972).

11. Cf. Robert T. Fortna, "Jesus and Peter at the High Priest's House: A Test Case for the Relation Between Mark's and John's Gospels," *New Testament Studies,* Vol. 24 (1978), pp. 371–383.

12. See the helpful articles by G. von Rad, K. G. Kuhn, and W. Gutbrod on *Israel* (Israel), *Hebraios* (Hebrew), *Ioudaios* (Jew), and related terms in Gerhard Kittel (ed.), *Theological Dictionary of the New Testament,* Vol. III, tr. by Geoffrey W. Bromiley et al. (Wm. B. Eerdmans Publishing Co., 1965), pp. 356–391.

13. The evidence is marshaled by Barrett, *The Gospel According to St. John,* pp. 255–256.

14. J. Louis Martyn, *Theology and History in the Fourth Gospel,* 2d ed., rev. and enl. (Abingdon Press, 1979). The first edition, from which the revision does not differ essentially, appeared in 1968.

15. Rudolf Bultmann, *The Gospel of John: A Commen-*

tary, tr. by G. R. Beasley-Murray et al. (Westminster Press, 1971), p. 63.

16. Cf. the observations in my article, "Johannine Christianity: Some Reflections on Its Character and Delineation," *New Testament Studies,* Vol. 21 (1975), esp. pp. 222–224.

17. Bultmann, *The Gospel of John,* p. 462.